Elgar Encyclopedia of International Sanctions

ELGAR ENCYCLOPEDIAS IN THE SOCIAL SCIENCES

Elgar Encyclopedias in the Social Sciences serve as the definitive reference works to their fields. Each *Encyclopedia* is overseen by an editor internationally recognised as a leading name within the field, and contains a multitude of entries written by key scholars, providing an accessible and condensed overview of the key topics within a given subject area. Volumes in the series are commissioned across the breadth of the social sciences, and cover areas including, but not limited to, Political Science, Sociology, Human Geography, Development Studies, Social Policy, Public Management and Public Policy. Individual entries present a concise and logical overview of a given subject, together with a list of references for further study. Each *Encyclopedia* will serve as an invaluable resource for practitioners, academics, and students, and should form an essential part of any research journey.

For a full list of Edward Elgar published titles, including the titles in this series, visit our website at www.e-elgar.com.

Elgar Encyclopedia of International Sanctions

Edited by

Clara Portela

Professor of Political Science, Department of Constitutional Law and Political Science, University of Valencia, Spain

Andrea Charron

Professor of International Relations and Director, Centre for Defence and Security Studies, University of Manitoba, Canada

Mirko Sossai

Professor of International Law, Department of Law, University Roma Tre, Italy

ELGAR ENCYCLOPEDIAS IN THE SOCIAL SCIENCES

Edward Elgar
PUBLISHING

Cheltenham, UK • Northampton, MA, USA

Cover image: Clara Portela

Published by

Edward Elgar Publishing Limited
The Lypiatts
15 Lansdown Road
Cheltenham
Glos GL50 2JA
UK

Edward Elgar Publishing, Inc.
William Pratt House
9 Dewey Court
Northampton
Massachusetts 01060
USA

Authorised representative in the EU for GPSR queries only: Easy Access System Europe – Mustamäe tee 50, 10621 Tallinn, Estonia, gpsr.requests@easproject.com

A catalogue record for this book is available from the British Library

Library of Congress Control Number: 2025945914

This book is available electronically in the Elgaronline
Political Science and Public Policy subject collection
https://doi.org/10.4337/9781035339532

FSC
www.fsc.org
MIX
Paper | Supporting responsible forestry
FSC® C013604

ISBN 978 1 0353 3952 5 (cased)
ISBN 978 1 0353 3953 2 (eBook)
ISBN 978 1 0353 7994 1 (ePub)

Printed and bound by CPI Group (UK) Ltd, Croydon, CR0 4YY

This Encyclopedia is dedicated to those pioneering sanctions scholars who led the way and inspired and supported future generations of researchers – in particular, to the memory of Prof Margaret Doxey, Dr Hadewych Hazelzet and Prof Vera Gowlland-Debbas, with gratitude.

Contents

List of abbreviations

ACP	African, Caribbean and Pacific
ARSIWA	Articles on Responsibility of States for Internationally Wrongful Acts
AU	African Union
CIS	Commonwealth of Independent States
CFSP (EU)	Common Foreign and Security Policy
CJEU	Court of Justice of the European Union
DPPA	UN Department of Political and Peacebuilding Affairs
DPRK	Democratic People's Republic of Korea
ECHR	European Convention on Human Rights
ECOWAS	Economic Community of West African States
EEC	European Economic Community
EPC	European Political Cooperation
EU	European Union
FARC	Fuerzas Armadas Revolucionarias de Colombia
FATF	Financial Action Task Force
FCDO	(UK) Foreign, Commonwealth and Development Office
GATS	General Agreement on Trade in Services
GATT	General Agreement on Tariffs and Trade
IAEA	International Atomic Energy Agency
ICAO	International Civil Aviation Organization
ICC	International Criminal Court
ICJ	International Court of Justice
ICTY	International Criminal Tribunal for the Former Yugoslavia
ILC	International Law Commission
INTERPOL	International Criminal Police Organisation
IWG	International Working Group on Russian Sanctions
JCPOA	Joint Comprehensive Plan of Action (for Iran)
JVCFOA	Canada's Justice for Victims of Corrupt Foreign Officials Act
MOFCOM	Ministry of Commerce People's Republic of China
NATO	North Atlantic Treaty Organization
NPT	Treaty on the Non-Proliferation of Nuclear Weapons
OAPEC	Organization of Arab Petroleum Exporting Countries
ODA	Official Development Assistance
OECD	Organisation for Economic Cooperation and Development
OFAC	(US) Office of Foreign Assets Control
OFSI	(UK) Office of Financial Sanctions Implementation
OTSI	(UK) Office for the Investigation of Trade Sanctions
PCA	(EU) Partnership and Cooperation Agreement
PSC	(AU) Peace and Security Council
REPO	Russian Elites, Proxies, and Oligarchs
RNBO	National Security and Defense Council of Ukraine
RUF	Revolutionary United Front (Sierra Leone)
SAMLA	(UK) Sanctions and Anti-Money Laundering Act
SBU	Security Service of Ukraine
SEMA	Canada's Special Economic Measures Act
START	Strategic Arms Reduction Treaty
TEU	Treaty on the European Union
TFEU	Treaty on the Functioning of the European Union
UCG	Unconstitutional changes of government
UN	United Nations
UNPROFOR	UN Protection Force I and II in the former Yugoslavia
UNSC	United Nations Security Council
WB	World Bank
WMDs	Weapons of mass destruction
WTO	World Trade Organization

List of contributors

John Agbonifo, Associate Professor of Sociology, Osun State University, Nigeria

Armend Bekaj, Researcher, Department of Peace and Conflict Research, Uppsala University, Sweden

Thomas Biersteker, Honorary Professor of International Relations/Political Science and Honorary Curt Gasteyger Chair, Geneva Graduate Institute, Switzerland

Iryna Bogdanova, Postdoctoral Researcher, University of Luxemburg, Luxembourg

Kristen Boon, Dean, University of Ottawa Faculty of Law (Common Law Section), Canada

Alix J. Boucher, Assistant Research Fellow, Africa Center for Strategic Studies, National Defense University, DC, USA

Michael Brzoska, Retired Professor, Department of Social Sciences, University of Hamburg, Germany

Antonio Bultrini, Associate Professor of International Law, University of Florence, Italy

Marco Bünte, Professor of Asian Politics, Friedrich-Alexander University (FAU) Erlangen-Nuremberg, Germany

Loren Bustos, Doctoral Researcher, Friedrich-Alexander University (FAU) Erlangen-Nuremberg, Germany

Martina Buscemi, Associate Professor of International Law, University of Milan, Italy

Maria Adele Carrai, Assistant Professor in Global China Studies, NYU Shanghai, China

Celia Challet, Assistant professor of Law, Ecole européenne de sciences politiques et sociales, Université Catholique de Lille, France

Andrea Charron, Professor and Director of the Centre for Defence and Security Studies, University of Manitoba, Canada

Rishika Chauhan, MacArthur-funded Postdoctoral Researcher at the Centre for Science and Security Studies (CSSS), King's College London, UK

Caty Clément, Senior Advisor at the International Advisory Team, Geneva Centre for Security Policy and Interpeace, Switzerland

Tiziana Corda, Research Fellow, Department of Social and Political Sciences, University of Milan, Italy

Martin Dawidowicz, Associate Professor of Public International Law, Faculty of Law, Uppsala University, Sweden

Laura Di Gianfrancesco, Research Fellow, Department of Law, Roma Tre University, Italy

Radka Druláková, Vice-Dean for Research and Doctoral Studies, Faculty of International Relations, Prague University of Economics and Business, Czechia

Bryan R. Early, Professor of Political Science, Political Science Department, University at Albany, SUNY, USA

Nickolas Eburne, Judicial Fellow, International Court of Justice, The Netherlands

Francesca Finelli, Visiting Researcher at the Court of Justice of the European Union, Luxembourg

Robert Fowler, Former Canadian Diplomat and Public Servant of the Government of Canada. Honorary Senior Fellow, University of Ottawa, Canada

Daniel Franchini, Lecturer in International Law, University of Sheffield, UK

Javier García Olmedo, Postdoctoral Researcher, University of Luxembourg, Luxembourg

Susanne Gratius, Professor of International Relations, Autonomous University Madrid (UAM), Spain

Francesco Giumelli, Associate Professor in International Relations, University of Groningen, The Netherlands

Manuel Herrera, Senior Policy Fellow, British-American Security Information Council, UK

Alexandra Hofer, Assistant Professor in Public International Law, Department of International and European Law, Utrecht University, The Netherlands

Zuzana Hudáková, Research Associate, Geneva Graduate Institute, Switzerland

Mathilde Jeantil, Doctor of Law, Centre Thucydide, Université Paris-Panthéon-Assas, France

Yifan Jia, Doctoral Researcher, Dickson Poon School of Law, King's College London, UK

Machiko Kanetake, Associate Professor of Public International Law, Utrecht University, The Netherlands

Kerim Can Kavaklı, Assistant Professor of Political Science, Department of Social and Political Sciences, Bocconi University, Italy

Ksenia Kirkham, Senior Lecturer, Department of War Studies, King's College London, UK

Iikka Korhonen, Director, Bank of Finland Institute for Emerging Economies (BOFIT), Finland

Thomas Kruiper, Associate Professor, Department of International Relations, Universidad Europea Valencia, Spain

Jan Lepeu, Postdoctoral Researcher, Centre for Transnational Governance, European University Institute, Italy

Meredith Lilly, Professor and Simon Reisman Chair in International Economic Policy, Norman Paterson School of International Affairs, Carleton University, Canada

Sascha Lohmann, Senior Associate, SWP, German Institute for International and Security Affairs, Germany

George A. Lopez, Rev. Theodore M. Hesburgh, C.S.C., Professor Emeritus of Peace Studies, Kroc Institute for International Peace Studies, University of Notre Dame, IN, USA

Yuliya Miadzvetskaya, Doctoral Researcher, Université Libre de Bruxelles, Belgium

Anna Miromanova, Assistant Professor of Economics, Lewis and Clark College, Portland, OR, USA

Anton Moiseienko, Senior Lecturer in Law, College of Law, Governance and Policy, Australian National University, Australia

Erica Moret, Senior Researcher Global Governance Centre and Coordinator, Geneva International Sanctions Network (GISN), Switzerland

T. Clifton Morgan, Albert Thomas Professor of Political Science, Department of Political Science, Rice University, TX, USA

Lisa Neal, Doctoral Researcher, University of Hamburg, Germany

Aurel Niederberger, State Secretariat for Economic Affairs (SECO), Switzerland

Jacob Öberg, Professor of European Law, Department of Law, University of Southern Denmark, Denmark

Stefano Palestini, Associate Professor, Department of Sociology and Social Research, School of International Studies, University of Trento, Italy

Paschalis Paschalidis, Counsel, Arendt & Medernach SA, Luxembourg

Anna Pau, Postdoctoral Research Fellow, European Union Law, University of Bologna, Italy

Clara Portela, Professor of Political Science, Law School, University of Valencia, Spain

Keith A. Preble, Teaching Assistant Professor of Political Science, East Carolina University, NC, USA

Luciano Quispe, Doctoral Researcher, Instituto de Ciencia Política, Pontificia Universidad Católica de Chile, Chile

Lukas Regli, Project Lead FATF Mutual Evaluation, State Secretariat for International Finance (SIF), Switzerland

Alice Riccardi, Associate Professor of International Law, Department of Law, Roma Tre University, Italy

Andrei Richter, Professor Researcher, Comenius University, Slovakia and Visiting Professor of Russian Studies, Charles University, Czechia

Loraine Rickard-Martin, Cofounder of Compliance and Capacity Skills and former Secretary of the UN Secretary-General's High-Level Panel on Threats, Challenges and Change, USA

Felipe Rodríguez Silvestre, Doctoral Researcher, University of Ghent, Belgium

Cedric Ryngaert, Professor of Public International Law, Utrecht University, The Netherlands

Franziska F.N. Schreiber, Doctoral Researcher, Peace Research Institute Frankfurt, Germany

Francesco Seatzu, Professor of International Law, University of Cagliari, Italy

Peter Seeberg, Associate Professor, Center for Modern Middle East and Muslim Studies, Department of Culture and Language, University of Southern Denmark, Denmark

Stefano Silingardi, Associate Professor of International Law, Department of Italian and Supranational Public Law, University of Milan, Italy

Mirko Sossai, Professor of International Law, Department of Law, Roma Tre University, Italy

Lindsay Speirs, MA Candidate and Research Fellow at the Centre for Defence and Security Studies, University of Manitoba, Canada

Gavin Sullivan, Reader in International Human Rights Law, Edinburgh Law School, University of Edinburgh, UK

Björn ten Seldam, Associate, Arendt & Medernach SA, Luxembourg

Sasha Tiaglei, Undergraduate and Research Fellow at the Centre for Defence and Security Studies, University of Manitoba, Canada

Nathanael Tilahun, Senior Lecturer in International Law, University of Essex, UK

Jo-Ansie van Wyk, Research Professor, Department of Political Sciences, University of South Africa, South Africa

Maruša T. Veber, Assistant Professor, Faculty of Law, University of Ljubljana, Slovenia

Daniel Ventura, Associate Professor, Université Côte d'Azur, France

Pierre-Hugues Verdier, Sullivan and Cromwell Professor of Law, University of Virginia School of Law, VA, USA

Martijn C. Vlaskamp, Ramón y Cajal Assistant Professor, Institut Barcelona d'Estudis Internacionals (IBEI), Spain

Judith Vorrath, Senior Associate, SWP, German Institute for International and Security Affairs, Germany

Dawid Walentek, Postdoctoral Researcher, Ghent Institute of International and European Studies, University of Ghent, Belgium

Charmaine N. Willis, Assistant Professor in Political Science, Old Dominion University, VA, USA

Oliver Windridge, Senior Adviser, The Sentry and Senior Counsel, International Lawyers Project, UK

Štěpánka Zemanová, Head of the Department of International and Diplomatic Studies, Faculty of International Relations, Prague University of Economics and Business, Czechia

Yuleng Zeng, Assistant Professor of International Political Economy, University of Groningen, The Netherlands

Introduction

ANDREA CHARRON, CLARA PORTELA AND MIRKO SOSSAI

Sanctions are the most frequently used tool to deal with violent conflicts and international norms violations. By virtue of their nature as coercive measures, international sanctions are of interest to political science and legal studies alike. Due to their often economic character, they are equally an object of research for economists and international political economy scholars. And yet, despite the confluence of interests in the phenomenon of international sanctions, very little interconnection has been established between different disciplines examining the same subject. The disconnection between them is such that it lacks a common language (Sossai et al. [2024]). Each discipline has different ideas on what sanctions are, what they are meant to achieve and when they are effective. Absent a common language, interdisciplinary collaboration and possible synergies are extremely difficult to achieve. Such collaboration, however, has never been more necessary, at a time when international sanctions are achieving unprecedented prominence on the geopolitical agenda. Facilitating the emergence of such a common language is the ambition of the *Encyclopedia of International Sanctions*.

The first task is to establish a definition of sanctions, which is far from straightforward. Here, the divergence is not merely between disciplines but even within disciplines different variants coexist. In general, political science and international relations scholarship regard sanctions as coercive instruments that pursue political ends, be they in the context of power politics or in support of international governance structures and standards. Legal studies adopt a similar perspective, focusing on sanctions as temporary measures taken in reaction to violations of international obligations. These measures aim to re-establish international legality and are meant to terminate once the violation stops. A stricter conception within legal literature distinguishes between sanctions as "centralised" measures adopted in accordance with the constituent instrument of some international organisations (including the UN Charter), and "decentralised" measures, called countermeasures, which are taken by a state individually or a group of states, to respond to wrongful acts. Another fundamental distinction concerns the types of measures that qualify as sanctions. Lawyers and political scientists alike consider sanctions as the withdrawal of a benefit that would otherwise be granted, including diplomatic restrictions, visa bans or the suspension of membership of international arrangements. For economists and industry experts, by contrast, sanctions are invariably economic restrictions designed to affect trade and investment flows. In the spirit of inclusiveness, the present work adopts a broad understanding of sanctions, which includes economic and non-economic measures alike. Lastly, sanctions can be either multilateral or autonomous depending on the authority that enacted them. If they are required by the United Nations Security Council, they are considered multilateral sanctions. While the term unilateral is often used to mean sanctioned by one state, the preferred term is autonomous. In cases when multiple states apply autonomous sanctions, they are often coordinated to mirror the effect of multilateral measures (Charron and Portela [2022]).

The area where these diverging perspectives have experienced some interaction is the evaluation of sanctions. A coherent body of research, however, has yet to be achieved. Far from being a merely anecdotal issue, the questions of the goals of sanctions and the nature of the measures remain central to the key debates in sanctions scholarship, i.e., whether or not they are successful in achieving their aims. The evolution of the study of sanctions is illustrative. Early studies on sanctions rendered a bleak, pessimistic picture of sanctions effectiveness. Political scientists claimed that sanctions were futile exercises or simply gestures lacking the potential to affect change (Doxey [1971]; Galtung [1967]; Wallensteen [1968]). It was not until a group of economists published a large-N study, *Economic Sanctions Reconsidered* (Hufbauer et al. [1985]), in the mid-1990s, claiming that sanctions proved successful one-third of the time that scholarship launched an endeavour to identify the conditions of sanctions success. Although this claim had the merit of revolutionising the field by confirming sanctions' coercive potential, it neglected the idea that sanctions pursue multiple, sometimes changing objectives, where coercion may not feature prominently – or not even feature at all. In so doing, it neglected a modest strand of research that had identified a variety of sanctions objectives (Barber [1979]; Doxey [1987]; Hoffman [1967]; Lindsay [1986]), which became marginalised from mainstream sanctions research for decades, until interest in the issue resurfaced in the twenty-first century (Biersteker et al. [2016]; Giumelli [2008]; Jones and Portela [2020]). Similarly, it took some time for non-economic measures such as membership suspensions or visa bans to receive researchers' attention (Charron and Portela [2015]) or to study the threat of sanctions as having its own impacts (Morgan et al. [2009]; Kruiper [2024]). Still, none of these aspects have become fully integrated in sanctions scholarship yet. Nevertheless, we consider them in our volume in order to render as complete a picture as possible of the sanctions world.

By contrast, legal scholarship displays different foci. During the 1990s, the reactivation of the multilateral United Nations (UN) collective security system brought the legality and legitimacy of sanctions to the forefront of legal debate. Central to this discussion were the scope of the UN Security Council's powers and issues of accountability, particularly regarding the humanitarian impact of sanctions on civilian populations (Gowlland-Debbas [2001]; Picchio Forlati and Sicilianos [2004]). A new area of research emerged concerning the domestic implementation of sanctions, which requires individual countries to translate international or regional sanctions into their own laws and regulations. In the 2000s, the shift from comprehensive to targeted sanctions introduced new challenges. Legal scrutiny of UN sanctions intensified, particularly in response to questions of due process within the Al-Qaeda counterterrorism sanctions regime (Ronzitti [2016]; van den Herik [2017]). Litigation before EU courts, especially after 9/11, highlighted concerns about human rights and procedural deficiencies in the targeted sanctions process. The *Kadi* saga before the Court of Justice underscored these issues, prompting procedural reforms in the Al-Qaeda sanctions regime, including the establishment of the UN Office of the Ombudsperson. In more recent years, the deadlock in the UN Security Council has triggered discussions about the legality of unilateral measures adopted by individual states and as part of the foreign policy of a regional organisation like the European Union (EU). In Western legal scholarship, these measures are often justified as lawful responses to serious breaches of *erga omnes* obligations, as obligations owed to the international community for the protection of collective interests. To enhance their effectiveness, various techniques have emerged to extend the reach of unilateral sanctions. Notably, the United States has increasingly relied on extraterritorial legislation. However, the legality of such measures has been a point of contention, particularly across the Atlantic (Beaucillon [2021]; Ruys et al. [2024]).

However, in order to provide researchers with the tools to explore this universe to the full, adopting an inclusive, comprehensive approach emerges as a necessity. The growing prominence of sanctions measures, and the prolific and often creative practice of senders, both traditional powers and newcomers – not to mention the concerted efforts of targets to evade sanctions – have increased the diversity of restrictions and the challenges associated with their categorisation, measurement, comparison, monitoring and assessment. The standard format of databases, popularised by the authors of *Economic Sanctions Reconsidered*, has become inadequate to capture individual sanctions such as visa bans or bans on payments (Portela and Charron [2023]). Both researchers and policymakers are increasingly interested in implementation and enforcement issues, such as detecting and preventing evasion (Early and Preble [2020]). With the growing diversity of sanctions tools and sanctions senders, and the insufficiency of traditional research tools, exploring the potential of interdisciplinary approaches emerges as a promising avenue. Our contribution to the interdisciplinary endeavour is this encyclopedia: a compendium combining a political science with a legal studies perspective, aimed to encourage some initial steps towards the framing of an interdisciplinary approach. The volume is designed to provide an up-to-date reference to international sanctions, satisfying the needs of researchers while facilitating an understanding of the topic from multiple disciplinary perspectives and assisting scholars of social sciences writ large.

The entries in this encyclopedia are organised into five main parts. Part I focuses on individual states, groups of states and international organisations as senders of sanctions. Part II delves into the specific content of these measures, providing a comprehensive overview of sanctions design and the various typologies of the measures used. Part III highlights key sanctions episodes, covering both UN and non-UN regimes. These entries explore the essential features of each sanctions regime, addressing both substantive and procedural issues, and shedding light on the multiple layers of measures applied to specific scenarios. Part IV, devoted to cross-cutting issues, examines critical questions related to the legitimacy, implementation and effectiveness of international sanctions, including evasion and circumvention, and judicial review, among others. Finally, Part V explores the objectives of sanctioning measures, analysing the rise of thematic sanctions alongside geographically focused sanctions.

The editors extend their gratitude to the authors for their enthusiastic contributions to this project. The authors bring diverse scientific perspectives and represent multiple generations of sanctions expertise. Many entries reflect their personal experiences and professional insights. Special thanks are also due to Benedetta Panagia, Pietro Salvatici, Lindsay Speirs and Sasha Tiaglei for their invaluable editorial assistance.

Bibliography

Literature

Barber J, 'Economic Sanctions as a Policy Instrument' (1979) 55 *International Affairs* 367.

Beaucillon C (ed.), *Research Handbook on Unilateral and Extraterritorial Sanctions* (Edward Elgar 2021).

Biersteker T, Eckert S and Tourinho M, *Targeted Sanctions: The Impacts and Effectiveness of United Nations Action* (Cambridge University Press 2016).

Charron A and Portela C, 'The UN, Regional Sanctions and Africa' (2015) 91(6) *International Affairs* 1369.

Charron A, Portela C and Eckert S, 'Multilateral Sanctions Revisited: An Overview' in Charron A and Portela C (eds), *Multilateral Sanctions Revisited: Lessons Learned from Margaret Doxey* (McGill-Queen's University Press 2022) 15.

Doxey M, *Economic Sanctions and International Enforcement* (Oxford University Press 1971).

Doxey M, *International Sanctions in Contemporary Perspective* (McMillan 1987).

Early B and Preble K, 'Going Fishing versus Hunting Whales: Explaining Changes in How the US Enforces Economic Sanctions' (2020) 29(2) *Security Studies* 231.

Galtung J, 'On the Effects of International Economic Sanctions, with Examples from the Case of Rhodesia' (1967) 19(3) *World Politics* 378.

Giumelli F, 'New Analytical Categories for Assessing EU Sanctions' (2010) 45(3) *International Spectator* 131.

Gowlland-Debbas V (ed.), *United Nations Sanctions and International Law* (Nijhoff 2001).

Hoffman F, 'The Functions of Economic Sanctions' (1967) 4 *Journal of Peace Research* 140.

Hufbauer G, Schott J and Elliott K, *Economic Sanctions Reconsidered* (Institute for International Economics 1985).

Jones L and Portela C, 'Evaluating the Success of International Sanctions: A New Research Agenda' (2020) 125 *Afers Internacionals* 39.

Kruiper T, *United Nations Sanctions Regimes and Selective Security* (Routledge 2024).

Lindsay J, 'Trade Sanctions as Policy Instruments: A Re-examination' (1986) 30(2) *International Studies Quarterly* 153.

Morgan TC, Bapat N and Krustev V, 'The Threat and Imposition of Economic Sanctions, 1971–2000' (2009) 26(1) *Conflict Management and Peace Science* 92.

Picchio Forlati L and Sicilianos L (eds), *Economic Sanctions in International Law/Les sanctions économiques en droit international* (Nijhoff 2004).

Portela C and Charron A, 'The Evolution of Databases in the Age of Targeted Sanctions' (2023) 25(1) *International Studies Review.*

Ronzitti N (ed.), *Coercive Diplomacy, Sanctions and International Law* (Nijhoff 2016).

Ruys T, Ryngaert C and Rodríguez Silvestre F (eds), *The Cambridge Handbook of Secondary Sanctions and International Law* (Cambridge University Press 2024).

Sossai M, Giumelli F and Portela C, 'Conclusions' in Bultrini A, Giumelli F, Portela C and Sossai M (eds), *International Sanctions in Practice: An Interdisciplinary Perspective* (Routledge 2024) 197.

ANDREA CHARRON, CLARA PORTELA AND MIRKO SOSSAI

van den Herik L (ed.), *Research Handbook on UN Sanctions and International Law* (Edward Elgar 2017).
Wallensteen P, 'Characteristics of Economic Sanctions' (1968) 5(3) *Journal of Peace Research* 247.

Andrea Charron, Clara Portela and Mirko Sossai

PART I

PROFILE OF SENDERS

1. African Union and ECOWAS

Kristen Boon and Nickolas Eburne

I Introduction

The African Union (AU) and the Economic Community of West African States (ECOWAS) can take action to uphold democratic norms and respond to unconstitutional changes of government (UCG) by imposing sanctions on their member states. The AU primarily imposes political sanctions, but occasionally applies targeted sanctions against individuals responsible for UCG. ECOWAS, in contrast, utilizes economic sanctions to safeguard democratic principles among its membership.

II Sanctions under the AU

The AU is made up of 55 member states representing all the countries on the African continent. AU member states are divided into five geographic regions, encompassing Northern, Eastern, Western, Southern, and Central Africa. Typical AU sanctions involve suspending a member state's participation in AU activities following UCG. The AU institutes these sanctions through its Peace and Security Council (PSC), which serves as the standing decision-making organ of the AU for the prevention, management, and resolution of conflicts. The PSC assesses a particular situation to determine whether UCG has occurred and, if so, recommends the suspension of that member to the Assembly of Heads of State and Government, which makes the final decision on suspension. As for targeted sanctions in response to actions by members that threaten peace, security, or stability in Africa, the PSC has the authority to both identify the specific individuals or entities to be sanctioned and determine which sanctions to apply (which can range from travel bans to asset freezes and arms embargoes).

Since 2019, the PSC has suspended seven member states: Sudan (June 2019 and October 2021), Mali (August 2020), Guinea (September 2021), Burkina Faso (January 2022), Niger (August 2023), and Gabon (August 2023) (Etyang et al. [2024]). On occasion, the AU has also imposed targeted sanctions in the form of asset freezes and travel bans against leaders and members of military juntas (PSC [2012]).

The AU's responses are guided by its Constitutive Act, the protocol establishing the Peace and Security Council of the African Union, and the Lomé Declaration, which emphasize zero tolerance for unconstitutional changes. The definition of a UCG is codified in Article 23 of the African Charter on Democracy, Elections and Governance, 2007:

> [T]he following illegal means of accessing or maintaining power constitute an [UCG] and shall draw appropriate sanctions by the Union:
>
> 1. Any putsch or coup d'état against a democratically elected government.
> 2. Any intervention by mercenaries to replace a democratically elected government.
> 3. Any replacement of a democratically elected government by armed dissidents or rebels.
> 4. Any refusal by an incumbent government to relinquish power to the winning party or candidate after free, fair, and regular elections; or
> 5. Any amendment or revision of the constitution or legal instruments, which is an infringement on the principles of democratic change of government.

As the AU relies on the collective agreement of its member states for enforcement, the effectiveness of AU sanctions has been limited by inconsistencies in commitment among member states and challenges in enforcement. For example, the AU did not impose sanctions on Chad after the 2021 seizure of power by senior military officers following the death of the Chadian president. The AU was critiqued for this inaction, which some claim emanates from concerns around security in the region (ISS [2021]; see Corda [2024] 168).

III ECOWAS sanctions

ECOWAS, in contrast, demonstrates a more proactive stance, with a history of enforcing sanctions and, in some cases, deploying military interventions to restore constitutional order. ECOWAS's smaller membership (15 states) and regional focus on West Africa allow for more cohesive and decisive actions.

ECOWAS was initially formed to facilitate trade between its members, but soon after began to act on UCGs in the region. In pursuing this objective, ECOWAS members are guided by the 2001 Supplementary Protocol on Democracy and Good Governance (the Protocol), the goal of which is to ensure that all West African countries have transparent elections, respect for human rights, and non-military interference in governance. The Protocol states that good governance, the rule of law, and human rights are the foundations of democracy.

ECOWAS acts through its Authority of Heads of State and Government (the Authority) for both the suspension of ECOWAS membership and targeted sanctions. The Authority determines whether claims of UCG occurring are substantiated and then has the ability to suspend the membership of the affected country. The decision is usually taken by consensus, but it can also be taken by a two-thirds majority vote. As for targeted sanctions in response to actions threatening peace and security in the region, the Authority determines the specific sanctions to be imposed (travel bans, asset freezes, trade restrictions), and these are then implemented by member states.

Article 45(1) of the Protocol provides that sanctions can be imposed if a democracy is "abruptly brought to an end" or where massive violations of human rights are committed in a member state. In recent years, countries like Mali, Guinea, and Burkina Faso have faced ECOWAS sanctions following military coups, reflecting the organization's commitment to democratic principles (Charron and Portela [2015] at 1377). In February 2024, ECOWAS eased sanctions on Guinea, Mali, and Niger, citing humanitarian reasons (ECOWAS [2024]). At the date of writing, ECOWAS has lifted most of its economic and financial sanctions against member states that experienced military coups between 2020 and 2023. However, some targeted sanctions and political sanctions remain in place in several of these countries, such as Niger. Additionally, even though some sanctions were lifted against Mali, Burkina Faso, and Guinea, all three are still suspended from ECOWAS until elections are held. As tensions between ECOWAS and its suspended members escalated further, Mali, Burkina Faso, and Niger declared their intention to withdraw from the organization in January 2024. The subsequent lifting of most sanctions failed to convince them to reconsider their decision. Instead, the three countries solidified their alignment by signing an agreement to establish a confederation among themselves (Sossai [2024] 102).

IV Relationship with UN sanctions

There is certainly interplay between the AU and the United Nations (UN) sanction regimes, the latter wielded by the United Nations Security Council (UNSC). The AU sometimes aligns its sanctions with UNSC measures, especially in cases where UN sanctions target specific individuals or groups posing a regional threat. The opposite is also true: UNSC sanctions have also been used to serve as reinforcement for AU sanctions. This was the case, for example, in the Central African Republic, Côte d'Ivoire, Guinea-Bissau, and Libya (Charron and Portela [2015] 1376).

Similarly, ECOWAS may work in concert with UN sanctions, particularly when addressing global security, such as terrorism or transnational crime. For instance, sanctions on militant groups in West Africa and the Sahel often align with UN listings. Côte d'Ivoire, Guinea-Bissau, and Sierra Leone all faced UN and ECOWAS sanctions in the past (Charron and Portela [2015] at 1376).

In summary, both the AU and ECOWAS aim to uphold democratic principles through sanctions. While ECOWAS's targeted financial sanctions aim to bring their members back into the fold when it comes to democratic principles, the AU favors an approach where sanctioned states are excluded from the benefits of AU membership, and rely on a unified community to implement the sanctions.

Disclaimer

The views expressed in this article are solely those of the authors and do not represent or reflect the views, positions, or policies of the International Court of Justice.

Bibliography

Literature

Charron A and Portela C, 'The UN, Regional Sanctions and Africa' (2015) 91(6) *International Affairs* 1369.

Corda T, 'Democratic Sanctions in Africa: A Reassessment of Their Selective and Inconsistent Use Across Multiple Senders' in Bultrini A, Giumelli F, Portela C and Sossai M (eds), *International Sanctions in Practice: An Interdisciplinary Perspective* (Routledge 2024) 161.

Etyang O, Abdulkadir T, Masah C and Mapiro T, *Evaluation of the African Union Peace and Security Council: Lessons from 20 Years of Intervention and Recommendations for the Future* (Accord Policy & Practice Brief No. 65, August 2024) <https://www.accord.org.za/publication/evaluation-of-the-african-union-peace-and-security-council-lessons-from-20-years-of-intervention-and-recommendations-for-the-future/> accessed 15 November 2024.

ISS, 'The AU Reneges on Its Stance against Coups d'État' (PSC Insights 27 May 2021) <https://issafrica.org/pscreport/psc-insights/the-au-reneges-on-its-stance-against-coups-detat> accessed 15 November 2024.

Sossai M, 'Regional Sanctions Against Member States: A Comparative and Relational Approach' in Adinolfi G, Lang A and Ragni C (eds), *Sanctions by and against International Organizations* (Intersentia 2024) 93.

Documents

African Charter on Democracy, Elections and Governance (adopted 30 January 2007, entered into force 15 February 2012).

Constitutive Act of the African Union (adopted 11 July 2000, entered into force 26 May 2001).

Protocol A/SP1/12/01 on Democracy and Good Governance Supplementary to the Protocol Relating to the Mechanism for Conflict Prevention, Management, Resolution, Peacekeeping and Security (adopted 21 December 2001 entered into force 20 February 2008).

ECOWAS, Final Communiqué of the Extraordinary Summit of the ECOWAS Authority of Heads of State and Government on the Political, Peace and Security Situation in the Region (Abuja 24 February 2024).

Peace and Security Council of the African Union, Communiqué, Doc. PSC/PR/COMM. (CCCXVI) (3 April 2012).

Protocol Relating to the Establishment of the Peace and Security Council of the African Union (adopted 9 July 2002, entered into force 26 December 2003).

KRISTEN BOON AND NICKOLAS EBURNE

2. Arab states

Mirko Sossai

I Introduction

Arab States have traditionally been perceived as sceptical regarding the use of sanctions. This is unsurprising, given that respect for state sovereignty and the prohibition of interference in the internal affairs of other states have long formed the foundation of their mutual relations (Barnett [1995] 482) and are core principles of the League of Arab States (LAS), a regional organization comprising 22 Middle Eastern and African countries. However, the League's constituent instrument – the 1945 Pact of the LAS – does provide, in Article 18(2), that the Council of the League can unanimously decide to consider any state failing to fulfil its obligations under the pact "as excluded from the League".

II The boycott of Israel and the sanctions against Egypt (1979)

Since its establishment in 1945, the LAS (also known as the Arab League) has maintained an official boycott of Israeli goods and companies. This policy has been more emblematic of the League's political stance than any other single initiative. Although the boycott targets a non-member state, it should not be regarded as a typical sanctioning tool against third states, comparable to European Union (EU) measures. Instead, it reflects the League's territorial conception, which considers Palestine an integral part of the Arab region and views the creation of Israel as an unacceptable external interference (Hellquist [2014] 24).

The only episode prior to the Arab Spring in which the LAS imposed sanctions against a member state was directly tied to the Arab–Israeli conflict. This occurred in 1979 when Egypt was suspended following the Camp David peace accords with Israel, which were seen as a violation of pan-Arab solidarity (Debre [2021] 519). In addition to Egypt's suspension from the League and affiliated organizations, political and economic measures were taken, including severing diplomatic relations, imposing an economic embargo, and terminating financial assistance. The League's headquarters were transferred from Cairo to Tunis (UN Doc. A/34/160 – S/13216 [1979]). In 1989, Egypt was readmitted to the League and the following year the headquarters returned to Cairo.

III The Arab Spring and the Arab League's sanctions against Libya and Syria (2011)

The events connected to the Arab uprisings marked not only a process of revitalization of the LAS but also a change in the previous policy of non-interference in the conduct of its member states, particularly regarding human rights violations. On 22 February 2011, during an emergency meeting in Cairo, the Council of the League agreed by unanimous vote to suspend Libya from its membership (see chapter), a decision "welcomed" by the United Nations Security Council (UNSC) (SC/10180 [2011]) and the General Assembly (UNGA Res 65/265 [2011]). In November 2011, the LAS took further unprecedented steps by suspending Syria (see chapter) and imposing broader sanctions later that month. These measures included cutting off transactions with the Syrian Central Bank, a travel ban on senior Syrian government officials travelling to other Arab countries, a freeze on the assets of the Assad government, and an embargo on investments into the country. Syria was subsequently readmitted in May 2023.

The suspension of Syria was passed with 18 votes in favour, while Lebanon and Yemen voted against, and Iraq abstained. This decision is notable because the LAS Pact requires unanimity and does not explicitly condition membership on respect for human rights. Additionally, the League applied economic sanctions against the Assad government, despite the pact providing no specific power for imposing such measures. It follows that these measures did not completely follow established procedures and rules. Some argued that the LAS acted *ultra vires* (i.e. beyond the competences given to the organization) and, therefore, the decisions were invalid (Hofer [2024] 122). Others, however, categorized these actions as third-party countermeasures (see chapter) (Dawidowicz [2017] 220). From another perspective, it could be suggested that the LAS possesses an implied or inherent power to impose sanctions on its members when circumstances necessitate such measures.

IV The "Quartet" sanctions against Qatar (2017)

The measures imposed by the LAS against Syria highlighted the enduring significance of pan-Arabism. However, at the time, it was observed that beneath this pan-Arab rhetoric lay a fragmented group of states. For some members, sanctions could serve as instruments to assert prominence in the competition for regional leadership (Hellquist [2014]). A significant regional crisis unfolded in June 2017, when Saudi Arabia, the United Arab Emirates (UAE), Bahrain, and Egypt (the "Quartet") severed all relations with Qatar. These measures included not only breaking off diplomatic relations but also closing their land, sea, and airspace to the movement of Qatari persons and goods. The Quartet justified the measures as lawful countermeasures (see chapter) in response to Qatar's alleged violations of the Riyadh Agreements, concluded under the aegis of the Gulf Cooperation Council (GCC). Under these agreements, Qatar committed "to cease supporting, financing or harbouring persons or groups presenting a danger to national security, in particular terrorist groups". Shortly after imposing these measures, the Quartet issued a list of 13 demands to Qatar, including shutting down Al Jazeera and its affiliate stations. Qatar, however, denied the accusations that it was supporting terrorism, arguing that the measures undermined its sovereignty by attempting to dictate Qatar's international relations, as well as interfering with its internal affairs (Abusedra [2021]).

A significant aspect of the 2017 Gulf crisis is that Qatar engaged in various dispute settlement mechanisms in order to invoke the international responsibility of the Quartet. Two key measures imposed by the Quartet – the repatriation of Qatari nationals from their territories and the closure of their airspace to Qatari civil aviation – formed the basis for international legal proceedings before several forums, including the International Court of Justice, the International Civil Aviation Organization (ICAO), the World Trade Organization (WTO), and the UN Committee on the Elimination of Racial Discrimination (Gaver [2020]). In January 2021, the coercive measures were lifted following extensive mediation efforts between Saudi Arabia and Qatar, led by Kuwait, which succeeded in December 2020. This mediation culminated in a solidarity and stability deal, signed in January 2021 (Hofer [2021]).

V Conclusion

The Arab Spring marked a turning point in the use of sanctions by Arab states, occurring during a period of widespread legitimacy crises for all of them. The imposition of coercive measures not only reflected a struggle for regional leadership but also underscored the inherent tension between two core objectives: fostering Arab cooperation to maintain regional security and upholding the founding principle of non-interference in the domestic affairs of sovereign states. The sanctions imposed by the LAS and individual states extended beyond the suspension of membership. They included economic and financial measures, which tended to be more comprehensive in nature compared to the targeted sanctions adopted in other regional contexts.

Bibliography

Literature

Abusedra A, 'The Impact of Unilateral Sanctions on Regional Integration Treaties with Special Reference to the Gulf Cooperation Council' in Subedi SP (ed.), *Unilateral Sanctions in International Law* (Hart 2021) 137.

Barnett MN, 'Sovereignty, Nationalism, and Regional Order in the Arab States System' (1995) 49 *International Organization* 479.

Dawidowicz M, *Third-Party Countermeasures in International Law* (Cambridge University Press 2017).

Debre MJ, 'Legitimation, Regime Survival, and Shifting Alliances in the Arab League: Explaining Sanction Politics during the Arab Spring' (2021) 42 *International Political Science Review* 516.

Gaver CD, 'Déjà Vu All Over Again: ICJ Rules on the Jurisdiction of the ICAO Council in Relation to the Gulf Dispute' (*Opinio Juris*, 29 July 2020) <https://opiniojuris.org/2020/07/29/deja-vu-all-over-again-icj-rules-on-the-appellate-jurisdiction-of-the-icao-council-in-relation-to-the-gulf-dispute/>.

Hellquist E, 'Regional Organizations and Sanctions Against Members – Explaining the Different Trajectories of the African Union, the League of Arab States, and the Association of Southeast Asian Nations', KFG Working Paper Series, No. 59 (2014).

Mirko Sossai

Hofer A, 'Regional Organizations and the Non-Mandated Sanctioning of Member States: The Case of the League of Arab States Sanctions Against Syria' in Adinolfi G, Lang A and Ragni C (eds), *Sanctions by and against International Organizations* (Intersentia 2024) 111.

Hofer A, 'Sanctioning Qatar: The Finale?' (*EJIL:Talk!*, 16 June 2021) <https://www.ejiltalk.org/sanctioning-qatar-the-finale/>.

Documents

Pact of the League of Arab States (adopted 22 March 1945, entered into force 10 May 1945).

Resolutions adopted by the Council of the League of Arab States at the level of Arab Ministers for Foreign Affairs, Economy and Finance (31 March 1979) Annex to UN Doc. A/34/160 – S/13216 (3 April 1979).

UNGA Res 65/265 'Suspension of the Rights of Membership of the Libyan Arab Jamahiriya in the Human Rights Council' (1 March 2011) UN Doc. A/RES/65/265.

Security Council press statement on Libya (22 February 2011) UN Doc. SC/10180.

MIRKO SOSSAI

3. Canada

ANDREA CHARRON AND MEREDITH LILLY

I Introduction

Since the days of the League of Nations, Canada has supported the idea of sanctions to signal disapproval and criticize a target's bad behavior, even if its enforcement record was decidedly mixed. Indeed, lack of monitoring of sanctions' efficacy is a perennial problem for the Government of Canada. Sanctions are Canada's most applied foreign policy tool since the 1990s. Canada seeks to apply sanctions either via a multilateral organization like the United Nations (UN), or autonomously with a coalition of like-minded states, especially the European Union, the United States and the United Kingdom. On only very rare occasions has Canada sought to sanction unilaterally.

In 2007, the then Department of Foreign Affairs and International Trade (now Global Affairs Canada) outlined its definition of and approach to sanctions. Sanctions are

> measures, not including the use of armed force, that are intended to bring about changes in the policies or behaviour of a specific state. Sanctions can encompass a wide variety of measures, including limitations on official and diplomatic contacts or travel, the imposition of legal measures to restrict or prohibit trade or other economic activity between Canada and the target state, or the seizure or freezing of property situated in Canada. *In order to maximise the effectiveness of any sanctions regime, particularly one involving trade and economic measures, Canadian policy and legislative instruments seek to ensure that, wherever possible, sanctions measures are applied multilaterally.* (emphasis added) (cited in Charron [2008])

II Standing legislation

Canada has standing legislation to apply sanctions. The minister of foreign affairs is responsible for the application of sanctions, including the granting of permits or certificates as exemptions to sanctions. The Parliament of Canada may authorize the imposition of sanctions through the United Nations Act (UNA),[1] the Special Economic Measures Act (SEMA) and/or the Justice for Victims of Corrupt Foreign Officials Act (JVCFOA). On at least eight occasions, the Governor in Council has invoked two or even all three of the Acts in the same situation.[2] Regulations are created under the appropriate Act to tailor measures to specific circumstances. While the UNA supports multilateral sanctions only, the SEMA can support either multilateral or autonomous sanctions and the JVCFOA autonomous measures only. Sanctions may apply against any actors but reach for enforcement purposes is limited to Canadians or Canadian companies regardless of their location in the world, or to foreign individuals, entities, or assets located in Canada. Unlike the United States, which also applies sanctions in an extraterritorial manner (potentially to foreign actors in foreign countries), Canada does not apply this practice.

III The SEMA

The SEMA (adopted in 1992 and updated in 2017 and 2023) and the JVCFOA (adopted in 2017 and updated in 2023) are most often applied in concert with allies.[3] Both are designed to address different situations. The SEMA can be used to deal with four situations:

> 1. where an international organization to which Canada belongs calls on its members to take economic measures against a foreign state;
> 2. where a grave breach of international peace and security has occurred and is likely to result in a serious international crisis;
> 3. where gross and systematic human rights violations have been committed in a foreign state; or
> 4. where a national of a foreign state, who is either a foreign public official or an associate of such an official, is responsible for or complicit in acts of significant corruption. (SEMA [1992])

Like sanctions under the UNA, the SEMA can be applied against individuals, entities, states or even regions and can accommodate any measure that the sanctioning authority deems necessary such as the sanctioning of Russia's shadow fleet.

IV The JVCFOA

The JVCFOA, in contrast, is more circumspect and applies only to individuals deemed responsible for or complicit in gross violations of internationally recognized human rights (Kustra et al. [2024]; Lilly and Arabi [2020]). It can also apply to foreign public officials, or their associates, who are responsible for or complicit in acts of significant corruption.

One of the reasons why Canada's Parliament wished to adopt the JVCFOA – a Magnitsky-style legislation – was to keep pace with allies if they imposed such sanctions. Prior to 2017, Canada could not act autonomously to impose sanctions targeting individual acts of human rights violations or corruption (Nault [2017]). The proposed JVCFOA was designed to address this perceived gap and to allow for more options to coordinate with allies. The JVCFOA was the first avenue established for targeting foreign nationals who had acted in ways that were not strongly connected to broader circumstances occurring in the state of origin of the crime(s), or which fell below SEMA's threshold of constituting a threat to international peace and security. For example, acts of corruption might reasonably be considered serious or punishable acts but might not constitute a threat to peace and security of the international community (McTaggart [2019]). At the same time, the proposed bill was described as a "bare minimum" measure meant to prevent the circulation of "dirty money" in Canada, and as a way to ensure that Canada would not be a safe haven for individuals implicated in egregious acts (Nault, [2017]). Therefore, even if the sanctions themselves were deemed ineffective at coercing a change in behavior, at least, in theory, they might deter criminals from finding refuge in Canada.

V Conclusion

Canada continues to enact new legislation to apply sanctions in a myriad of scenarios. Canadian autonomous sanctions activity escalated dramatically in 2017 and, by September 2025, more than 5000 individuals and entities were targeted by Canada, the majority associated with Russia's illegal war in Ukraine (Global Affairs Canada [2025]). Despite this increased activity, enforcement remains low. Canada has only prosecuted one entity to date and rarely reports on the level of assets immobilized through its sanctions.[4] Canada's key contribution to the field are three Canadians who have instrumentally changed global thinking on the nature and application of sanctions, including academics David Malone and the "doyenne" of sanctions Margaret Doxey, and Ambassador Robert Fowler's active investigation into sanctions-busting activity against UN Angolan sanctions (Charron [2010]).

Notes

1. United Nations Act (R.S.C. 1985, c. U-2). The UNA was first adopted in 1947. Offenses and punishments include (a) on summary conviction, a fine of not more than $100 000 or imprisonment for a term of not more than one year, or both; or (b) on conviction on indictment, to imprisonment for a term of not more than 10 years.
2. Against the situations in Iran, Libya, North Korea, South Sudan and Haiti (SEMA and UNA) and Myanmar, Russia, and Venezuela (SEMA and JVCFOA). Iran and South Sudan have been subject to all three (UNA, SEMA, and JVCFOA)
3. Special Economic Measures Act (S.C. 1992, c. 17) and Justice for Victims of Corrupt Foreign Officials Act (Sergei Magnitsky Law) (S.C. 2017, c. 21). For both Acts, every person who knowingly contravenes or fails to comply with an order or regulation: (a) is guilty of an indictable offense and is liable to imprisonment for a term of not more than five years; or (b) is guilty of an offense punishable on summary conviction and is liable to a fine of not more than $25 000 or imprisonment for a term of not more than one year, or both.
4. On 15 April 2014, Lee Specialties Ltd of Alberta, Canada, pleaded guilty to charges and was fined $90 000 for unlawful exports of Viton O-rings to Iran in contravention of the SEMA. Additionally, two judicial review cases were requested of individuals targeted by the SEMA including the former prime minister of Haiti filed in December 2022 and Dimitry Mazepin (former Formula 1 driver and Russian) filed an application for judicial review in Federal Court in April 2023.

Bibliography

Literature

Charron A, 'Canada's Domestic Implementation of UN Sanctions' (2008) 14(2) *Canadian Foreign Policy Journal* 1.

Charron A, 'Three Canadians and Their Contribution to United Nations Sanctions: A Tribute to Margaret Doxey, David Malone and Robert Fowler' (2010) 16(3) *Canadian Foreign Policy Journal* 1.

Kustra, T and James P, 'The Importance of Immigrants on American Intervention in International Crises' (2024) *Conflict Management and Peace Science* 131.

Lilly M and Arabi D, 'Symbolic Act, Real Consequences: Passing Canada's Magnitsky Law to Combat Human Rights Violations and Corruption' (2020) 75(2) *International Journal* 163–78.

McTaggart S, 'Sanctions: The Canadian and International Architecture Background Paper' (2019) Economics, Resources and International Affairs Division 2; Special Economic Measures Act, S.C. 1992, c 17.

Documents

Global Affairs Canada 'Consolidated Canadian Autonomous Sanctions List' (*Global Affairs Canada,* 2025) <https://www.international.gc.ca/world-monde/international_relations-relations_internationales/sanctions/consolidated-consolide.aspx?lang=eng> accessed 10 October 2025.

Justice for Victims of Corrupt Foreign Officials Act (Sergei Magnitsky Law) (S.C. 2017, c. 21).

Nault, R.D. 'A Coherent and Effective Approach to Canada's Sanctions Regimes: Sergei Magnitsky and Beyond' 42nd Parliament 1st Session (House of Commons 2017) <https://www.ourcommons.ca/DocumentViewer/en/42-1/FAAE/report-7>.

Special Economic Measures Act (S.C. 1992, c. 17).

United Nations Act (R.S.C. 1985, c. U-2).

ANDREA CHARRON AND MEREDITH LILLY

4. China

MARIA ADELE CARRAI

I Introduction

China's approach to international sanctions has been shaped by its own experiences as a target of such measures, particularly following the Tiananmen Square incident in 1989, when many Western countries imposed arms embargoes and other restrictions in response to the government's actions against protesters. It is also rooted in its understanding of sovereignty articulated in the Five Principles of Peaceful Coexistence (Carrai [2019]). China tends to oppose unilateral international sanctions, especially those with extraterritorial reach, which it views as manifestations of "long-arm jurisdiction" that encroach upon sovereignty (MFA [2023]). The repercussions of sanctions on nations like China or Iran, exemplified by the case of Huawei, underscore the tangible impacts of these measures (McDonald [2021]). Consequently, instead of initiating sanctions, China has developed policies framed as "anti-sanctions" or "countermeasures". These policies were initially a response to the proliferation of American sanctions, bans, and other trade tensions, evolving significantly over the past few years. By framing its actions as countermeasures or anti-sanctions, China positions itself not as an aggressor, but as a defender of national sovereignty against what it perceives as overreach by other states, particularly in the context of international trade and diplomacy.

II The unreliable entity list

China's sanctions regime is rudimentary, primarily defensive, and reactive to the sanctions imposed by the United States and the European Union (EU). While China does participate in and implement United Nations (UN)-mandated international sanctions (Fung [2019]), it has developed its own toolbox for imposing unilateral sanctions. In response to sanctions from Western nations, China in the past five years has swiftly developed a robust counter-sanction strategy, particularly criticizing the application of extraterritorial jurisdiction by the United States (see also chapter on Secondary sanctions and the extraterritorial effects of sanctions). China first unveiled its foreign anti-sanction policy in 2019, responding to a global economic climate marked by uncertainty and rising protectionism. In 2020, the Ministry of Commerce established the system of unreliable entities under the directives of the State Council (MOFCOM [2020]). The provisions on the unreliable entity list target foreign enterprises, organizations, and individuals engaged in activities deemed detrimental to China's national sovereignty, security, or development interests. They also address actions that discriminate against Chinese entities, potentially infringing on their legitimate rights. Entities can be labeled as "unreliable" if they threaten China's national interests, disrupt normal transactions, or apply discriminatory measures against Chinese parties contrary to standard market practices. This mechanism aims to deter foreign companies from severing ties with Chinese companies as a way to support Western sanctions (Wang and Dai [2020]). To date, Lockheed Martin Corporation and Raytheon Missiles & Defense have been listed for their arms dealings with Taiwan (MOFCOM [2023]). The list serves not only as a sanction but also as a deterrent, imposing minimal yet significant threats (Zhang [2020] 229).

III Blocking rules and the anti-foreign sanctions law

In January 2021, China enacted the Rules on Counteracting Unjustified Extraterritorial Application of Foreign Legislation and Other Measures. These blocking measures aim to mitigate the impact of foreign sanctions, particularly from the United States, on Chinese entities. Under these regulations, individuals and companies affected by foreign sanctions are required to report these incidents to Chinese authorities (MOFCOM [2021]). A designated working mechanism then evaluates the legitimacy of the sanctions and, if deemed unjustified, issues orders to annul their legal effects. However, the effectiveness of these measures remains questionable, and there have been no instances where reports to the courts have led to the application of these blocking rules (Webster [2022] 189).

Subsequently, in June 2021, Beijing introduced the Law of the People's Republic of China on Countering Foreign Sanctions. This national-level legislation extends the scope of countermeasures similar to those in the unreliable entity list and the blocking measures. It expands targets to include spouses and family members of individuals already listed, as well as those in control or senior management positions within the sanctioned organizations (NPC [2021]). This broadened approach reflects a comprehensive effort to shield Chinese interests from external judicial overreach.

IV China's strategic and symbolic approach to sanctions

As China's global influence grows, so too does its assertiveness, including in the domain of international sanctions. Unlike traditional Western sanctions regimes or those enforced by the UN Security Council (UNSC), China's sanctions feature unique legal and political nuances. According to Webster ([2022] 182), China's sanctions often serve anti-democratic purposes, such as deflecting criticisms of human rights abuses and stifling scrutiny of China's internal affairs. Interestingly, China has mainly targeted high-profile political figures critical of its policies rather than corporations, except for those involved with Taiwan. Moreover, the enforcement of counter-sanctions is largely non-coercive, targeting individuals and typically failing to cause economic harm (Li [2024]). This has led scholars like Li ([2024]) to suggest that China's use and rhetoric of sanctions are more performative than punitive, aimed at signaling resilience to and defiance of both international and domestic audiences.

Angela Poh's recent work on how Chinese decision-makers handle sanctions both within the framework of the UNSC and through unilateral actions revealed how China's very rhetoric on sanctions has significantly influenced its behavior, often limiting its capacity to use sanctions fully in line with its immediate interests (Poh [2021]). In addition to formal sanctions, China often employs measures that, while not officially labeled as sanctions, effectively serve the same purpose. For instance, China has imposed import restrictions on Canadian beef and Australian products, citing safety concerns. However, these actions coincide with diplomatic disputes, suggesting that they are responses to foreign policy disagreements rather than genuine safety issues. The inclusion of Chinese authorities in the EU human rights sanctions regime led to significant diplomatic repercussions, including Beijing's cancellation of a long-negotiated investment treaty with the EU that was on the verge of being signed. This incident underscores the broader geopolitical implications of sanctions and the interconnectedness of economic and political strategies.

V Conclusion

China's anti-sanction laws are likely to remain largely symbolic, strategically implemented to avoid overt confrontations. The real impact is likely to be felt through China's economic statecraft—actions that are more subtle and carried out quietly, rather than through overt legal channels (Li [2017]). This method allows China to exert influence and respond to international pressures without overt confrontations, reflecting a strategic preference for less visible yet potentially impactful maneuvers in global diplomacy. Still, the increasing deployment of sanctions by China raises concerns about transparency, due process, and the potential for escalating retaliations, which could impair global cooperation and dialogue. While China's significant market size offers leverage, its heavy reliance on international trade means that any sanctions it imposes could also adversely affect its own economy.

Bibliography

Literature

Carrai MA, *Sovereignty in China: A Genealogy of a Concept since 1840* (Cambridge University Press 2019).

Fung CJ, *China and Intervention at the UN Security Council: Reconciling Status* (Oxford University Press 2019).

Li KX, 'Performative Economic Sanctions: How Sanctions Work Without Economic Harm' (2024) 15 *Harvard Law School National Security Journal* 327.

Li M, *China's Economic Statecraft. Co-optation, Cooperation, and Coercion* (World Scientific 2017).

McDonald J, 'Huawei Revenue Sinks as Smartphones Hurt by US Sanctions', *Associated Press* (2021) <https://apnews.com/article/technology-business-13737ab7a59484a536066d5b2fab153a> accessed 6 August 2021.

Poh A, *Sanctions with Chinese Characteristics: Rhetoric and Restraint in China's Diplomacy* (Amsterdam University Press 2021).

Maria Adele Carrai

Wang F and Dai M, 'Four Key Issues on China's Unreliable Entity List' (2020) China Law Insights <https://www.chinalawinsight.com/2020/10/articles/u-s/four-key-issues-on-chinas-unreliable-entity-list/> accessed 16 October 2020.

Webster T, 'Retooling Sanctions: China's Challenge to the Liberal International Order' (2022) 23(1) *Chicago Journal of International Law*.

Zhang AH, *Chinese Antitrust Exceptionalism: How the Rise of China Challenges Global Regulations* (Oxford University Press 2020).

Documents

'Law of the PRC on Countering Foreign Sanctions' of the National People's Congress (*China Law Translate*, 2021) <https://chinalawtranslate.com/en/counteringforeignsanctions/> accessed 10 June 2021.

'MOFCOM Order No. 4 of 2020 on Provisions on the Unreliable Entity' (Ministry of Commerce People's Republic of China, 2020) <http://english.mofcom.gov.cn/article/policyrelease/questions/202009/20200903002580.shtml> accessed 19 September 2020.

'The U.S. Willful Practice of Long-Arm Jurisdiction and Its Perils' (Ministry of Foreign Affairs of the People's Republic of China, 2023) <https://www.mfa.gov.cn/eng/wjbxw/202302/t20230203_11019281.html> accessed 3 February 2023.

'不可靠实体清单工作机制关于将洛克希德·马丁公司 雷神导弹与防务公司列入不可靠实体清单的公告' (Ministry of Commerce People's Republic of China, 2023) <http://www.mofcom.gov.cn/article/zwgk/gkzcfb/202302/20230203391289.shtml> accessed 16 February 2023.

5. Coalitions of the willing

Mirko Sossai

I Introduction

The term 'coalitions of the willing' refers to informal coordination mechanisms among like-minded states (Benvenisti [2007]). In the post-9/11 era, this concept has reflected the strategies and objectives of the US administration in addressing the threats posed by international terrorism and the proliferation of weapons of mass destruction (WMDs). Although it is strongly associated with the Iraq war of 2003, the coalition of the willing identifies a model of cooperation characterized by informality, focusing on the creation of ad hoc transnational networks rather than formal institutions, and relying on voluntary adherence to non-binding principles (Rodiles [2018]). Early examples of these informal, non-treaty-based arrangements include the five multilateral weapon and technology export control regimes: the Australia Group (AG), the Zangger Committee, the Missile Technology Control Regime (MTCR), the Nuclear Suppliers Group (NSG), and the Wassenaar Arrangement on Export Controls for Conventional Arms and Dual-Use Technologies. Other prominent manifestations of the coalition-of-the-willing approach include the Financial Action Task Force (see chapter on FATF recommendations) and the proliferation security initiative.

The catchphrase 'coalition of the willing' has been used to describe the phenomenon of the coordination among like-minded countries in imposing sanctions, often acting outside formal institutional frameworks. This cooperation can take various forms. In some instances, it involves the simultaneous adoption of sanctions by multiple senders against a common target, such as those taken by the United States, the European Union (EU), and the United Kingdom on Myanmar (see chapter) and Syria (see chapter), in the absence of United Nations (UN) sanctions. In addition, the EU has developed a consistent practice of inviting certain neighbouring European states to align with its sanctions regimes (Cardwell and Moret [2023]). In other cases, coordination occurs within the context of more structured political initiatives, such as the G7, or through the establishment of ad hoc 'coalitions' or 'partnerships'.

II The informal coordination between like-minded countries

During a United Nations Security Council (UNSC) meeting in February 2022 on the humanitarian and intended consequences deriving from the use of sanctions, the UK representative stressed that 'where collective UN action is blocked', the United Kingdom is 'prepared to act with allies and partners, or unilaterally, to apply sanctions'. The United States emphasized that sanctions by 'groups of Member States' are consistent with international law (UNSC [2022]). One of the most far-reaching regimes ever imposed by a group of countries against another one, because the UNSC became deadlocked, was directed at Syria. Following the outbreak of civil war in 2011, countries such as Australia, Canada, Japan, Switzerland, and Turkey joined the United States and the EU in enacting targeted and sectoral measures. In other cases (see also chapter on Iran; and chapter on Democratic People's Republic of Korea; Ballbach [2023]), coordinated sanctions were introduced to supplement and strengthen existing UN regimes, often referring back to the relevant UNSC decisions to legitimize these measures.

In most episodes where multiple measures overlap against the same target, each sender independently decides and enforces sanctions under its own national laws. Coordination remains informal, ad hoc, and lacks a centralized authority, often resulting in fragmented and poorly orchestrated efforts (Moret [2021] 35). Still, these measures are characterized by their similar content and shared objective of safeguarding collective interests. When multiple sanctions are applied to the same target, questions arise regarding the consideration of their cumulative intensity. It has been suggested that the customary principle of proportionality could serve as a coordination criterion when applying different regimes to a specific context (Farrall [2007] 223). For instance, this principle would ensure a comprehensive evaluation of the overall impact of the imposed measures. Sanctions applied by a group of like-minded countries are sometimes called 'plurilateral', a term borrowed from the vocabulary of the World Trade Organization (WTO).

III International coalitions and partnerships

The coordination of sanctions has become more structured in certain contexts, leading to the establishment of specific 'coalitions' and 'partnerships'. One notable example is the establishment by the G7 countries of an enforcement coordination mechanism (ECM) in 2023, aimed at strengthening the enforcement of their measures against Russia, also by sharing typologies of circumvention and evasion and other relevant information. A key area of focus has been the development of regulatory standards for export controls, particularly regarding the implementation of restrictions on dual-use goods and technologies. The G7 has also coordinated these control efforts in the wider context of the Global Export Control Coalition (GECC), a coalition of 39 members that includes Australia, Canada, the 27 EU member states, Iceland, Japan, Liechtenstein, New Zealand, Norway, South Korea, Switzerland, Taiwan, the United Kingdom, and the United States.

Moreover, a French government initiative highlights the continued relevance of the coalition-of-the-willing approach in fostering international cooperation with respect to combating the use of chemical weapons in Syria and beyond. Established in 2018, the International Partnership against Impunity for the Use of Chemical Weapons includes 40 countries and the EU and serves as an informal platform for collaboration and information exchange, dedicated solely to addressing impunity for chemical weapon perpetrators worldwide. Open to all states parties of the Chemical Weapons Convention, the partnership aims at enhancing accountability by strengthening the legal and operational capacities of participating states to identify, sanction, and prosecute individuals and entities involved in the proliferation or use of chemical weapons. Notably, the founding declaration emphasizes the role of a consolidated sanctions list, naming individuals, entities, groups, and governments sanctioned by both the EU and individual states (including the United States) for their involvement in chemical weapon–related crimes in Syria (Aloklah [2022]).

IV Conclusion

The evolution of plurilateral sanctions regimes reflects a broader trend towards the use of informal and flexible mechanisms for international coordination and cooperation, particularly when institutionalized forums and international organizations, including the UN, face political deadlock. The coalition-of-the-willing approach exemplifies this trend, enabling like-minded states to act collectively in the application of sanctions, in response to global challenges. Reasons of speed and flexibility certainly contribute to explain why states have relied on informal initiatives. However, these mechanisms are not without challenges: risks of fragmentation, lack of proportionality, and varying national legal frameworks can hinder coordination and effectiveness.

Bibliography

Literature

Aloklah WA, 'International Efforts Against Impunity for the Use of Chemical Weapons in Syria: Is There Hope for International Justice?' (2022) 20 *Journal of International Criminal Justice* 541.

Ballbach EJ, *Sanctions against North Korea: From the UN Security Council to a Coalition of the Willing?* (GCSP Policy Brief No. 12, December 2023).

Benvenisti E, 'Coalitions of the Willing and the Evolution of Informal International Law' in Calliess C, Nolte G and Stoll P-T (eds), *Coalitions of the Willing: Avantgarde or Threat?* (Carl Heymanns Verlag 2007) 1.

Cardwell PJ and Moret E, 'The EU, Sanctions and Regional Leadership' (2023) 32 *European Security* 1.

Farrall J, *United Nations Sanctions and the Rule of Law* (Cambridge University Press 2007).

Moret E, 'Unilateral and Extraterritorial Sanctions in Crisis: Implications of Their Rising Use and Misuse in Contemporary World Politics' in Beaucillon C (ed.), *Research Handbook on Unilateral and Extraterritorial Sanctions* (Edward Elgar 2021) 19.

Rodiles A, *Coalitions of the Willing and International Law: The Interplay between Formality and Informality* (Cambridge University Press 2018).

Documents

UNSC, General Issues Relating to Sanctions (7 February 2022) UN Doc. S/PV.8962.

Mirko Sossai

6. The Commonwealth

RISHIKA CHAUHAN

I Introduction

The Commonwealth, a voluntary association of 56 states, has adeptly employed sanctions to impel its members to observe the group's core values. While the association's commitment to principles of supporting democracy, human rights and freedom of expression is expected, the prospect of the Commonwealth attaining them through sanctions is unlikely. The group follows voluntary and consensus-based decision-making as outlined in the Harare Declaration of 1991 (The Commonwealth [1991]), making securing compliance to sanctions challenging. Moreover, without concrete collective economic or defence programmes, the Commonwealth lacks any means to threaten or enforce sanctions (McBride [2020]). However, the group has utilized economic and arms restrictions, along with membership suspension as sanctions to effectively change the behaviour of target states. The Commonwealth Ministerial Action Group (CMAG) is entrusted with the task of dealing with "persistent or serious violations" of the group's values by adopting "appropriate steps" (The Commonwealth [2024] and [2012] 20). Comprising ten members—eight foreign ministers from different countries, as well as two other representatives from the offices of the Commonwealth Chair and previous host of the Heads of Government meeting—the CMAG has the mandate to suspend a member, as well as recommend expulsion (The Commonwealth [2024]). Established in November 1995 by the Commonwealth Heads of Government, the first member that the CMAG suspended was Nigeria in 1999. Before 1995, however, decisions regarding sanctions were made at the Commonwealth Heads of Government meetings, and announced through communiques, as in the case of South Africa in 1986 (The Commonwealth [1986]).

II Membership suspension as a form of sanction

The suspension of the rights of membership is "the complete or partial suspension of rights and privileges in organs in which a member is represented" (Mathias and Trengove [2016] 979; see also chapter on Membership sanctions). In the Commonwealth, when a state is partially suspended, it is excluded from the "Councils of the Commonwealth",[1] which bars the concerned government from participating in intergovernmental meetings, ministerial meetings, and the CMAG (The Commonwealth [2023]). Moreover, new Commonwealth technical assistance is also blocked, although aid towards the "restoration of democracy" remains uninterrupted (The Commonwealth [2011] 21 and [2023]). In 2000, the CMAG first distinguished between "suspension from the Councils of the Commonwealth" and "full suspension": when a state is fully suspended, it is excluded from the Councils of the Commonwealth, Commonwealth meetings as well as official events, and its country's coat of arms is removed from the Commonwealth Secretariat building. The state is also barred from participating in Commonwealth sport and cultural activities (The Commonwealth [2011] 13). So far, there have only been two cases of full suspension—Nigeria in 1995 and Fiji in 2009. However, at times, member states have voluntarily withdrawn from the Commonwealth. The threat of sanctions caused South Africa to withdraw in 1961, while continued suspension from the Commonwealth drove Zimbabwe to withdraw in 2003. In each case, sanctions are applied on a case-by-case basis. On occasion, suspension is used in conjunction with other measures, while at other times, suspension is the only sanction employed against a state to press its government to follow the core principles and values of the Commonwealth.

III Economic sanctions and arms embargo

Of all the sanction regimes initiated by the Commonwealth, sanctions against South Africa and Nigeria are noteworthy for their focus on specific economic sectors. To coerce South Africa to change its policy of apartheid, the Commonwealth imposed sanctions against Pretoria in 1986. The Commonwealth found the African state's policy was counter to the 1971 Singapore Declaration of Commonwealth Principles (preceded by the Harare Declaration in 1991), which recognized "racial discrimination as an unmitigated evil of society" (The Commonwealth [1971]). The economic sanctions package included a ban on travel, investments, bank loans, and agricultural imports (The Commonwealth [2017]). However, the organization was ready to "review" and "rescind" the measures if there was a change in the behaviour of the target (Manby [1992] 203). Suspension could not be used as a sanction in this case as South Africa had withdrawn from the Commonwealth in 1961 over the organization's criticism of apartheid and the possibility of Pretoria's suspension. The sanctions applied by the United Nations (UN) and the Commonwealth (Manby [1992] 204) continued to draw attention to South Africa's policy of discrimination, leading to more sanctions and inflicting greater cost for non-adherence. Only after South Africa conducted elections in 1994 was it readmitted to the group.

In the case of Nigeria, an arms embargo followed the state's full suspension from the Commonwealth. Nigeria was suspended from the Commonwealth in 1995, while an arms embargo was initiated on foot of those applied by the European Union in 1996, in response to the ruling military junta's refusal to allow inspections to ascertain the promotion of human rights and democratic reforms (SIPRI [2012]). The suspension was lifted in May 1999 following the establishment of civilian rule. In November 1999, the arms embargo also ended.

IV Suspension and readmittance

Partial suspensions from the Commonwealth were enforced in the cases of Pakistan (1999, 2007), Fiji (1987, 2000, 2006, 2009), Sierra Leone (1997), and Zimbabwe (2002). Pakistan was suspended twice over a period of eight years for its failure to maintain democracy. The first time, a military coup, led by General Pervez Musharraf, was the reason for its suspension (Rizvi [2000] 217). Pakistan was readmitted to the Councils of the Commonwealth in May 2004, but was suspended again in November 2007 because of Islamabad's failure to end emergency rule and conduct elections (Wintour [2007]). In 2008, giving credit to the Pakistani government's constructive action to establish democracy and follow the values and principles of the Commonwealth, Pakistan was readmitted to the association.

Fiji was suspended four times, partially in 1987, 2000, 2006, and fully in 2009, over its failure to maintain democracy. The first suspension from the Councils of the Commonwealth occurred after a civilian government was dislodged in a military coup, led by Colonel Sitiveni Rabuka. The island state was accepted back after a decade, but was subsequently suspended a second time in 2000, following another military coup but reinstated in 2001. In 2006, Fiji was suspended a third time after military commander Commodore Voreqe Bainimarama deposed the elected Prime Minister Laisenia Qarase. Fiji was fully suspended from the Commonwealth in May 2009 after Bainimarama failed to honour the agreed deadline to hold elections (Hayward-Jones [2011] 3). Fiji was also banned from participating in the Commonwealth Games in 2010 as a result (The Hindustan Times [2009]). Finally, in March 2014, the state was accepted back into the Commonwealth after a democratic government was reinstated.

Sierra Leone and Zimbabwe were other cases of partial suspensions. The former was suspended from October 1997 to July 1998, when a coup ousted its then President Ahmad Tejan Kabbah. The state was accepted back by the Commonwealth only after President Ahmad Tejan Kabbah returned to power (Reuters [2007]). Zimbabwe was suspended for a year in 2002 after President Robert Mugabe assumed power amid reports of vote rigging and fraudulent elections, and episodes of political violence. The following year, when the Commonwealth refused to readmit the state, President Robert Mugabe decided to withdraw from the association (Winchester [2023]).

V Conclusion

While all the cases cannot be understood as successes, the Commonwealth's sanctions have contributed immensely to instituting democracy and preventing human rights violations in the developing world. Given the diversity in the Commonwealth, the interpretation of global norms can sometimes vary, and the developed Global North can have a different view from the developing Global South on a range of issues. Moreover, as it is a group of both, the former colonizer and the colonized states, their experiences and opinions might differ, making it hard to coordinate. Furthermore, regional foreign policy interests could eclipse the need to support global norms, articulated as the Commonwealth's core values and principles. However, despite the setbacks and the different identities of member states, the Commonwealth has established a strength in its diversity that is visible in its sanctioning history.

Note

1. Several organizations are affiliated to the Commonwealth that support its activities in different fields, for example the Council for Education in the Commonwealth, the Commonwealth Enterprise and Investment Council and the Commonwealth Council for Education Administration and Management. However, in the context of partial suspension, the focus is on the member's exclusion from the CMAG and other forums that conduct meetings at different levels.

Bibliography

Literature

Early BR and Spice R, 'Economic Sanctions, International Institutions, and Sanctions Busters: When Does Institutionalized Cooperation Help Sanctioning Efforts?' (2015) 11 *Foreign Policy Analysis* 339.

Hayward-Jones J, 'Fiji at Home and in the World: Public Opinion and Foreign Policy' (The Lowy Institute, 6 September 2011) <https://www.lowyinstitute.org/publications/fiji-home-world-public-opinion-foreign-policy> accessed 14 July 2024.

HT Correspondent, 'Fiji Banned from 2010 Commonwealth Games' (*The Hindustan Times*, 2 December 2009) <https://www.hindustantimes.com/india/fiji-banned-from-2010-commonwealth-games/story-2WnsO1OXfFofXTpMVHQXuI.html> accessed 14 July 2024.

Kirby M, 'The Commonwealth of Nations Today: Historical Anachronism or Focus for Universal Values?' (2011) 37(1) *Commonwealth Law Bulletin* 39.

Manby B, 'South Africa: The Impact of Sanctions' (1992) 46(1) *Journal of International Affairs* 193.

Mathias S and Trengove S, 'Membership and Representation' in Cogan JK, Hurd I and Johnstone I (eds), *The Oxford Handbook of International Organizations* (Oxford University Press 2016) 962.

McBride J, 'The Commonwealth of Nations: Brexit and the Future of "Global Britain"' (Council on Foreign Relations, 5 March 2020) <https://www.cfr.org/backgrounder/global-britain-and-commonwealth-nations> accessed 14 July 2024.

Reuters, 'Factbox: Commonwealth Suspensions since 1949' (*Reuters*, 23 November 2007) <https://www.reuters.com/article/world/factbox-commonwealth-suspensions-since-1949-idUSSP148135/> accessed 14 July 2024.

Rizvi H, 'Pakistan in 1999: Back to Square One' (2000) 40 *Asian Survey* 208.

SIPRI, 'Commonwealth Arms Embargo on Nigeria' (*SIPRI*, 29 October 2012) <https://www.sipri.org/databases/embargoes/eu_arms_embargoes/nigeria_commenwealth/commonwealth-arms-embargo-on-nigeria> accessed 14 July 2024.

Sohn LB, 'Expulsion or Forced Withdrawal from an International Organization' (1964) *Harvard Law Review* 1381.

Winchester N, 'The Commonwealth: Zimbabwe's Return?' (House of Lords Library, 9 January 2023) <https://lordslibrary.parliament.uk/the-commonwealth-zimbabwes-return/> accessed 10 July 2023.

Wintour P, 'Pakistan Suspended from Commonwealth' (*The Guardian*, 22 November 2007) <https://www.theguardian.com/politics/2007/nov/22/foreignpolicy.uk> accessed 10 July 2023.

Documents

Sharma K, 'Report of Commonwealth Ministerial Action Group as adopted by the Commonwealth Heads of Government Meeting' (*The Commonwealth*, 31 January 2012) <https://thecommonwealth.org/news/strengthening-role-commonwealth-ministerial-action-group> accessed 14 July 2024.

The Commonwealth, 'Commonwealth Ministerial Action Group' (The Commonwealth 2024) <https://thecommonwealth.org/commonwealth-ministerial-action-group> accessed 15 August 2024.

The Commonwealth, 'From the Archive: Sanctions Agreed against Apartheid-Era South Africa January 25, 2017' (The Commonwealth 2017) <https://thecommonwealth.org/news/archive-sanctions-agreed-against-apartheid-era-south-africa> accessed 10 July 2023.

The Commonwealth, 'Gabon Partially Suspended from the Commonwealth

RISHIKA CHAUHAN

Pending Restoration of Democracy' (The Commonwealth 2023) <https://thecommonwealth.org/news/gabon-partially-suspended-commonwealth-pending-restoration-democracy> accessed 14 July 2024.

The Commonwealth, 'Harare Declaration of Commonwealth Principles' (The Commonwealth 1991) <https://thecommonwealth.org/harare-declaration-1991> accessed 14 July 2024.

The Commonwealth, 'Singapore Declaration of Commonwealth Principles' (The Commonwealth 1971) <https://production-new-commonwealth-files.s3.eu-west-2.amazonaws.com/migrated/history-items/documents/Singapore%20Declaration.pdf> accessed 14 July 2024.

The Commonwealth, 'Southern Africa: Commonwealth Heads of Government Review Meeting's Communique' (1986) 12(4) *Commonwealth Law Bulletin* (The Commonwealth 1986) 1059.

The Commonwealth, 'Strengthening the Role of the Commonwealth Ministerial Action Group (CMAG) Report by CMAG as adopted by the Commonwealth Heads of Government Meeting' (The Commonwealth 2011) <https://production-new-commonwealth-files.s3.eu-west-2.amazonaws.com/migrated/news-items/documents/120131.pdf> accessed 10 July 2023.

7. European Union

Jan Lepeu

I Introduction

Over the last few decades, the European Union (EU) has emerged as one of the most important senders of international sanctions. As such, EU sanctions are not only a key subcategory of the overall study of international sanctions, but also a key angle to investigate how the EU acts in the world. Because of its *sui generis* nature, neither a federal state nor a purely intergovernmental international organization, the EU lacks some of the other instruments that states have at their disposal. Sanctions, therefore, have an outsized importance in EU foreign policy. Furthermore, they are often perceived as the embodiment of a value-driven EU foreign policy, based on the universal ideals cited in European treaties (Articles 3.5 and 21, Treaty on the European Union [TEU]) that, purportedly, distinguish the Union's foreign policy from the interest-driven ones of states. After all, the institutionalization of the EU coincided with the first 'Sanctions Decade' of the 1990s and emerged from the same post–Cold War liberal zeitgeist.

II Historical overview

Historically, sanctions sat uneasily in the institutional architecture of the European integration. Prior to the Maastricht Treaty (1992), European cooperation was divided institutionally and, to an extent, philosophically. On the one hand, economic integration, including international trade, partially supranationalized under the European Economic Community (EEC). On the other hand, foreign policy coordination under European Political Cooperation (EPC) was a purely intergovernmental framework with no secretariat and little role for any supranational institution. Economic sanctions—economic tools used to achieve foreign policy objectives—sat in between the two institutional frameworks, creating controversies regarding whether such measures should be adopted collectively through EEC legal acts or through national instruments (Nuttall [1992] 261–5). The first sanctions regimes adopted in concert by ECC/EPC member states were a collection of national instruments, first to implement United Nations Security Council (UNSC) sanctions, as was the case of the 1965 UN Rhodesia sanctions (S/RES/216 [1965]), and later for autonomous European sanctions, the first case being the 1980 Iranian hostage crisis. Yet, those national instruments sometimes differed widely among European states, undermining not only the effectiveness of the sanctions regimes, but also the cohesiveness of the Common Market at the centre of the European integration project.

The creation of the EU through the Treaty of Maastricht, which succeeded both the old EEC and the EPC, led to the institutionalization of EU 'restrictive measures', as sanctions are commonly referred to in EU terminology. Conversely, the supranationalization of intra-EU policy fields such as trade, finance, transport and communications increasingly restricted the ability of EU member states to independently impose their own economic sanctions outside of the EU framework (De Waele [2022]). In the post-Maastricht era, EU sanctions became anchored in the newly created EU competence to develop its own foreign policy, the Common Foreign and Security Policy (CFSP). The CFSP, succeeding the EPC, was now officially integrated into the core vehicle of European integration, the EU, albeit following different rules. Indeed, traces of the old policy fields divisions remain, and the hybrid nature of economic sanctions, as a foreign policy instrument relying on market forces, can still be read in the institutional process through which they are adopted.

III The decision-making process

In most cases, the adoption of EU restrictive measures necessitates two legal acts. Like any other CFSP decision, sanctions necessitate a decision of the Council (Article 29 TEU) adopted by the unanimity of the member states (Article 31 TEU). Such a decision attributes to sanctions their 'foreign policy quality' and locates it within the general EU competency to act under its CFSP. But unlike other CFSP Decisions, most EU sanctions necessitate a second legal act—a Council Regulation, adopted on the basis of Article 215 of the Treaty on the Functioning on the European Union (TFEU). The regulations are directly applicable in all member states and entirely binding also on their economic operators. The regulations are therefore the texts rendering implementable most EU sanctions, stipulating, for example, which bank accounts ought to be frozen as well as spelling out the harmonized system (HS) codes of the goods that will not be traded with specific countries. This second legal act highlights the unique nature of sanctions within the EU's foreign policy toolbox and the necessity of directly applicable EU legal acts to weaponize Europeanized intra-EU policy fields for foreign policy purposes. Unlike the CFSP Council decision, the Council regulations do not necessitate unanimity, testifying to EU sanctions' embedment in the rules and practices attached not only to EU foreign policy, but also, in the case of the regulations, to the governance of the single market.

In practice, the two legal acts are usually negotiated and adopted simultaneously. Therefore, EU sanctions ought to be at least tacitly accepted by all member states, ensuring that the effectiveness of EU sanctions relies not only on the market power of the entire Union, but also on the symbol of a united political front. Once imposed, EU sanctions have to be implemented by the EU member states and incorporated into their national foreign policies, by virtue of the principles of loyal cooperation and mutual solidarity (Article 24.3 TEU). EU sanctions, therefore, create a legally binding common position where previously sometimes none existed. Furthermore, the Union's sanctions are usually implemented by more than just its members, as other European states tend to replicate, in parts or in totality, EU sanctions in their own legislation on a voluntary basis (Cardwell and Moret [2022]).

IV The ongoing transformations of the EU restrictive measures

Nowadays, the EU has in place around 50 sanctions regimes targeting nearly 40 countries (EU Sanctions Map [2024]), with the number of individual designations amounting to almost 5000 individuals and entities (EC Sanctions Tracker [2024]), to which ought to be added more comprehensive forms of sanctioning, such as sectoral trade measures. A limited number of those regimes are implementing sanctions taken by the UNSC (see chapter on United Nations). In other cases, the EU adopts supplementary measures to reinforce UNSC sanctions, usually referred to as 'UN+' sanctions (Portela [2012]). Nonetheless, most of the EU sanctions regimes nowadays consist of 'autonomous' or 'unilateral' sanctions, independent EU actions taken completely outside of the UN framework. Although they cannot rely on the authority and legitimacy of the UN Charter, those autonomous sanctions are often taken in concert with 'like-minded' partners such as the United States, the United Kingdom (since Brexit), other regional organizations and increasingly through coordination in the G7 or 'G7+' formats (see chapter on Coalitions of the willing). EU sanctions are distinguished from others by the important level of judicial review exercised by the Court of Justice of the EU. This has resulted in a substantial body of judgments addressing various fundamental aspects (see chapter on Judicial review [European Union]). In addition to its CFSP sanctions ('EU restrictive measures'), the EU possesses other tools of economic coercion through its generalized scheme of preferences (GSP) and the different conditionality clauses included in its various trade and/or associations agreements with third parties (Portela [2012]).

In the last decade, EU sanctions have undergone important transformations. Initially, EU sanctions were very much anchored in the practice of 'smart' or 'targeted' sanctions, favouring light-touch measures tailored to directly affect the 'wrongdoers' themselves rather than entire countries. Historically, the most common type of EU sanctions consisted of asset freezes and travel bans applied to a small number of individuals and entities, while sectoral sanctions were mainly arms embargoes (Giumelli et al. [2020]). However, since 2010, a number of EU sanctions regimes (see chapters on Iran, Syria, Russia) have demonstrated a return to a more comprehensive type of sanctioning, with the superposition of an important number of layers of ostensibly targeted measures mixing large numbers of individual listings with severe sectoral trade and financial restrictions to produce an overall effect approaching the more comprehensive types of sanctioning of old (Lepeu [2025]). A second transformation has been the rise of 'horizontal' sanctions regimes alongside the continuous existence of country-specific sanctions. Those horizontal sanctions regimes are not directed at a specific country and/or situation, but are thematically organized (cyber, global human rights, chemical weapons) and enable the listing of 'wrongdoers' regardless of their nationalities or the location of their misdoings (see chapter on Sanctions for human rights and democracy). Finally, the full-scale invasion of Ukraine has transformed EU sanctioning practices. The European Commission has played an increased role not only in drafting the instruments but also in coordinating with other sanctions senders (Portela [2024]), while the question of the implementation of the sanctions, historically delegated to the member states with little EU supervision (Giumelli et al. [2022]), has come to the fore. While it is too early to say for certain if the exceptional nature of the post-2022 Russia sanctions, in terms of both process and substance, will have lasting effects on other EU sanctions regimes, it is likely to become an important turning point for EU sanctioning practices as a whole.

Bibliography

Literature

Cardwell PJ and Moret E, 'The EU, Sanctions and Regional Leadership' (2022) 32(1) *European Security* 1.

De Waele H, 'Unilateral Measures of Member States Affecting the Internal Market and the Law/Politics Divide in External Relations: Commission v Greece (FYROM)' in Butler G and Wessel RA (eds), *EU External Relations Law: The Cases in Context* (Hart Publishing 2022) 321.

EU Sanctions Map (*European Union*, last updated 3 July 2024) <https://www.sanctionsmap.eu> accessed 8 July 2024.

EU Sanctions Tracker (*European Commission*, last updated July 2024) <https://data.europa.eu/apps/eusanctionstracker/> accessed 8 July 2024.

Giumelli F, Hoffmann F and Książczaková A, 'The When, What, Where and Why of European Union Sanctions' (2020) 30(1) *European Security* 1.

Giumelli F, Geelhoed W, de Vries M and Molesini A, 'United in Diversity? A Study on the Implementation of Sanctions in the European Union' (2022) 10(1) *Politics and Governance* 36.

Lepeu J, 'Ukraine, the De-targetization of EU Sanctions, and the Rise of the European Commission as Architect of EU Foreign Policy' (2025) *International Politics* <https://doi.org/10.1057/s41311-024-00649-7> accessed 14 January 2025.

Nuttall S, *European Political Co-operation* (Clarendon Press 1992).

Portela C, 'Sanctions and the Geopolitical Commission: The War over Ukraine and the Transformation of EU Governance' (2023) 8(3) *European Papers – A Journal on Law and Integration* 1125 <https://doi.org/10.15166/2499-8249/706> accessed 9 July 2024.

Portela C, *European Union Sanctions and Foreign Policy: When and Why Do They Work?* (Routledge 2012).

Documents

Treaty on European Union [2016] OJ C202/1.

Treaty on Functioning of the European Union [2016] OJ C202/1.

JAN LEPEU

8. France

MATHILDE JEANTIL

I Introduction

As a permanent member of the United Nations Security Council (UNSC) and as a member of the European Union (EU), France plays an active role in the imposition of international sanctions. In this regard, France has established a legal and institutional framework to respond effectively to challenging international situations, without compromising its own interests.

II France's legal and institutional framework for effective sanctions enforcement

France implements three types of sanctions. First, as a member of the UN, France must apply the coercive measures adopted by the UNSC (see chapter) under Chapter VII of the Charter. Second, as a member of the EU (see chapter), France must implement the restrictive measures decided within the framework of the EU Common Foreign and Security Policy (CFSP). Finally, France can impose autonomous asset freezes at the national level in specific circumstances under the Monetary and Financial Code and restrict access to its territory (ACPR, DGT [2021]).

French legislation incorporates a series of provisions designed to guarantee the effective enforcement of international sanctions (Hotte et al. [2012]; François and Weissberg [2023]). In particular, Article 459 of the Customs Code, which regulates trade between France and other countries, provides the basis for the prosecution and punishment of violations of international sanctions, including asset freeze measures. Meanwhile, breaches of domestic asset freeze measures are addressed under Article L 574-3 of the Monetary and Financial Code. Those who infringe, circumvent, or engage in fraudulent activities in violation of international sanctions are liable to face a maximum sentence of five years' imprisonment and a fine equal to twice the value of the proceeds obtained through such illicit actions. The exportation of dual-use items or military equipment without the requisite license is subject to similar penalties (respectively, Art. 414 of the Customs Code and Art. 2331-1 et seq. of the Defence Code).

The implementation of sanctions in France involves numerous authorities and administrations (Hotte et al. [2012]). While the Ministry of Foreign Affairs is primarily responsible for designing sanctions regimes, the Ministry of the Economy and Finance ensures the implementation of coercive measures. La Direction Générale du Trésor is thus the competent authority for the enforcement of sectoral and financial sanctions, as well as asset freezes. Moreover, French customs authorities – in particular the Direction nationale du renseignement et des enquêtes douanières (DNRED) – are instrumental in the enforcement of trade restrictions, asset freezing, and the countering of sanctions circumvention (Cornevin [2024]). Finally, export licences are issued by the Service des biens à double usage (SBDU) for dual-use goods, and by the Secrétariat général de la défense et de la sécurité nationale (SGDSN), after interministerial consultations.

III French perspective on sanctions: Upholding rule of law, multilateralism, and diplomacy

France's approach to international sanctions is guided by its determination to defend the rule of law and its core values. Consequently, sanctions are a key instrument in addressing human rights violations, military aggression, support for international terrorism, and the proliferation of weapons of mass destruction (WMDs).

Notwithstanding its capacity for unilateral sanctions, France prioritizes the adoption of sanctions within a multilateral framework. From the French perspective, collective action is essential to enhance the legitimacy and effectiveness of coercive measures. France's primary objective is to implement sanctions through the UNSC, when it can collaborate with other permanent members to address global security concerns. In particular, France played a significant role in the adoption of sanctions against Iran and North Korea by the Security Council in response to their proliferating nuclear programmes (Nicoullaud [2021]). When UNSC members fail to reach a consensus, France advocates for the implementation of sanctions at the EU level (Viaud [2019]). For example, France played a pivotal role in the introduction of restrictive measures against Syria following the repression against the population by Bashar al Assad's regime in 2011. Similarly, France spearheaded the adoption of sanctions against Russia following the annexation of Crimea in 2014 and the subsequent invasion of Ukraine in 2022 (Mitrofanova and Plouchart [2023]).

Finally, France decides on autonomous asset freezes as part of the fight against terrorism (Art. L 562-2 of the Monetary and Financial Code) or to punish individuals likely to violate UN or EU sanctions pending the adoption of a European regulation (Art. L 562-3). For instance, in 2018, the French government enacted a freeze on the assets of around 30 Syrian, French, Lebanese, and Chinese entities and company directors, who were suspected of involvement in the supply of materials and expertise to the Syrian chemical weapons design and production programme (Le Drian and Lemaire [2018]). The sanctions were decided in France as a means of condemning the Bashar Al Assad regime and retaliating against Russia's veto in the Security Council. France also enacts administrative bans on entering the territory against individuals if their presence would pose a serious risk to public order, internal security, or France's international relations (Art. 222-1 and Art. 320-1 et seq. of the Code for Entry and Residence of Foreigners and Right of Asylum). In 2018, the French Ministry of the Interior prohibited the admission of 18 Saudi nationals, who were suspected of involvement in the murder of Saudi journalist Jamal Khashoggi in Istanbul, which undermined freedom of the press and the most fundamental rights (FranceInfo [2018]). The French government also adopted similar unilateral sanctions in February 2024 against extremist Israelis who had perpetrated violence against Palestinians in the West Bank, followed by the EU in July (Ministry of Foreign Affairs [2024]).

From the French perspective, sanctions represent a compromise between inaction and the use of force (François and Weissberg [2023]). France only considers the imposition of sanctions when diplomatic efforts alone have proven unsuccessful in inducing a change in the target's behaviour. Nevertheless, under no circumstances should sanctions terminate diplomatic negotiations, but instead facilitate constructive dialogue. Consequently, France has been one of the ardent proponents of the dual-track approach to resolving the Iran nuclear crisis, advocating for the use of pressure through sanctions and diplomatic engagement (Nicoullaud [2021]; Jeantil [2023]). Similarly, France has long sought to act as mediator in the conflict between Russia and Ukraine while also implementing sanctions against Moscow. Following the annexation of Crimea in 2014, diplomatic meetings were convened between Russia and Ukraine under the auspices of France and Germany (the so-called Normandy format), resulting in the Minsk Agreements. President Emmanuel Macron has continued such a policy of 'dialogue and firmness' since the invasion of Ukraine in 2022, even though he has recently hardened the tone towards Russia (Mitrofanova and Plouchart [2023]; Minic [2024]).

IV Navigating sanctions: France's defence of sovereignty and strategic interests

While France consistently advocates for a multilateral approach to sanctions, it also safeguards its sovereignty and interests when exerting economic pressure on a third country. For instance, France has rejected the imposition of EU sanctions on the Russian nuclear sector, given the significant dependence of the French nuclear industry on Russia for the supply of essential materials (Collen [2023]).

Furthermore, France firmly rejects the use of extraterritorial sanctions by third countries, notably the United States, on the grounds that such actions infringe upon its sovereignty and violate international law. Indeed, secondary sanctions penalize foreign companies, notably French ones, for engaging in trade and investment with countries subject to US sanctions. For instance, US authorities imposed an $8.9 billion penalty on French bank BNP Paribas in 2014 for allegedly violating sanctions against Sudan, Cuba (see chapter), and Iran (see chapter). Following the US withdrawal from the Joint Comprehensive Plan of Action (JCPOA), the Europeans, France in particular, failed to protect their companies from renewed US sanctions, either by reinforcing the Blocking Statute or by setting up INSTEX (Bonnecarrère [2018]; Jeantil [2023]).

V Conclusion

France's approach to international sanctions reflects its commitment to the preservation of international peace and security, as well as the promotion of human rights. Additionally, it illustrates France's attachment to multilateralism and diplomatic engagement to address international crises.

Disclaimer

Mathilde Jeantil holds a PhD in International Relations from the Université Paris Panthéon-Assas, where she worked on economic sanctions in response to the Iranian nuclear crisis. Her research focuses on economic sanctions and nuclear non-proliferation. Any views expressed in this text are those of the author and do not necessarily reflect the view of the French administration.

Bibliography

Literature

ACPR, DGT, 'Lignes directrices conjointes de la Direction Générale du Trésor et de l'Autorité de contrôle prudentiel et de résolution sur la mise en œuvre des mesures de gel des avoirs' (2021) 47.

Bonnecarrère P, 'L'extraterritorialité des sanctions américaines' Rapport d'information fait au nom de la commission des affaires européennes (2018) no. 17, Sénat, 65.

Collen V, 'Russie: pourquoi certains secteurs échappent aux sanctions européennes' (22 June 2023) *Les Echos* <https://www.lesechos.fr/monde/europe/russie-pourquoi-certains-secteurs-echappent-aux-sanctions-europeennes-1954735> accessed 12 October 2024.

Cornevin C, 'Moteurs, éléments électroniques... Les Douanes démantèlent un tentaculaire trafic à destination de la Russie sous embargo' [2024] *Le Figaro* <https://www.lefigaro.fr/actualite-france/moteurs-de-voitures-camions-elements-electroniques-les-douanes-demantelent-un-tentaculaire-trafic-a-destination-de-la-russie-frappee-par-l-embargo-20240524#> accessed 19 August 2024.

Cornevin C, 'Comment Bercy et les Douanes « piègent » la fortune des oligarques russes' (2024) *Le Figaro* <https://www.lefigaro.fr/actualite-france/comment-bercy-et-les-douanes-piegent-la-fortune-des-oligarques-russes-20240620> accesssed 19 August 2024.

FranceInfo, 'Affaire Khashoggi: la France sanctionne 18 Saoudiens liés à l'assassinat du journaliste' (2018) <https://www.francetvinfo.fr/monde/proche-orient/disparition-d-un-journaliste-saoudien/affaire-khashoggi-la-france-sanctionne-18-saoudiens-lies-a-l-assassinat-du-journaliste_3047029.html> accessed 12 October 2024.

François T and Weissberg C, 'La politique des sanctions internationales' Rapport, Assemblée nationale (2023) 66.

Hotte D, Morlet D, Sauteret S, Soulignac V and Baumard P, *Les sanctions financières internationales* (Revue Banque, Paris 2012) 238.

Jeantil M, 'Les sanctions économiques dans la réponse apportée à la crise nucléaire iranienne' (PhD thesis, Université Paris-Panthéon-Assas 2023).

Le Drian J-Y and Lemaire B, 'Communiqué de presse conjoint sur des sanctions contre des individus et des entités impliqué dans des transferts de matériaux sensibles pouvant entrer dans la fabrication d'armes de destruction massive à destination de la Syrie' (23 January 2018).

Minic D, 'La politique russe d'Emmanuel Macron: étapes et racines d'une nouvelle approche, 2017–2024' IFRI (2024) no. 133.

Ministry of Foreign Affairs, 'Israel/Palestinian Territories – France Adopts Sanctions against Violent Israeli Settlers (13 February 2024)' <https://www.diplomatie.gouv.fr/en/country-files/israel-palestinian-territories/news/2024/article/israel-palestinian-territories-france-adopts-sanctions-against-violent-israeli> accessed 19 August 2024.

Ministry of Foreign Affairs, 'Liste des autorités compétentes', <https://www.diplomatie.gouv.fr/fr/autorites-sanctions/> accessed 19 August 2024.

Ministry of Economy and Finances, Direction générale du Trésor <https://www.tresor.economie.gouv.fr/services-aux-entreprises/sanctions-economiques> accessed 19 August 2024.

Mitrofanova O and Plouchart J, 'La France face à la guerre en Ukraine (Entretien)' (2023) 54(2) *Etudes internationales* 311–33.

Nicoullaud F, *Des atomes, des souris et des hommes, France–Iran: leurs relations nucléaires jusqu'à l'accord de Vienne* (Hémisphères 2021) 372.
Viaud A, 'France et Royaume-Uni: adoption des sanctions onusiennes et européennes (Iran, Syrie, Russie)' (2019) 3(818) *Revue Défense Nationale* 99.

Documents

Code for Entry and Residence of Foreigners and Right of Asylum (France).
Customs Code (France).
Defence Code (France).
Monetary and Financial Code (France).

MATHILDE JEANTIL

9. Japan

Machiko Kanetake

I Introduction

It was only at the beginning of the twenty-first century that the Japanese government decided to take a proactive approach to economic sanctions by amending a legislative framework and applying it to instigate sanctions for the country's national security. In Japan, sanctions had traditionally been applied under the auspices of the United Nations Security Council (UNSC) (see chapter) or as part of the consorted initiatives of like-minded states (see chapter on Coalitions of the willing). Yet, the Japanese government's approaches to sanctions became more proactive in response to North Korea's missile tests from the mid-1990s and domestic support for the strategic use of sanctions for the country's national security. The turning point in this regard arrived in July 2006, when the Japanese government instituted its first autonomous sanctions outside the framework of international cooperation.

This entry provides a brief overview of legal and administrative frameworks on the implementation of economic sanctions (Sections II and III). This is followed by a brief description of the country's autonomous sanctions against North Korea, taken outside of the UN's framework or the initiatives of like-minded states (Section IV). Japan's legal frameworks on sanctions must be understood together with the presence of international pressure, especially that from the Financial Action Task Force (FATF), which necessitated or justified domestic legal changes (Section V).

II Development of Japan's approaches to sanctions

The use of sanctions by the Japanese government has traditionally been characterized by the spirit of 'international cooperation' with the United Nations (UN) or like-minded states. Although the government applied certain restrictive measures outside of the UN's framework, such measures were taken as part of the international initiatives of several like-minded states. For example, in line with the initiatives of the United States and other like-minded states, Japan introduced sanctions against Iraq in August 1990 shortly before the adoption of UNSC Resolution 661. Japan has also imposed a series of sanctions against Russia since 2014 and more extensively in response to Russia's full-scale invasion of Ukraine since 24 February 2022. Beyond the international initiatives of like-minded states, however, the Japanese government was traditionally reluctant to impose 'autonomous' economic sanctions. The government's first unilateral sanctions outside the framework of international cooperation were introduced in July 2006, in response to North Korea's launch of ballistic missiles.

The development of the Japanese government's approaches to sanctions is best illustrated by the incremental changes made with regard to the Foreign Exchange and Foreign Trade Act (FEFT Act), which is the main domestic legal basis to give effect to economic sanctions. The Act was enacted in 1949 to ensure equilibrium in the international balance of trade and currency stability by controlling foreign exchange, foreign trade, and other foreign transactions (FEFT Act, Act No. 228 [1949] Article 1). The concept of 'peace and security' did not initially form part of the overall legislative purpose of the FEFT Act. The same holds true for the Export Trade Control Order, an administrative instrument enacted according to the FEFT Act. Under the Order, the minister could deny an export license if it was found necessary for ensuring 'the maintenance of equilibrium in the international balance of trade and the sound development of foreign trade and national economy' (Export Trade Control Order, Cabinet Order No. 378 [1949], as amended in 1968, Article 1(6)). As a result, the strategic trade controls that Japan introduced under the Coordinating Committee for Multilateral Export Control (COCOM) during the Cold War were regarded in 1969 by the Tokyo District Court as falling outside the purview of the Export Trade Control Order inasmuch as the export controls pursued political, as opposed to economic, objectives (Case No. 1969 (Gyo U) 30 [1969]).

The FEFT Act's objectives were amended in 1979 to acknowledge non-economic objectives as grounds for imposing licensing requirements. The 1979 amendment enabled the government to restrict capital and service transactions if they 'prevent the sincere fulfilment of treaties and other international agreements Japan has concluded' or 'impair international peace and security' (FEFT Act,

Act No. 228 [1949], as amended by Act No. 65 of 18 December 1979, Articles 23(2)(iv), 25(ii)). A further legislative change came in 1987, following substantial political backlash against Toshiba Machine Co. involving the company's breach of COCOM export control rules. By the 1987 amendment to the FEFT Act, 'the maintenance of international peace and security' had become one of the explicit bases for restricting the export of goods in general. However, the overall legislative purpose of the FEFT Act under Article 1 remained confined to economic rationales.

It was only in 2004 that Article 1 of the FEFT Act was amended to include the element of 'peace and security' as part of its overall legislative purpose. The 2004 amendment added 'the maintenance of peace and security in Japan and in the international community' to Article 1. Given that the amendment referred to peace and security 'in Japan', this legislative change also enabled the government to impose restrictions for the maintenance of 'national'—and not merely international—peace and security. These series of amendments set the scene for the first autonomous sanctions imposed against North Korea in July 2006, which are explained in Section IV.

III Legal and administrative frameworks

As already indicated in the previous section, Japan does not have general enabling legislation equivalent to the United Nations Act 1946 in the United Kingdom or the United Nations Participation Act 1945 in the United States to implement UN economic sanctions regimes (see chapter on Domestic implementation). Instead, Japan implements UN sanctions (or instigates other non-UN sanctions, either autonomously or as part of international initiatives of like-minded states) on a patchwork basis by applying existing pieces of legislation, which have a much wider use than in the context of economic sanctions. Among such pieces of legislation, the FEFT Act has been the primary vehicle for the imposition of both UN and non-UN sanctions.

For example, Article 16(1) of the FEFT Act allows the government to restrict payments to a foreign state or non-resident. Article 16(1) is implemented together with Article 6(1) of the Foreign Exchange Order issued by the cabinet. In addition to the payment restriction, Article 21(1) of the FEFT Act provides the basis for restricting capital transactions within the framework of economic sanctions. Furthermore, if sanctions regimes aim to restrain the export and import of goods in general, Article 48 of the FEFT Act serves as a basis for restricting exports, while Article 52 provides a ground for regulating imports. The FEFT Act, however, does not serve as an adequate legal basis for certain circumstances envisaged by UN sanctions. This became particularly evident with regard to the implementation of the UN's counterterrorism sanctions. The FEFT Act, which literally aims to regulate certain 'foreign' transactions, could not be invoked by the government to restrict payments made for the benefit of its own nationals who have residency in Japan. Partly in response to the 2008 report of the FATF, the Japanese Diet took steps to remedy the gaps between the UN's counterterrorism sanctions and Japan's legal frameworks. One of such legislative reforms was the 2014 Terrorist Asset Freezing Act, which enabled the government to regulate domestic transfers involving international terrorists. Furthermore, pursuant to the 2022 amendment, the 2014 Asset Freezing Act was extended to cover the implementation of UN sanctions under Security Council Resolutions 1718 and 2231 against North Korea and Iran, respectively, concerning the development of weapons of mass destruction (WMDs). The 2022 amendment also strengthened the restrictions on the transfer of crypto assets.

Multiple governmental agencies are involved in the implementation of UN and non-UN sanctions, which also complicates the domestic oversight of sanctions. As in the case of many other states, the national legislature plays a very limited role when it comes to the implementation of sanctions. The Ministry of Foreign Affairs (MOFA) plays a role in disseminating the general information on sanctions, yet the MOFA is by no means the only ministry involved. For example, an entry ban on individuals is administered by the Ministry of Justice, while an entry ban on ships is controlled by the Ministry of Land, Infrastructure, Transport, and Tourism. When it comes to arms embargo and asset freeze measures, the Ministry of Economy, Trade, and Industry (METI) and the Ministry of Finance are responsible for administering the FEFT Act in order to give effect to such restrictive measures.

In addition to these ministries regularly working for the implementation of economic sanctions, the 2014 Asset Freezing Act entrusted the National Public Safety Commission, which is part of Japan's national police apparatus, with the authority to implement the UN's sanctions regimes on counterterrorism and the prevention of the development of WMDs. The 2014 Asset Freezing Act does not contain any provision that obliges the relevant ministries to report to the Diet. The limited involvement of the legislative body is problematic, especially in light of the fact that the legislation may impose significant restrictions on the fundamental rights of individuals subject to asset freeze measures.

With regard to penalties, violations of restrictive measures that give effect to economic sanctions can trigger both criminal penalties and administrative dispositions. Over the years, the penalties have been strengthened by a series of amendments to the FEFT Act, which reflect the greater political weight given to the prevention of export control violations. In addition, administrative dispositions can be taken by the METI minister against those who have exported or imported goods without the necessary license.

IV Implementation of 'autonomous' sanctions against North Korea

As noted in the introduction and Section II, the Japanese government applied its autonomous sanctions pursuant to the revised FEFT Act to respond to North Korea's launch of a series of ballistic missiles on 6 July 2006. Shortly after the launch of missiles, the Japanese government took steps to ban the entry of a North Korean cargo-passenger ship (Man Gyong Bong 92) into Japanese ports. The government also prohibited the entry of North Korean officials and decided to assess the entry of non-officials in a more stringent manner. While the UNSC also condemned the launch of missiles by North Korea, it did not go as far as imposing economic sanctions. In October 2006, the unilateral sanctions were further expanded in response to North Korea's first nuclear test on 9 October. After North Korea conducted its second nuclear test on 25 May 2009, the Japanese government imposed a general export ban on goods destined for North Korea, except for those for humanitarian purposes. Sanctions were briefly relaxed in 2014 due to diplomatic talks but were reinstated in 2016 after North Korea resumed nuclear and missile activities. In February 2016, the Japanese government introduced a prohibition on payment to individuals who have domiciles in North Korea and expanded the scope of targets subject to asset freeze measures. In September 2016, the government strengthened the scope of entry bans and prohibited the entry of Japanese-flagged ships that stopped at a North Korean port. These restrictive measures have been extended multiple times.

V Conclusion

Overall, it is fair to say that the Japanese approaches to sanctions are predominantly supported by the UNSC's legal mandate as well as the political support given to Japan's allies with regard to non-UN sanctions. Japan's autonomous sanctions against North Korea were instigated in response to mounting domestic pressure due not only to ballistic missile launches but also to the lack of progress regarding the abduction of Japanese nationals by North Korea. Yet, the way that the government proceeded with the amendments to the FEFT Act and the ultimate imposition of sanctions was decisively cautious. Caution was exercised to limit the restrictions on the freedom of foreign exchange, which was the underlying economic rationale for the FEFT. At the same time, the cautious approach was presumably also tied up with the general legal uncertainty about the legality of unilateral sanctions under international law. Such uncertainty translates into a matter of political risks, which are relatively smaller if non-UN sanctions are taken as part of the concerted efforts of like-minded states.

Among a series of legislative changes, the most significant pertained instead to the implementation of UN sanctions on counterterrorism and the prevention of the development of WMDs. Behind such substantive changes lay a series of recommendations from the FATF, which have been used as a technique for standard setting among FATF members. The FATF's 2008 and 2021 evaluation reports on Japan motivated and justified the enactment of the 2014 Asset Freezing Act and its amendments.

While the changes to legal frameworks were made in a rather cautious manner, what is clearly missing from the domestic implementation of sanctions are systematic oversight mechanisms, including those of the legislative body. The involvement of multiple agencies at times complicates the exercise of robust oversight. Furthermore, little attention has been given to the implications of counter-terrorism sanctions on the human rights of the affected individuals.

Declaration

This entry builds on the author's following publication:

Kanetake M, 'Implementation of Sanctions: Japan' in Asada M (ed.), *Economic Sanctions in International Law and Practice* (Routledge 2020) 136–54.

Bibliography

Literature

Asada M (ed.), *Economic Sanctions in International Law and Practice* (Routledge 2020).

Asada M, 'Arms Control Law in Crisis? A Study of the North Korean Nuclear Issue' (2004) 9 *Journal of Conflict and Security Law* 331.

Fukushima S, 'How Japan Implements UN Financial Sanctions' in Yoshimura S (ed.), *United Nations Financial Sanctions* (Routledge 2021) 67.

Hayashi M, 'Russia: The Crimea Question and Autonomous Sanctions' in Asada M (ed.), *Economic Sanctions in International Law and Practice* (Routledge 2020).

Hook GD, *Militarisation and Demilitarisation in Contemporary Japan* (Routledge 2003).

Kanehara A, 'The Incident of an Unidentified Vessel in Japan's Exclusive Economic Zone' (2002) 45 *Japanese Annual of International Law* 116.

Kanetake M, 'United Nations Security Council 1267 on Measures Against the Taliban, 15th October 1999 (UN Doc. S/RES/1267 (1999))' Oxford International Organisations (OXIO) 33 (Oxford University Press 2016).

Kanetake M, *The UN Security Council and Domestic Actors: Distance in International Law* (Routledge 2018).

Kawashima F, 'Trade Sanctions Against Russia and Their WTO Consistency: Focusing on Justification Under National Security Exceptions' in Asada M and Tamada D (eds), *The War in Ukraine and International Law* (Springer 2024) 157.

Kim C, 'The CoCom Case' (1970) 4 *Journal of World Trade Law* 604.

Murase S, 'Trade versus Security: The COCOM Regulations in Japan' (1988) 31 *Japanese Annual of International Law* 1.

Owada H, 'Japan' in Gowlland-Debbas V (ed.), *National Implementation of United Nations Sanctions: A Comparative Study* (Martinus Nijhoff Publishers 2004) 265.

Tamada D and Achilleas P (eds), *Theory and Practice of Export Control: Balancing International Security and International Economic Relations* (Springer 2017).

Documents

Act on Special Measures concerning the Freeze of Assets of International Terrorists and Other Measures Conducted by the Government Taking into Consideration United Nations Security Council Resolution 1267, etc., Act No. 124 of 27 November 2014.

Export Trade Control Order, Cabinet Order No. 378 of 1 December 1949.

Financial Action Task Force, 'Anti-Money Laundering and Counter-Terrorist Financing Measures, Japan, Mutual Evaluation Report' (August 2021) <https://www.fatf-gafi.org/en/publications/Mutualevaluations/Mer-japan-2021.html>.

Financial Action Task Force, 'Third Mutual Evaluation Report: Anti-Money Laundering and Combating the Financing of Terrorism, Japan' (17 October 2008) <https://www.fatf-gafi.org/en/publications/Mutualevaluations/Mutualevaluationofjapan.html>.

Foreign Exchange and Foreign Trade Act, Act No. 228 of 1 December 1949.

Foreign Exchange Order, Cabinet Order No. 260 of 11 October 1980.

Import Trade Control Order, Cabinet Order No. 414 of 29 December 1949.

Judgment of 22 March 1988, Tokyo District Court, Case No. wa-1547 (1987), *Hanrei-jiho (Judicial Reports)*, No. 1271, p. 30, translation in (1988) 31 *Japanese Annual of International Law* 206.

Judgment of 8 July 1969, Tokyo District Court, Case No. 1969 (Gyo U) 30.

United Nations Act 1946, 9 and 10 Geo 6, Chapter 45.

Machiko Kanetake

United Nations Participation Act 1945, Public Law 79–264.
UNSC Res 1267 (15 October 1999) UN Doc. S/RES/1267.
UNSC Res 1333 (19 December 2000) UN Doc. S/RES/1333.
UNSC Res 1718 (14 October 2006) UN Doc. S/RES/1718.
UNSC Res 2140 (26 February 2014) UN Doc. S/RES/2140.
UNSC Res 2231 (20 July 2015) UN Doc. S/RES/2231.
UNSC Res 2321 (30 November 2016) UN Doc. S/RES/2321.
UNSC Res 661 (6 August 1990) UN Doc. S/RES/661.

Machiko Kanetake

10. League of Nations

Mirko Sossai

I Introduction

Created at the end of the First World War, the League of Nations was the first attempt to establish an international organization with permanent institutions aimed at promoting international cooperation and achieving global peace and security: any war or threat of war was considered a matter of concern to the international community as a whole. Its founding document – the Covenant of the League of Nations, which was integrated into the Peace Treaty of Versailles – sought to introduce limitations on the general liberty at that time to "resort to war" and envisaged the possibility of imposing sanctions on member states that violated its provisions. Unfortunately, the practice of the League soon showed that Article 16 would have had only a limited role in the maintenance of peace.

II The legal framework

With the League of Nations, war was no longer regarded as "a private duel" but as a "breach of the peace" that affected the whole community (Brownlie [1963] 57). Articles 12, 13, and 15 of the Covenant introduced a new distinction under international law, between legal and illegal wars, providing a general basis for determining the "aggressor". This distinction was based on whether member states complied with obligations to use procedures for the pacific settlement of disputes. If a state resorted to war in violation of these provisions, Article 16 of the Covenant envisaged the application of sanctions: its paragraph 1 empowered member states to subject "the covenant-breaking State" to "the severance of all trade or financial relations" and to prevent its nationals from "all financial, commercial or personal intercourse" with nationals of other states. The so-called "economic weapon" was celebrated as "the great discovery and the most precious possession of the League": it meant "the substitution of economic pressure for actual war" (Bertram [1931] 169). Article 16(2) also envisaged military sanctions "to protect the covenants of the League", recommended by the League Council and executed by the forces of the member states. Additionally, its paragraph 4 provided for the expulsion of members that violated their obligations under the Covenant: while this provision did not qualify the types of breaches that could give rise to it, the decision required a unanimous vote of the League Council, in which the member concerned was not, however, entitled to participate. The only state to be expelled from the League was the Union of Soviet Socialist Republics (USSR), following its invasion of Finland in December 1939 (*League of Nations Official Journal* [1939] 506; see chapter on Membership sanctions).

Article 16 rested upon the idea of "collective security" as a substitute for unilateral measures. In this sense, it constituted the precursor of and a partial model for Article 41 of the UN Charter. Nevertheless, the interpretation of Article 16 provoked a debate marked by the delicate balance between the obligations of member states and the powers of the League (White [2020] 107). The understanding of US President Woodrow Wilson, one of the greatest supporters of the creation of the League of Nations, was that a member state that resorted to war in violation of the Covenant would immediately and automatically be subject to sanctions. Great faith was placed on economic measures. However, this framework was compromised by the way that member states subsequently interpreted the provision, raising two controversial questions: first, who could make the determination that there had been a resort to war; second, whether, after such a determination had been made, states were obligated to apply sanctions (Farrall [2007] 53). In October 1921, the Assembly proposed several amendments to Article 16, which never entered into force but kept the character of non-binding "rules for guidance": although the Assembly made clear that it was "the duty of each Member of the League to decide for himself whether breach of the Covenant [had] been committed" ("Resolutions regarding the economic weapon", reproduced in Williams [1936] 148), the proposed amendments recognized a role for the Council "to give an opinion whether or not a breach of the Covenant has taken place" and to invite the members to take action accordingly. Furthermore, the Council was tasked with recommending to member states the appropriate timing "for the application of the economic pressure" (League of Nations [1927]).

III A limited practice

The role of Article 16(1) of the Covenant was, in any case, constrained by political considerations. While the mere threat of sanction enforcement had a deterrent effect during the Yugoslavia–Albania border war of 1921, in other instances, economic measures were widely debated but ultimately not applied. This was evident in the context of the response of the League of Nations to the Japanese invasion of Manchuria and Northern China in 1931–32 (De Fiedorowicz [1937]; Mulder [2022] 186). Therefore, the only experiment of the League's sanctions took place during the Italian occupation of Abyssinia in 1935–36.

A few days after Italian troops invaded the empire of Haile Selassie on 3 October 1935, the members of the League Council unanimously agreed that Italy had resorted to war in violation of its obligations under the Covenant. The Assembly reached the same conclusion and established a coordinating committee to recommend measures for member states that had agreed to apply sanctions against the aggressor. The recommended measures, subsequently adopted by the Assembly in November, included an arms embargo, a freeze on financial transactions, export prohibitions on a number of raw materials vital for war production (but significantly, they did not include steel, coal, or oil, which were initially considered to be included in the list), as well as a ban on all imports from Italy (League of Nations [1935] 80). Although these measures impacted the Italian economy, they ultimately failed to compel Mussolini's government to withdraw from Abyssinia. By July 1936, less than eight months after the sanctions were first implemented, the League Assembly officially terminated them. Of the 45 member states that voted, only Abyssinia itself opposed ending the sanctions (League of Nations [1936] 62–3).

IV The ineffectiveness of the sanction system

The failure of the League of Nations can be attributed in part to the inadequacy of its sanction system (Kelsen [1946]). This ineffectiveness stemmed from several factors: the League's lack of universality, particularly due to the US refusal to join; the absence of a competent central authority to definitively determine whether an act of war had occurred; and a decentralized decision-making process that left the application of sanctions to the discretion of individual member states. The drafting of the United Nations (UN) Charter sought to address these shortcomings by granting greater powers to the new organization, including the establishment of an executive body empowered to impose sanctions or take military action under Chapter VII. However, writing at the dawn of the UN era and reflecting on its predecessor, Brierly ([1946] 85) observed that this shift toward greater institutionalization in the Charter came with its own set of challenges, including the use of the veto and the concentration of significant powers in the hands of the United Nations Security Council. Unlike the League's system, which allowed for sanctions to be imposed by members, under the UN Charter the negative vote of a permanent member blocks collective action, leading states to take unilateral measures outside the UN system.

Bibliography

Literature

Bertram A, 'The Economic Weapon as a Form of Peaceful Pressure' (1931) 17 *Problems of Peace and War* (Grotius Society Papers) 139.

Brierly JL, 'The Covenant and the Charter' (1946) 23 *British Yearbook of International Law* 83.

Brownlie I, *International Law and the Use of Force by States* (Oxford University Press 1963).

De Fiedorowicz G, 'Historical Survey of the Application of Sanctions' (1936) 22 *Transactions of the Grotius Society* 117.

Farrall J, *United Nations Sanctions and the Rule of Law* (Cambridge University Press 2007).

Kelsen H, 'Sanctions under the Charter of the United Nations' (1946) 12 *The Canadian Journal of Economics and Political Science* 429.

Mulder N, *The Economic Weapon: The Rise of Sanctions as a Tool of Modern War* (Yale University Press 2022).

White ND, 'The League of Nations, Autonomy and Collective Security' (2020) 8 *London Review of International Law* 89.

Williams JF, 'Sanctions under the Covenant' (1936) 17 *British Yearbook of International Law* 130.

Mirko Sossai

Documents

Covenant of the League of Nations (adopted 28 June 1919, entered into force 10 January 1920).

League of Nations, 'Reports and Resolutions on the Subject of Article 16 of the Covenant', League Doc. A. 14.1927 (1927).

League of Nations, *The League from Year to Year* (1935).

League of Nations, *The League from Year to Year* (1936).

MIRKO SOSSAI

11. Russian Federation (as a sender of sanctions)

Anna Miromanova

I Introduction

Russia's approach to sanctions is characterised by a curious duality. On the one hand, Russia strongly opposes unilaterally imposed sanctions without the authorisation of the United Nations Security Council (UNSC) (Doraev [2015] 394). On the other hand, Russia has and does use retaliatory economic, financial, and diplomatic measures against "unfriendly" states to reinforce its role and position in its sphere of political influence. The imposition of sanctions by Russia was, until 2006, guided primarily by Article 1194 of Russia's Civil Code, which stated that the government may establish reciprocal measures against entities that enact similar measures against Russian citizens. The subsequent enactment of the Federal Law "On special economic measures" number 281-FZ (Doraev [2015] 395) allowed the Russian government to use sanctioning measures against "unfriendly" states without explicitly defining unfriendly actions, thus leaving them up to subjective interpretation. The following cases demonstrate the duality of Russia's approach to sanctions.

II Sanctions against Abkhazia, Georgia

Following the dissolution of the Soviet Union, in a tumultuous time of uncertainty and internal conflicts, several former Soviet Republics created the Commonwealth of Independent States (CIS) in 1991. One such conflict took place in the Georgian territory of Abkhazia in 1992–93, when Abkhazia declared independence from Georgia, leading to a violent conflict between Abkhaz separatists and Georgian government forces. The conflict resulted in the displacement of people, destruction, and loss of life (Kvarchelia [2008]). In response, several peacekeeping missions were authorised by the United Nations (UN) and CIS. Additionally, Georgia joined the CIS in 1993 in hopes that its membership could help it regain the separatist territory (Kvarchelia [2008]). In 1996, CIS, under the charge of Russia, imposed sanctions on Abkhazia to pressure the separatist authorities to negotiate a peaceful resolution to the conflict. The sanctions included trade embargoes, a geographic blockade, and financial and economic measures. In the aftermath, sanctions restricted Abkhazia's access to development funds originating only from Georgia, based on economic concessions made by the Abkhazian government (Kvarchelia [2008]). This led to increased poverty and isolation in the region.

In 2000, Russia ceased the strict enforcement of sanctions without officially lifting them. Due to a shared border with Russia, economic, trade, and business cooperation sprung up between Russian and Abkhazian businesses. Russia is the biggest trade partner for Abkhazia: 80 per cent of its imports originate there (Gerrits and Mader [2016] 301). Additionally, the Russian ruble is used as a primary currency and many Abkhazians hold Russian passports (although many do so involuntarily, after Russia stopped acknowledging Abkhazian passports), essentially ending the travel blockade. In 2008, Russia officially lifted its sanctions against Abkhazia and recognised its statehood. To date, only Russia and its close allies – Venezuela, Nauru, Nicaragua, and Syria – recognise Abkhazia's independence from Georgia (Jones [2024]). Russia is a patron state of Abkhazia, supporting its economy through trade and subsidies. Abkhazia has remained independent, rejecting the option of integration into Russia. This case illustrates how sanctions brought a sender and a target of sanctions closer by creating legal uncertainties (Bugajski and Assenova [2016] 21) and the initial economic isolation created by sanctions. By removing the sanctions before other CIS states, recommending that the sanctions be removed by the international community, and recognising Abkhazia as an independent state, Russia solidified its role as Abkhazia's protector and ally and secured multiple benefits for itself, such as military bases positioned in the region, as well as an independent territory through which goods can be smuggled during the wave of anti-Russian sanctions in the wake of hostilities against Ukraine (2014 onward; 2022 onward).

III Retaliatory sanctions

A second strand concerns Russia's tendency to use sanctions as a retaliatory measure in the form of "countersanctions". Russia has been under sanctions since March 2014, following its invasion of Crimea, but these sanctions have evolved from relatively simple travel bans and asset freezes to arms embargoes and bans on exports of dual-purpose equipment. As soon as the Western countries imposed the first round of sanctions in March 2014, Russia retaliated by "mirroring" the sanctions. It started by imposing travel bans on several officials from the sanctioning countries. After the intensification of anti-Russian sanctions following the shooting down of Malaysian flight MH17 in July 2014, Russia further retaliated by imposing an import embargo on many agricultural products, including meat, dairy, fruits, and vegetables from the United States, the European Union (EU), Canada, Norway, and Australia. The embargoed products were chosen strategically to hurt the economies of smaller EU countries that relied on exports of agricultural products to Russia (Miromanova [2022]), potentially pressuring the EU to remove anti-Russian sanctions. Both anti-Russian sanctions and Russian retaliatory sanctions weakened the Russian economy by slowing down economic growth (Kholodilin and Netšunajev [2018]), raising prices (Hinz and Monastyrenko [2022]), and putting significant pressure on domestic manufacturing need for import substitution, frequently leading to lower-quality substitutes.

New rounds of economic, diplomatic, and financial sanctions against the Russian government, officials, and businesses continued during the period between 2015 and 2022 due to Russia's interference in the US presidential elections and the poisoning of Sergei and Yulia Skripal in the United Kingdom in 2018, as well as Russian opposition leader Alexey Navalny in 2020, who tragically died after being imprisoned for three years. The largest wave of sanctions against Russia and Russian retaliatory measures came after 24 February 2022, when Russia launched a full-scale military attack on Ukraine. For the first time, Western sanctions targeted Russian oil and gas, blocking the Russian Central Bank's access to its foreign reserves, as well as banning Russian exports of agricultural and military equipment and nuclear reactors. Finally, purchase of Russian oil and gas can only be made in rubles, forcing sanctioning countries to purchase Russian currency on foreign exchange markets. Russia's response to the most recent episode of sanctions included restricting travel to Russia issued to officials, politicians, and business owners from the sanctioning states, revoking tax treaties with the United States, prohibiting exports of dual-purpose equipment to the sanctioning countries, and closing Russia's aerospace to European and US airlines (Reuters [2022]).

The Russian economy has survived under sanctions since 2014, allowing it to "sanction-proof" its economy. Among the sanction-proofing strategies used by the Russian government are import substitution (Connolly [2023]), building up significant foreign exchange reserves to maintain confidence in the Russian ruble, and deepening cooperation with allied countries, most prominently China (Preble and Willis [2024]). Russia's assault on Ukraine continues to this day (June 2024), and the sanctions so far have not been successful in stopping the conflict. Russian countersanctions are also still in place, further cementing its status as an international pariah.

Bibliography

Literature

Bugajski J and Assenova M, *Eurasian Disunion: Russia's Vulnerable Flanks* (The Jamestown Foundation 2022).

Connolly R, 'Western Sanctions on Russia and Strategic Stability' (CAN Corporation Report, October 2023).

Doraev M, 'The Memory Effect of Economic Sanctions Against Russia: Opposing Approaches to the Legality of Unilateral Sanctions Clash Again' (2015) 37(1) *University of Pennsylvania Journal of International Law* 355.

Gerrits AWM and Bader M, 'Russian Patronage over Abkhazia and South Ossetia: Implications for Conflict Resolution' (2016) 32(3) *East European Politics* 297 <https://doi.org/10.1080/21599165.2016.1166104> accessed 9 July 2024.

Hinz J and Monastyrenko E, 'Bearing the Cost of Politics: Consumer Prices and Welfare in Russia' (2022) 137 *Journal of International Economics* 103581 <https://doi.org/10.1016/j.jinteco.2022.103581> accessed 9 July 2024.

Jones P, 'Russia's Tightening Abkhazian Stranglehold Threatens Western and Georgian Interests' (2024) *Harvard International Review* <https://hir.harvard.edu/washington-must-not-idle-as-russia-tightens-its-abkhazian-stranglehold/> accessed 9 July 2024.

ANNA MIROMANOVA

Kholodilin KA and Netšunajev A, 'Crimea and Punishment: The Impact of Sanctions on Russian Economy and Economies of the Euro Area' (2018) 19(1) *Baltic Journal of Economics* 39 <https://doi.org/10.1080/1406099X.2018.1547566> accessed 9 July 2024.

Kvarchelia L, 'Sanctions and the Path Away from Peace' in Griffiths A and Barnes C (eds), *Powers of Persuasion: Incentives, Sanctions and Conditionality in Peacemaking* (Conciliation Resources 2008) <https://www.c-r.org/accord/incentives-sanctions-and-conditionality/sanctions-and-path-away-peace> accessed 9 July 2024.

Miromanova A, 'The Effectiveness of Embargoes: Evidence from Russia' (2022) 46(4) *World Economy* 1 <https://doi.org/10.1111/twec.13344> accessed 9 July 2024.

Preble KA and Willis CN, 'How Russia has Managed to Shake Off the Impact of Sanctions – with a Little Help from Its Friends' (The Conversation, 2024) <https://theconversation.com/how-russia-has-managed-to-shake-off-the-impact-of-sanctions-with-a-little-help-from-its-friends-223632>.

Reuters, 'Russia's Response to Western Sanctions' (*Reuters*, 13 May 2022) <https://www.reuters.com/world/russias-response-western-sanctions-2022-05-13/>.

Anna Miromanova

12. Switzerland

Aurel Niederberger and Lukas Regli

I Introduction

Switzerland's sanctions policy emerged against the backdrop of its distinct historical, political, and economic characteristics. It is a close partner but not a member of the European Union (EU) (see chapter), an outspoken supporter of multilateralism and the United Nations (UN) (see chapter), which it joined in 2002, and a steady advocate of international law. Furthermore, it hosts relatively large financial and trading sectors and is home to other relevant industries, ranging from manufacturers of high-tech items to gold refineries to cryptocurrency startups (SECO [2024]). These traits influence and shape Switzerland's policy choices with regard to sanctions.

Switzerland's foreign policy strategy 2024–27 describes sanctions as an "important instrument to enforce international law". As it is neither an EU member nor a candidate for accession to the EU, Switzerland is neither legally nor politically bound by EU sanctions. Instead, it decides on a case-by-case basis whether to fully or partially align itself with EU sanctions. As a UN member, it implements sanctions imposed by the UN Security Council (UNSC) based on Chapter VII of the UN Charter. As of January 2025, Switzerland has 26 active sanctions regimes: eight regimes are based exclusively on UNSC resolutions, 12 exclusively on EU coercive measures, and 6 involve both UN-based and EU-based measures or designations.[1]

II Switzerland and EU sanctions

According to Swiss law – namely the 2002 Embargo Act – the government may adopt sanctions mirroring those of Switzerland's most significant trading partners. These sanctions serve to secure "compliance with international law, in particular the respect of human rights". In practice, Switzerland equates "most significant trading partners" with the EU (Federal Council [2019]). When the EU adopts new sanctions measures, the Swiss government decides on a case-by-case basis whether to align with none, some, or all of those measures. Likewise, the government decides whether to adopt none, some, or all designations of individuals and organisations targeted by EU sanctions measures. To make this decision, it considers different criteria regarding foreign policy, foreign economic policy, and legal issues (Federal Council [2019]). In other words, the Swiss Embargo Act does not empower the government to impose sanctions independently from decisions on an international level. Switzerland has never aligned with sanctions from countries or organisations other than the EU and the UN.

The Swiss sanctions architecture therefore builds on a specific interplay between legislative and executive branches. Parliament defines the general framework of Switzerland's sanctions policy through the Embargo Act (aim, criminal provisions, responsible authorities, etc.). Acting on the basis of the Embargo Act, the government is solely responsible for adopting specific sanctions. Once adopted, different federal authorities are responsible for sanctions implementation – including enforcement and prosecution – with no formal role for the authorities of the constituent states of the Swiss federation ("cantons").

Sanctions are compatible with international law on neutrality, as defined in the 1907 Hague Conventions on the rights and duties of neutral powers (Conventions V and XIII). The conventions preclude neutral states from giving preferential military support to a state involved in interstate conflict but do not mention sanctions. The legal requirements regarding neutrality therefore only become relevant when sanctions include restrictions on military goods; in this case, a neutral state must apply equivalent restrictions to all belligerent states.

Switzerland has aligned itself with multiple EU regimes targeting internal conflicts and violations of humanitarian law and human rights law (Democratic Republic of Congo, Myanmar [see chapter], Sudan, Syria [see chapter], and others), some of which are hybrid EU/UN regimes. Switzerland's largest, EU-based sanctions regime concerns Russia's military aggression against Ukraine. Between 2014 and 2022, Switzerland did not take over EU sanctions related to Russia's actions in Ukraine but imposed measures to prevent sanctions evasion through Switzerland, notably by prohibiting the establishment of new business relationships with persons or entities designated under the respective EU sanctions regime (*Ordonnance du 2 avril 2014 instituant des mesures visant à empêcher le contournement de sanctions internationales en lien avec la situation en Ukraine*).

Material consequences as well as exposure of the Swiss economy and financial markets to sanctioned countries vary across sanctions regimes. For instance, as of August 2024, 7.1 billion CHF[2] (7.7 billion USD) linked to persons and entities designated under the sanctions regime related to Russia's military aggression against Ukraine were frozen (SECO [2025]). As of January 2025, 99 million CHF were frozen due to sanctions concerning Syria and 18 million concerning Belarus. Amounts are negligible for sanctions relating to other countries (figures provided by SECO as of December 2024). Trade volume likewise varies significantly across concerned countries.[3]

III Switzerland and UN sanctions

Although Switzerland joined the UN in 2002, it had already contributed to the improvement of sanctions design. Switzerland initiated the Interlaken Process in 1998, which brought together diplomats, the UN, the private financial sector, and academia to develop a framework for targeted financial sanctions (Biersteker et al. [1998]; see also chapter on Targeted sanctions and sanctions reform process). Among the goals of the Interlaken Process was to avoid the high humanitarian costs linked to comprehensive sanctions.

Switzerland sought to further minimise any humanitarian consequences of UN sanctions by advocating comprehensive exemptions for humanitarian action. With Resolution 2664 (2022), the UNSC introduced such comprehensive humanitarian exemptions for all UN sanctions regimes. In December 2024, Switzerland, together with the United States, drafted and led the negotiations on UNSC Resolution 2761 (2024), which made these exemptions permanent in the sanctions regime against ISIL, Al-Qaida, and affiliated groups, replacing the two-year limit set by Resolution 2664.

Switzerland continuously demanded fair and clear procedures to list and delist individuals for sanctions. Since 2005, Switzerland has worked together with the Group of Like-Minded States on UN Targeted Sanctions to demand the improvement of procedural rights of individuals targeted by UN sanctions. The group welcomed the creation of the Ombudsperson in 2009, an independent office that receives and evaluates delisting requests directly from sanctioned individuals under the UN sanctions regime against ISIL, Al-Qaida, and affiliated groups (see chapter on UN focal points and UN Office of the Ombudsperson). Since then, the group has been calling for the extension of the mandate of the Ombudsperson to other sanctions regimes (Group of Like-Minded States on UN Targeted Sanctions [2018]).

Court proceedings further invigorated Swiss engagement for due process in UN sanctions. For instance, in *Nada v Switzerland* i (2012) and ii (2013), the European Court of Human Rights ruled that the absence of an adequate review mechanism to be removed from the list of sanction targets violated the rights of sanctioned persons. Such court decisions revealed the conflicting obligations resulting from UNSC resolutions on the one hand and international human rights law on the other (Cockayne et al. [2018] 15). A motion by the Swiss lawyer and politician Dick Marty in the Council of States, deposited in 2009, demanded the Federal Council take action to remedy the situation (Marty [2009]).

As a member of the UNSC 2023–24, Switzerland sought to advance the issue of the lack of procedural rights in UN sanctions. After several states opposed the proposition to expand the Ombudsperson to other sanctions regimes, Switzerland advocated a complete reform of the Focal Point for Delisting. Created in 2006, the Focal Point constituted a weak alternative to the Ombudsperson, applicable to all other UN sanctions regimes. As a point of contact, it simply forwarded delisting requests to the UNSC members (see also chapter on UN focal point and UN Office of the Ombudsperson). During bilateral expert-level talks with the United States in Washington (2 February 2024) and the ensuing negotiation of UNSC Resolution 2744, Switzerland proposed ways to turn the Focal Point into an independent institution with the power to engage with petitioners and provide the Security Council with an evaluation of delisting requests (Security Council Report [2024]). While the outcome fell short of some of the Swiss preferences (such as the ability to make recommendations), it still constituted an important improvement (Fontana [2024]).

Whereas Switzerland thus frequently criticised the shortcomings of UN sanctions, it also stressed that UN sanctions are an important tool to safeguard international peace and security. From Switzerland's point of view, fair and clear procedures as well as humanitarian exemptions increase rather than constrain the effectiveness of UN sanctions (see chapter on Measuring sanctions effectiveness) by bolstering their legitimacy, keeping them tailored toward the right targets and intended purpose, and preventing contradictions between different sources of international law (S/PV.9689 [2024]). With its steady engagement, Switzerland has contributed to change in UN sanctions. In a world where multilateral institutions are in retreat and where sanctions are increasingly imposed autonomously, it remains unclear which platforms Switzerland will be able to use in future to act as a "norm shaper" on sanctions the way it has in the past.

IV New challenges

Alongside sanctions norms and policies, sanctions implementation is becoming ever more important and complex, notably in light of the extraterritorial effects of especially US sanctions regimes. Many businesses choose to implement foreign sanctions issued by the countries in which they operate – this is particularly true in an open and well-connected economy like Switzerland's. In the past, the Swiss government reacted with initiatives such as the Swiss Humanitarian Trade Arrangement, a payment mechanism for Swiss companies to export humanitarian goods to Iran despite US sanctions, established in coordination with the United States (US Department of the Treasury [2020]; SECO [2020]). Going forward, governments and businesses will have to account for the increasingly intricate global effects of sanctions regimes by various actors.

Given Russia's military aggression against Ukraine, Switzerland's sanctions policy became the object of sometimes heated public and parliamentary debate. Some politicians and political groups advocate for an end to Swiss EU-based sanctions against belligerent states, invoking a strict notion of neutrality that goes beyond the obligations that neutral states hold according to international law (Federal Council [2024]). Others advocate for a more proactive sanctions policy, be it by aligning more closely with EU sanctions (Walder [2022]; Molina [2023]) or by adopting sanctions independently of the EU or any other international organisations or trading partners. An attempt to revise the Swiss Embargo Act to enable such autonomous sanctions was accepted by Switzerland's lower chamber but rejected by its upper chamber in 2022 (Dépêche ATS [2022a], [2022b]). As voices calling for changes to Swiss sanctions policy grow more numerous, the future direction of Switzerland's sanctions policy remains open.

Disclaimer

All views and findings expressed in this text are those of the authors and do not necessarily reflect the views of the State Secretariat for International Finance (SIF), the State Secretariat for Economic Affairs (SECO), or the Swiss government.

Notes

1. An overview of ongoing sanctions regimes can be found on the website of the State Secretariat for Economic Affairs (SECO): <https://www.seco.admin.ch/seco/fr/home/Aussenwirtschaftspolitik_Wirtschaftliche_Zusammenarbeit/Wirtschaftsbeziehungen/exportkontrollen-und-sanktionen/sanktionen-embargos/sanktionsmassnahmen.html>.
2. The total value of frozen funds may vary due to fluctuations in asset valuations and other reasons, such as new listings and delistings.
3. Swiss foreign trade statistics can be found at <https://www.gate.ezv.admin.ch/swissimpex/>.

Bibliography

Literature

Biersteker T, Eckert SE, Romaniuk P, Halegua A and Reid N, *Targeted Financial Sanctions: A Manual for Design and Implementation. Contributions from the Interlaken Process* (The Thomas J. Watson Jr Institute for International Studies, Brown University 1998).

Biersteker T, Brubaker R and Lanz D, *UN Sanctions and Mediation: Establishing Evidence to Inform Practice* (United Nations University Centre for Policy Research, 2019) <https://collections.unu.edu/eserv/UNU:7257/UN_Sanctions_and

_Mediation_WEB_FINAL.pdf> accessed 26 January 2025.

Cockayne J, Brubaker R and Jayakody N, *Fairly Clear Risks: Protecting UN Sanctions' Legitimacy and Effectiveness Through Fair and Clear Procedures* (United Nations University Centre for Policy Research, 2018) <https://collections.unu.edu/eserv/UNU:6450/UNU_FairlyClearRisks_FINAL_Web.pdf> accessed 26 January 2025.

Fontana K, 'Dick Martys Vermächtnis: Die Schweiz erzielt einen Erfolg bei den schwarzen Listen der Uno' (*Neue Zürcher Zeitung*, 17 September 2024) <https://www.nzz.ch/schweiz/dick-martys-vermaechtnis-die-schweiz-erzielt-einen-erfolg-bei-den-schwarzen-listen-der-uno-ld.1848765> accessed 26 January 2025.

Documents

Convention (V) respecting the Rights and Duties of Neutral Powers and Persons in Case of War on Land (adopted 18 October 1907, entered into force 26 January 1910).

Convention (XIII) concerning the Rights and Duties of Neutral Powers in Naval War (adopted 18 October 1907, entered into force 26 January 1910).

Council of the European Union 'Sanctions Guidelines' (2018) Document 5664/18 <https://data.consilium.europa.eu/doc/document/ST-5664-2018-INIT/en/pdf>.

Dépêche ATS, 'Berne doit pouvoir prendre des sanctions de manière autonome: Délibérations au Conseil national' (2022a) <https://www.parlament.ch/fr/ratsbetrieb/suche-curia-vista/geschaeft?AffairId=20190085>.

Dépêche ATS, 'Le Conseil des États ne veut pas de sanctions autonomes suisses: Délibérations au Conseil national' (2022b) <https://www.parlament.ch/fr/ratsbetrieb/suche-curia-vista/geschaeft?AffairId=20190085>.

Federal Council, 'Response to the Motion by Fabian Molina: "Kohärente Schweizer Sanktionspolitik. Rechtsgrundlage für den Umgang mit thematischen Sanktionen der EU" of 29 September 2023' (29 November 2023) <https://www.parlament.ch/de/ratsbetrieb/suche-curia-vista/geschaeft?AffairId=20234278>.

Federal Council, 'Response to the interpellation by Nicolas Walder: "La Suisse va-t-elle imposer à son tour des sanctions contre les autorités et institutions chinoises au Turkestan oriental?" of 19 March 2021' (12 May 2021) <https://www.parlament.ch/fr/ratsbetrieb/suche-curia-vista/geschaeft?AffairId=20213408>.

Federal Council, 'Message concernant la modification de la loi sur les embargos (FF 2020 625)' (13 December 2019); <https://www.fedlex.admin.ch/eli/fga/2020/65/fr>.

Federal Council, 'Response to the interpellation by Nicolas Walder: "Le Conseil fédéral prendra-t-il des sanctions contre les violations graves des droits humains?" of 28 February 2022' (25 May 2022) <https://www.parlament.ch/fr/ratsbetrieb/suche-curia-vista/geschaeft?AffairId=20223029>.

Federal Council, 'Message concernant l'initiative populaire fédérale «Sauvegarder la neutralité suisse (initiative sur la neutralité)' (27 November 2024) <https://www.fedlex.admin.ch/eli/fga/2024/3136/fr>.

Group of Like-Minded States on Targeted Sanctions, 'Proposal for fair and clear procedures for a more effective UN sanctions system', Annex to UN Doc. S/2018/1094 (11 December 2018).

Marty D, 'Les fondements de notre ordre juridique court-circuités par l'ONU' Motion in the Swiss Council of States' (12 June 2009) <https://www.parlament.ch/de/ratsbetrieb/suche-curia-vista/geschaeft?AffairId=20093719>.

Molina F, 'Kohärente Schweizer Sanktionspolitik. Rechtsgrundlage für den Umgang mit thematischen Sanktionen der EU' Parliamentary motion (29 September 2023) <https://www.parlament.ch/de/ratsbetrieb/suche-curia-vista/geschaeft?AffairId=20234278>.

Parlamentarische Verwaltungskontrolle, 'Beteiligung des Bundes an Wirtschaftssanktionen. Bericht der Parlamentarischen Verwaltungskontrolle zuhanden der Geschäftsprüfungskommission des Ständerates' (9 November 2017).

SECO, 'Payment mechanism for humanitarian supplies to Iran in effect' (press release, 27 February 2020) <https://www.seco.admin.ch/seco/en/home/seco/nsb-news/medienmitteilungen-2020.msg-id-78251.html>.

SECO, 'National Risk Assessment (NRA): Proliferation Financing. Report of the

Interdepartmental Coordinating Group on Combating Money Laundering and the Financing of Terrorism (CGMF)' (2024) State Secretariat for Economic Affairs SECO, Money Laundering Reporting Office Switzerland MROS; efd.admin.ch/en/nsb?id=103476.

SECO, '*FAQ – Sanctions contre la Russie*' (website as of 14 January 2025); <https://www.seco.admin.ch/seco/fr/home/Aussenwirtschaftspolitik_Wirtschaftliche_Zusammenarbeit/Wirtschaftsbeziehungen/exportkontrollen-und-sanktionen/sanktionen-embargos/sanktionsmassnahmen/faq_russland_ukraine.html>.

Security Council Report 'Sanctions: Vote on a Draft Resolution on the Focal Point for Delisting and Informal Working Group on UN Sanctions' What's in Blue (17 July 2024) <https://www.securitycouncilreport.org/whatsinblue/2024/07/sanctions-vote-on-a-draft-resolution-on-the-focal-point-for-delisting-and-informal-working-group-on-un-sanctions.php>.

Statement after the vote by Switzerland at the 9689th meeting of the Security Council on general issues relating to sanctions (19 July 2024) <https://www.aplusforpeace.ch/statement-after-vote-general-issues-relating-sanctions>.

US Department of the Treasury, 'United States and Switzerland Finalize the Swiss Humanitarian Trade Arrangement' (press release, 27 February 2020) <https://home.treasury.gov/news/press-releases/sm919>.

Walder N, 'Le Conseil fédéral prendra-t-il des sanctions contre les violations graves des droits humains?' (parliamentary interpellation of 28 February 2022) <https://www.parlament.ch/fr/ratsbetrieb/suche-curia-vista/geschaeft?AffairId=20223029>.

AUREL NIEDERBERGER AND LUKAS REGLI

13. Ukraine

Andrei Richter

I Introduction

In the initial eight years of the Russian aggression against Ukraine (2014–22), the formal side of bilateral relations seemed to be normal: the leaders spoke on the phone, there were diplomatic relations, trade and economic links, free travel of tourists across their borders, even the law enforcement agencies cooperated with each other on crime. At the same time, the Ukrainian authorities understood the need to escape Moscow's influence while keeping the national economy in operation.

To facilitate these contradictions, Ukraine resorted to a national law 'On Sanctions', adopted in August 2014. The proclamation by the Supreme Rada of Ukraine (the Parliament) that the Russian Federation was an 'aggressor state' (2015) and, later, a 'terrorist state' (2022) were other formal bases for restrictions selectively introduced against certain Russian and pro-Russian actors abroad and within Ukraine. The adoption of the law also allowed the national policies of Ukraine to align with those of the Western states that introduced economic sanctions against Russia in response to its annexation of Crimea in March 2014.

II Law 'On Sanctions'

The Law 'On Sanctions' has become the legal foundation for all national sanctions in Ukraine. It was adopted in order to provide the means for

> an urgent and effective response to existing and potential threats to the national interests and national security of Ukraine, including hostile acts, armed attack by other states or non-state entities, harm to the life and health of the population, hostage-taking, expropriation of the property of the state, individuals and legal entities, causing property losses, creating obstacles to sustainable economic development and exercise by Ukrainian citizens of their rights and freedoms to the full extent. (On Sanctions [2014] Preamble)

It defines sanctions as 'special economic and other restrictive measures' that 'may be imposed by Ukraine against a foreign state, a foreign legal entity, a legal entity controlled by a foreign legal entity or a non-resident individual, foreigners, stateless persons, and entities engaged in terrorist activities' (On Sanctions [2014] Art. 1). The law provides an open list of 24 types of restrictive measures that the authorities may impose against sanctioned individuals or entities, such as asset blocking, cancelling or suspending licences and permits, terminating trade agreements, as well as cultural exchanges, academic cooperation, educational and sports contacts and entertainment events, and depriving individuals of state awards of Ukraine (On Sanctions [2014] Art. 4).

According to the law, the procedure to impose (or amend/reverse) sanctions is as follows. It begins with a formal proposal submitted to the National Security and Defense Council of Ukraine (RNBO, the coordinating body in matters pertaining to national security and defence under the President of Ukraine), by the Supreme Rada, the president, the cabinet of ministers, the national bank, or the Security Service of Ukraine (SBU). Upon formal review by RNBO, the individual and entity sanctions are then introduced by its decision, which becomes enforced through a decree of the President of Ukraine. Sectoral sanctions are introduced in the same manner with a follow-up approval by the Supreme Rada. So far, the president has issued more than 100 decrees enacting sanctions. The RNBO has discretion as to the specific type(s) of sanctions to be imposed in each case, as well as their terms (currently typically ten years).

In May 2022, the Supreme Rada adopted broad additions to the existing sanction regime. The law enacted a new type of sanction that results in the foreclosure of assets in the state's favour. It may be imposed on both companies and individuals that cause significant damage to the national security of Ukraine. Observers believe that these provisions 'may set an example to other jurisdictions of a response aimed at protecting national security and making Russia accountable' (Vorozhbyt and Bogachenko [2023] at 76).

The penalties for violating the sanctions include criminal liability. Under certain circumstances, violations may be treated as collaboration with the aggressor state, financing terrorism and/or financing the violent overthrow of the regime, as well as other criminal offences, which include imprisonment of up to 12 years (Shtepa [2023]).

III Case law

Several times, the legality of specific presidential decrees on sanctions was challenged in the Administrative Cassation Court, a chamber of the Supreme Court of Ukraine, as the first instance on presidential acts (Richter [2022] at 14–18). For example, in the case challenging the decree on sanctions in relation to certain Russian social media and electronic mail service providers, claimant N, a citizen of Ukraine and in possession of accounts on Russian social network platforms, as well as a mailbox on Mail.ru, argued that the sanctions violated his right to receive information and to freedom of expression, as guaranteed by Article 10 of the European Convention on Human Rights (ECHR). The Supreme Court ruled that the presidential decree had the legitimate aim of an 'urgent and effective response to the threats to the national security of Ukraine', which corresponded to the possible restrictions under the ECHR. They were prescribed by the national law, including 'On Sanctions', and 'necessary in a democracy', as there was an urgent need to introduce and continue them in view of the 'facts of aggression against Ukraine'. The Supreme Court ruled that the claimant had not substantiated a violation of his rights by the sanctions against the particular companies as other 'comparable' online services remained free from governmental interference in Ukraine. Therefore, the President of Ukraine had acted in a lawful and legal manner when introducing these necessary and proportionate restrictions. On 4 November 2020, the Grand Chamber of the Supreme Court of Ukraine upheld the decision taken by the Administrative Cassation Court and dismissed the appeal (Case N. 9901/138/20 [2020] paras 42, 44, 45, 48).

IV Coordination and impact of the sanctions

All RNBO decisions on sanctions prescribe informing the authorities of the European Union (EU), the United States and other states on the new subjects of Ukrainian actions, as well as raising the issue of replicating them by the third parties. Moreover, by decree of the president, all anti-Russian sanctions introduced by the EU and the states from the Group of Seven should be fully implemented in Ukraine through synchronising them by the RNBO within 15 days of their original enforcement abroad. Ukrainian authorities should also urge their international partners to target the entities and individuals already sanctioned by Ukraine because of the Russian aggression (On the decision… [2025]).

Additionally, in 2022, the President of Ukraine called for the establishment of the International Working Group on Russian Sanctions (IWG) with the participation of independent experts on sanctions. The group has been co-chaired by the head of the Office of the President, Andriy Yermak, and Stanford University Professor Michael McFaul.

The IWG aims to strengthen international sanctions against Russia by proposing new sanctions strategies and packages to like-minded governments, as well as mechanisms aimed at monitoring compliance and preventing possible sanction circumvention. It facilitates the Ukrainian authorities in synchronizing national sanctions with those introduced abroad, with the reverse happening as well (Vorozhbyt and Bogachenko [2023] at 76).

Among other things, the IWG facilitated the launching of the State Sanctions Registry (in Ukrainian and English) in 2024. This comprehensive registry is operated by the RNBO and provides free public access to the up-to-date and reliable information about entities and individuals subject to sanctions. Their total number currently exceeds 20,000 (as of September 2025). Information is available in Ukrainian and in English.

The IWG claims that more than half of the measures proposed by it have been partially or fully implemented (Shtepa [2023]). As to their impact, the IWG acknowledged that while the current sanctions regime is 'imperfect', it has helped reduce Russia's capacity to conduct its aggression against Ukraine: 'Moving forward, we cannot fatalistically declare that sanctions aren't working and then do nothing new. Instead, we must identify new actions and better enforcement mechanisms to make sanctions more effective as a means to accelerating the end of Russia's invasion of Ukraine' (Action Plan 3.0 [2024] at 18).

V Conclusion

Following Russia's annexation of Crimea in 2014, Ukraine followed Western countries and developed a comprehensive regime of sanctions. Based on the Law 'On Sanctions' and numerous decrees and decisions by the authorities, backed by the expert community and the public at large, the sanctions regime supplements military and diplomatic efforts to help Ukraine repel the aggression by putting economic pressure on Russia and its allies and protecting the population from malicious propaganda.

Bibliography

Literature

Richter A, 'Sanction Law against Russian and Belarusian Audiovisual Media' (European Audiovisual Observatory [Council of Europe] 2022) <https://rm.coe.int/iris-extra-2022-sanction-law-against-russian-and-belarusian-audiovisua/1680a8ff9f> accessed 2 September 2025.

Shtepa H, 'Blog Series: Sanctions Enforcement Around the World, the Ukrainian Perspective' (Baker McKenzie blog, 4 May 2023) <https://sanctionsnews.bakermckenzie.com/blog-series-sanctions-enforcement-around-the-world-the-ukrainian-perspective/> accessed 2 September 2025.

Vorozhbyt O and Bogachenko P, 'Ukraine: Sanctions – the Edge of War and Beyond' (*CEE Legal Matters*, 9 December 2023) <https://ceelegalmatters.com/Magazines/ISSUE_CEELM_9.12_free.pdf> accessed 2 September 2025.

Law (national)

On Sanctions, Law of Ukraine (*The Official Bulletin of the Verkhovna Rada of Ukraine*, 2014, No. 40, Article 2018, as of 17 July 2020) 14 August 2014, No. 1644-VII, Official translation into English <https://zakon.rada.gov.ua/laws/show/en/1644-18?lang=en#Text> accessed 2 September 2025.

Про санкції (On Sanctions), Law of Ukraine, 14 August 2014, N 1644-VII, (Відомості Верховної Ради, 2014, N. 40, ст.2018 as of 1 August 2025) <https://zakon.rada.gov.ua/laws/show/en/1644-18?lang=uk#Text> accessed 2 September 2025.

Про внесення змін до деяких законодавчих актів України щодо підвищення ефективності санкцій, пов'язаних з активами окремих осіб (On amendments to several legal acts so as to increase effectiveness of sanctions, related to the assets of certain persons), Law of Ukraine, 12 May 2022, N 2257-IX (*Holos Ukraïny*, N. 109 as of 23 May 2022) <https://zakon.rada.gov.ua/laws/show/2257-20#Text> accessed 2 September 2025.

Про рішення Ради національної безпеки і оборони України від 27 червня 2025 року «Про синхронізацію санкційного тиску України, Європейського Союзу та інших учасників Групи семи на Російську Федерацію і пов'язаних з нею суб'єктів (On the decision of the National Security and Defence Council of Ukraine of 27 June 2025 "On synchronization of sanctions pressure of Ukraine, the European Union and other members of the Group of Seven on the Russian Federation and entities related to it"), decree of the President of Ukraine No. 422/2025, 27 June 2025 <https://www.president.gov.ua/documents/4222025-55429> accessed 2 September 2025.

Case law (national)

Case N. 9901/138/20, Decision, Grand Chamber of the Supreme Court of Ukraine (4 November 2020) <https://reyestr.court.gov.ua/Review/93217974> accessed 2 September 2025.

Document

Action Plan 3.0: Strengthening Sanctions Against the Russian Federation, *Working Group Paper #19*, Stanford University. 15 May 2024 <https://fsi.stanford.edu/working-group-sanctions> accessed 2 September 2025.

Database

State Sanctions Registry <https://drs.nsdc.gov.ua/> accessed 2 September 2025.

14. United Kingdom

Yifan Jia

I Overview of the sanctions regimes

The United Kingdom has a long-standing history of participating in sanctions as a sender state. Prior to the UK's formal withdrawal from the European Union (EU) in 2020 (Brexit), the United Kingdom only implemented sanctions mandated by the United Nations (UN) and the EU. Following Brexit, the UK has continued to implement UN sanctions while also establishing its own autonomous sanctions framework. This framework is primarily underpinned by the Sanctions and Anti-Money Laundering Act 2018 (SAMLA), supplemented by other legislation, including the Immigration Act 1971 and the Export Control Order 2008.

Coming into effect in 2020, SAMLA marks the beginning of a new era for the UK's independent sanctions framework. It has been amended twice since then. The first amendment, introduced by the Economic Crime (Transparency and Enforcement) Act 2022, establishes an 'urgent procedure' for implementing sanctions for a defined period (provided they align with designations made by UK partners), enforces stricter liability for imposing penalties, and removes parliamentary oversight of government sanctions powers. The second amendment, under the Sanctions (EU Exit) (Miscellaneous Amendments) (No. 2) Regulations 2024, expands reporting obligations related to financial sanctions and revises licensing and exception provisions within sanctions legislation. While these changes aim to strengthen the sanctions framework, they also raise concerns regarding checks and balances. The lack of transparency has become one of the most criticised aspects of the UK sanctions regimes (Collins [2024]).

As a recently developed sanctions framework, the United Kingdom has drawn on lessons from other sender states, striving to address common criticisms by ensuring its measures comply with both domestic and international legal obligations. This is evident in its framework of exceptions and licences designed to minimise unintended consequences from sanctions. The framework includes general licences that apply to all individuals and entities meeting certain requirements, as well as specific licences that individuals and entities can apply for to gain permission.

The United Kingdom has also established a system of remedies to ensure due process. The designated individuals or entities can 'request key relevant information, request a ministerial review or bring a challenge in court' (FCDO and the Rt Hon Lord Cameron [2024]). There are no successful judicial review cases against the government in relation to sanctions under the SAMLA so far. Notably, the first sanctions case under SAMLA, *Shvidler (Appellant) v Secretary of State for Foreign, Commonwealth and Development Affairs (Respondent)*, was dismissed by the UK Supreme Court in July 2025. Following this, there remains the possibility of escalation to the European Court of Human Rights.

The United Kingdom published its first sanctions strategy in 2024, outlining the objectives and approaches for its sanctions policy. The United Kingdom identified three key purposes of sanctions: 'to deter future or continued malign activity, to disrupt current malign activity, and to demonstrate the [UK's] readiness to defend international norms'. The strategy positions sanctions within a broader context, emphasising their role as a critical instrument of UK foreign, national, and security policy (FCDO and the Rt Hon Lord Cameron [2024]).

As of 2024, the United Kingdom has 36 active autonomous sanctions regimes, which can be classified into thematic and geographic regimes. Thematic sanctions relate to issues such as chemical weapons, counterterrorism, cyber activity, anti-corruption, and human rights. The UK geographic sanctions focus on over 20 countries or regions, including Afghanistan, the Republic of Belarus, the Democratic People's Republic of Korea, Iran, Myanmar, Russia, Syria, Venezuela, and Zimbabwe (FCDO [2019]). Each sanctions regime is supported by specific regulations outlining its purposes, designation criteria, and restrictive measures. Up to 2024, the United Kingdom had imposed sanctions on over 3000 individuals and entities under its autonomous sanctions framework (GOV.UK [2024]).

II The enforcement framework

The United Kingdom has various types of sanctions, including trade sanctions, such as arms embargoes; financial sanctions, such as asset freezes; immigration sanctions, such as travel bans; and aircraft and shipping sanctions. The Foreign, Commonwealth and Development Office (FCDO) is responsible for formulating the overall sanctions policy of the United Kingdom, while the enforcement of specific sanctions falls under the remit of different government departments: the Department for Business and Trade oversees trade sanctions, HM Treasury handles financial sanctions, the Department for Transport manages transport sanctions, and the Home Office is responsible for immigration sanctions.

The United Kingdom has established two dedicated agencies for sanctions enforcement: the Office of Financial Sanctions Implementation (OFSI) and the Office of Trade Sanctions Implementation (OTSI). All individuals and businesses operating within the territory and territorial sea of the United Kingdom, as well as UK nationals and businesses established under UK law, regardless of their location globally, need to comply with sanctions (FCDO [2019]).

The OTSI is under the Department for Business and Trade, which oversees the enforcement of trade sanctions. Most violations of trade sanctions are considered strict liability, meaning that the OTSI does not need to prove intentionality or knowledge of the violations. The enforcement actions resulting from a breach can include the issuance of a warning letter, referral to the appropriate regulatory authority, notification of other relevant organisations, public disclosure of the breach, imposition of a monetary penalty, and referral to HM Revenue & Customs (HMRC) for further action (Department for Business and Trade and OTSI [2024]).

The OFSI is under HM Treasury, responsible for enforcing financial sanctions. The OFSI has expanded rapidly in recent years, especially following the establishment and implementation of sanctions regimes in response to Russia's invasion of Ukraine (Branch [2024]). The OFSI has the power to impose monetary penalties for violations of sanctions. As of 2024, the OFSI had issued penalties against ten companies. The most significant fine, amounting to £20.47 million, was imposed on Standard Chartered Bank for providing funds to a designated person without the necessary licence. Breaches of financial sanctions can also constitute a serious criminal offence, punishable by up to seven years' imprisonment upon conviction on indictment (HM Treasury and OFSI [2024]).

The United Kingdom is often criticised for poor sanctions enforcement. A non-governmental organisation (NGO) report points out that 'there have been zero breaches of financial sanctions imposed since 2022, zero convictions for sanctions evasion since 2012, and zero assets permanently seized through civil or criminal action related to sanctions violations' (Taylor [2024]). The Foreign Affairs Committee of the House of Commons also highlights concerns about the UK government's inadequate resources and expertise for the effective implementation and enforcement of sanctions, including the ability to trace and freeze targeted assets (Foreign Affairs Committee [2024]).

As a new independent sanctions sender, the United Kingdom places significant importance on international cooperation. Following Brexit, the United Kingdom has maintained regular engagement with EU institutions and member states through various channels, including the Sanctions Coordinators Forum (FCDO and the Rt Hon Lord Cameron [2024]). However, after four years of Brexit, the United Kingdom and the EU have increasingly divergent approaches to sanctions (Ovsiannikova [2024]). Meanwhile, the United Kingdom is increasingly learning from another key global sanctions power, the United States. The United Kingdom has strengthened its collaboration with the United States through the Atlantic Declaration in 2023 and the Memorandum of Understanding in 2024, particularly through the partnership between the OFSI and the US Office of Foreign Assets Control (OFAC). The United Kingdom also plays an important role in some sanctions coalitions, including among the G7 nations and Five Eyes (FCDO and the Rt Hon Lord Cameron [2024]).

III Conclusion

The UK autonomous sanctions framework, despite being established in recent years, is evolving rapidly. The foundational legislation underpinning sanctions has been amended twice, with a range of regulations and statutory instruments introduced to enhance enforcement. To support these developments, the government has expanded the existing offices and created new ones. On the global stage, the

United Kingdom has played an active role in coordinating and implementing multilateral sanctions. Having only been operational for four years, the UK sanctions policy's impact on global affairs is still unfolding.

Bibliography

Literature

Branch S, 'Evolution of the UK Financial Sanctions Framework Following the UK's Withdrawal from the EU' in Zilioli C, Bismuth R and Thévenoz L (eds), *International Sanctions: Monetary and Financial Law Perspectives* (Brill Nijhoff 2024) 146.

Ovsiannikova I, 'EU and UK Sanctions Policies After Brexit: Divergent Allies? The Case Study of Belarus' (2024) 30 *European Journal on Criminal Policy and Research* 277.

Documents

GOV.UK, 'The UK Sanctions List' <https://search-uk-sanctions-list.service.gov.uk/> accessed 26 December 2024.

Collins D, 'Market-Based Reforms to the UK Economic Sanctions Regime' (*Adam Smith Institute*, 2024).

Department for Business and Trade and OTSI, 'How Suspected Breaches of Trade Sanctions are Assessed by the Office of Trade Sanctions Implementation (OTSI)' (12 September 2024) <https://www.gov.uk/guidance/how-suspected-breaches-of-trade-sanctions-are-assessed-by-the-office-of-trade-sanctions-implementation-otsi> accessed 26 December 2024.

FCDO and Rt Hon Lord Cameron D, 'Deter, Disrupt and Demonstrate – UK Sanctions in a Contested World: UK Sanctions Strategy' (22 February 2024) <https://www.gov.uk/government/publications/deter-disrupt-and-demonstrate-uk-sanctions-in-a-contested-world-uk-sanctions-strategy> accessed 26 December 2024.

FCDO, 'Post-Legislative Scrutiny Memorandum: Sanctions and Anti-Money Laundering Act 2018' (4 March 2024) <https://www.gov.uk/government/publications/post-legislative-scrutiny-memorandum-sanctions-and-anti-money-laundering-act-2018/post-legislative-scrutiny-memorandum-sanctions-and-anti-money-laundering-act-2018> accessed 26 December 2024.

FCDO, 'UK Sanctions' (28 August 2019, last updated 10 October 2024) <https://www.gov.uk/guidance/uk-sanctions> accessed 26 December 2024.

Foreign Affairs Committee, 'The Cost of Complacency: Illicit Finance and the War in Ukraine' (UK Parliament, 30 June 2022) <https://publications.parliament.uk/pa/cm5803/cmselect/cmfaff/168/report.html> accessed 26 December 2024.

HM Treasury and OFSI, 'Enforcement of Financial Sanctions' (25 February 2019, last updated 27 September 2024) <https://www.gov.uk/government/collections/enforcement-of-financial-sanctions> accessed 26 December 2024.

OFSI, 'Strengthening Global Sanctions: Two Years of Enhanced Partnership' (19 November 2024) <https://ofsi.blog.gov.uk/2024/11/19/strengthening-global-sanctions-two-years-of-enhanced-partnership/> accessed 26 December 2024.

Taylor H, 'New Report Finds UK's Enforcement of Sanctions is "All Bark and No Bite"' (*Spotlight on Corruption*, 24 July 2024) <https://www.spotlightcorruption.org/sanctions-all-bark-and-no-bite/> accessed 26 December 2024.

Yifan Jia

15. United Nations

Andrea Charron and Lindsay Speirs

I Introduction

United Nations (UN) mandatory multilateral sanctions are the most frequently applied tool of the UN Security Council (UNSC) to address threats to and breaches of international peace and security. Although the term sanctions is never referenced in the UN Charter, they include "measures, not involving the use of armed force" that could result in a "complete or partial interruption of economic relations and of rail, sea, air, postal, telegraphic, radio and other means of communication and the severance of diplomatic relations" (UN Charter, Article 41; de Wet [2024]). Mandatory UNSC sanctions remain at the apex of legitimacy, whereas sanctions applied by coalitions of states in an ad hoc manner against external targets are at the bottom (Portela and Charron [2023] 17).

Inspired by the League of Nations' "terrible remedy" (Wilson [1919]), sanctions post-WWI were meant to be applied automatically should a League member state resort to aggression. Member states would, in theory, immediately ensure

> the severance of all trade or financial relations, the prohibition of all intercourse between their nationals and the nationals of the covenant-breaking State, and the prevention of all financial, commercial or personal intercourse between the nationals of the covenant-breaking State and the nationals of any other State whether a Member of the League or not. (Covenant of the League of Nations, Article 16(1))

In practice, this was not the case (see also chapter on League of Nations).

The measures imposed by the UNSC have been as varied as the cases in which they were required. Between 1968 and 2025, the UNSC adopted 31 mandatory sanctions regimes. The UNSC has applied voluntary measures under Chapter VI of the Charter, as well as mandatory comprehensive sanctions, commodity sanctions, diplomatic measures, arms embargoes, travel and financial asset freezes and has even banned luxury goods. Sanctions have been applied to address interstate conflict, civil wars, terrorism, weapons proliferation, rogue state behaviour, unconstitutional changes of government and to protect civilians (Charron [2011]; Security Council Report [2013] 7; see also chapter on Sanctions for conflict resolution). What remains constant is the need for agreement or acquiescence among the five permanent members to apply the measures. Enforcing them is another matter entirely. It is up to member states to give effect to sanctions, including in their domestic legal orders. The record on effectiveness is decidedly mixed. While the failure to implement UNSC measures has occasionally been due to indifference or even direct opposition to them, it is often the result of a lack of capacity (Hufbauer et al. [2009]; Pape [1998]; Biersteker et al. [2012]; see also chapter on Domestic implementation).

II The few sanctions regimes of the Cold War period

The first mandatory sanctions applied by the UNSC were targeted against the white minority regime of Ian Smith, who, in 1965, declared Southern Rhodesia's unilateral independence from the United Kingdom (Doxey [1972]). The measures recommended by the UNSC began as voluntary (or hortatory) sanctions to ban the sale of arms, limit economic relations and the export of oil products to the Smith regime (S/RES/217 [1965]) but soon became mandatory (S/RES/232 [1966]). It was the first time the UNSC created a sanctions committee to advise the UNSC on the efficacy of the measures. The committee noted that neighbouring Zambia would be affected by the sanctions and would require economic assistance, invoking the spirit of Article 50 of the UN Charter (S/RES/253 [1968] para. 15). Layers of sanctions were applied first as suggested measures, then as a requirement for member states to take all possible further action under Article 41 to deal with the situation in Southern Rhodesia (S/RES/253 [1968] para. 9; S/RES/277 [1970] para. 12). Many states, including South Africa, were slow and/or simply refused to enforce the sanctions against Ian Smith's regime. By December 1979, the "Bush War" for liberation prevailed, and Ian Smith was replaced by insurgent leader Robert Mugabe. With the signing of the Lancaster House Agreement ([1979]), the UNSC lifted all sanctions via S/RES/460 ([1979]). Ironically, Mr Mugabe was subject to US, EU, Canadian and other autonomous sanctions beginning in 2003 for his refusal to step down after rigged elections and an expropriation campaign against white farmers.

The only other mandatory UN sanctions regime agreed to during the Cold War was against South Africa (see also chapter on South Africa). It too began as a voluntary arms embargo in 1963 (UNSC Res 181 [1963]). In 1964, the Council expressed grave concern at the policy of apartheid and decided to establish an expert committee of UNSC members to study the measures that could be adopted, inviting input from member states (UNSC Res 191 [1964] paras 8 and 10). It wasn't until 1977 that the arms embargo was made mandatory (UNSC Res 418 [1977]), declaring South Africa's acquisition of arms and related material a threat to international peace and security. Following the adoption of a new constitution and the election of President Nelson Mandela in 1994, the mandatory arms embargo was lifted (UNSC Res 930 [1994]). Many scholars have noted that the autonomous, additional measures applied by member states (such as the numerous sports boycotts) were more effective in ending the apartheid regime than the mandatory UNSC measures (Hanlon [1990] 88).

III The 1990s: the "Sanctions Decade"

The 1990s were rightfully dubbed the "Sanctions Decade" by David Cortright and George Lopez [2000]. With the end of the Cold War and a reinvigorated P5, civil wars around the world were addressed by the imposition of sanctions, often as the teeth to support UN peacekeeping missions (Charron [2011]). Africa was the subject of the greatest number of sanctions regimes and was therefore the test case for sanctions' innovations. Canadian Ambassador Robert Fowler, chair of the Angola Sanctions Committee, revolutionized how sanctions were monitored and, for the first time, against a non-state actor – UNITA (see chapter on Angola). Liberia was first sanctioned in 1992 and again in 1997 based on the recommendations of Panels of Experts for Sierra Leone sanctions (UNSC Res 1132 [2000]). The Panel concluded that President Charles Taylor of Liberia was financially supporting rebels in Sierra Leone – the Revolutionary United Front – prolonging the civil war in Sierra Leone. In addition to travel, arms and diamond sanctions, timber restrictions were applied against Liberia (UNSC Res 1343 [2001]; see also chapter on Sierra Leone). Sanctions against African states, non-state actors, individuals and entities have been some of the most inventive but also the least effective. From charcoal (against Somalia) to due diligence requirements for mining (DRC), from sanctioning whole states (Rwanda and CAR, for example) to regions within provinces (Ituri and Kivu in the DRC), to applying sanctions at the behest of a target state to improve forest management practices (in Liberia's third sanctions regime), the UNSC has tried to limit the unintended consequences of sanctions' potentially coercive effect against innocent civilians. This, however, was a lesson learned far too late.

The other issue tackled by the UNSC sanctions in the 1990s was state-sponsored terrorism, which morphed into tackling non-state-sponsored forms as well. Libya's implication in the bombing of two international flights (American Pam Am flight 103 in 1988 and French Union de Transports Aériens or UTA flight 772 in 1989) resulted in a suite of measures that were instituted after it was evident that Libya was uncooperative with investigations (UNSC Res 731 [1992]). Sudan was sanctioned next for its role in the assassination attempt of Egyptian President Hosni Mubarak in 1995. When Egypt was on the UNSC in 1996, it recommended rather anaemic sanctions in deference to its close ties to Sudan (UNSC Res 1044 [1996]). Sudan was known to harbour more than a few terrorists, including Carlos the Jackal and Osama bin Laden (who later fled to Afghanistan). In 1998, a week after US embassies in Nairobi, Kenya and Dar es Salaam, Tanzania, were bombed by bin Laden's group Al Qaeda, the UNSC unanimously passed a resolution condemning the acts as indiscriminate and outrageous (UNSC Res 1189 [1998]). The voluntary sanctions applied against the Taliban in Afghanistan in 1996 became mandatory via UNSC Res 1267 ([1999]).

Comprehensive (or dumb) sanctions applied against Iraq, Haiti and the former Yugoslavia precipitated a rethink of the purpose and consequences of sanctions. So grave were the impacts of these sanctions that the P5 penned a non-paper to the President of the Security Council in 1995 in which they pledged that "future sanctions regimes should be directed to minimize the unintended, adverse side-effects of sanctions on the most vulnerable segments of targeted countries"

(S/1995/300 [1995] 2). Hereafter, exemptions for foodstuffs and medicines became commonplace (see chapter on Humanitarian carveouts).

IV The advent of targeted sanctions

So important is the potential of UN sanctions that the UNSC sought outside assistance in the form of committees, panels of experts and academics. Three state-led processes aimed to improve the effectiveness of UN sanctions by focusing on standardizing resolution language and best practices. The Interlaken, Bonn/Berlin and Stockholm processes tackled various issues with targeted UN sanctions which were presented to the UNSC's General Working Group on Sanctions for future consideration. The Swiss government sponsored best practices for financial sanctions (Biersteker and Watson [2001]), the German government tackled arms, travel and aviation sanctions (Brzoska [2001]) and the Swedish government studied the implementation and monitoring of sanctions (Wallensteen et al. [2003]). The Watson Institute initiated sanctions training for new UNSC members, and professional sanctions associations around the world always include an examination of UN sanctions compliance.

The balance to limit the humanitarian consequences of sanctions has been tested by North Korea and Iran given their proliferation activity. North Korea's continued defiance and missile testing have resulted in layers of sanctions since 2006 that now include mandatory inspection of any cargo into North Korea. It, in return, has found many ways to defy the sanctions (see also chapter on North Korea)

Increasingly, the UNSC takes its cue to apply sanctions after a regional organization has initiated measures. In the case of sanctions applied by various African regional organizations often because of an unconstitutional change of government, the UNSC follows with mandatory sanctions measures targeting one of the parties to the conflict and providing more teeth to the regional measures (Charron and Portela [2015] 12; see also chapter on Sanctions for human rights and democracy).

Mounting legal challenges with respect to UNSC sanctions in national, regional and international courts have centred on the infringement of the human rights of targets, the over-legislation by the UNSC, the lack of due process, the overlap of sanctions lists and the confluence of sanctions with International Criminal Court indictments (see also chapter on International criminal justice and sanctions). Many of the initial legal cases were prompted by the expanding "blacklists" resulting from the 9/11 terrorist attacks, which barred thousands from travelling or accessing their funds as suspected members or accomplices of Al Qaeda and the Taliban (see chapter on Sanctions in the fight against terrorism). In response, the UN created the position of Ombudsperson and Focal Point (see chapter on Focal Point and Ombudsperson) to serve as liaisons between individual targets and the UNSC sanctions committees. Graft and corruption have also been connected to the evasion of sanctions – infamously as part of the Oil-for-Food programme to manage sanctions against Iraq in the 1990s (UNSC Report [2013]).

V Conclusion

The rate of adoption of sanctions has decreased considerably since the decade of sanctions. This is especially the case post-2014 when geopolitical tensions between Russia and the Western P5 members made agreement on many needed sanctions to deal with Russia's aggression against Ukraine impossible.

Of all the studies on UN sanctions, their "effectiveness" or lack thereof tops this list of subjects. Many databases have been created to help measure effectiveness, but methodological challenges often obstruct a clear picture of the degree of innovation introduced by UNSC practice (Portela and Charron [2023]). Thankfully one database is dedicated to targeted UN sanctions (TSC [2025]) (Note to editors: need to add this in the biblio (Targeted Sanctions Consortium Database found at https://www.graduateinstitute.ch/research-centres/global-governance-centre/targeted-sanctions-initiative) More research is needed on the threat stage of UN sanctions (Kruiper [2024]; see also chapter on Sanction threats) and the UNSC's selectivity in addressing some but not all crises with sanctions when the P5 is unable to agree on sanctions measures (Charron [2011]; Eriksson and Wallensteen [2015]). Given past trends, the UNSC is most likely to sanction cases of civil wars in Africa, while regional and increasingly autonomous measures sanction other objectives.

Bibliography

Literature

Biersteker T, Eckert SE and Tourinho M, *Designing United Nations Targeted Sanctions* (The Graduate Institute/Targeted Sanctions Consortium/Watson Institute 2012).

Biersteker TJ and Watson S, *Targeted Financial Sanctions: A Manual for Design and Implementation* (The Swiss Confederation 2001).

Brzoska M (ed.), *Design and Implementation of Arms Embargoes and Travel and Aviation Related Sanctions: Results of the Bonn-Berlin Process* (Bonn International Center for Conversion in cooperation with the Auswartiges Amt and the United Nations Secretariat 2001).

Charron A, *UN Sanctions and Conflict: Responding to Peace and Security Threats* (Routledge 2011).

Charron A and Portela C, 'The UN, Regional Sanctions and Africa' (2015) 91 *International Affairs* 1369.

Cortright D and Lopez GA, *The Sanctions Decade: Assessing UN Strategies in the 1990s* (Lynne Rienner Publishers, 2000).

de Wet E, 'Article 41' in B Simma and others (eds), *The Charter of the United Nations: A Commentary* (4th edn, Oxford University Press 2024) 1665.

Doxey M, 'International Sanctions: A Framework for Analysis with Special Reference to the UN and Southern Africa' (1972) 26 *International Organization* 527.

Eriksson M and Wallensteen P, 'Targeting Sanctions and Ending Armed Conflicts: First Steps towards a New Research Agenda' (2015) 91 *International Affairs* 1387.

Hanlon J, 'Successes and Future Prospects of Sanctions Against South Africa' (1990) 17 *Review of African Political Economy* 84.

Hufbauer GC, Schott J, Elliot KA and Oegg B, *Economic Sanctions Reconsidered* (3rd edn, Peterson Institute 2009).

Kruiper T, *United Nations Sanctions Regimes and Selective Security* (Routledge 2024).

Pape R, 'Why Economic Sanctions Still Do Not Work' (1998) 23 *International Security* 66.

Portela C and Charron A, 'The Evolution of Databases in the Age of Targeted Sanctions' (2023) 25 *International Studies Review* <https://academic.Oxford University Press.com/isr/article-abstract/25/1/viac061/6987069> accessed 7 January 2025.

Volker PA, 'Independent Inquiry Committee into the United Nations Oil-for-Food Programme, Manipulation of the Oil-for-Food Programme by the Iraqi Regime' (United Nations 2005).

Wallensteen P, Staibano C and Eriksson M, *Making Targeted Sanctions Effective: Guidelines for the Implementation of UN Policy Options* (Department of Peace and Conflict Research, Uppsala University 2003).

Documents

Charter of the United Nations (adopted 26 June 1945, entered into force 24 October 1945).

Security Council Report, 'UN Sanctions' (No. 3, Security Council Report 2013).

UNSC Res 181 (7 August 1963) UN Doc. S/RES/181.

UNSC Res 191 (18 June 1964) UN Doc. S/RES/191.

UNSC Res 217 (12 November 1965) UN Doc. S/RES/216.

UNSC Res 232 (16 December 1966) UN Doc. S/RES/232.

UNSC Res 253 (19 March 1968) UN Doc. S/RES/253.

UNSC Res 277 (11 March 1970) UN Doc. S/RES/277.

UNSC Res 418 (4 November 1977) UN Doc. S/RES/418.

UNSC Res 460 (21 December 1979) UN Doc. S/RES/460.

UNSC Res 731 (21 January 1992) UN Doc. S/RES/731.

UNSC Res 930 (27 June 1994) UN Doc. S/RES/930.

UNSC Res 1044 (31 January 1996) UN Doc. S/RES/1044.

UNSC Res 1189 (13 August 1998) UN Doc. S/RES/1189.

UNSC Res 1267 (15 October 1999) UN Doc. S/RES/1267.

UNSC Res 1132 (8 October 1997) UN Doc. S/RES/1132.

UNSC Res 1343 (7 March 2001) UN Doc. S/RES/1343.

ANDREA CHARRON AND LINDSAY SPEIRS

UNSC 'Letter Addressed to the President of the Security Council' (13 April 1995) S/1995/300.
Wilson W, 'Address at the Coliseum at the State Fair Grounds in Indianapolis, Indiana' (The American Presidency Project, 1919) <https://www.presidency.ucsb.edu/documents/address-the-coliseum-the-state-fair-grounds-indianapolis-indiana?>.

ANDREA CHARRON AND LINDSAY SPEIRS

16. United States

Bryan R. Early

I Introduction

The United States employs economic sanctions more than any other country. Its sanctions have far-reaching effects on the global economy that extend beyond the sanctions' targets. No other country has the capacity to impose sanctions that are as economically debilitating as US sanctions, and no other country uses extraterritorial measures and secondary sanctions as frequently as the United States to coerce third-party cooperation. The United States also has an unparalleled ability to enforce its sanctions, imposing fines that can cost violators tens or even hundreds of millions of dollars. Despite having the world's most potent sanctions capabilities, US sanctions often fail to achieve their objectives and are associated with numerous harms. This entry offers insight into how and why the United States imposes sanctions and what effects its sanctions have.

II Summarising US sanctions policies

The US government issues various forms of economic sanctions and has a robust strategic trade control system that manages transactions involving dual-use goods and munitions with strategic implications. US sanctions can apply to entire states or broad sectors of their economies, or they can focus on individuals and entities via sanctions lists, such as the Specially Designated Nationals and Blocked Persons (SDN) list. The US President can impose sanctions using congressional authority through legislation like the Trading with the Enemy Act (1917) and the International Emergency Economic Powers Act (1977). The US Congress can also adopt legislation that imposes national sanctions regimes or obligates the imposition of economic sanctions on parties for undesired behaviours related to specific issues. For example, the Countering America's Adversaries Through Sanctions Act (2017) mandated extensive new sanctions against North Korea, Iran, and Russia. National-level sanctions adopted by Congress tend to be much harder to repeal than those adopted under the US President's discretion, making them last longer and more challenging to resolve. The United States tends to impose only a handful of new national-level sanctions per year. Issue-focused legislation like the Global Magnitsky Act (2016) empowers the US President to impose sanctions on individuals who engage in human rights abuses and corruption. Analysis by Rowan Scarpino and Jocelyn Trainer indicates that the United States added approximately 815 entities and individuals per year to its SDN list between 2017 and 2021, with the number skyrocketing up to 2500 in 2023 because of the sanctions imposed on Russia and Belarus. The US Department of the Treasury's Office of Foreign Assets Control (OFAC) oversees placing parties on the SDN list with interagency input. US sanctions policies are unique in that many include extraterritorial provisions, and the United States also adopts secondary sanctions against foreign individuals and entities that undercut its sanctions. Finally, the United States employs sanctions for environmental and commercial reasons, such as trade disputes.

III Why does the United States impose so many sanctions?

US policymakers employ sanctions for a myriad of reasons. Structurally, the United States has several advantages in employing sanctions over most other countries. Its large economic size and interconnectedness within the global economy mean it has economic leverage that it can exploit via sanctions. Being cut off from US markets and products will hurt most countries and many companies. The United States's large internal market and expansive trade network also mean that the US economy is resilient to the disruptions imposed by its sanctions. The centrality of the United States in the global financial system and the use of the US dollar in the settlement of international transactions also provide US policymakers with significant advantages in employing financial sanctions. Legislation adopted after the September 11 terrorist attacks in 2001 also empowered the US government to wield a wide array of new powers to "weaponise" its regulation of financial transactions for national security and foreign policy purposes. Lastly, the United States' position as the world's lone superpower following the end of the Cold War has given it a global portfolio of political and security interests and, some would argue, a responsibility to intervene to uphold global norms and protect civilians from violence and abuse. The

United States's use of sanctions thus reflects its expansive international interests and its structural capabilities that make sanctions an efficient policy instrument.

Domestic political factors also influence why the US government frequently uses economic sanctions. US presidents possess broad discretionary authority in adopting sanctions. Adopting sanctions is often the easiest, fastest political option for presidents when they confront international crises or security threats requiring a more potent response than diplomacy alone. Sanctions are also a cheap but relatively high-profile way for US presidents to uphold international norms and stigmatise bad behaviours. Research by Taehee Whang has also shown that US presidents can use sanctions to gain domestic political support.

IV Who does the United States sanction?

The United States imposes sanctions at the country level and on non-state actors. The United States imposes sanctions for two primary reasons that can overlap: norms violations and security threats. Norms violators include governments, non-state entities, and individuals engaged in human rights abuses, undermining democratic institutions, drug trafficking, corruption, or illicit economic activities. Security threats may include the same set of actors that are engaged in the proliferation of conventional munitions or weapons of mass destruction (WMD)-related goods, involved in civil wars and interstate disputes, or engaged in or support terrorism. As of 2023, the United States had 14 country-specific sanctions regimes and had imposed targeted sanctions on individuals or entities from most countries in the world. The leading targets of US sanctions—at the country and targeted levels—include Belarus, Burma, China, Iran, Mexico, North Korea, and Russia.

V Obtaining cooperation for and enforcing US sanctions

The United States employs both unilateral and multilateral sanctions regimes. The United States frequently seeks support for its sanctioning efforts through informal coordination, coerced cooperation, and international organisations. The United States informally coordinates its sanctions policies with allies and partners like the European Union. In politically salient sanctions episodes, it may also use secondary sanctions and other coercive threats to gain the cooperation of third parties—both at the state and non-state levels—that would prefer not to join sanctioning efforts or engage in sanctions-busting. As a permanent member of the United Nations Security Council, the United States frequently seeks the body's backing for sanctioning efforts it supports. Notably, the United States often imposes more comprehensive sanctions than its multilateral coalition partners adopt, and it will undertake unilateral measures when cooperation is not forthcoming. In the cases of US sanctioning efforts against both Cuba and Iran, for example, the United States experienced periods when its sanctions had broad multilateral support and were solely unilateral.

The United States invests significantly more resources in its capacity to implement, monitor, and enforce its sanctions than any other country. OFAC manages the implementation of US economic sanctions, promoting compliance with the policies both domestically and internationally. The body also gained substantial enforcement powers in 2008, enabling it to impose massive civil penalties against firms that violate US sanctions. The OFAC leveraged these powers to become a powerful regulatory body whose enforcement actions alter how both US and foreign firms do business with the targets of US sanctions. US sanctions enforcement efforts are also supported by the Department of Homeland Security, the Federal Bureau of Investigation, various prosecutorial offices, and the Department of Commerce's Bureau of Industry and Security, which handles strategic trade control violations (these cases often overlap with sanctions violations). Many firms around the world are more afraid of running afoul of US sanctions than their own governments' sanctions policies.

VI The success and harms of US sanctions

National-level sanctions imposed by the United States tend to follow the same general patterns as sanctions imposed by all senders, but the US sanctions have some advantages. Various databases that track sanctions outcomes differ with respect to the success rates of sanctions. Analyses by Daniel Drezner and

Elizabeth Rosenberg and her colleagues suggest that US sanctions and US financial sanctions, in particular, work more effectively. The United States also has advantages in obtaining concessions from sanctions threats when target countries receive high levels of US foreign aid or depend on the United States for their security. Less research has been conducted on how effective US sanctions are at constraining their targets' military and economic strength or their capacity to engage in WMD proliferation. For example, Nicholas Miller finds that US sanctions imposed for non-proliferation purposes have a mixed track record of success.

US economic sanctions may also have unintended consequences and side effects that run counter to US goals. Scholarship shows that US sanctions have immiserating effects on their targets' populations when the United States imposes severe sanctions and when it imposes them for human rights purposes. US sanctions in concert with OFAC sanctions enforcement actions also appear strongly linked to de-risking behaviours that cut off countries from otherwise legitimate trade and finance networks due to the compliance risks of doing business in places subject to US sanctions. Given that the United States subjects most countries or their citizens to some degree of sanctions, the consequences of US sanctions on the global economy are significant. This helps explain why a backlash to US sanctions has taken place, and countries and companies have begun building and employing systems for international exchange that no longer use the US dollar. US sanctions thus impose costs and harms not only on their intended targets but also on third parties and US interests.

For the foreseeable future, economic sanctions will remain an essential tool of US foreign policy. Policymakers must be careful not to over-implement sanctions and be wary of alienating foreign governments and businesses. Global backlash against US sanctions could threaten the US dollar's role as an international reserve currency and the primary currency used to settle international transactions. Alternatives to the dollar are less efficient and more costly, but parties may find the benefits of being outside the reach of US financial sanctions worth the cost. US sanctions may also drive other countries and businesses to become more reliant upon US rivals, like the People's Republic of China. This, in turn, could weaken the United States's ability to use sanctions to counter future security threats. US sanctions are a powerful tool that should be employed judiciously. The long-term utility of US sanctions and the health of the US economy will depend upon US policymakers' ability to exercise restraint in how they use sanctions.

Bibliography

Literature

Arnold A, 'Curbing China's Resilience to US Coercive Economic Statecraft' (2023) 46 *The Washington Quarterly* 153.

Bapat N, Early B, Grauvogel J and Kleinberg K, 'The Currency Constraint: Explaining the Selective Enforcement of U.S. Financial Sanctions' (2024) 20 *Foreign Policy Analysis*.

Casey C, Rennack D and Elsea J, 'The International Emergency Economic Powers Act: Origins, Evolution, and Use' (Congressional Research Service 2024) <https://sgp.fas.org/crs/natsec/R45618.pdf> accessed 5 December 2024.

Drezner D, 'Targeted Sanctions in a World of Global Finance' (2015) 41 *International Interactions* 755.

Early B and Jadoon A, 'Using the Carrot as the Stick: U.S. Foreign Aid and the Effectiveness of Sanctions Threats' (2019) 15 *Foreign Policy Analysis* 350.

Early B and Peksen D, 'Does Misery Love Company? Analyzing the Global Suffering Inflicted by U.S. Economic Sanctions' (2022) 2 *Global Studies Quarterly* 1.

Early B and Peterson T, 'Does Punishing Sanctions Busters Work? Sanctions Enforcement and U.S. Trade with Sanctioned States' (2022) 75 *Political Research Quarterly* 782.

Early B and Peterson T, 'The Enforcement of U.S. Economic Sanctions and Global De-Risking Behavior' (2024) 68 *Journal of Conflict Resolution* 2048.

Early B and Preble K, 'Enforcing US Economic Sanctions: Why Whale Hunting Works' (2020) 43 *The Washington Quarterly* 159.

Early B and Preble K, 'Going Fishing Versus Hunting Whales: Explaining Changes in How the U.S. Enforces Economic Sanctions' (2020) 29 *Security Studies* 231.

Early B and Spice R, 'Economic Sanctions, International Institutions, and Sanctions

Busters: When Does Institutionalized Cooperation Help Sanctioning Efforts?' (2015) 11 *Foreign Policy Analysis* 339.

Early B, 'Making Sanctions Work: Promoting Compliance, Punishing Violations, and Discouraging Sanctions Busting' in Bergeijk P (ed.), *Research Handbook on Economic Sanctions* (Edward Elgar 2021).

Early B, *Busted Sanctions: Explaining Why Economic Sanctions Fail* (Stanford University Press 2015).

Jentleson B, *Sanctions: What Everyone Needs to Know* (Oxford University Press 2022).

McDowell D, *Bucking the Buck* (Oxford University Press 2023).

Miller NL, 'The Secret Success of Nonproliferation Sanctions' (2014) 68 *International Organization* 913.

Morgan TC, Syropoulos Cz and Yotov Y, 'Economic Sanctions: Evolution, Consequences, and Challenges' (2023) 37 *Journal of Economic Perspectives* 3.

Nephew R, *The Art of Sanctions* (Columbia University Press 2017).

Newman A and Farrell H, *Underground Empire: How America Weaponized the World Economy* (Henry Holt and Co 2023).

Peksen D, 'When Do Imposed Economic Sanctions Work? A Critical Review of the Sanctions Effectiveness Literature' (2019) 30 *Defense and Peace Economics* 635.

Rosenberg E, Goldman Z, Drezner D and Solomon-Strauss J, 'The New Tools of Economic Warfare: Effects and Effectiveness of Contemporary U.S. Financial Sanctions' (Center for New American Security, 15 April 2016) <https://www.cnas.org/publications/reports/the-new-tools-of-economic-warfare-effects-and-effectiveness-of-contemporary-u-s-financial-sanctions> accessed 5 December 2024.

Scarpino R and Trainer J, 'Sanctions by the Numbers: 2023 Year in Review' (Center for New American Security, 27 June 2024) <https://www.cnas.org/publications/reports/sanctions-by-the-numbers-2023-year-in-review> accessed 5 December 2024.

Whang T, 'Playing to the Home Crowd? Symbolic Use of Economic Sanctions in the United States' (2013) 55 *International Studies Quarterly* 787.

Zarate J, *Treasury's War: The Unleashing of a New Era of Financial Warfare* (Public Affairs 2013).

Documents

Countering America's Adversaries Through Sanctions Act (2017).

Global Magnitsky Human Rights Accountability Act (2016).

International Emergency Economic Powers Act (1977).

Trading with the Enemy Act (1917).

17. World Bank

Francesco Seatzu

I Introduction

The World Bank (WB) developed its sanctions system in 1996 in response to growing concerns about corruption and fraud in the execution of its projects. The creation of this framework was driven by a need to protect the integrity of its development initiatives and was part of a broader effort to enhance governance standards (Seatzu [2019] 420). James Wolfensohn, then president of the WB, underscored the threat of corruption in his 1996 speech, which highlighted the need for a strong sanctions framework to preserve the effectiveness of the WB's funding efforts. In this context, the system also drew from the recommendations of Richard Thornburgh, former US Attorney General, who emphasized the importance of impartiality and transparency in addressing misconduct.

The WB's sanctions framework, much like the suspension and debarment procedures in the United States, not only addresses the current conduct of entities but also ensures that past actions, such as fraud and corruption, are dealt with adequately. Its core purpose is to safeguard the credibility and integrity of the WB and ensure that its funds are directed appropriately toward development efforts.

II The WB's sanctioning process

The WB's sanctions system serves as a critical mechanism for maintaining the integrity of its development initiatives by addressing misconduct in its funded projects through rigorous investigations and administrative proceedings. At the heart of this system is the Integrity Vice Presidency (INT), an internal body responsible for investigating allegations of fraud, corruption, and other forms of malfeasance. Through its systematic and transparent approach to addressing violations, the INT fosters accountability and trust in the bank's operations. This commitment is closely tied to the principles enshrined in Article III, Section 5(b) of the WB's Articles of Agreement, which require that loans be used exclusively for their intended purposes and managed with efficiency and economy. Implicitly, this provision obligates the bank to ensure that its resources are protected against fraud, corruption, and other prohibited practices. Together, these mechanisms underscore the WB's dedication to upholding ethical and effective management of its global development efforts.

The WB's sanctions system is an integral part of ensuring accountability and integrity within its financed projects, targeting a range of entities and individuals found to engage in prohibited practices such as fraud, corruption, collusion, coercion, or obstruction. Central to this approach is the principle that accountability applies irrespective of an entity's status, thereby reinforcing the bank's commitment to equitable enforcement. By addressing misconduct systematically, the sanctions system not only protects the bank's reputation but also ensures that its funds are utilized efficiently to achieve their intended development objectives. This proactive stance helps prevent resource misallocation, fostering trust in the international financial system and promoting adherence to ethical standards in global development initiatives.

III Human rights considerations in the sanctioning process

While the WB's sanctions system has been successful in protecting its development agenda, concerns have been raised regarding the protection of human rights. Critics argue that the procedural safeguards provided to entities under investigation may not always meet international human rights standards (Boisson de Chazournes and Fromageau [2011] 255). Key issues raised include the right to a fair trial and the protection of property rights, as sanctions can result in severe reputational damage and loss of business opportunities.

Despite these concerns, the WB strives to incorporate basic human rights principles into its sanctions system, such as the right to a fair hearing (Seatzu [2019] 430). However, the classification of sanctions as either administrative or criminal has been a point of contention. Many argue that the consequences of sanctions, such as reputational harm, bear resemblance to criminal penalties, necessitating a more formal judicial review process to ensure fairness and due process.

IV Potential reforms to the sanctions system

The WB's sanctions framework has been continuously refined, but proposals for reform persist. One proposed reform is the abolition of the current system and the transfer of sanctioning powers to WB member states (Seatzu [2019] 430). This would decentralize the enforcement process but might risk inconsistency across the bank's operations.

Another suggestion is to strengthen the current system by establishing an independent review body with judicial authority. Such a body would be tasked with overseeing sanctions, thus enhancing transparency, fairness, and objectivity in the process. This approach could potentially address criticisms regarding the concentration of power in the WB's decision-making process.

A third proposal is a hybrid model that combines WB oversight with independent reviews. This model would ensure that sanctions comply with international legal standards and benefit from the support of national legal frameworks. It would balance the need for WB integrity with an assurance of fairness for those subject to sanctions.

Each of these proposals requires careful consideration of how to balance the WB's need to enforce its rules and safeguard its development agenda with the protection of the rights of individuals and entities involved. Transparent, fair, and proportionate measures will be key to ensuring the continued credibility of the WB's sanctioning process.

V Conclusion

The WB's sanctioning system plays a pivotal role in preserving the integrity and credibility of the bank's operations. However, it also raises significant questions about the balance between sanctioning misconduct and protecting fundamental human rights. While the WB has been successful in combating fraud and corruption, concerns regarding fairness, transparency, and due process persist. Moving forward, proposals for reform will need to ensure that the bank's sanctions framework remains a robust tool for protecting development efforts, while upholding international human rights standards and enhancing the fairness of the process (Seatzu [2019] 430).

Bibliography

Literature

Boisson de Chazournes L and Fromageau E, 'Le mécanisme de sanction de la banque mondiale contre la fraude et la corruption: le droit administratif global comme outil d'élaboration et de consolidation d'une procédure' in Bories C (ed.), *Un droit administratif global? = A global administrative law?* (Pédone 2011) 255.

Bradlow DD and Grossman C, 'Limited Mandates and Intertwined Problems: A New Challenge for the World Bank and the IMF' (1995) 17 *Human Rights Quarterly* 411.

Dubois P, Ezzeddin P and Swan CD, 'Suspension and Debarment on the International Stage: Experiences in the World Bank's Sanctions System' (2016) 25 *Public Procurement Law Review* 61.

Canni TJ, 'Debarment is No Longer Private World Bank Business: An Examination of the Bank's Distinct Debarment Procedures Used for Corporate Procurements and Financed Projects' (2010) 40 *Public Contract Law Journal* 147.

Seatzu F, 'A Human-Rights-Based Approach to the World Bank Sanctions Regimes' (2019) *Rivista di diritto internazionale* 420.

PART II

TYPES OF MEASURES

18. Arms embargo

JUDITH VORRATH

I Introduction

Arms embargoes are used to constrain access to arms, ammunition and other military material in a specific geographical area or for certain actors. The main purpose is to restrict the ability to use military force or commit violent acts – in the context of an armed conflict or other threats to peace and security. Thus far, this specific type of sanction has been the most commonly used by the United Nations (UN). As of 31 July 2024, 12 of the existing 14 UN sanctions regimes comprise an arms embargo (UN DPPA [2023]). These are mandatory arms embargoes imposed by resolutions of the UN Security Council (UNSC), in contrast to voluntary arms embargoes that merely call upon member states to cease deliveries without being binding. In addition, the European Union (EU) imposes autonomous arms embargoes or builds on existing UN embargoes by extending their scope or reach. Other regional organizations, like the Economic Community of West African States (ECOWAS), have used arms embargoes, though in a much more limited way. Countries, most notably the United States and the United Kingdom, frequently also apply their own arms embargoes.

II The notion of "arms and related material"

In the case of a mandatory UN arms embargo, all UN member states are obliged to prevent the direct or indirect sale, supply or transfer of arms and military equipment to the target area or to targeted actors. Some arms embargoes in the UN context are two-way embargoes like the one imposed on North Korea in 2006 (at the time limited to major conventional weapons) and on Libya in 2011. These include not only the import of arms and related material, but also their export from the same country. The term "arms and related material" is used in many of the current UN arms embargoes, but the scope and types of material are subject to interpretation. The initial wording in the respective UN resolutions used to be very general; however, it has become clearer over the years, now often including the financing of arms supplies, technical advice and military training. Some embargoes also explicitly prohibit the provision of armed mercenary personnel. Yet, there are no general lists of prohibited goods – apart from those for the non-proliferation regimes on Iran and North Korea that have been set up based on lists of export control forums (Dörfler [2021] 23–31).

In contrast, the EU has established a common military list to define the scope of rules for controlling the export of military technology and equipment for its member states (EU [2024]). It comprises a broad range of goods designed specifically for military use and is frequently updated to cover new or modified technology, such as software designed for military offensive cyber operations. In the absence of a similar practice for UN arms embargoes, the reference to "arms and related material" is generally understood to cover all types of weapons, components, spare parts, ammunition and weapons accessories (Watson Institute for International and Public Affairs and CCSI [2015]). There are some indirect reference points; for example, the list of conventional weapons and goods in the international Arms Trade Treaty (UN 2014), which are prohibited in cases of existing UN arms embargoes, or lists that specify exemptions to certain UN arms embargoes. However, these only indicate what weapons and material are clearly covered by embargoes without being comprehensive.

III Evolution of arms embargoes

Arms embargoes have evolved in many respects over time. Significant change has occurred with regard to the combination of arms embargoes with other types of sanctions. Initially, the UNSC tended to impose arms embargoes as a stand-alone measure, as in the early case of the embargo against apartheid South Africa in 1977. In some cases, other sanctions were added later. This practice of imposing arms embargoes only – at least in the initial phase of a regime – remained common over the course of the 1990s – the so-called sanctions decade when the UNSC increasingly used coercive measures under Article 41 of the UN Charter. Afterwards, arms embargoes were normally part of a package including other sanctions, such as travel bans or assets freeze, right from the start. The main reason is that it became increasingly clear by the end of the 1990s that stand-alone embargoes were ineffective.

The Bonn-Berlin Process in 1999/2000, which was part of a larger reform effort on sanctions, provided important recommendations on improving the design and implementation of arms embargoes at the time (Brzoska [2001]). Even though not all of these were taken up, there have clearly been improvements, perhaps most noticeably in the monitoring. Today, most UN regimes contain a panel of experts or monitoring team with specific arms expertise in case an embargo is in place. They investigate, among others, (potential) violations of arms embargoes and report to the UNSC and the respective sanctions committee as the UNSC's subsidiary body. They can also make recommendations to improve the effectiveness of sanctions, for example, closing relevant loopholes in arms embargoes or designating individuals or entities for violations of the respective arms embargo. It was most likely also due to these reforms that multilateral arms embargoes significantly reduced the arms imports of affected states and groups, in some cases even if the ultimate goal of changing the target's behaviour was not met (Brzoska and Lopez [2009]). Yet, the challenges of implementation and enforcement remained.

Thus, the UNSC has repeatedly authorized member states to inspect suspicious cargo on their territory in the direction of the target area and to confiscate and destroy prohibited weapons or other military equipment seized. In cases like Somalia and Libya, it has gone a step further and authorized other member states or regional organizations to inspect suspicious ships off the coasts of these states to enforce the respective embargo. Some UN peacekeeping missions also had or have a mandate to support the implementation of arms embargoes, for example, by confiscating and collecting weapons and other goods that were imported in violation of the embargo (Vorrath [2024]).

IV Challenges in implementation

There are indications that the effects of the initial improvements may have waned. Some adjustments of UN arms embargoes have made monitoring them more difficult, especially as panels have come under increasing political and budgetary pressure. First, there are not just general, but also targeted arms embargoes that only apply to individuals or entities designated on a sanctions list. Those embargoes focus on specific actors like the Taliban in Afghanistan or the Houthis in Yemen and those associated with them. The global counterterrorism regime by the UN includes an arms embargo for those designated on the ISIL (Da'esh) and Al-Qaida sanctions list. While they are meant to weaken these particular groups, they are very difficult to monitor and control. Apart from this, the lifting of targeted arms embargoes – for single designated actors or generally – can hardly be used as a bargaining chip vis-à-vis non-state-armed actors since they are not supposed to receive weapons uninhibited in general.

Moreover, of the existing general embargoes in the context of armed conflict, almost all have exemptions or exceptions or – in the case of Somalia – a partial lift for the federal government issued in 2013 and extended since. Allowing the provision of certain arms, military material or training for specific international actors like peacekeepers or international training missions has become almost standard practice in order to allow them to function according to their mandate. A more controversial step is the exceptions or exemptions for national authorities to import certain arms and military material for their security forces – often under specific provisions like notification of or approval by the respective sanctions committee. While this is meant to support stabilization and counterterrorism efforts, without effective safeguards there is a high risk that weapons and military items are diverted and end up in the hands of non-state armed groups. This has repeatedly been reported by different expert panels. Another problem is that, in such contexts, the line between state and non-state actors can be blurred and thus, between those who are and those who are not allowed to receive weapons under specific conditions. At the same time, conditional exemptions for government security forces have become increasingly controversial in the UNSC and with the national governments concerned. Thus, the provisions under several UN arms embargoes for state authorities have been dropped; for example, the notification requirements for deliveries to the government of the DRC and the Central African Republic were lifted in 2022 and 2023, respectively (UNSC Res 2667 [2022]; UNSC Res 2693 [2023]).

Conflict-related arms embargoes that are time-limited – meaning they have to be renewed regularly, usually on an annual basis – have been adapted more frequently. The consensus at the UNSC has mostly worked towards easing arms embargoes for national authorities. Yet, if the underlying political objectives were not (fully) achieved, it has proven difficult to change course, in particular by tightening embargoes again. Moreover, strong interests from permanent and elected UNSC members have at times collided with arms embargo provisions.

V Conclusion

Overall, the implementation and enforcement of UN arms embargoes remain key for their credibility. Under most UN regimes to end armed conflict, there is a listing criterion for those acting in violation of the arms embargo. Yet, despite extensive reporting on violations and a lack of compliance with approval or notification provisions, few persons or entities are listed for such breaches (Vorrath [2022]). There are other options to improve enforcement. For example, the EU designated entities responsible for violating the arms embargo on Libya as an autonomous measure. Panel reports in and of themselves can also have an impact by naming and shaming specific actors or by providing information that can be used by member states to become active with regard to companies or other actors under their jurisdiction. Ultimately, however, arms embargoes need better political guidance and connection with other relevant instruments beyond sanctions.

Bibliography

Literature

Brzoska M (ed.), *Design and Implementation of Arms Embargoes and Travel and Aviation Related Sanctions: Results of the Bonn-Berlin Process* (BICC 2001).

Brzoska M and Lopez GA, 'Putting Teeth in the Tiger: Policy Conclusions for Effective Arms Embargoes' in Brzoska M and Lopez GA (eds.), *Putting Teeth in the Tiger: Improving the Effectiveness of Arms Embargoes* (Emerald Group 2009) 243.

Dörfler T, 'Interface Challenges of UN Sanctions with Forums of Export Control: Towards Cohesion and Consistency in Non-proliferation Sanctions?' in Lohmann S and Vorrath J (eds), *International Sanctions: Improving Implementation through Better Interface Management* (SWP Research Division International Security and the Americas Division Working Paper 1/2021) 23.

Vorrath J, 'The Evolution of UN Arms Embargoes in Conflict Settings: Stumbling Blocks to Effective Implementation' in Charron A and Portela C (eds), *Multilateral Sanctions Revisited: Lessons Learned from Margaret Doxey* (McGill-Queen's University Press 2022) 133.

Vorrath J, 'UN Arms Embargoes under Scrutiny: Obstacles and Options for an Effective Contribution to Conflict Resolution' (SWP Research Paper 12/2024).

Documents

Arms Trade Treaty (entered into force 24 December 2014) 3013 UNTS 269.

Common Military List of the European Union (2024) OJ C/2024/1945.

UN Department of Political and Peacebuilding Affairs (DPPA), *Subsidiary Organs of the United Nations Security Council fact sheets* (UN 2023).

UNSC Res 2667 (20 December 2022) UN Doc. S/RES/2667.

UNSC Res 2693 (27 July 2023) UN Doc. S/RES/2693.

Watson Institute for International and Public Affairs and CCSI, *Compendium of the High-level Review of United Nations Sanctions* (November 2015).

19. Banking system

Daniel Franchini

I Introduction

The banking system plays a central role in the implementation of international sanctions. The interconnectedness of global banking has significantly contributed to the steady rise in the use of financial sanctions since the early 1980s (Syropoulos et al. [2024] 14). Among the sanctions that have gained prominence in recent years – particularly among those implemented unilaterally by states – are restrictions on access to financial institutions and infrastructures that execute international payments, including banking networks and messaging systems like the Society for Worldwide Interbank Financial Telecommunication (SWIFT) (Cipriani et al. [2023] 32). Sanctions have also increasingly targeted the foreign reserves held by central banks in foreign jurisdictions (Franchini [2024]).

Thanks to the dominance of the US dollar as a global currency, the United States has been a prominent user of such sanctions (McDowell [2023]). The European Union (EU) and other states have followed suit, most notably in response to Russia's aggression against Ukraine in February 2022. However, the dominant role of Western states, combined with the severe effects of these sanctions, has fuelled criticism regarding their proportionality and potential for abuse (Hofer [2020]; Tzouvala [2024]). As a result, some states have explored alternative banking arrangements to mitigate the impact of financial sanctions (Ramaswamy [2022]), though these efforts have had limited success to date.

II Dollar-based sanctions and correspondent banks

Since most international transactions are conducted in US dollars, non-US banks financing them rely on correspondent banking relationships with US banks to facilitate payments for goods and services. These arrangements involve a bank in one country, the respondent, engaging a bank in the United States, the correspondent, to handle certain financial services for the respondent and its customers (Robinson et al. [2023] 482).

These arrangements grant access to the US financial system for transactions that otherwise would not be subject to US jurisdiction. The flipside is that they have become a tool for the United States to enforce sanctions restricting transactions with little or no direct US connection. Access to the US financial system is so crucial that the mere threat of exclusion can be instrumental. For example, European firms have been known to wind down business with sanctioned states like Iran due to the risk of losing access to US financial services (Ruys and Ryngaert [2020] 16).

However, US sanctions have extended beyond mere access restrictions. On several occasions, non-US entities violating US sanctions have faced severe civil and criminal penalties. For instance, in 2014, French bank BNP Paribas paid a record $8.9 billion to settle alleged violations of US sanctions against Sudan, Iran, Cuba, and Myanmar (Office of Foreign Assets Control [2014]). These 'secondary sanctions' have been criticised for exceeding internationally accepted jurisdictional links and potentially violating the customary international law of state jurisdiction (see chapter on Secondary sanctions and extraterritorial effects; Ruys and Ryngaert [2020] 18).

The development of interoperable central bank digital currencies (CBDCs) – championed especially by BRICS states (Liu and Papa [2022]) – may offer an alternative to the US dollar in global financial markets, potentially limiting the reach of dollar-based sanctions. However, CBDCs are still in their early stages, and it is unclear whether the development of digital currencies alone will be able to challenge the dominance of the US dollar (Kuehnlenz et al. [2023]).

III SWIFT and alternative banking messaging systems

SWIFT is a messaging network used by banks and other financial institutions to securely transmit information and instructions through a standardised system of codes. Established in 1973 and headquartered in Belgium, SWIFT is essential for international trade and finance, facilitating cross-border payments and currency exchanges. Because of its importance, SWIFT can serve as a powerful tool for sanctions. Denying access to SWIFT significantly hinders the ability of a state or other entity to conduct international financial transactions.

As a cooperative of banks, SWIFT aims to act in the interest of its community and has resisted political pressure to disconnect states such as Myanmar in 2004 and Israel in 2014 (Cipriani et al. [2023] 47). However, in response to the 2012 US sanctions related to Iran's nuclear programme and subsequent EU regulation, SWIFT discontinued access to designated Iranian banks, including Iran's Central Bank.

Restrictions on SWIFT services in response to international sanctions have become more frequent in recent years. In 2017, Belgium blocked SWIFT services to UN-sanctioned North Korean banks, leading SWIFT to disconnect all North Korean banks. After the Iran nuclear deal in 2016, Iranian banks were reconnected to SWIFT, but they were disconnected again in 2018 following US pressure, despite EU regulations not mandating such action. In 2014, after Russia's annexation of Crimea, SWIFT initially resisted calls to exclude Russia but eventually disconnected several Russian and Belarusian banks in compliance with 2022 EU Council regulations.

The use of SWIFT as a vehicle for international sanctions has spurred some states to develop alternatives. Russia created SPFS in 2014, which now connects several Russian banks. France, Germany and the United Kingdom developed INSTEX in 2019 to facilitate transactions with Iran. China launched CIPS in 2015 to support the renminbi in international trade. However, these alternatives have not achieved global reach comparable to SWIFT, and their effectiveness in shielding transactions from international sanctions remains limited (Eichengreen [2022] 2).

IV Sanctions on central banks

Central banks play a vital role in a state's economy, acting as lenders of last resort, supporting the value of its currency, ensuring banking stability and sometimes managing sovereign wealth funds (Lastra [2014] 78). To fulfil their functions, they typically hold foreign currency reserves deposited with other central banks (Downes [1989]). This makes them vulnerable to sanctions in foreign jurisdictions, particularly in the form of asset freezing (Franchini [2024]).

The United States has a history of freezing foreign central bank assets held in the Federal Reserve Bank of New York. Examples include Iran in 1979 and 2012, Libya in 1986, Panama in 1988, Iraq in 1990, North Korea in 2017, Venezuela in 2019 and Afghanistan in 2022. In the past two decades, other states have enacted similar measures. The EU froze Iranian and Syrian Central Bank assets in 2012, with the Arab League targeting Syria's Central Bank the same year. Most notably, in response to Russia's aggression against Ukraine in 2022, the G7 states, France, Germany, Italy, the United Kingdom, Canada, the United States and Japan, together with the EU, froze an estimated $350 billion in foreign reserves of the Central Bank of Russia.

The legal basis for such measures under international law is debated. The 2004 United Nations Convention on Jurisdictional Immunities of States and Their Property – not yet in force – grants immunity from measures of constraint to central bank assets as property 'in use for sovereign non-commercial purposes' (Articles 19, 21(1)(c)). This is generally considered reflective of customary international law (Brunk [2019] 280). Thus, freezing these assets could amount to a breach of immunity.

Some argue that immunity only applies to judicial measures, thus no issue of immunity would arise when sanctions are imposed through executive means, such as is ordinarily the case with asset freezing (Ruys [2019] 677; Webb [2024] 11). This view is opposed by those who consider any interference with foreign state property as potentially triggering immunity considerations regardless of the implementing body (Thouvenin [2015] 212). Even under this view, the freezing of central bank assets could be lawful when taken in response to an internationally wrongful act. As a countermeasure, the immunity protecting these assets could be temporarily suspended with a view to inducing the wrongdoing state to comply with its international obligations (Franchini [2020]).

Confiscation of central bank assets is harder to justify from an international law standpoint. Given that it likely requires judicial review, it would breach state immunity even under the more permissible reading of these rules (see chapter on Confiscation; Brunk [2023] 1640). Additionally, because of its irreversible character, confiscation is likely at odds with the law governing countermeasures. Article 49 of the International Law Commission's (ILC) Articles on State Responsibility prescribes that countermeasures must be temporary in character and reversible. This is to preserve their function as coercive measures designed to induce compliance with international law rather than to punish wrongdoing states (ILC [2001] Art. 49 para. 9).

State practice offers only a few examples of measures of confiscation of state assets, including most notably measures taken by the United States and Canada against Iran upon labelling the latter a sponsor of terrorism. These measures have given rise to protests by other states, and their legality has been challenged before the International Court of Justice (Certain Iranian Assets [2016]; Alleged Violations of State Immunities [2023]).

V Conclusion

The centrality of the banking system to international sanctions is matched only by the controversy surrounding its use. Control of the global financial infrastructure by a limited number of Western states grants them outsized power to impose economic hardship on other states (Rotblat [2017]). Furthermore, concerns exist regarding the effectiveness and proportionality of sanctions that exclude entire countries from SWIFT or freeze central bank assets, with potential for unintended harm to the target state's population (Drezner [2015]). Despite these concerns, no meaningful alternatives exist that can shield states from such sanctions. Additionally, when applied within the boundaries of international law, sanctions leveraging the banking system can be a potent tool for enforcing the international rule of law.

Bibliography

Literature

Brunk (Wuerth) I, 'Central Bank Immunity, Sanctions, and Sovereign Wealth Funds' (2023) 91 *George Washington Law Review* 1616.

Brunk (Wuerth) I, 'Immunity from Execution of Central Bank Assets' in Ruys T, Angelet N and Ferro L (eds), *The Cambridge Handbook of Immunities and International Law* (Cambridge University Press 2019) 266.

Cipriani M, Goldberg LS and La Spada G, 'Financial Sanctions, SWIFT, and the Architecture of the International Payment System' (2023) 37 *Journal of Economic Perspectives* 3.

Downes P, 'Managing Foreign Exchange Reserves' (1989) 26 *Finance and Development* 20.

Drezner DW, 'Targeted Sanctions in a World of Global Finance' (2015) 41 *International Interactions* 755.

Eichengreen B, 'Sanctions, SWIFT, and China's Cross-Border Interbank Payments System' (2022) Center for Strategic & International Studies <https://www.csis.org/analysis/sanctions-swift-and-chinas-cross-border-interbank-payments-system> accessed 1 July 2024.

Franchini D, 'State Immunity as a Tool of Foreign Policy: The Unanswered Question of Certain Iranian Assets' (2020) 60 *Virginia Journal of International Law* 433.

Franchini D, 'When Finance Becomes a Weapon: The Challenge of Central Bank Sanctions under International Law' (2025) 24 *Journal of International Trade Law and Policy* 28.

Hofer A, 'The Proportionality of Unilateral "Targeted" Sanctions: Whose Interests Should Count?' (2020) 89 *Nordic Journal of International Law* 399.

Kuehnlenz S, Orsi B and Kaltenbrunner A, 'Central Bank Digital Currencies and the International Payment System: The Demise of the US Dollar?' (2023) 64 *Research in International Business and Finance* 101834.

Lastra RM, 'The Role of Central Banks in Monetary Affairs: A Comparative Perspective' in Thomas Cottier and others (eds), *The Rule of Law in Monetary Affairs* (Cambridge University Press 2014).

Liu ZZ and Papa M, *Can BRICS De-Dollarize the Global Financial System?* (Cambridge University Press 2022).

McDowell D, *Bucking the Buck: US Financial Sanctions and the International Backlash against the Dollar* (Oxford University Press 2023).

Ramaswamy S, 'The Threat of Financial Sanctions: What Safeguards Can Central Banks Build?' (2022) 30 *China & World Economy* 23.

Robinson G, Dörry S and Derudder B, 'Global Networks of Money and Information at the Crossroads: Correspondent Banking and SWIFT' (2023) 23 *Global Networks* 478.

Rotblat C, 'Weaponizing the Plumbing: Dollar Diplomacy, Yuan Internationalization, and the Future of Financial Sanctions' (2017)

21 *UCLA Journal of International Law and Foreign Affairs* 311.

Ruys T and Ryngaert C, 'Secondary Sanctions: A Weapon out of Control? The International Legality of, and European Responses to, US Secondary Sanctions' (2020) *British Yearbook of International Law*.

Ruys T, 'Immunity, Inviolability and Countermeasures' in Ruys T, Angelet N and Ferro L (eds), *The Cambridge Handbook of Immunities and International Law* (Cambridge University Press 2019) 670.

Syropoulos C and others, 'The Global Sanctions Data Base – Release 3: COVID-19, Russia, and Multilateral Sanctions' (2024) 32 *Review of International Economics* 12.

Thouvenin J-M, 'Gel des fonds des banques centrales et immunité d'exécution' in Peters A and others (eds), *Immunities in the Age of Global Constitutionalism* (Brill Nijhoff 2015) 209.

Tzouvala N, 'Sanctions, Dollar Hegemony, and the Unraveling of Third World Sovereignty' (2024) *Yale Journal of International Law* <https://www.yjil.yale.edu/sanctions-dollar-hegemony-and-the-unraveling-of-third-world-sovereignty/> accessed 1 July 2024.

Webb P, 'Legal Options for Confiscation of Russian State Assets to Support the Reconstruction of Ukraine' (European Parliamentary Research Service 2024) <https://www.europarl.europa.eu/thinktank/en/document/EPRS_STU(2024)759602> accessed 1 July 2024.

Documents

Alleged Violations of State Immunities (Islamic Republic of Iran v Canada) (Application instituting proceedings) [2023].

Certain Iranian Assets (Iran v USA) (Application instituting proceedings) [2016].

ILC, 'Draft Articles on Responsibility of States for Internationally Wrongful Acts with Commentaries' (2001) UN Doc. A/56/10.

Office of Foreign Assets Control, 'Treasury Reaches Largest Ever Sanctions-Related Settlement with BNP Paribas SA for $963 Million' (US Department of the Treasury, 30 June 2014) <https://home.treasury.gov/news/press-releases/jl2447> accessed 1 July 2024.

20. Commodity sanctions

MARTIJN C. VLASKAMP

I Introduction

Many economic sanctions packages target the commodities trade with the sanctioned country. For instance, the Western response to Russia's 2022 full-scale invasion of Ukraine involved numerous measures aimed at its oil, gas, and coal sectors. Commodity sanctions are defined as restrictive measures that limit trade in specific resources, primarily natural resources such as oil, gas, minerals, and agricultural products. They are often part of broader sanctions packages to coerce changes in behaviour, prevent engagement in prohibited activities, or signal violations of international norms. Commodity sanctions can be applied to states, individuals, or non-state actors (Biersteker et al. [2018] 407).

II Background

Sanctioning commodity trade as part of economic statecraft dates back to ancient times. A notable early example is Athens' ban in 432 BC on trade with Megara for aligning with Sparta (Carisch et al. [2017] 112). Modern export sanctions on commodities often hope to limit a rival's ability to wage war, particularly through oil restrictions (Carisch et al. [2017] 111). Key instances include the 1941 US oil embargo on Japan following its invasion of Indochina and the North Atlantic Treaty Organization's (NATO) 1999 oil embargo against Yugoslavia during the Kosovo War. Beyond warfare, export sanctions can serve political purposes if the targeted country relies on the commodity for its economy. The 1973 Arab oil embargo targeted nations supporting Israel during the Yom Kippur War. A more recent example is China's 2023 export restrictions on critical semiconductor metals in response to US, Dutch, and Japanese policies limiting the export of advanced chip-making equipment.

While export sanctions remain relevant, import sanctions have become more common today. These sanctions typically seek to harm a target economically by cutting off its revenues from commodities. Western actors, including the US and the European Union (EU), and multilateral institutions like the United Nations, are the primary enforcers (Global Sanctions Data Base [2023]). However, non-Western countries are increasingly using this policy tool as well. For instance, China restricted Australian coal, wine, and barley imports in 2020 in retaliation for Australia's call for a COVID-19 origins investigation. A specific case of commodity sanctions is the Kimberley Process, a trade regime for rough diamonds established in response to the issue of so-called conflict diamonds. When countries are excluded from the Kimberley Process Certification Scheme, their rough diamonds can no longer be traded globally, as all major trade actors are part of the regime.

III Types of commodity sanctions

Commodity sanctions can take various, sometimes overlapping forms. The most direct one is a complete ban on trading specific commodities with a targeted actor, such as the US bans on the import of Russian crude oil, liquefied natural gas, coal, and diamonds. These sanctions aim to harm a country's economy and undermine its regime by targeting critical exports. Typically, sanctions apply to commodities in their primary state, but increasingly, they extend to products incorporating those materials. For example, the EU has banned all items using Russian iron ores from its single market.

Another form of commodity sanctions targets individuals or entities involved in commodity production or trade rather than the commodities themselves. These sanctions may target, for example, state-owned extractive companies, ministers, or businesspeople and can overlap with financial sanctions, such as asset freezes or exclusions from the finance and trade systems. Other sanctions focus on restricting the export of technology and equipment necessary to produce the targeted commodity. Secondary sanctions may also target third-party actors that are suspected of evading sanctions, such as ship owners smuggling sanctioned commodities. Such sanctions leave third-state actors with the choice to support, remain neutral, or actively oppose them, while companies must choose between complying or ignoring them (Vlaskamp [2023]).

Another type of commodity sanction focuses on extraction-related behaviour, allowing exports only if commodities meet specific social or environmental standards. For example, the 2010 US Dodd–Frank Act and the 2017 EU Conflict Minerals Regulation aim at minerals that fund violent conflicts, primarily in the eastern Democratic Republic of the Congo. These sanctions can be accompanied by targeted measures against individuals and entities violating these standards, such as warlords or illegal trading houses.

IV Impact and effectiveness

Commodity sanctions can have significant short-term economic impacts on targeted economies. The decreasing oil revenues of Russia, Venezuela, and Iran following sanctions and, in the case of Russia, the G7 crude oil price cap demonstrate their disruptive power (Babina et al. [2023]; Nakhli et al. [2021]; Rodríguez [2022]). Iran's decision to negotiate the 2015 nuclear deal was at least partially influenced by severe economic strain from international sanctions (Maloney [2015]). The overall effectiveness of commodity sanctions, however, depends on several factors, including the degree of international cooperation, the level of economic interdependence between sender and target, the extent to which the commodity can be replaced on international markets, and the target regime's political structure (Early [2015]; Kavakli et al. [2020]; Peksen [2019]).

Assessing the specific effectiveness of individual commodity sanctions is challenging, as they are often part of broader sanction regimes (Peksen [2019]). Moreover, while, for example the Iran sanctions are widely seen as successful sanctions, there are also many instances where commodity sanctions have not achieved their intended objectives. Measures that target Russian and Venezuelan oil exports, as of fall 2025, have not led to a significant weakening of either regime or major behavioural shifts. Both countries have found ways to mitigate the effects, such as seeking alternative trading partners or leveraging domestic resources, highlighting the limitations of commodity sanctions when dealing with resilient or resource-rich states (Babina et al. [2023]).

V Controversies and criticisms

Commodity sanctions, like other economic sanctions, are often criticized for disproportionately harming the civilian population in targeted states, leading to increased poverty and inequality, worsening health conditions, excess deaths, and a deterioration in human rights and democracy (Rodríguez [2024]). For example, sanctions targeting Iraq's oil revenues after the 1990 invasion of Kuwait were blamed for increasing child mortality and contributing to a severe humanitarian crisis (Alnasrawi [2001]). Similarly, sanctions aimed at reducing conflict minerals from the eastern Democratic Republic of the Congo have been criticized for exacerbating violence and child mortality, as collapsing the mining economy deprived local communities of livelihoods (Parker et al. [2016]; Stoop et al. [2018]).

Another major criticism is that commodity sanctions often have limited effectiveness in a globalized economy. Countries under sanctions frequently find ways to circumvent restrictions through "sanctions busting," such as seeking alternative trading partners or covert methods of selling commodities (Early [2015]). For instance, despite Western oil sanctions, Russia has continued to sell oil to countries like China, India, and Turkey at discounted rates, reducing the impact on its economy (Demertzis [2024]). The buyers, at the same time, decreased their energy bills and gained economic competitiveness with respect to the sanctioning parties due to cheap energy (Donovan and Nikoladze [2024]). Confronted with higher energy prices in Europe, critics of the sanctions on Russia, such as some far-right political parties, have therefore argued that these measures are harming the economies of the sanctioning countries more than the economy of the targeted country (Deutsche Welle [2022]).

VI Conclusion

Commodity sanctions are a significant tool of economic statecraft with a wide range of applications and impacts. They can disrupt target economies by limiting access to critical resources or markets for their commodities. However, their effectiveness in achieving political change remains uncertain, especially when targets adapt to the restrictions or find alternative trading partners. Humanitarian concerns and potential self-harm to sanctioning countries further complicate their use. Looking ahead, the future of commodity sanctions will likely involve balancing traditional geostrategic goals with addressing an economically more multipolar world.

MARTIJN C. VLASKAMP

Bibliography

Literature

Alnasrawi A, 'Iraq: Economic Sanctions and Consequences, 1990–2000' (2001) 22(2) *Third World Quarterly* 205.

Babina T, Hilgenstock B, Itskhoki O, Mironov M and Ribakova E, 'Assessing the Impact of International Sanctions on Russian Oil Exports' (papers.ssrn.com 2023).

Biersteker TJ, Eckert SE, Tourinho M and Hudáková Z, 'UN Targeted Sanctions Datasets (1991–2013)' (2018) 55(3) *Journal of Peace Research* 404.

Carisch E, Martin LR and Meister SM, *The Evolution of UN Sanctions: From a Tool of Warfare to a Tool of Peace, Security and Human Rights* (Springer International Publishing 2017).

Demertzis M, 'The Limits of the Effectiveness of EU Sanctions on Russia' (*Bruegel*, 14 November 2023) <https://www.bruegel.org/comment/limits-effectiveness-eu-sanctions-russia> accessed 20 September 2024.

Deutsche W, 'Germany: Far-Right Demo Slams Russia Sanctions, Coalition' (*DW*, 8 November 2022) <https://www.dw.com/en/germany-far-right-demo-protests-russia-sanctions-energy-policy/a-63380291> accessed 20 September 2024.

Donovan K and Nikoladze M, 'The Axis of Evasion: Behind China's Oil Trade with Iran and Russia' (*Atlantic Council*, 28 March 2024) <https://www.atlanticcouncil.org/blogs/new-atlanticist/the-axis-of-evasion-behind-chinas-oil-trade-with-iran-and-russia/> accessed 20 September 2024.

Early BR, *Busted Sanctions: Explaining Why Economic Sanctions Fail* (Stanford University Press 2015).

Global Sanctions Data Base, 'Global Sanctions Data Base Website' (Global Sanctions Data Base, 2023) <https://www.globalsanctionsdatabase.com/> accessed 9 July 2023.

Kavakli KC, Chatagnier JT and Hatipoğlu E, 'The Power to Hurt and the Effectiveness of International Sanctions' (2020) 82(3) *The Journal of Politics* 879.

Maloney S, 'Sanctions and the Iranian Nuclear Deal: Silver Bullet or Blunt Object?' (2015) 82(4) *Social Research: An International Quarterly* 887.

Nakhli SR, Rafat M, Dastjerdi RB and Rafei M, 'Oil Sanctions and Their Transmission Channels in the Iranian Economy: A DSGE Model' (2021) 70 *Resources Policy*.

Parker DP, Foltz JD and Elsea D, 'Unintended Consequences of Sanctions for Human Rights: Conflict Minerals and Infant Mortality' (2016) 59(4) *The Journal of Law and Economics* 731.

Peksen D, 'When Do Imposed Economic Sanctions Work? A Critical Review of the Sanctions Effectiveness Literature' (2019) 30(6) *Defence and Peace Economics* 635.

Rodríguez F, 'Sanctions and Oil Production: Evidence from Venezuela's Orinoco Basin' (2022) 31 *Latin American Economic Review* 31.

Rodríguez F, 'The Human Consequences of Economic Sanctions' (2024) 51(4) *Journal of Economic Studies* 942.

Stoop N, Verpoorten M and Windt PVD, 'More Legislation, More Violence? The Impact of Dodd–Frank in the DRC' (2018) 13(8) *PLOS ONE*.

Vlaskamp MC, 'How Do Third Parties React to Commodity Sanctions?' in Kirkham K (ed.), *The Routledge Handbook of the Political Economy of Sanctions* (Routledge 2023).

MARTIJN C. VLASKAMP

21. Countermeasures

Martin Dawidowicz

I The role and function of countermeasures in international law

Countermeasures are a unilateral measure of self-help that have long been recognized as a feature of a decentralized international legal order in which the judicial settlement of disputes is still not guaranteed and injured states may take otherwise unlawful action of a peaceful character in order to enforce their rights against the responsible state (Alland [2010] 1127–36; Dawidowicz [2017] 3–4; Air Services Agreement [1978] para. 81).

As a unilateral self-help measure that entitles the state to act as judge and sheriff in its own cause, countermeasures are, however, ripe with the potential for abuse and this potential is exacerbated by the factual inequalities between states (ILC Commentary [2001] 128 para. 2). Thucydides's cautionary tale for the ages in the Melian Dialogue of 416 BC – "the strong do what they can and the weak suffer what they must" – remains apt today and, in large part, explains the still controversial nature of countermeasures in the international legal order. Indeed, the history of countermeasures has been marked by empire, power politics and gunboat diplomacy; the light that history shines on the topic is a lantern on the stern that continues to colour the whole approach to it (Dawidowicz [2017] 4–7; see also e.g. chapters on Cuba; Secondary sanctions and extraterritorial effects; Confiscation).

Still, countermeasures have generally been understood as a useful and necessary tool to enforce international law, albeit within strictly defined parameters (see chapter on Measuring sanctions effectiveness; see also chapter on Legality and legitimacy). In short, countermeasures are a reality of international relations but, as they risk causing conflict escalation, should be "a wager on the wisdom, not the weakness of the other Party … [and] should be used with a spirit of great moderation" (Air Services Agreement [1978] para. 91). Put differently, the regulation of countermeasures in international relations raises a serious normative dilemma. There is an inherent tension between the need for a more effective international legal order in spite of decentralization and the risks of abuse relating to the allocation of enforcement authority to individual states. As a result, countermeasures are subject to strict conditions governing their use (Dawidowicz [2017] 285–382; Paddeu [2024] paras 10–40; see also chapters on Termination of sanctions; Humanitarian carveouts; Sanctions and the use of force). Before turning to the most important developments in the modern law of countermeasures, the term must first be distinguished from other cognate concepts so that its role and function in the international legal order may be properly understood.

II Countermeasures and other types of unilateral measures

The modern notion of "countermeasures" is historically linked to the term "reprisals", which has an ancient pedigree in international law. In the Naulilaa Arbitration, which concerned the use of armed reprisals in the interwar period, the arbitral tribunal explained:

> Reprisals are an act of taking the law into its own hands (*Selbsthilfehandlung*) by the injured State … in response to an act contrary to the law of nations by the offending State. Their effect is to suspend momentarily, in the relations between the two States, the observation of a particular rule of the law of nations … They would be illegal if an earlier act, contrary to the law of nations, had not furnished the motive. (Naulilaa Incident Arbitration [1928] 1026)

The term "reprisals" was thus historically used to refer to otherwise unlawful action – whether forcible or non-forcible – taken by way of self-help in response to prior breaches of international law (see chapter on Sanctions and the use of force). In the modern United Nations (UN) Charter era, which prohibited armed reprisals, the term "reprisals" came to be replaced by the term "countermeasures", which covers otherwise unlawful unilateral measures of a peaceful or non-forcible character (ILC Commentary [2001] 128 para. 3; Air Services Agreement [1978] para. 81).

In a general sense, a countermeasure is clearly a sanction if by that term is meant a coercive reaction to illegality. As a unilateral self-help measure, a countermeasure may accordingly be described as a unilateral sanction (Alland [2010] 1134–5; Pellet and Miron [2011] paras 4–11; Dawidowicz [2017] 21–7; also ILC Commentary [2001] at Art. 1 para. 3). However, as the International Law

Commission (ILC) has explained, the term sanction has acquired a specific meaning in contemporary international law: it is reserved for various institutional reactions (including the use of force) taken in the framework of international organizations, notably under Chapter VII of the UN Charter (see ILC Commentary [2001] at Art. 22 para. 3; Introductory Commentary to Chapter II of Part Three, para. 3; Art. 54 para. 2). Sanctions are thus distinct from countermeasures in several respects. First, sanctions constitute a centralized reaction taken by states acting in a collective or institutional capacity through an international organization, whereas countermeasures constitute a decentralized or unilateral reaction taken by one state or a group of states, with each acting in an individual capacity. Second, as opposed to countermeasures, sanctions in the form of measures taken under Chapter VII of the UN Charter need not necessarily respond to a prior wrongful act. Third, in principle, their functions are different: measures under Chapter VII of the UN Charter have the broad aim to maintain or restore international peace and security, whereas countermeasures are a tool of law enforcement *stricto sensu*. In sum, sanctions and countermeasures are cognate concepts but remain analytically distinct and should not be conflated.

Although countermeasures form part of the broader category of unilateral self-help measures under international law, it is nonetheless a term of art that denotes a rather narrow legal category (Dawidowicz [2017] 15–31; Paddeu [2024] para. 3). Countermeasures should notably be distinguished from acts of retorsion, which are unfriendly though inherently lawful measures. Where relevant international obligations exist, countermeasures may, however, include a very wide range of otherwise unlawful conduct (see e.g. chapters on Arms embargo; Sanctions on transport (aviation, maritime, ground); Financial sanctions; Development aid cut-offs; Sanctions on transport; Commodity sanctions; Diplomatic sanctions; Membership sanctions; Banking system (SWIFT and Central Bank); andEnergy embargo). The distinction between countermeasures and retorsion is fundamental in legal terms but not always an easy one to draw in practice.

Traditionally, international law was based on a bilateral enforcement model that only permitted the use of countermeasures in the relations between the responsible state and the directly injured state *inter se*. This meant that only the directly injured state could resort to countermeasures against the responsible state (ILC Commentary [2001] Art. 1 paras 3–4). More recently, however, the international law of countermeasures appears to have widened, enabling all states to take countermeasures – that is to say, third-party countermeasures – in response to the most serious assaults on multilateral public order. The apparent recognition of third-party countermeasures marks the most important development in the modern law of countermeasures.

III Third-party countermeasures and the enforcement of fundamental norms

The post–UN Charter era witnessed the emergence of several fundamental norms that transformed international law, such as the prohibition on the use of force and the right to the self-determination of peoples. In particular, the 1960s and 1970s were a period marked by decolonization and a Cold War stalemate in the UN Security Council. These developments exposed the limitations of the traditional bilateral model of enforcement under international law – as witnessed by the (in) famous judgment of the International Court of Justice (ICJ) in the second phase of *South West Africa* (South West Africa [1966] 6). The ICJ's judgment in that case caused great consternation in the UN General Assembly, especially among newly independent states. A few years later, the ICJ seemingly provided a judicial mea culpa in the *Barcelona Traction* case by adopting the notion of obligations *erga omnes*, that is to say, obligations of a state towards the international community as a whole, the protection of which is in the legal interest of all states (Barcelona Traction [1970] para. 33). The ICJ's affirmation of obligations *erga omnes* in that case marked a "significant step" (ILC Commentary [2001] Art. 1 para. 4) away from the bilateral model of enforcement towards a multilateral (or communitarian) dimension of law enforcement in international law. Still, the ICJ was silent on the specific means by which obligations *erga omnes* could be enforced under international law.

During the ILC's work on state responsibility, the question of whether, as a matter of progressive development of international law, all states were allowed to take third-party countermeasures in response to breaches of fundamental norms was very controversial. The ILC ultimately reserved its position on the issue in 2001 (Articles on Responsibility of States for Internationally Wrongful Acts [2001] Art. 54) and the question of the legality of third-party countermeasures "remains uncertain" today (Crawford [2013] 703; Paddeu [2024] paras 45–6). Still, there is an abundance of state practice in support of the conclusion that third-party countermeasures are permissible under present-day international law (Tams [2005] 198–251; Katselli-Proukaki [2010] 90–209; Dawidowicz [2017] 111–238; Institut de Droit International [2005] Art. 5(c)). Already in the 1960s, states had adopted third-party countermeasures (see e.g. chapter on South Africa) and this practice has continued to grow over the last decades in response to massive human rights violations and other major international crises (see e.g. chapters on Iraq; Yugoslavia; Myanmar; Belarus; Libya; Syria; Russia; Venezuela; see also e.g. chapters on Sanctions for conflict resolution; Sanctions for human rights and democracy).

Most recently, the precise limitations governing the use of third-party countermeasures have been the subject of considerable debate in relation to the possible decision by EU member states, the United States and others to confiscate sovereign Russian financial assets and transfer them to Ukraine as compensation for the damage caused by Russia's war of aggression (see chapter on Russia). The confiscation (as opposed to the mere freezing) of sovereign Russian assets has raised a number of highly controversial issues related to the precise conditions governing the use of third-party countermeasures (see e.g. chapters on Confiscation; Termination of sanctions; see also chapter on Investment protection). The debate on third-party countermeasures continues unabated, not least in the cyberspace context (Dias [2024]). A recent issue that has received some attention in this regard concerns the possibility of collaboration in the taking of countermeasures (Jackson and Paddeu [2024] 231).

IV Conclusion

Countermeasures are a reality of international relations and yet they still pose a serious normative dilemma. On the one hand, as a unilateral self-help measure, countermeasures are ripe with the potential for abuse; and Thucydides reminds us that this risk is exacerbated by the factual inequalities between states. On the other hand, countermeasures are a useful and necessary tool to more effectively enforce international law. As international law has gradually moved away from the bilateral enforcement model, the apparent recognition of third-party countermeasures in defence of multilateral public order marks the most important development in the modern law of countermeasures. That said, as the arbitral tribunal in the *Air Services Agreement* case reminds us, countermeasures should always be a "wager on the wisdom" of the state(s) taking such unilateral action and "used with a spirit of great moderation" (Air Services Agreement [1978] para. 91).

Bibliography

Literature

Alland D, 'The Definition of Countermeasures' in Crawford J, Pellet A and Olleson S (eds), *The Law of International Responsibility* (Oxford University Press 2010) 1127.

Crawford J, *State Responsibility: The General Part* (Cambridge University Press 2013).

Dawidowicz M, *Third-Party Countermeasures in International Law* (Cambridge University Press 2017).

Dias T, 'Countermeasures in International Law and Their Role in Cyberspace' (Chatham House, Research Paper 2024) <https://www.chathamhouse.org/sites/default/files/2024-05/2024-05-23-countermeasures-international-law-cyberspace-dias.pdf> accessed 10 September 2024.

Jackson M and Paddeu F, 'The Countermeasures of Others: When can State Collaborate in the Taking of Countermeasures?' (2024) 118 *American Journal of International Law* 231.

Katselli-Proukaki E, *The Problem of Enforcement in International Law: Countermeasures, the Non-Injured State and the Idea of International Community* (Routledge 2010).

Paddeu F, 'Countermeasures' in *Max Planck Encyclopedia of International Law* (Oxford University Press 2024).

Pellet A and Miron A, 'Sanctions' in *Max Planck Encyclopedia of International Law* (Oxford University Press 2011).

Tams C, *Enforcing Obligations Erga Omnes in International Law* (Cambridge University Press 2005).

Documents

Air Services Agreement of 27 March 1946 (United States v France) [1978] 18 *Rep Intl Arbitral Awards* 417.

Barcelona Traction, Light and Power Company, Limited (Spain v Belgium) (Second Phase) [1970] *ICJ Rep* 3.

Institut de Droit International, 'Krakow Resolution' (2005) ('Obligations Erga Omnes in International Law') <https://www.idi-iil.org/app/uploads/2017/06/2005_kra_01_en.pdf>.

ILC, 'Draft Articles on Responsibility of States for Internationally Wrongful Acts with Commentaries' in *Yearbook of the International Law Commission* (2001) Vol II (Part Two) UN Doc. A/56/10.

Naulilaa Incident Arbitration (Portugal v Germany) [1928] 2 *RIAA* 1011.

South West Africa (Ethiopia v South Africa; Liberia v South Africa) (Second Phase) [1966] *ICJ Rep* 6.

Martin Dawidowicz

22. Development aid cut-offs

Franziska F.N. Schreiber

I Definition

Development aid cut-offs (also referred to as aid suspensions or aid sanctions) involve the temporal suspension or perpetual withdrawal, in part or in full, of official development assistance (ODA) by a donor towards an aid recipient (Crawford [2001]). ODA is the main source of funding for development aid (or development assistance), which constitutes concessional government aid directed at the promotion of economic development and welfare in receiving low- and middle-income countries. ODA is primarily granted via bilateral grants from a donor to a recipient country or can be directed through international organizations and non-governmental organizations. Donors can cut off the provision of development aid, for instance, in response to a particular incident or development in the recipient country, such as human rights violations, democratic regression, or unconstitutional transfers of power. Aid sanctions represent a means for donors to enforce respect for international norms such as human rights, democracy, and the rule of law (Portela and Mora-Sanguinetti [2023]), to restore compliance with the obligations agreed upon in international agreements, and to signal their norm commitment.

II Senders

The senders of both aid and economic sanctions often overlap as both are located in the Global North. Besides the World Bank Group, Western states and members of the Organisation for Economic Cooperation and Development's (OECD) Development Assistance Committee (DAC), such as the United Kingdom and Sweden, constitute "traditional" donors. The European Union (EU) and the United States represent the largest aid donors and generally subject their aid provision to certain conditions and terms to be met by the aid recipient. The concept of conditionality was first introduced by the International Monetary Fund (IMF) in 1952 and became popular during the EU enlargement waves (Mushi [2013]). The conditionality of aid represents a conventional property of aid (Forster [2013]), but since the 1990s it has increasingly developed towards political conditionality by linking aid to political reforms and the promotion of democracy and human rights (Stokke [2013]). In recent years, the global aid regime has experienced a pluralization of donors beyond the "traditional" donors. "Non-traditional", emerging donors such as Russia and China are not necessarily new actors in development assistance but have grown in importance due to shifting wealth proportions among countries over the years (Koch [2015]). The BRICS countries' disbursement schemes, for instance, differ from those of the "traditional" donors in that they tend to be flexible, non-conditional, and built on partnerships on equal footing with the recipients. This not only results in "aid competition" among donors but may also undermine the leverage of aid conditionality. Nevertheless, these "non-traditional" donors have also cut off their aid in some cases (Cheeseman et al. [2024]).

III Targets

The addressees of both economic sanctions and aid suspensions are often located in the Global South. Development aid cut-offs require a respective financial relationship between a donor and a recipient. Aid has been found to be selectively and inconsistently suspended (e.g. Nielsen [2013]), as sanctions frameworks tend to leave leeway for political maneuvering. A broad literature has confirmed the influence of geopolitics and donor interests on aid suspensions (e.g. Stokke [2013]; Dunning [2004]; Del Biondo [2015]; Bermeo [2016]). However, self-interest fails to explain all inconsistencies and variations in the sanctioning behavior (Del Biondo [2012]; Swedlund [2017]). Under the Cotonou Agreement (2000–23) between the EU and the African, Caribbean and Pacific (ACP) states (Portela [2016]), Article 96 allowed for the interruption of development aid and trade preferences ("appropriate measures") as a measure of last resort if preceding political dialogues and consultations failed to result in an agreement between the parties. Since 2023, the subsequent Samoa Agreement includes an equivalent procedure for dispute settlement and the fulfilment of obligations in Article 101. Such sanctions can only be instigated against the ACP states, although these may also be subjected to other kinds of sanctions (Portela [2010]). In the past years, Article 96 has been applied in response to military coups, flawed elections, or human rights violations in different countries, such as Fiji (2000, 2007), Zimbabwe (2002), Guinea (2004, 2009), and Burundi (2015).

IV Conceptual distinction

Development aid cut-offs match the definitional requirements to constitute a subtype of sanctions and frequently represent one component of larger sanction packages (Portela and Mora-Sanguinetti [2023]). Aid sanctions restrict the flow of foreign aid, whereas economic sanctions comprise broader measures to restrict the exchange of money, goods, and services. Economic sanctions are generally costly for both sanction sender and target; aid cut-offs are mostly costly for the recipients, given the relationship of dependency between aid donor and recipient, whereas the cut-offs are economically beneficial for the senders. While aid sanctions are capable of exerting pressure on the recipient governments, the sanctioned country's population is likely not to be the primary addressee of aid suspensions, which attenuates the common criticism of economic sanctions to cause suffering to the population (Jeong [2020]). Aid sanctions are further to be distinguished from budget support cuts, with budget support constituting medium-term and fungible aid directly given to the recipient government's budget (Swedlund and Lierl [2020]).

V Effectiveness

Aid cut-offs are not free of criticism and side effects. Aid conditionality has been criticized for perpetuating asymmetric relations, for encroaching on the principle of non-intervention, and for its limited effectiveness. Current research reports on different factors that impinge on the effectiveness of aid sanctions, among them the kind of international engagements, the regime type in the recipient country, the degree of aid dependency of the recipient state, the kind of aid that is being cut off, as well as the degree of donor coordination and competition in the field (Cheeseman et al. [2024]). Aid sanctions may exacerbate regional instability and repression in the target state, enable the sanctioned government to garner support if resentment against such foreign interference is stirred up, or jeopardize the relationship between donor and recipient at large. The effectiveness of aid sanctions may be further impaired by the fact that, following the developmental logic, suspending development aid is an unfavorable act. The administration of aid suspensions may be tedious in "red tape" organizations or hampered if they are delegated to intermediaries such as aid agencies with institutional preferences that potentially diverge from those of the aid donors (Swedlund [2017]). Although research assessing the effectiveness of aid suspensions states conflicting evidence, recent contributions point towards their relative effectiveness (Crawford [1997]; Portela and Mora-Sanguinetti [2023]; Mertens [2024]).

Bibliography

Literature

Bermeo SB, 'Aid is Not Oil: Donor Utility, Heterogeneous Aid, and the Aid-Democratization Relationship' (2016) 70(1) *International Organization* 1.

Cheeseman N, Swedlund HJ and O'Brien-Udry C, 'Foreign Aid Withdrawals and Suspensions: Why, When and Are They Effective?' (2024) 178 *World Development.*

Crawford G, 'Foreign Aid and Political Conditionality: Issues of Effectiveness and Consistency' (1997) 4(3) *Democratization* 69.

Crawford G, *Foreign Aid and Political Reform. A Comparative Analysis of Democracy Assistance and Political Conditionality* (Palgrave 2001).

Del Biondo K, 'Norms, Self-Interest and Effectiveness: Explaining Double Standards in EU Reactions to Violations of Democratic Principles in Sub-Saharan Africa' (2012) 25(2) *Afrika Fokus* 109.

Del Biondo K, 'Donor Interests or Developmental Performance? Explaining Sanctions in EU Democracy Promotion in Sub-Saharan Africa' (2015) 75 *World Development.*

Dunning T, 'Conditioning the Effects of Aid: Cold War Politics, Donor Credibility, and Democracy in Africa' (2004) 58(2) *International Organization* 409.

Forster J, 'Conditionality in Swiss Development Assistance' in Stokke O (ed.), *Aid and Political Conditionality* (Taylor & Francis 2013) 201.

Jeong JM, 'Economic Sanctions and Income Equality: Impacts of Trade Restrictions and Foreign Aid Suspension on Target Countries' (2020) 37(6) *Conflict Management and Peace Science* 674.

FRANZISKA F.N. SCHREIBER

Koch S, 'A Typology of Political Conditionality beyond Aid: Conceptual Horizons Based on Lessons from the European Union' (2015) 75 *World Development*.

Mertens C, 'Carrots as Sticks: How Effective Are Foreign Aid Suspensions and Economic Sanctions?' (2024) 68(2) *International Studies Quarterly*.

Mushi SS, 'Determinants and Limitations of Aid Conditionality: Some Examples from Nordic-Tanzanian Co-operation' in Stokke O (ed.), *Aid and Political Conditionality* (Taylor & Francis 2013).

Nielsen RA, 'Rewarding Human Rights? Selective Aid Sanctions against Repressive States' (2013) 57(4) *International Studies Quarterly* 791.

Portela C, *European Union Sanctions and Foreign Policy. When and Why do they Work?* (Routledge 2010).

Portela C, 'Are European Union Sanctions "Targeted"?' (2016) 29(3) *Cambridge Review of International Affairs* 912.

Portela C and Mora-Sanguinetti JS, 'Sanctions Effectiveness, Development and Regime Type. Are Aid Suspensions and Economic Sanctions Alike?' (2023) 172 *World Development*.

Stokke O, 'Aid and Political Conditionality: Core Issues and State of the Art' in Stokke O (ed.), *Aid and Political Conditionality* (Taylor & Francis 2013).

Stokke O, 'Aid and Political Conditionality: The Case of Norway' in Stokke O (ed.), *Aid and Political Conditionality* (Taylor & Francis 2013).

Swedlund HJ, 'Can Foreign Aid Donors Credibly Threaten to Suspend Aid? Evidence from a Cross-National Survey of Donor Officials' (2017) 24(3) *Review of International Political Economy* 454.

Swedlund HJ and Lierl M, 'The Rise and Fall of Budget Support: Ownership, Bargaining and Donor Commitment Problems in Foreign Aid' (2020) 38 *Development Policy Review* 50.

23. Diplomatic sanctions

Lisa Neal

I Introduction

All types of sanctions are "largely (but not completely) a function of the relations with the target [the receiver of sanction policies]" (Drury [2001] 500). Therefore, all types of sanctions can be part of a diplomatic strategy, but they are not a strategy per se.

This also applies to diplomatic sanctions. Three key elements distinguish diplomatic sanctions from other types of sanctions:

1. Diplomatic sanctions have diplomatic objectives. They focus primarily on political disengagement and are specifically used as means of "isolating and delegitimizing regimes" (Maller [2010] 61).
2. Diplomatic sanctions have a narrow scope of action because they focus on specific diplomatic measurements. Biersteker et al. ([2016] 25) define diplomatic sanctions as "restrictions on the diplomatic activity of a governing body".
3. Diplomatic sanctions exceed routine negotiations otherwise used in diplomatic disputes. They include limiting diplomatic accreditation and representation. This can occur in both directions; a host country may expel an ambassador, or another country may withdraw them. Diplomatic sanctions can also include individual travel bans, suspension from international events and organisations, social exclusion, and withholding recognition of a regime or even a state (Biersteker et al. [2016] 25; Brooks [2002] 11 and 30).

II The benefits of diplomatic sanctions

Comparing their discriminatory potential with other measures identifies diplomatic sanctions as targeted sanctions. They may not be as targeted as individual sanctions because they often include a government. However, they are less comprehensive than transportation sanctions and economic sanctions (Biersteker et al. [2016] 27).

Diplomatic sanctions are imposed by international organisations, such as the United Nations (UN). The European Union (EU) mainly focuses on economic sanctions while simultaneously arranging for political dialogue (Portela [2010] 165). Unilateral diplomatic sanctions are imposed by different states, with the United States a frequent inaugurator (Drury [2001]).

The use of diplomatic sanctions is a principal means of enforcing compliance with international law. They are designed to influence the policies and actions of a target. Diplomatic sanctions are an evolving practice, primarily used to condemn human rights violations and "to target states for issues related to terrorism, proliferation, and an accompanying desire for regime change in some cases" (Maller [2010] 63). A review of the practice by prominent senders reveals that the most common forms of diplomatic sanctions employed are individual listings, which lead to travel bans and asset freezes. A pertinent example is the imposition of restrictions by the EU and the United States on Burmese diplomats.

Diplomatic sanctions are considered low-cost means of foreign policy, primarily from the sender's perspective. Economically, diplomatic sanctions are cheaper than military expenditures. Politically, diplomatic sanctions attract less attention from the domestic audience than military action. For example, restricting a high-level Iranian representative from entering Canada or withdrawing the German ambassador from Russia "may capture some fleeting attention in the media and with the public, but it will not produce the same level of attentiveness [or opposition] in the domestic arena as dropping bombs on another country" (Drury [2001] 489).

The low-cost argument expands to the target's perspective as well. Diplomatic sanctions seem to cause less harm to the civilian population. "[D]iplomatic sanctions that specifically aim at the repressive political leaders [...] mitigate the negative impact of sanctions on the disadvantaged segments of the target society" (Drury and Peksen [2014] 484). This may point towards future sanction designs that avoid, for example, gender-specific consequences.

III The potential costs of diplomatic sanctions

The assessments in favour of diplomatic sanctions as a low-cost tool or modest policy change are, however, challenged by research. "Modest changes are not trivial changes" (Hufbauer et al. [2009] 66) and there are potential limitations to diplomatic sanctions.

Diplomatic sanctions that reduce or terminate diplomatic activities may lead to a loss of information and intelligence. Having an operating embassy provides valuable insights. The on-the-ground presence allows close monitoring of events, facilitates awareness of minor details, and grants access to first-hand "information about the attitudes and actions of foreign governments and societies" (Maller [2010] 64). Intelligence collected through alternative sources, such as UN staff and journalists, is harder to fact-check and significantly endangers those professionals.

Direct relationships and ongoing communication offer the potential to de-escalate emerging tensions. If there is little or no communication between two conflicting parties due to diplomatic sanctions, miscommunication or misperceptions become more likely (Maller [2010] 66). For example, in 1979, the increasing tensions between the United States and Iran were visibly manifested when the US embassy in Iran was closed, and diplomatic channels were blocked. Today, there are still no direct diplomatic ties between the United States and Iran (June 2024). This has led to several incidents that could have escalated into full-scale conflicts. With ongoing US military manoeuvres in the Persian Gulf, there is a significant potential for reactions without formal channels to verify information. Communication through third parties is not a sufficient alternative, as there is less trust in indirectly conveyed messages (Maller [2010] 66).

Findings by Hufbauer et al. ([2009]) indicate that sanctions are most successful between friendly (democratic) states, as the relations prior to sanctions determine how much a potential sanction target could lose (Hufbauer et al. [2009] 67, 161, 163). Limiting direct diplomatic interactions between governments without friendly relations may "increase the likelihood of further disagreements between two states in the future" (Maller [2010] 68). The limited access to a foreign population reduces the ability of a state to promote its interests or strengthen a positive image.

Diplomatic sanctions not only cause a backlash but may also counter other coercive policy tools. According to Maller ([2010] 68), other policies, such as economic sanctions, may be crafted based on incomplete assessments due to limited access. The costs of diplomatic sanctions also depend on the target's reactions. For example, a travel ban on a single state representative could lead that person to sever ties with the sanctioning entity, depriving the population of much-needed supplies.

IV Conclusion

In summary, diplomatic sanctions are not a harmless measure. Contrary to common perceptions, they do impose costs. At the same time, they have targeting discriminatory potential that could be used to reduce unintended consequences.

Bibliography

Literature

Biersteker TJ, Tourinho M and Eckert SE, 'Thinking about United Nations Targeted Sanctions' in Biersteker TJ, Eckert SE and Tourinho M (eds), *Targeted Sanctions. The Impacts and Effectiveness of United Nations Action* (Cambridge University Press 2016) 11.

Brooks RA, 'Sanctions and Regime Type. What Works, and When?' (2011) 11(4) *Security Studies* 1.

Drury CA and Peksen D, 'Women and Economic Statecraft: The Negative Impact International Sanctions Visit on Women' (2014) 20(2) *European Journal of International Relations* 463.

Drury CA, 'Sanctions as Coercive Diplomacy: The U.S. President's Decision to Initiate Economic Sanctions' (2001) 54(3) *Political Research Quarterly* 485.

Hufbauer GC, Schott JJ, Elliot KA and Oegg B, *Economic Sanctions Reconsidered* (3rd edn, Peterson Institute for International Economics 2009).

Maller T, 'Diplomacy Derailed: The Consequences of Diplomatic Sanctions' (2010) 33(3) *The Washington Quarterly* 6.

Portela C, *European Union Sanctions and Foreign Policy. When and Why Do They Work?* (Routledge 2010).

24. Energy embargo

KSENIA KIRKHAM

I Definition

An energy embargo, or energy sanctions, in its simplest form is a complete or partial ban on the trade of energy resources, such as hydrocarbons (oil, natural gas, coal), by one party (predominantly a state or group of states) against a rival party that belongs to a jurisdiction of a rival state. It could be applied against energy exporters to undermine revenues from sales, as well as against energy importers to limit their access to vital energy resources.

Like other types of sanctions, an energy embargo is an economic weapon that is used for multiple objectives: (1) political: to enforce change in the political behaviour of a sanctioned state; (2) signalling: to signal to allies and enemies the disagreement with a political course of the sanctioned state (to isolate the target state); (3) deterrence: to weaken the economic and military capabilities of a sanctioned state, or to dissuade it from acting; (4) geo-economic (i.e. neo-protectionism): to promote national economic interests by securing leading positions in the global markets and undermining strategic competitors' economic capabilities (Kirkham [2024]).

II History

Notable historical examples of energy embargoes include the nineteenth-century Napoleonic Wars, when Britain imposed a naval blockade on France to weaken its military capabilities by restricting access to coal imports. In the early twentieth century, oil substituted coal as a strategic commodity. This dramatic shift was famously noted by Britain's Lord Curzon in 1918 when he announced that 'the Allied cause floated to victory on a wave of oil' (Yergin [2023]). Indeed, oil embargoes were crucial economic weapons that shaped the outcome of both the First and Second World Wars, with the most prominent cases being the British oil and coal blockade on the 'Central Powers' Germany and Austria-Hungary from 1914 to 1919, and the US oil embargo on Japan from 1941 to 1945. Importantly, the effectiveness of energy embargoes during the world wars in Europe was enhanced by strategic bombing campaigns targeting energy facilities and infrastructure. Later, the disruption of oil supplies to Europe was witnessed in other military conflicts, such as the 1956 Suez Crisis and the 1967 Six-Day War.

In 1973, the Organization of Arab Petroleum Exporting Countries (OAPEC) states, except for Iraq, imposed an oil embargo on states that supported Israel during the Yom Kippur War, marking a turning point in energy geopolitics by provoking an extensive oil crisis and ending the era of 'cheap' energy (Kirkham [2021]). The oil shock triggered a total revision of national energy security strategies by Western states and the creation of the International Energy Agency in 1974, to combine efforts to secure a continuous flow of hydrocarbons. After the Soviet Union's invasion of Afghanistan and the Iranian Revolution in 1979, the UK institutionalised legal mechanisms, such as the UK Rapid Deployment Force, or the UK Central Command embedded in the Carter Doctrine of 1980 to justify the application of military force in regions beyond original UK and the North Atlantic Treaty Organisation (NATO) reach in case of disruption of supplies (Dannreuther [2010]).

Energy embargoes were used as part of a broader framework of international sanctions. The most prominent example was the United Nations (UN) sanctions on the oil sector of Iraq in 1990, following Iraq's invasion of Kuwait. However, the devastating humanitarian consequences of comprehensive UN sanctions led to the revision of policies and initiated the 'smart sanctions movement' in the 1990s.

III Energy security and neo-protectionism

Since the oil crisis in the 1970s, energy embargoes have been conceptualised within the broader context of energy security – one of the most important parameters of contemporary national security strategies. The availability and sufficiency of supplies of energy resources at minimum costs (Yergin [2006]) is the simplest definition of energy security. It stresses the strategic importance of energy sources to the functioning of national economies.

Between 1980 and the 2000s, as energy warfare expanded beyond trade, sanctions acquired an extraterritorial character, especially when it came to targeting energy transport infrastructure, such as pipelines (e.g.

secondary sanctions against 'third parties' outside the jurisdiction of sender or target states). Sanctions on oil, and since the 1990s power generation revolution also on natural gas, have become a strategic tool in the arsenal of economic and military warfare, spurring a 'New Great Game' in Eurasia after the dissolution of the Soviet Union. Another turn in the weaponisation of energy resources was triggered by the shale gas revolution in 2006 and an expansion of liquefied natural gas (LNG) projects. The 'New Great Game' rotated 180°, 'from competition among consumers over upstream assets and transportation routes towards rivalry between producers over sales markets in Europe and China' (Kirkham [2021]).

In 2017, the United States, self-sufficient in its energy needs since the fracking boom, used the Polish-led 'Three Seas Initiative' to expand its infrastructure for exporting liquefied natural gas (LNG) to Europe, while the Countering America's Adversaries Through Sanctions Act (Section 232 of CAATSA) was designed to oust the main competitor in the lucrative European energy market by imposing sanctions against entities involved in the construction and financing of the Nord Stream 2 and Turk Stream gas pipelines from Russia to Europe. This was not the first case in history. In 1981, UK President Ronald Reagan enacted the Export Administration Act of 1979 (i.e. a ban on the use of American equipment and technology) to introduce sanctions against the ongoing construction of the Urengoy–Pomary–Uzhgorod 'Brotherhood' gas pipeline from the Soviet Union to Western Europe. In both cases, energy sanctions were seen as a violation of international law and the sovereignty of European partners (European Parliament [2020]).

IV War in Europe and paradoxical effects

In 2022, Russia's invasion of Ukraine was followed by a total energy embargo by the United States. The EU followed the US lead, introducing a partial embargo on Russian oil and gas, sacrificing their economic prosperity for NATO's solidarity. Expensive LNG, coupled with high infrastructure costs, reduced gross domestic product (GDP) growth and manufacturing activity (a more important indicator than GDP) in most states, with Germany as an extreme case, where industrial output dropped by 9 per cent over the period 2018–2023 (followed by France [–5 per cent] and Italy [–3 per cent]) (Deutsche Bank [2024]). For the EU, except Poland, which replaced Germany as a new energy and military hub in Europe, energy sanctions caused significant disruptions to production, higher energy prices, and higher inflation and unemployment across multiple sectors. Apart from sanctions against Russia, other prominent examples are the US oil embargoes against Venezuela, Syria, and Iran. However, devastating economic and humanitarian consequences with minimal disruptive effects on governing elites spurred debates over the effectiveness and legality of such measures (Ameli [2024]).

Another contentious point relates to the impact of energy embargoes on sustainable development. As natural gas plays a key role in the transition phase to Net Zero, the most vivid paradox of sanctions has been its detrimental effect on environmental sustainability policies. Clean energy technologies need far more minerals than the traditional hydrocarbon-based energy system. The securitisation of supply chains of energy sources and critical minerals to support sustainable development with the aid of energy embargoes contradicts this very objective (Kirkham [2024]).

V Conclusion

Although energy embargoes have been used actively throughout history as an effective economic weapon, the exponential growth of secondary sanctions as a contemporary geo-economic tool is becoming riskier for the sending states: energy embargoes not only affect the target states but also hit hard third parties caught in the sanctions crossfire and have a boomerang effect for the sending states.

The use of sanctions against some states in the Middle East and Latin America, where the export of energy resources is the major source of government revenues, can have a devastating effect on populations, with minimal chances of a desired regime change. Resource-rich states risk repeating the destiny of Iraq, whose abundant oil and gas reserves served as a geopolitical curse and a bringer of war rather than a blessing for the nation.

Overall, while ongoing economic militarisation drains critical resources away from green technologies, global capitalism has entered a vicious circle – the growth in military expenditures and energy embargoes to address security risks, and the growth in security risks due to excess militarisation and economic warfare in the energy sphere. Ultimately, more wars in new regions (i.e. Africa, the Pacific) risk having unprecedented environmental consequences.

Bibliography

Literature

Ameli V, 'Unilateral Sanctions as Sustainable Development Decelerators' in Kirkham K (ed.), *The Routledge Handbook of the Political Economy of Sanctions* (Routledge 2023).

Dannreuther R, 'Energy Security' in Burgess P (ed.), *The Routledge Handbook of New Security Studies* (Routledge 2010) 144.

Kirkham K, 'The Paradox of the New Great Game: Do Europe and China Need More Pipelines from Eurasia?' (2021) 24(1) *Journal of Balkan and Near Eastern Studies* 1.

Kirkham K, 'The Role of Sanctions in Global Politics: How Do Sanctions (Not) Work?' in Fasulo F and Gili A (eds), *The Rise of Fragmentation. A New Economic Security Era?* (Ledizioni 2024) 105.

Yergin D, 'Ensuring Energy Security' (2006) 85(2) *Foreign Affairs* 69.

Documents

Deutsche Bank, 'German Industrial Production: The Decline Is Not Over Yet' (2024) <https://www.dbresearch.com/PROD/RPS_EN-PROD/PROD0000000000531908/German_industrial_production%3A_The__decline_is_not_.PDF?undefined&realload=NpQSfiGroIQhL1ueUFRMcSklkiwUD7ByLblUGjzQoeDd3wMlkJ5kc4Yo//fxRqE/>.

European Parliament, 'Extraterritorial Sanctions on Trade and Investments and European Responses' (2020) <https://www.europarl.europa.eu/RegData/etudes/STUD/2020/653618/EXPO_STU(2020)653618_EN.pdf>.

Yergin D, 'The 1973 Oil Crisis: Three Crises in One – and the Lessons for Today' (Centre on Global Energy Policy 2023) <https://www.energypolicy.columbia.edu/publications/the-1973-oil-crisis-three-crises-in-one-and-the-lessons-for-today/>.

Ksenia Kirkham

25. Financial Action Task Force Recommendations

Anton Moiseienko

I Introduction: overview

The Financial Action Task Force (FATF) is an intergovernmental forum made up of member states and organisations. Despite not being binding in international law, FATF Recommendations form the de facto global standard in anti-money laundering (AML), counterterrorist financing (CTF) and counter-proliferation financing (CPF). Their implementation is underpinned by a mutual evaluation system that creates tangible incentives for states to comply with the FATF Recommendations.

There are several dimensions to the overlap between the FATF Recommendations and sanctions. First, the FATF Recommendations facilitate the implementation of the UN Security Council's (UNSC) terrorism-related and proliferation-related sanctions. Second, domestic AML controls set up in accordance with the FATF Recommendations can facilitate the implementation by states of unilateral/autonomous sanctions. Third, and finally, the FATF's 'blacklisting' and 'greylisting' processes can be seen as involving a form of international sanctions.

II History and content of the FATF Recommendations

The first edition of the FATF Recommendations was published in 1990 and stems from a meeting held in Paris in 1989 to coordinate an international approach to the finances of drug trafficking organisations (Pieth [2018]). Consistent with the focus of that first meeting, the first set of FATF Recommendations was limited to measures against the laundering of the proceeds of drug trafficking (FATF [1990]). During the 1990s, it was expanded to include the proceeds of most types of profit-generating crimes. In 2001, after the attacks of 9/11, nine Special Recommendations were added, focusing on terrorist financing. In 2012, the implementation of proliferation-related sanctions was also included within the FATF Recommendations (FATF [2023]).

The FATF currently consists of 40 members, including 38 countries, the European Commission and the Gulf Cooperation Council. Other countries take part in the FATF's global network via membership in FATF-style regional bodies, which participate in the mutual evaluation of their members (see below) and contribute to the development of the FATF Recommendations.

The FATF Recommendations prescribe a range of measures that countries and regulated private-sector organisations should take ('countries' is the FATF's preferred term: some countries that the FATF treats as distinct jurisdictions for its purposes are not independent states, e.g. Hong Kong). Countries should, among other things, criminalise money laundering and terrorist financing; enable confiscation of the proceeds and instrumentalities of crime; assess the risks of money laundering, terrorist financing and proliferation financing and ensure a coordinated response to those risks; implement UN-imposed terrorism-related and proliferation-related sanctions (see chapter on Sanctions in the fight against terrorism); ensure adequate supervision of private-sector compliance; provide for the transparency of corporate and trust ownership; and ensure international cooperation against money laundering, terrorist financing and proliferation financing. In turn, regulated private-sector organisations – including financial institutions, designated non-financial businesses and professions and virtual asset service providers – should conduct customer due diligence and report suspicious activities.

The FATF Recommendations of greatest relevance to sanctions are Recommendation 6 (concerning UN-imposed terrorism-related sanctions) and Recommendation 7 (concerning UN-imposed proliferation-related sanctions). Both these Recommendations require countries to implement respective sanctions without delay. They also require countries to either have the mechanism in place to propose relevant sanctions designations to the UN (Recommendation 6) or at least consider developing such a mechanism (Recommendation 7).

While the FATF Recommendations do not expressly deal with unilateral/autonomous (non-UN-imposed) sanctions, many elements of the Recommendations – including those dealing with the confiscation of the proceeds or instrumentalities of crime, customer due diligence, suspicious activity reporting and beneficial ownership transparency – can support the implementation of such sanctions.

For instance, an increasing number of countries confiscate property involved in sanctions evasion as 'proceeds' of such evasion, which is similar to the approach the FATF requires countries to take to the 'proceeds' of tax evasion.

III Blacklisting and greylisting

Compliance with the FATF Recommendations is underpinned by the FATF's mutual evaluation mechanism. Mutual evaluation involves countries being 'peer reviewed' by other countries' representatives, and the resulting review is made publicly available. Each country's review is adopted at a plenary meeting of the FATF. Prior to 2013, mutual evaluation only assessed countries' technical compliance, i.e. the implementation of the FATF Recommendation in domestic law. Since 2013, mutual evaluation assesses technical compliance alongside countries' effectiveness of implementation, as measured against a set of 11 Immediate Outcomes (FATF [2024]).

Countries falling short of the FATF Recommendations, whether in relation to technical compliance or effectiveness, risk finding themselves on one of the two 'name and shame' lists operated by the FATF (FATF, 'Black and Grey Lists').

One of them, colloquially known as the 'blacklist', is a list of 'High-Risk Jurisdictions subject to a Call for Action'. As of August 2024, this list consists of North Korea, Iran and Myanmar. The FATF's blacklist can be further subdivided into two categories. In relation to some countries, namely North Korea and Iran, the FATF identifies specific 'countermeasures' that should be applied by all other countries, e.g. a prohibition on the operation of any branches or subsidiaries of North Korean banks within their territories. In relation to other countries, namely Myanmar, only the general requirement to 'apply enhanced due diligence measures proportionate to the risks arising from the jurisdiction' is in place. The 'countermeasures' required by the FATF are different from, and are not to be confused with, countermeasures as understood in the international law of state responsibility.

The FATF's greylist is formally known as the list of 'Jurisdictions under Increased Monitoring'. This includes countries that exhibit significant deficiencies in compliance with the FATF Recommendations but have made a high-level political commitment to address such deficiencies. There is no formal sanction associated with placement on the FATF's greylist. However, domestic regulators, including in major international financial centres, are likely to treat being on the greylist as an indicator of the country presenting an elevated financial crime risk (Morse [2022]). This, in turn, makes it more expensive and cumbersome to transact with businesses and customers based in greylisted countries, with deleterious effects for the economic development and investment levels in greylisted countries (Collin et al. [2016]; De Kokeret al. [2023]).

IV Conclusion

Despite their non-binding status, the FATF Recommendations constitute the de facto global standard in the fight against money laundering, terrorist financing and proliferation financing – including as relates to the implementation of UN-imposed terrorism-related and proliferation-related sanctions. Compliance with the FATF Recommendations is underpinned by a mutual evaluation mechanism whose influence is underwritten by domestic regulators around the world treating blacklisted and greylisted countries as presenting high levels of financial crime risk.

Bibliography

Literature

Collin M, Cook S and Soramaki K, 'The Impact of Anti-Money Laundering Regulation on Payment Flows: Evidence from SWIFT Data' (2016) Center for Global Development Working Paper No. 445, 2016 <https://papers.ssrn.com/sol3/papers.cfm?abstract_id=2893790#> accessed 24 August 2024.

De Koker L, Howell J and Morris M, 'Economic Consequences of Greylisting by the Financial Action Task Force' (2023) 11(5) *Risks* 81.

Morse JC, *The Bankers' Blacklist: Unofficial Market Enforcement and the Global Fight against Illicit Financing* (Cornell University Press 2022).

Pieth M, 'Finance and the "Shadow Economy"' in Heimann F and Pieth M (eds), *Confronting Corruption: Past Concerns, Present Challenges, and Future Strategies* (Oxford University Press 2018) 119.

ANTON MOISEIENKO

Documents

FATF, 'Black and Grey Lists' <https://www.fatf-gafi.org/en/countries/black-and-grey-lists.html> accessed 24 August 2024.

FATF, *International Standards on Combatting Money Laundering and the Financing of Terrorism & Proliferation*, updated November 2023 <https://www.fatf-gafi.org/content/dam/fatf-gafi/recommendations/FATF%20Recommendations%202012.pdf.coredownload.inline.pdf> accessed 24 August 2024.

FATF, *Methodology for Assessing Technical Compliance with the FATF Recommendations and the Effectiveness of AML/CFT/CPF Systems*, updated July 2024 <https://www.fatf-gafi.org/en/publications/Mutualevaluations/Fatf-methodology.html> accessed 24 August 2024.

FATF, *The Forty Recommendations of the Financial Action Task Force on Money Laundering* (1990).

26. Financial sanctions

SASCHA LOHMANN

I Introduction

The use of financial sanctions in international relations, pioneered by the US and UK governments during World War I and II, can be an alternative to, a precursor of, or complement the use of military force. Encompassing a variety of restrictions on the financial elements of cross-border trade in goods and services, including commodities as well as technology, financial sanctions enable contemporary policymakers in international institutions and nation states to interrupt economic exchange with state and non-state actors beyond borders without using kinetic force. Previously, soldiers had to be sent in harm's way in order to enforce physical land or naval blockades, which inflicted devastating loss and damage on economic and civilian life throughout history (Davis and Engerman [2006]). This changing use of international sanctions from physical to non-physical means was facilitated by a transformative process known as financialization, whereby the creation and supply of financial instruments took on paramount importance for the production and trade of goods and services in North America and Europe from the mid-twentieth century. Against this backdrop, the use of financial sanctions has evolved as the go-to instrument for policymakers to pursue various national security and foreign policy objectives. Its rising unilateral application without a resolution under Article 41 of the Charter of the United Nations (UN) correlates with an increasingly deadlocked Security Council (UNSC).

II Design

In general, financial sanctions inhibit economic exchange involving liabilities and assets (stocks), as well as capital transactions (flows). Specific measures include, but are not limited to, restrictions on the use and (cross-border) transfer of monetary instruments such as funds in any form like cash or bank deposits. Moreover, restrictions can limit other uses of debt, including, but not limited to, securities, bonds, grants, loans, letters of credit, guarantees, or any form of financial assistance or investment by private or public organizations. Furthermore, financial sanctions can curtail access to financial services, including banking transactions, financial messaging services, as well as (re-)insurance (see chapter on Banking system) (Baldwin 1985 [2020]).

Until the late 1990s, the comprehensive use of financial sanctions directed against entire countries had produced devastating unintended consequences for affected civilian populations, as in the case of Iraq (see chapter) (Gordon [2010]). In response, a transnational reform movement emerged to prevent unintended negative consequences by targeting the use of international sanctions at the immediate perpetrators of incriminated behaviour. With respect to financial sanctions, this collective effort was channelled through the so-called Interlaken Process, which consisted of a series of discussions and workshops organized by the Swiss government at Interlaken in 1998 and 1999. Participants, hailing from the public, private, and non-profit sectors, eventually produced operational documents serving as a blueprint for the targeted use of financial sanctions (Watson Institute for International Studies [2001]).

Branded as 'smart sanctions', this targeted use of financial sanctions centres on the age-old practice of blacklisting persons (both individuals and entities) holding key positions in a political regime or serving critical functions in an economy. As a result, any asset owned or controlled by individual state and non-state actors can be immobilized ('frozen'). In addition, any transaction directly or indirectly benefiting them can be fully or partially prohibited. Both 'asset freezes' and the prohibition of making assets available to listed persons have emerged as primary types of financial sanctions employed by the UNSC and individual UN member states, most notably from North America and Europe. The targeted use of financial sanctions is widely credited by its supporters as a preventive and proportionate measure because it would only be temporary, while leaving title to, and ownership of, assets unaffected. However, its compatibility with legal obligations under international customary and conventional law has been subject to controversial debates. This is primarily due to the absence of a right to commerce between nations, as well as broad exceptions for national security reasons enshrined in bilateral friendship, navigation, and commerce treaties, as well as in multilateral agreements.

III Output

Financial sanctions are put into effect through different legal instruments created by legislative or executive bodies. The immediate addressees tasked with implementation are first and foremost financial and credit institutions (see chapter on Domestic implementation). Non-compliance in the case of detected violations may entail different legal and economic consequences. Depending on the assertion of a jurisdictional claim by a legislative or executive body, enforcement actions by competent agencies may reach persons or acts well beyond borders. Primary financial sanctions constitute a legal obligation to comply with applicable provisions for natural and legal persons subjected to the jurisdiction of the respective issuing body. Violations entail civil fines or criminal punishment (see chapter on Criminalisation of sanctions violation). Secondary financial sanctions apply to foreign persons acting outside the jurisdiction of an issuing body for engaging in conduct construed as sanctionable (see chapter on Secondary sanctions and extraterritorial effects of sanctions). This typically includes the circumvention and evasion of, or any act otherwise prohibited by, primary financial sanctions. As a result, various market access restrictions may follow related to the use and movement of funds, among others.

IV Outcome

Financial sanctions generate a broad spectrum of effects on political and economic life, even up to the obstruction of trade in specific instances. This is because financial stocks and flows, such as for payment or insurance, are necessary preconditions for imports and exports of military and dual-use goods, technology, or non-financial services. By introducing legal and reputational risks, especially to international banks, financial sanctions could potentially create widespread chilling effects by encouraging risk-averse behaviour among immediate addressees or other market participants. These effects can also backfire in the case of excessive de-risking, which describes the withdrawal of financial institutions from jurisdictions to which a plethora of financial sanctions apply, and where high reputational, legal, and operational risks greatly outweigh any profit (see chapter on Overcompliance). With the blacklisting of systemically relevant entities such as key commercial actors, including even central banks, the use of financial sanctions seems to have come full circle. This re-comprehensivation also manifests itself in the current debate about moving beyond immobilization (freezing) toward confiscation (seizing) of private and sovereign assets (see chapter on Confiscation) in the context of the unilateral sanctions imposed by the US government and its allies against Russia in response to the invasion of Ukraine since March 2014.

V Impact

The impact (see chapter on Measuring sanctions effectiveness) of financial sanctions depends on the degree to which pursued policy goals are approximated or attained. Initially, the primary goal was custodial, as the US Department of the Treasury utilized its then-novel freezing powers to protect the foreign assets of European countries from the occupying forces of Nazi Germany (Domke [1943]). This defensive approach turned increasingly offensive in the following years, starting with the Korean War and continuing today. The track record of effectiveness has remained mixed so far. While eliciting the desired behaviour change of targets remains elusive, financial sanctions contribute to resource denial or the deterrence of relevant third parties from emulating an incriminated behaviour. Quantitative empirical studies claim that financial sanctions are more effective than trade sanctions to advance national security or foreign policy goals (Hufbauer et al. [2007]). At the dawn of a geo-economic age, in which economic interdependence appears (yet again) as a risk rather than an opportunity, the frequency and intensity of financial sanctions targeting individual state and non-state actors, economic sectors, or entire regions will likely increase in response to protracted crises and escalating conflicts around the world.

Bibliography

Literature

Baldwin DA, *Economic Statecraft: New Edition* (Princeton University Press 2020 [1985]).

Davis LE and Engerman S, *Naval Blockades in Peace and War: An Economic History Since 1750* (Cambridge University Press 2006).

SASCHA LOHMANN

Domke M, *Trading with the Enemy in World War II* (Central Book Company, 1943).

Gordon J, *Invisible War: The United States and the Iraq Sanctions* (Harvard University Press, 2010).

Hufbauer GC, Schott JJ, Elliott KA and Oegg B, *Economic Sanctions Reconsidered* (3rd edn, Peterson Institute for International Economics 2007).

Watson Institute for International Studies, *Targeted Financial Sanctions: A Manual for Design and Implementation: Contributions from the Interlaken Process* (Brown University 2001).

Sascha Lohmann

27. Media sanctions

Anna Pau

I Introduction

Media sanctions consist of a ban on designated legal persons from carrying out broadcasting activities directly or indirectly (e.g., through subsidiaries) in any form (audio and/or audiovisual) to audiences in a given territory. Such measures may also order the suspension of any broadcasting licenses and distribution agreements with the above legal persons. In addition to media outlets, a number of persons may also be affected by media sanctions (in the form of visa bans or asset freezes): most notably journalists, but also other key figures in leadership positions, such as the media outlet's editor-in-chief or director.

Media sanctions have been adopted with the aim of countering government propaganda and disinformation, understood as "verifiably false or misleading information that is created, presented and disseminated for economic gain or to intentionally deceive the public, and may cause public harm" (European Commission [2018]). Yet, the object of such measures is not content-specific, but rather amounts to the obscuration of the entire media channel, with a focus on their lack of independence (for instance, in consideration of their ties to an authoritarian regime) (Lattanzi [2023]).

Media sanctions seriously encroach on fundamental human rights and, in particular, on freedom of expression and its corollaries, including freedom of the press and of communications, the right of citizens to be informed, as well as fundamental values such as democracy, media diversity and pluralism. For a better understanding of these sanctions, the practice of the European Union's (EU) (see chapter) restrictive measures targeting Russian media outlets is examined. Although the EU is not the only international actor to sanction Russia's media (e.g., see chapters on Canada, the United Kingdom and the United States do as well), they are indeed noteworthy for their widespread effects and were also the subject of recent case law.

II Sanctions v Russian media

The material scope of the EU restrictive measures against Russia (see chapter) has expanded considerably since the full invasion of Ukraine by Russia in February 2022. Following the adoption of media sanctions by the EU (Council Decision 2022/351 [2022]; Council Regulation 2022/350 [2022]), the broadcasting activities of several Russian media outlets (e.g., *Sputnik*, *Russia Today* [RT] and others) were banned in EU member states. There are no other cases at the EU level of sanctions affecting information, except for some restrictive measures adopted against foreign journalists considered responsible for government propaganda (*Sarafraz v Council* [2015]; *Kiselev v Council* [2017]). Media sanctions constitute one example of EU atypical individual restrictive measures in consideration of their targets, as well as their content (Poli [2024]).

The EU was not the first to adopt such restrictions: some EU member states preceded the Council in banning the broadcasting activities of Russian TV channels in their territory (e.g., Lithuania and Latvia since 2015). Canada aligned with the EU in imposing sanctions on arms-length and state-owned entities that host and support various platforms used for disseminating Russian disinformation, including mass media. The United States initially designated three Russian state-owned TV stations for their governmental ties and subsequently adopted further sanctions against Russian state media for allegedly undermining democracy in the United States. Norway adopted a different stance from that of the EU and decided not to restrict freedom of expression. The United Kingdom imposed, *inter alia*, an asset freeze against a journalist for his propaganda activities regarding the war in Ukraine (*Phillips v Secretary of State* [2024]).

Media sanctions were adopted by the EU under extraordinary circumstances. The threat that sanctions are intended to address is hybrid by nature, since it consists of disinformation activity aimed at promoting an act of aggression. Blacklisted media or individuals, while not the direct perpetrators of such serious violations, nevertheless provide active political support to the latter. Indeed, according to the Council, their actions "constitute a significant and direct threat to the Union's public order and security" (Council Decision 2022/351, Recital 8). The latter represents an unprecedented justification: it is indeed the first time that the Council refers to this concept in a Common Foreign and Security Policy (CFSP) measure (Poli and Finelli

[2023]) and is dependent on the extended notion of "hybrid threats" adopted by the Council (Council Decision [2022] Recital 5). Consequently, these measures "should be maintained until the aggression against Ukraine is put to an end, and until the Russian Federation, and its associated media outlets, cease to conduct propaganda actions against the Union and its Member States" (Council Decision [2022] Recital 10). The restrictive measures should thus be lifted if one of these conditions is no longer met. In June 2024, the Council decided that media service providers in the EU would no longer be allowed to accept funding from the Russian state and its proxies.

Media sanctions raised concerns among legal scholars and experts and were the target of severe reproaches by organizations of journalists. Such measures have been defined as acts of censorship, or otherwise criticized as they would excessively limit certain fundamental rights or violate the principles on which the EU itself is founded. The validity of EU media sanctions has recently been challenged in an annulment action before the General Court (GC) of the EU (*RT France v Council* [2022]). However, the action was rejected. The following section briefly dwells on the interferences of these measures with freedom of expression and information.

III Media sanctions: freedom of expression and information

Freedom of expression and information is a fundamental human right, as well as an essential foundation of a democratic society (EU Charter [2010] Art. 11; Convention for the Protection of Human Rights and Fundamental Freedoms [1953] Art. 10; International Covenant on Civil and Political Rights [1976] Art. 19) (ICCPR). The activities of media outlets are covered by this freedom and, in general, the media play an essential role in ensuring its effective realization as a "public watchdog" (*Thoma v Luxembourg* [2001] para. 45). In this context, media diversity is a key aspect of democracy and pluralism (*Informationsverein Lentia and others v Austria* [1993] para. 38).

Media freedom is not, however, absolute. Based on the case law of the European Court of Human Rights (ECtHR), all opinions must be able to be expressed by natural or legal persons in accordance with the ethics of journalism and within the limit of "hate speech", which represents an abuse of freedom of expression (*Bladet Tromsø and Stensaas v Norway* [1999] para. 65). Moreover, any propaganda for war will be prohibited by law under Article 20 ICCPR; the latter "is one of the international instruments (…) of which the Courts of the European Union take account in applying the general principles of EU law" (*RT France v Council* [2022] para. 208). However, according to EU law, any limitation on the exercise of freedom of expression must be subject to precise conditions: it must be provided for by law, be proportionate, respect the essence of this right and freedom, as well as meet an objective of general interest recognized by the Union (EU Charter [2010] Art. 52(1)).

The GC found that the Council satisfied all of these strict conditions necessary to adopt media sanctions (*RT France v Council* [2022]). In particular, such measures have passed the "essence test" in that they are temporary and reversible and do not prevent media service providers and their staff from carrying out other activities in the EU – such as research and interviews – as well as broadcasting outside the EU. The EU judges also confirmed that media sanctions may pursue a general interest recognized by the Union, namely the preservation of its values, fundamental interests and security, and also respond to the general interest of the international community to put the conflict to an end (Poli [2024]). Ultimately, by relying on the case law of the ECtHR, the GC confirmed that the measure is also proportionate. Pending the appeal, RT France's bankruptcy was declared by a French court and the case was thus dismissed (*RT France v Council* [2023] Order). This is a clear illustration of the far-reaching consequences of this type of sanction.

Russian media sanctions triggered retaliatory measures: indeed, Russia decided to ban many EU media outlets from broadcasting in Russian territory. This will certainly limit, among other things, media pluralism in Russia. The measures under comment represent a severe reaction to an exceptional context and are justified only as long as they adhere to precise criteria. A serious interference with individuals' freedoms should imply the most penetrating judicial review. The balancing exercise carried out by the Luxembourg judges ultimately weighs in favour of EU security and public order, to the detriment of some fundamental rights.

Bibliography

Literature

Baade B, 'The EU's "Ban" of RT and Sputnik: A Lawful Measure Against Propaganda for War' (*Verfassungsblog*, 8 March 2022) <https://verfassungsblog.de/the-eus-ban-of-rt-and-sputnik/> accessed 22 July 2024.

BBC, 'US Imposes New Sanctions on Russian State Media' (*BBC*, 13 September 2024) <https://www.bbc.com/news/articles/cvglrrz95zzo> accessed 22 October 2024.

Lattanzi S, 'On Propaganda and Public Order in Europe' (2023) 3 *Politica del diritto* 297.

Lonardo L, 'Censorship in the EU as a Result of the War in Ukraine. Case T-125/22 RT France v Council' (2023) 48(6) *European Law Review* 707.

Poli S and Finelli F, 'Context Specific and Structural Changes in EU Restrictive Measures Adopted in Reaction to Russia's Aggression to Ukraine' (2023) 3 *Eurojus* 19.

Poli S, 'Judicial Challenges to EU Restrictive Measures by Individual State Organs, "Emanations of non-EU Member States" and Third Countries: The Limits to the Council's Discretion' in Lang A, Adinolfi G and Ragni C (eds), *Sanctions By and Against International Organizations* (Intersentia 2024) 203.

Politico, 'RT France Declared Bankrupt by French Court' (*Politico*, 8 April 2023) <https://www.politico.eu/article/french-court-declares-rt-france-bankrupt/> accessed 22 October 2024.

Szép V and Wessel R, 'Balancing Restrictive Measures and Media Freedom: RT France v. Council' (2023) 60(5) *Common Market Law Review* 1384.

Documents

Bladet Tromsø and Stensaas v Norway App No. 21980/93 (ECtHR, 29 January 1999).

Case T-125/22 *Russia Today France v Council* (GC, 27 July 2022) ECLI:EU:T:2022:483.

Case T-262/15 *Kiselev v Council* (GC, 15 June 2017) ECLI:EU:T:2017:392.

Case T-273/13 *Sarafraz v Council* (GC, 4 December 2015) ECLI:EU:T:2015:939.

Charter of Fundamental Rights of the European Union [2010] OJ C83/389.

European Commission, 'Communication from the Commission, Tackling Online Disinformation: A European Approach' COM (2018) 236 final.

Convention for the Protection of Human Rights and Fundamental Freedoms (European Convention on Human Rights, as amended) (ECHR) (adopted 4 November 1950, entered into force 3 September 1953) ETS No. 5.

Council Decision (CFSP) n 2022/351 of 1 March 2022 amending Decision 2014/512/CFSP concerning restrictive measures in view of Russia's actions destabilising the situation in Ukraine [2022] OJ L65/5.

Council Regulation (EU) 2022/350 of 1 March 2022 amending Regulation (EU) No. 833/2014 concerning restrictive measures in view of Russia's actions destabilising the situation in Ukraine [2022] OJ L65/1.

European Federation of Journalists, 'Fighting Disinformation with Censorship is a Mistake' (European Federation of Journalists, 1 March 2022) <https://europeanjournalists.org/blog/2022/03/01/fighting-disinformation-with-censorship-is-a-mistake/> accessed 22 October 2024.

Government of Canada, 'RT and RT France can no Longer be Distributed by Canadian Television Service Providers' (Government of Canada, 16 March 2022) <https://www.canada.ca/en/radio-television-telecommunications/news/2022/03/rt-and-rt-france-can-no-longer-be-distributed-by-canadian-television-service-providers.html> accessed 22 October 2024.

Informationsverein Lentia and others v Austria App No. 13914/88; 15041/89; 15717/89; 15779/89 (ECtHR, 24 November 1993).

International Covenant on Civil and Political Rights (adopted 16 December 1966, entered into force 23 March 1976) 999 UNTS 171.

International Federation of Journalists, 'Russia: 81 EU Media Outlets Blocked from Broadcasting Inside the Country' (International Federation of Journalists, 26 June 2024) <https://www.ifj.org/media-centre/news/detail/category/press-releases/article/russia-81-eu-media-outlets-blocked-from-broadcasting-inside-the-country> accessed 22 October 2024.

Munch E, 'Latest Reactions by Media Regulatory Authorities to the War in Ukraine' (European Platform of Regulatory

Authorities, 9 June 2022) <https://www.epra.org/news_items/the-latest-reactions-by-media-regulatory-authorities-to-the-situation-in-ukraine> accessed 22 October 2024.

Phillips v Secretary of State for Foreign, Commonwealth and Development Affairs [2024] England and Wales High Court 32.

Russia Today France v Council (Order of the President of the Court of 28 July 2023) Case C-620/22 P, ECLI:EU:C:2023:615.

Thoma v Luxembourg App No. 38432/97 (ECtHR, 29 March 2001).

US Department of the Treasury, 'U.S. Treasury Takes Sweeping Action Against Russia's War Efforts' (US Department of the Treasury, 8 May 2022) <https://home.treasury.gov/news/press-releases/jy0771> accessed 22 October 2024.

ANNA PAU

28. Membership sanctions

Martina Buscemi

I Introduction

In case of non-compliance with obligations deriving from membership, international organizations (IOs) may adopt sanctions to pressure the errant member back into line. Unlike countermeasures, which represent acts of "private justice" and fall into a relational and horizontal paradigm, membership sanctions are measures taken in execution of a decision of a competent social organ that fit into an institutional and vertical dimension (Abi-Saab [1987] 309).

Membership sanctions consist of depriving the disobedient member of its rights, privileges and benefits. Typically, they are set out in the IO's rules, namely in the constitutive instrument. Yet, constitutive instruments do not always provide for disciplining powers against the outlawed members: they may be silent on the issue or they may envisage sanctions but only in limited circumstances, such as for default in payments of financial contributions or for serious breaches of the core principles of the IO.

II Overview of the sanctions

Membership sanctions may take different forms, varying from the most serious to the least serious ones. At one end of the spectrum is the expulsion of the member or the request to withdraw (compulsory withdrawal), as stipulated, for example, respectively, in Article 6 of the UN Charter and Article XXVI(c) of the Articles of Agreement of the International Monetary Fund. Unlike expulsion, the suspension of all privileges and rights of the member is a temporary sanction laid down in several constitutive instruments (e.g., Article 34 of the Statutes of the World Tourism Organization).

Less severe than the suspension of the entire membership is the temporary curtailment of *certain* rights and privileges: typically, the right to vote, the right to be represented in the organs or the right to hold elective offices of the IO. Some treaties specifically indicate the kind of rights that can be suspended, such as the Convention Establishing the World Intellectual Property Organization (Article 11 para. 5), while others, such as the Treaty of the European Union (via the notorious "nuclear option" enclosed in Article 7), provide only an illustrative but not exhaustive list of suspendable rights. In a limited number of cases, offending members can be excluded from single IO bodies, without necessarily being suspended from the entire membership of a given IO. The suspension from the UN Human Rights Council, based on General Assembly Resolution 60/251, is an eloquent example.

Another conventional sanction is the interruption of the *services* provided by the IO, in particular technical and financial assistance (e.g., Article VI of the Articles of Agreement of the International Bank for Reconstruction and Development). Finally, at the opposite end of the spectrum, one finds the partial restriction of services furnished by the IO (e.g., Article 131 para. 1 of the INTERPOL Rules on the Processing of Data).

Besides these typical sanctions, in practice, some IOs have resorted to the credentials procedure in order to exclude the representatives of the defiant member from participating in the institutional activities of the IO, without formally suspending or terminating the membership. This (ab)use of the credentials procedure appears rather controversial (Klabbers [2012] 120).

From a procedural point of view, differences exist in terms of the organ competent to impose the sanctions, as well as the voting majority required: a qualified majority is usually the rule, at times a relative majority, while unanimity is less frequently prescribed. Usually, the procedural guarantees offered to the member under accusation in the sanctioning process are rudimentary, if not entirely absent. The targeted member can hardly challenge the sanctions decisions, nor can the targeted member be heard or defend against accusations before judicial bodies: the sanctioning procedure is nearly always in the hands of the political bodies of the IO. The judicial means of settling disputes between a member and the IO can potentially provide a remedy to challenge the sanctions: yet, those means are not always available and there is no record of their concrete use in this matter. This has brought scholars to conclude that, when imposing sanctions, IOs act as "*judex in causa sua*" (Leben [1979] 270). Indeed, the sanctioning procedure, often bereft of any judicial check, has a marked political nature and may carry the risk of possible abuses.

From a political angle, membership sanctions may represent a double-edged sword: on the one side, they may constitute an effective remedy against non-compliance and may successfully discipline the disobedient member; on the other side, they may antagonize, diminish or induce to terminate the cooperation of the member (as well as that of like-minded states), thus bearing the risk of polarizing the whole membership (Steininger [2021] 548).

Not surprisingly, IOs tend to be particularly cautious when handling this tool. While recently, regional IOs have increasingly adopted sanctions (namely, the suspension of membership), especially within the African context, in response to unconstitutional governmental changes or gross human rights violations allegedly committed by members (Closa [2017]; Sossai [2020]), IOs having universal membership are more reluctant to make use of their disciplining powers. Well-known instances of suspension or expulsion from universal IOs have occurred in the past, particularly during the 1960s and 1970s against South Africa's apartheid regime, Portugal's colonialization policy and Franco's dictatorship in Spain (Leben [1979]). Other cases have occurred over time, but tended to be sporadic (Magliveras [1999]). In the past few years, the picture has partially changed. Sanctions have been adopted, in particular, as a reaction to egregious violations of international law and in the face of the Security Council's paralysis due to the exercise of the veto power (e.g., membership sanctions taken amid the Syrian conflict (Buscemi [2023])). More notably, the recent military aggression against Ukraine has led several IOs, having political or technical mandates, regional or universal membership, ranging in size and level, to unleash membership sanctions against the Russian Federation (Buscemi [2022]).

III Legal issues: the case of sanctions lacking an institutional basis

Sanctions that an IO adopts against its members according to its own rules are lawful (Yearbook of the International Law Commission (2011) Vol II Part Two 46, 72). Yet, more problematic is the situation – far from infrequent – in which IOs exercise the sanctioning power in an "exorbitant" manner, that is without a legal basis in institutional rules, or not adhering to these rules, or for breach of norms that have little or nothing to do with their institutional mandate. The question of the legality of "non-mandated" or "exorbitant" sanctions has been widely addressed in scholarship. Different grounds have been put forward to justify sanctions taken outside the institutional perimeter, which in the first place would be unlawful as they breach one or more rights accruing to the member (e.g., the right to vote, to receive technical assistance or to participate in the institutional life of the IO). The various justifications that have been brought forward rely on controversial notions of the law of IOs, such as the doctrine of implied powers or the existence of inherent powers to take self-help measures based on general international law, thus challenging the idea of the autonomy of IOs' legal orders.

In particular, with regard to sanctions lacking an institutional basis, it has been maintained that the IO can claim to suspend the rights of the member who has breached one of the obligations set forth in the constitutive instrument based on the general rule *inadimplenti non est adimplendum* (Magliveras [1999] 231). Alternatively, it has been argued that IOs have the power to resort to countermeasures under general international law, provided that the special mechanisms of the IO have been unsuccessfully exhausted, either as a party affected by the breach of the constitutive instrument, or as a third party in relation to violations of *erga omnes* obligations (Dopagne [2010] 180; Magliveras [1999] 241; Dawidowicz [2017] 224).

In this regard, however, the International Law Commission's (ILC) final position has drastically limited the possibility for an IO to take countermeasures against its members. In fact, Article 22 of the Draft Articles on the Responsibility of International Organizations (ARIO) distinguishes – rather problematically – the hypothesis of the violation of an obligation under international law (Article 22 para. 2 ARIO) from that of the violation of an obligation under the rules of an IO (Article 22 para. 3 ARIO), such as the constitutive instrument. In that latter case, in the view of the ILC, the IO can adopt countermeasures only if the "rules of IOs provide so". This formula seems to imply that if the rules of the IO do not explicitly authorize it to take countermeasures – rules formulated in this way appear unknown – the possibility to take countermeasures is barred. This restrictive stance has been justified in light of the "obligations of close cooperation that generally exist between an [IO] and its members" (Yearbook of the International Law Commission (2011) vol II Part Two 72). The ILC's position has given rise to doubts and criticisms, especially for conflating the notion of sanctions with that of countermeasures (Kerbrat [2013] 108), and it is doubtful whether it reflects customary international law.

Moreover, it should be mentioned that there is a general reluctance on the part of IOs to rely on general international law (be it the law of treaties or the law of international responsibility) to justify "exorbitant" sanctions. The scarcity of legal objections from members does not contribute to clarifying the picture. In the end, one is left with the impression that sanctions lacking an institutional basis highlight the transparency of the institutional veil of the IOs, under which members use and twist institutional rules to collectively react against the defiant member through the institutional apparatus.

IV Conclusion

When discussing the adoption of membership sanctions, IOs are faced with difficult decisions and conflicting interests, namely, the need to keep recalcitrant members engaged in the IO, hoping that this will entail more social control, and the need to safeguard the reputation of the IO by drawing red lines (Steininger [2021] 565). As IOs today, even the most technical ones, are increasingly concerned about their reputation in the court of public opinion, they seem more inclined to make use of their disciplining powers against the outlawed member in order to reassert legality, especially in the face of serious violations of international law and the Security Council's paralysis. The adoption of membership sanctions amid the Syrian and Ukrainian conflicts are telling examples.

In those contexts, membership sanctions serve a particular moral function that consists of stigmatizing and banning the ostracized member, who is treated as a "pariah" in the eyes of the community. This function can be devalued when the IO is perceived as applying "double standards". Yet, the risk of selectivity is unavoidable as membership sanctions are the result of a political procedure, often bereft of any judicial oversight.

Bibliography

Literature

Abi-Saab GM, 'Cours général de droit international public' (1987) 207 *Recueil des Cours* 9.

Buscemi M, 'Outcasting the Aggressor: The Deployment of the Sanction of "Non-Participation"' (2022) 116 *American Journal of International Law* 764.

Buscemi M, 'Institutional Sanctions and Functionalism: Insights from the Most Recent Practice' (2023) 20 *International Organizations Law Review* 52.

Closa C, 'Securing Compliance with Democracy Requirements in Regional Organizations' in Kochenov D and Jakab A (eds), *The Enforcement of EU Law and Values: Ensuring Member States' Compliance* (Oxford University Press 2017) 379.

Dawidowicz M, *Third-Party Countermeasures in International Law* (Cambridge University Press 2017).

Dopagne F, *Les contre-mesures des organisations internationales* (Anthemis 2010).

Dopagne F, 'Sanctions and Countermeasures by International Organizations: Diverging Lessons for the Idea of Autonomy' in Collins R and White ND (eds), *International Organizations and the Idea of Autonomy: Institutional Independence in the International Legal Order* (Routledge 2011) 178.

Forlati Picchio ML, *La sanzione nel diritto internazionale* (CEDAM 1974).

Kerbrat Y, 'Sanctions et contre-mesures: risques de confusion dans les articles de la CDI sur la responsabilité des organisations internationales' (2013) 46 *Revue Belge de Droit International* 103.

Klabbers I, *An Introduction to International Institutional Law* (Cambridge University Press 2012).

Leben C, *Les sanctions privatives de droits ou de qualité dans les organisations internationales spécialisées: recherches sur les sanctions internationales et l'évolution du droit des gens* (Bruylant 1979).

Magliveras KD, *Exclusion from Participation in International Organisations. The Law and Practice behind Member States' Expulsion and Suspension of Membership* (Kluwer Law International 1999).

Ruzié D, *Organizations internationales et sanctions internationales* (Armand Colin 1971).

Schermers HG and Blokker NM, *International Institutional Law: Unity with Diversity* (Brill Nijhoff 2018).

Sossai M, *Sanzioni delle Nazioni Unite e organizzazioni regionali* (Roma TrE-Press 2020).

Steininger S, 'With or Without You: Suspension, Expulsion, and the Limits of Membership Sanctions in Regional Human Rights Regimes' (2021) 81 *Zeitschrift für ausländisches öffentliches Recht und Völkerrecht* 533.

Document

ILC, Yearbook of the International Law Commission (2001) vol II (Part Two) UN Doc. A/CN.4/SER.A/2011/Add.1.

Martina Buscemi

29. Sanctions on transport (air, ship, ground)

MICHAEL BRZOSKA

I Introduction

Transport sanctions impose restrictions on the ownership, registration, insurance, movement, availability and use of vessels, as well as ground transport and aircraft by certain companies, for select purposes and/or in certain countries.

Transport sanctions can target the whole or parts of the transport sector. More frequently, however, has been the addition of transport sanctions as an element in international sanctions packages with other primary purposes, such as restricting trade or preventing designated persons or groups of persons from traveling internationally.

Transport sanctions have taken many and diverse forms. They have often been conceived of and designed to address particular cases and circumstances and have found limited application beyond their original intention. Having been an element in the international sanctions portfolio for decades, they have attained additional prominence through the recent cases against North Korea, Iran and Russia. The following section provides an overview of key practices.

II Types of transport sanctions

Direct transport sector sanctions

On 21 January 1992, the United Nations Security Council (UNSC) mandated an aviation ban against Libya in Resolution 731; the first modern case of an internationally mandated transport sanction. The sanctions were in response to the shooting down of two Western passenger aircraft by Libyan operatives (UNSC Res 731 [1992]). The sanctions package included a ban on aircraft traffic between Libya and other countries, as well as the servicing, maintenance and insurance of Libyan-owned aircraft.

Other notable cases were the revocation of landing rights given to JAT Yugoslav Airlines by European and North American governments prior to and during the Bosnian War 1991/1992, the European Union's (EU) ban on flights of the national Yugoslav airline to EU member states during the Kosovo War in 1998 and the ban on the Afghan airline Aviana mandated by the UNSC in Resolution 1267 (1999). The latter case included the explicit purpose of reducing the foreign currency income of the ruling Taliban.

Since 2006, aviation-related sanctions have become rare while those related to shipping have become more frequent. Primary targets have been North Korea and Iran, triggered by their nuclear programs. While shipping sanctions have focused on sanction evasion (see below), they have also affected the commercial viability of the country's shipping sector.

After the Russian invasion of Ukraine in 2014, the EU mandated a very extensive case of transport-related sanctions, hurting both the Russian shipping and ground transport sectors – as well as supporting the EU's overall sanctions package against Russia.

Sanctions package supporting transport-related sanctions

Many types of sanctions, such as comprehensive and selective trade sanctions as well as travel bans for designated persons or groups of persons, have a transport dimension. Original senders of such sanctions often do not mention provisions on transport explicitly. One broad exception is arms embargoes that often explicitly prohibit the use of "flag vessels and aircraft" for arms sales. When implementation problems have arisen, however, additional mandates specifically addressing transport have been added in a number of cases. An early example is the ban on shipping to the former Yugoslavia in UNSC Resolution 787 (1992) to support the trade embargo mandated in UNSC Resolution 757 (1992). Other cases include provisions on bunkering services, as well as the right to inspect cargo vessels and airplanes when violations of sanctions are suspected, such as North Korea and Iran.

Transport sanctions extending the reach of sanctioners

The implementation of sanctions, whether mandated by individual states, groups of states or the UNSC, is a matter for states, which can, in principle, only act in their territories, as well as on their flagged vessels and aircraft.

The high seas are therefore a problem for implementation. The UNSC has been reluctant to allow the (legal) inspection of cargo vessels, as well as the seizure of prohibited goods, on the high seas without the vessel's flag state's consent. In the case of the sanctions against North Korea, the UNSC has decided that non-consenting flag states will direct vessels to a port where inspections can be conducted (UNSC Res 2375 [2017] para. 8). In the case of Libya, the UNSC authorized the inspection of designated ships after seeking consent from flag states (UNSC Res 2146 [2014]), while in the case of the Iran sanctions, the UNSC called on flag states to cooperate with other states intending to inspect cargo (UNSC Res 1929 [2010] para. 15). Outside the realm of UN mandates, the United States has formed an informal coalition of states willing to cooperate on preventing the transport of goods related to weapons of mass destruction (WMDs), the Proliferation Security Initiative, which can only act within international law concerning the high seas.

Beyond the high seas, senders have attempted to extend the implementation of sanctions that are not binding for third countries through provisions relevant to the transport sector. The insurance business for ships, for instance, is highly concentrated in Western countries, making it more costly, or even impractical, for shipping companies from any country to provide transport services when insurance is not available for them (Leloulas [2021]). One example of such actions was Western sanctions on Iran; another case is Western sanctions following the Russian invasion of Ukraine.

Implementation of transport sanctions

Addressing transport has been an important element in the implementation of sanctions packages. Modes of transport, such as aircraft and ships, are often large and comparatively easy to detect, at least if larger quantities of supplies need to be transported. Still, sanctions implementation provisions for the transport of prohibited goods and persons have deliberately been violated or undermined by a lack of sufficient means of control over airspace and shipping. In some cases, measures, including additional sanctions, have been adopted to address these deficiencies.

III Side effects

Among transport sanctions, aviation bans have been the most controversial, raising humanitarian as well as cultural concerns. In the Libyan case, for instance, the hardship faced by devout Muslims to travel to Mecca was a highly contentious issue. The aviation ban on Sudan was mandated in principle by the UNSC in Resolution 1070 (1996) but suspended for humanitarian reasons (Bruderlein [1997]).

A further concern in the context of aircraft-related sanctions and shipping-related sanctions against Iran is safety. When a US-supplied helicopter with Iranian President Raisi on board crashed in early 2024, the Iranian government blamed the US embargo on aircraft services and spare parts. Other safety concerns had earlier been raised about Western restrictions on servicing Iranian ships transporting oil to third states.

IV Effectiveness of transport sanctions

Transport sanctions are, with few exceptions, closely tied to other sanctions. Explicit transport sanctions serve the implementation of trade sanctions, and sometimes the ban on the travel of persons. Their contribution is usually only modest. Still, as the wide range of types of transport sanctions demonstrates, they remain an attractive addition to the international sanctions toolbox in various dimensions.

Bibliography

Literature

Bruderlein C, 'DHA Report on the Potential Humanitarian Impact of a UN Flight Ban against Sudan: Note of the Expert to the UN Security Council' (1997) *UN Department of Humanitarian Affairs.*

Brzoska M, 'Design and Implementation of Arms Embargoes and Travel and Aviation Related Sanctions: Results of the "Bonn-Berlin Process"' (Bonn International Center for Conversion 2001) <https://digitallibrary.un.org/record/801765> accessed 6 November 2024.

Kilpatrick RL, 'The Impact of UN Sanctions on Commercial Shipping Activities' in Ribeiro M, Bastos L and Henriksen F (eds), *Global Challenges and the Law of the Sea* (Springer 2020) 159.

Leloulas G, 'The Role of Insurance in Sanctions Regimes' in Soyer B and Tettenborn A (eds), *Ship Operations. New Risks, Liabilities and Technologies in the Maritime Sector* (Informa Law from Routledge 2021) 3.

MICHAEL BRZOSKA

Documents

UNSC Res 731 (21 January 1992) UN Doc. S/RES/731 (1992).

UNSC Res 757 (30 May 1992) UN Doc. S/RES/757 (1992).

UNSC Res 787 (16 November 1992) UN Doc. S/RES/787 (1992).

UNSC Res 1267 (15 October 1999) UN Doc. S/RES/1267 (1999).

UNSC Res 1929 (9 June 2010) UN Doc. S/RES/1929 (2010).

UNSC Res 2146 (19 March 2014) UN Doc. S/RES/2146 (2014).

UNSC Res 2375 (11 September 2017) UN Doc. S/RES/2375 (2017).

MICHAEL BRZOSKA

30. Trade embargoes

Dawid Walentek

I Introduction

Policymakers can craft detailed sanctions to achieve their foreign policy objectives, as previous entries to this volume have shown, for example with sanctions on specific commodities (see also chapter on Commodity sanctions) or focusing on individuals and their assets (see also chapter on Financial sanctions). Yet, at times, leaders see sector-specific measures or sanctions linked to individuals as insufficient and opt for a comprehensive alternative. Trade embargoes, initially understood as trade blockades, are meant to prohibit all, or nearly all, economic exchanges between the sender and the target state, and typically encompass both exports and imports of goods and services, while also forbidding financial transactions with entities in (or related to) the target state. Thus, the underpinning idea is to stop the economic exchange between the sender and the target, whether it involves exporting cars or IT solutions or importing oil or agricultural products.

II The evolution and modern use of trade embargoes

Historically, trade embargoes accompanied military efforts – for example, during the Napoleonic Wars, the French Emperor Napoleon I set out to destabilise the British economy by blocking trade between continental Europe and Britain, albeit with limited effects, as circumvention and alternative trading routes offered sufficient alternatives for Britain (Marzagalli [2022]). Trade embargoes were a feature of the First and Second World Wars. For example, between 1914 and 1919, the Entente engaged in an economic blockade of the Central Powers, and Britain issued a trade embargo against Germany in 1939, while the United States issued a trade embargo against Japan and Germany in 1941. Typically, the terms trade embargoes and economic blockades were used interchangeably.

In the decades since the Second World War, trade embargoes have continued to accompany military efforts; yet, they also began to appear as independent policy tools and became a product of US foreign policy. For example, the United States imposed a trade embargo on China in 1950, after China's intervention in Korea, and kept the embargo in place following the end of the Korean War. The United States also imposed a trade embargo on (North) Vietnam in 1964 and kept it in place for 30 years (Chen [2006]), while the trade embargo on Cuba issued by the United States in 1962 still holds and is currently the longest economic blockade in place. The United States also issued a trade embargo on Nicaragua in 1985, hoping to undermine the Sandinista regime, and has been building the measures against Iran towards an actual trade embargo since 1987, reaching its peak during the Maximum Pressure Campaign conducted by the Trump administration in 2018.

It took the United Nations Security Council (UNSC) 21 years to put in place its first sanctions regime, targeting Southern Rhodesia and all Rhodesian exports and key imports (e.g., oil, arms and vehicles), while also forbidding all UN members (122 countries in 1965) from offering financial aid to Rhodesia. This was the first UNSC call for sanctions close to a trade embargo, albeit passed with no penalty for ignoring the measure – a course taken by, for example, South Africa (see chapter), a target of UNSC-designated (and voluntary) sanctions itself. On the other hand, the UNSC trade embargo against Iraq, issued in 1990 after Iraq's invasion of Kuwait, was enforced by both legal and military means – with the US-led Multinational Interception Force in charge of patrolling the sea off Iraq's coast. This mission was unprecedented in its scope, covering all aspects of economic activity in Iraq (Gordon [2012]).

Currently, the United States is the biggest issuer of trade embargoes – targeting Cuba (see chapter), Iran (see chapter), North Korea, Sudan and Syria (see chapter). The US effort in respect of embargoes is supervised by the US Treasury Department's Office of Foreign Assets Control (OFAC), which is able to pursue both criminal and financial penalties for violations of existing measures (see also chapter on United States) and by the Bureau of Industry and Security (BIS) at the US Department of Commerce. For all five listed countries, there is a degree of variation, occasional changes and lessening of the restrictions issued by the United States that are in place, making the distinction between targeted sanctions and trade embargoes increasingly blurred. What is more, organisations like OFAC do not specify whether a particular country is under a trade embargo, but comprehensive sanctions are typically understood as trade embargoes.

While the United States plays a leading role in the use of trade embargoes, other countries have used this policy too. For example, India imposed a trade embargo on Nepal in 1989 and again in 2015, and Qatar was subject to a trade embargo in 2017 issued by Saudi Arabia, Bahrain, Egypt and the United Arab Emirates. Interestingly, the European Union (EU) is far from issuing trade embargoes and typically engages in target-specific and detailed measures, even in respect of economic ties with Russia after its invasion of Ukraine, although the measures taken against Iran and Syria may be seen as approaching a trade embargo (Moret [2015]). This occurs against a rapid increase in the frequency of the use of sanctions by the EU and with sanctions being an explicit tool of the European Commission to pursue the EU's foreign policy objectives (see also chapter on European Union).

III Effectiveness and humanitarian implications

While trade embargoes are typically all-encompassing, their effectiveness is mixed and debated in the scholarly community. For example, the trade embargo against Rhodesia was not successful in either undermining the Rhodesian economy or in forcing a change in policy by the target state. Equally, the trade embargo on Cuba and Nicaragua has not achieved the expected regime change, nor did the trade embargo against Vietnam aid the military efforts of the United States in the 1960s and 1970s. The more recent efforts to induce policy change in Iran and North Korea have also observed limited effects. At the same time, trade embargoes are typically introduced in cases of high political salience, where the target is highly determined – as in the case of North Vietnam – or has a key ally helping to alleviate the pain of the trade embargo – as in the case of Rhodesia, supported by South Africa for nearly 15 years.

At the same time, the humanitarian toll of trade embargoes has been widely acknowledged by the scholarly community, with the most notorious case being the trade embargo against Iraq – noted to substantially undermine access to healthcare, bring a large share of the population into poverty and result in hundreds of thousands of deaths (Gordon [2012]), albeit the exact number has recently been questioned (Dyson and Cetorelli [2017]). In general, researchers find consistent negative effects of trade embargoes on the well-being of targeted populations – for example, measures introduced by India on Nepal (Chakravarty et al. [2021]) or the US policy of sanctions against Cuba (Garfield [2000]).

IV Conclusion

Trade embargoes are measures intended to cut all trade relations between the target and the sender, unlike sanctions that can be specific to a particular sector of the economy or individuals/entities. Trade embargoes may be issued as a unilateral effort, for example, as in the case of Nepal and India, multilateral and under the guidance of the UN, as in the case of Iraq, or in the form of coalitions of the willing (i.e., multinational but without coordination or approval from an international organisation), as in the case of the trade embargo on Qatar issued by its neighbours. While trade embargoes have a long history in the policy toolkit of states, they have traditionally accompanied war efforts. Only after the Second World War did trade embargoes become a policy choice in their own right and the United States is the most frequent user of trade embargoes. Despite frequently generating substantial economic and human costs for the target populations, their effectiveness is at best mixed, with the case of Iraq frequently serving as an example of the enduring suffering of the Iraqi population and no policy change, while the case of Cuba shows how the duration of the trade embargo by no means predicts its ability to achieve the desired effect. In general, we see trade embargoes becoming an increasingly rare policy choice and being replaced by targeted measures; however, for highly salient cases, they still remain an attractive choice for policymakers.

Bibliography

Literature

Chakravarty A, Parey M and Wright GC, 'The Human Capital Legacy of a Trade Embargo' (2021) 19 *Journal of the European Economic Association* 1692.

Chen X-Z, 'China and the US Trade Embargo, 1950–1972' (2006) 13 *American Journal of Chinese Studies* 169.

DAWID WALENTEK

Dyson T and Cetorelli V, 'Changing Views on Child Mortality and Economic Sanctions in Iraq: A History of Lies, Damned Lies and Statistics' (2017) 2(2) *BMJ Global Health.*

Garfield R, 'The Public Health Impact of Sanctions: Contrasting Responses of Iraq and Cuba' (2000) 215 *Middle East Report* 16.

Gordon J, *Invisible War: The United States and the Iraq Sanctions* (Harvard University Press 2012).

Marzagalli S, 'Napoleonic Wars and Economic Imperialism', in Broers M, Dwyer P (eds) *The Cambridge History of the Napoleonic Wars* (Cambridge University Press 2022) 232.

Moret ES, 'Humanitarian Impacts of Economic Sanctions on Iran and Syria' (2015) 24 *European Security* 120.

DAWID WALENTEK

PART III

KEY SANCTIONS EPISODES

31. Angola

ROBERT FOWLER

I Introduction

United Nations (UN) sanctions were imposed on the National Union for the Total Independence of Angola (UNITA) for nine years between 1993 and 2002. This was the first time that the UN Security Council (UNSC) had imposed sanctions on a non-state actor. The UNSC maintained that UNITA and its leader Jonas Savimbi were largely responsible for the civil war in Angola. As Chair of the Angola Sanctions Committee between 1 January 1999 and August 2000, I and the Council sought to apply new initiatives to improve the effectiveness of sanctions, including the creation of panels of experts. The final report of the Panel of Experts published in 2000 was a damning report outlining the many ways that criminal and UN states contributed to sanctions busting. This is my personal account of my two years as Chair of the Angola Sanctions Committee.

II The war

Much of the time I spent representing Canada on the Security Council in 1999 and 2000 was devoted to making sanctions against UNITA work so that the murderous 27-year civil war could finally be brought to an end. That war was the quintessential "proxy war" through which East/West rivalries played out on this foreign field with brutal indifference. It was also the "perfect civil war". One side had oil and the other diamonds, so neither could outspend the other into submission. Well over half a million Angolans had been killed and by the summer of 1998, the number of displaced people in Angola had risen to 1.3 million; some 10 per cent of the country's population.

Jonas Malheiro Savimbi, founder and leader of UNITA, ran and lost the 1992 Angolan presidential elections. Incumbent President José Eduardo dos Santos, President of the People's Movement for the Liberation of Angola (MPLA), who had ruled Angola since it won independence from Portugal in 1975, clearly won in what the UN declared to be a free and fair election. With the 1992 election, there was finally an internationally recognised winner and loser so, at least theoretically, the UN could engage to stop the war. To this end, the Security Council put in place:

1. An arms and petroleum embargo in 1993 (UNSC Res 864 [1993] para. 19), which also established the Security Council's Angolan Sanction Committee;
2. Travel sanctions against senior UNITA officials (UNSC Res 1127 [1997] operative para. 4) and, later, in October 1997, UNSC Res 1135, which requested member states to provide information on the measures they had adopted to implement the travel ban (few did); and
3. Financial sanctions against UNITA and the prohibition of direct or indirect export from Angola of all diamonds originating from territories not controlled by the Government of Angola (UNSC Res 1173 [1998] operative para. 12b).

All of these measures had largely been ignored by a wide range of sanctions busters, as they – and everybody else – believed that there was no cohesion, no sense of purpose and no will within the Security Council to see these measures enforced, thereby bringing the murderous civil war to an end.

The Angolan civil war seemed destined to go on indefinitely, all the while exacting a terrible human toll that few knew much about. In 1999, the United Nations International Children's Emergency Fund (UNICEF) announced that Angola was the worst place in the entire world in which to be a child (Save the Children [1999]).

III Canada's role on the Sanctions Committee

The UNSC Angolan Sanctions Committee played a determinate role in bringing peace to Angola. Angola was subject to Western and Soviet influences throughout the Cold War and did not benefit from the peace dividend at its termination. Civil war continued to rage. When Canada was elected to a sixth term on the Security Council in October 1998, I was chosen Chair of the Angolan Sanctions Committee. I knew we would share our term with Namibia, a staunch supporter of the Angolan ruling party's Movement for the Liberation of Angola (MPLA) and a steadfast opponent of Savimbi's UNITA. My Namibian colleague was Martin Andjaba, Namibia's

Permanent Representative to the UN from 1996 to 2010. From the first meeting I chaired of the Angolan Sanctions Committee on 1 January 1999, it became clear, however, that vestigial East/West tensions and mistrust continued to inform the way many members of the Council approached the Angolan civil war.

Further, I knew that we Canadians did not have the resources to know who was doing what to whom with regard to the non-application of the various sanctions that had been passed over the previous six years. However, if we were to make those measures work, we were going to have to be able to access that kind of information.

We had to develop our own research and investigative capabilities, and to come up with ones that would be at least somewhat independent of the political pressures which member states exert on their own diplomats, as well as by friends and foes alike through classic diplomatic pressure.

Rather quickly, we came up with the concept of an "Expert Panel" that would report to me as Chair of the Committee and would study the effectiveness of all of the relevant sanctions in place. It was formalised when we proposed and the Security Council adopted Resolution 1237 on 7 May 1999, deploring the deteriorating situation in Angola and establishing an "independent" expert panel.

IV Creation of a Panel of Experts

The essential essence of the Expert Panel was its independence (including from the Canadian Government). A Panel of Experts was formalised when the Security Council adopted Resolution 1237 on 7 May 1999, "deploring the deteriorating situation in Angola, which is primarily due to the refusal of UNITA, under the leadership of Mr. Jonas Savimbi, to comply with its obligations under the 'Acordos de Paz,' the *Lusaka Protocol*, and relevant Security Council resolutions" (UNSC Res 1237 [1999] operative para. 3).

The resolution condemned the continued "indiscriminate attacks by UNITA against the civilian population of Angola" (UNSC Res 1237 [1999] operative para. 4) and decided to establish "independent" expert panels for a period of six months (later extended) with the mandate to:

i) collect information and investigate reports, including through visits to the countries concerned, relating to the violation of the measures imposed against UNITA with respect to arms and related war matériel, petroleum and petroleum products, diamonds and the movement of UNITA funds and information on military assistance, including mercenaries;
ii) identify parties aiding and abetting the violations of the above-mentioned measures; and
iii) recommend measures to end such violations and to improve the implementation of the above-mentioned measures. (UNSC Res 1237 [1999] operative para. 6a–c)

V Access to the Angolan government

I travelled to Angola, Botswana, the DRC, Namibia, South Africa, Zambia and Zimbabwe in May 1999 reported in S/1999/644 as a 23-page report to the Council on 4 June 1999. Fourteen specific recommendations were made, many of which sought to inform, manage and direct the work of the expert panels (subsequently collapsed into a single panel).

A month later, in July 1999, I travelled to Europe (Belgium, France, Ukraine, the United Kingdom) and Algeria (to address the Organization for African Unity (OAU) Council of Ministers), and reported to the Council in a second report (S/1999/829) which made 5 additional recommendations, bringing the total to 19 recommendations.

Just before Christmas 1999, I learned from a small piece in *Jeune Afrique* that General Jacinto Bandua, Savimbi's chief of logistics, had crossed over to the MPLA side. I immediately called then Angolan Foreign Minister Joao Bernardo de Miranda, asking if I might have immediate access to General Bandua the following week in Angola.

Minister Miranda arranged for General Bandua and other key defectors from UNITA to be made available, and in Luanda we filmed 15 hours of their videotaped testimony in a makeshift studio, gaining a detailed appreciation of the scope and detail of how UN sanctions were being violated.

On 10 March 2000, we presented the Council with a 50-page "Report of the UN Panel of Experts on Violations of Security

Council Sanctions Against UNITA" (S/2000/203), otherwise known as the Fowler Report, which contained 39 specific recommendations. Using rigorous rules of evidence, the Panel named the most egregious sanctions busters – including sitting heads of government – thereby discouraging them and others from such activities. It concluded:

> It is clear from information received by the Panel during the course of its investigations [...], together with recent actions taken by Governments, and efforts by non-governmental organizations and others, that these measures have already made it harder for UNITA to sell its diamonds, and more expensive for UNITA to acquire arms and military equipment as a result of the increased risks of exposure to its suppliers and transporters.
>
> It is hoped that this effect will be significantly magnified by the release of the Panel's findings, conclusions, and recommendations.
>
> The Panel [...] hopes that the Council will now seize this opportunity to demonstrate that international sanctions **can be made to work effectively**, that Member States and others **will** be held accountable to the international community for their actions, and that the Council **means what it says** when it passes resolutions and takes action in support of peace. (emphasis added) (S/2000/203 [2000] para. 182)

A month later, on 18 April 2000, the Security Council passed Resolution 1295, which operationalised the Panel's recommendations, thereby lending them the force and authority of the Council. A Monitoring Mechanism was established to ensure adequate follow-up.

VI Conclusion

The Expert Panel could do and say things that national delegations and individual diplomats could not. Additionally, the vehicle of the "Expert Panel" allowed us to ensure that all key countries on the Security Council were represented, making it more difficult for them to distance themselves from the Panel's findings and conclusions.

What did we achieve?

1. First, we exposed and explained the link between Savimbi's dirty diamonds and his ability to continue to wage his merciless war.
2. Using rigorous rules of evidence, we named the most egregious sanctions busters – including sitting heads of government – thereby discouraging them and others from such activities.
3. The full-service international arms merchants, who had also been Savimbi's principal diamond traders, became much less interested in supplying UNITA in the field.
4. Once Savimbi's UNITA was no longer able to meet its materiel needs, Angola's armed forces defeated him in battle early in 2002, thereby ending the 27-year civil war.

We would, however, not have been able to do these things without the active and prior engagement of outstanding non-governmental organisations. Indeed, to a significant extent, they had initiated investigations into the sanctions busting activity. Without their input and constant pressure, it is doubtful that the Committee would have improved the efficacy of the sanctions. Specifically, Global Witness published a seminal paper titled "A Rough Trade – The Role of Companies and Governments in the Angolan Conflict" in 1998, and Human Rights Watch [1999] offered invaluable expertise and advice.

The successes were many, including: (1) Savimbi found it increasingly difficult to find markets for his diamonds; (2) governments and leaders in Eastern Europe and Africa were embarrassed by being named and shamed as sanctions busters and international criminals in the Panel's report; and (3) governments in Western Europe and the United States began to rethink their policies of turning a blind eye to the activities of Savimbi's international representatives and fundraisers.

The international arms merchants, who had also been Savimbi's principal diamond traders (including Russian arms dealer Viktor Bout), became – considering the significantly enhanced scrutiny occasioned by our report – much less interested in supplying UNITA with military capabilities. The risk began to exceed the benefit for them, and they sought other, less visible, less exposed clients. Once Savimbi's UNITA was no longer able to meet its logistics' needs, Angola's armed forces defeated him in battle, thereby ending the 27-year civil war.

In April 2012, Viktor Bout, known as the "merchant of death", was sentenced by a New York judge to a 25-year jail term. Readers of the report of the 2000 UN Panel of Experts on Violations of Security Council Sanctions Against UNITA will note that Mr Bout is mentioned several times (see paragraphs 26, 29 and 165 and footnote 7). There is no doubt in my mind that he was a significant contributor to the misery suffered by the people of Angola over a generation.

Bibliography

Literature

Global Witness, 'Rough Trade: The Role of Companies and Governments in the Angolan Conflict' Global Witness, London (December 1998) <https://www.globalwitness.org/en/archive/rough-trade/> accessed 13 July 2024.

Human Rights Watch, 'Angola Unravels: The Rise and Fall of the Lusaka Peace Process' Human Rights Watch, (13 September 1999) <https://www.hrw.org/report/1999/09/13/angola-unravels/rise-and-fall-lusaka-peace-process> accessed 13 July 2024.

Save the Children, 'Save the Children Hotline News' *Relief Web* (1 October 1999) <https://reliefweb.int/report/angola/save-children-hotline-news-01-oct-1999> accessed 7 June 2024.

Documents

UNSC Res 864 (15 September 1993) UN Doc. S/RES/864.

UNSC Res 1127 (28 August 1997) UN Doc. S/RES/1127.

UNSC Res 1173 (12 June 1998) UN Doc. S/RES/1173.

UNSC Res 1237 (7 May 1999) UN Doc. S/RES/1237.

UNSC Res 1295 (18 April 2000) UN Doc. S/RES/1295.

UNSC, 'Letter Dated 10 March 2000 from the Chairman of the Security Council Committee Established pursuant to Resolution 864 (1993) concerning the Situation in Angola addressed to the President of the Security Council' (10 March 2000) UN Doc. S/2000/203.

UNSC, 'Report of the Chairman's visit to Central and Southern Africa, May 1999' (4 June 1999) UN Doc. S/1999/644.

UNSC, 'Report on the Chairman's visit to Europe and participation in the 70th ordinary session of the Organization of African Unity, July 1999' (28 July 1999) UN Doc. S/1999/829.

32. Belarus

Yuliya Miadzvetskaya

I The vicious circle of sanctions imposition and relaxation (1996–2016)

Relations between Belarus under Aliaksandr Lukashenka and the West have been caught in a vicious circle of sanctions imposition and relaxation. The first sanctions episode against Belarus included a set of diplomatic measures by the European Union (EU) in response to the consolidation of presidential powers by Lukashenka following the 1996 constitutional referendum, which fell short of democratic standards (Silitsky [2005] 87–9), and the expulsion of Western diplomats from their residences in the Drazdy complex in 1998. As a result, the EU suspended the ratification of the Partnership and Cooperation Agreement (PCA) with Belarus, withdrew its support for Belarus's accession to the Council of Europe, reduced its contacts with Minsk to a technical level and enacted over 100 temporary travel bans against Belarusian officials (Van Elsuwege [2010] 5; Portela [2011] 490).

The second sanctions episode against Belarus is linked to the country's continued shift towards autocracy (Silitsky [2005] 92–4). Indeed, in 2004, the EU sanctioned four Belarusian officials allegedly involved in forced disappearances and the subsequent obstruction of justice in 1999–2000 (Council Common Position 2004/661/CFSP [2004]). The same year, the EU targeted more individuals responsible, respectively, for the fraudulent parliamentary elections and referendum of 2004 (Council Common Position 2004/848/CFSP [2004]). The United States, in turn, enacted into law the Belarus Democracy Act (2004), which provided for the introduction of sanctions against Belarus. Both the EU and the United States added to their Belarus sanctions lists those involved in the flawed 2006 presidential elections, which were accompanied by the repression of peaceful demonstrations (Council Common Position 2006/362/CFSP [2006]; Executive Order 13405 [2006]). In contrast to the EU, which mainly sanctioned Belarusian officials, the United States targeted large Belarusian enterprises such as the Belarusian State Concern for Oil and Chemistry "Belneftekhim", which unites petrochemical companies in Belarus (OFAC [2007]).

This sanctions episode did not last long. Both the EU and the United States partially relaxed their sanctions against Belarus in 2008 following the country's rapprochement with the West. In 2008, the Belarusian authorities released political prisoners and slightly distanced themselves from Russia by refusing to recognise the breakaway regions of Abkhazia and South Ossetia in the aftermath of the Russo-Georgian war (Portela [2011] 493–5). However, Belarus's rapprochement with the West pursued exclusively an economic rationale and did not bring any substantial changes to the country's political system. In fact, Minsk sought to regain its Western foreign policy vector in order to compensate for the decline in Belarus–Russia relations as a result of the 2007 energy crisis and, consequently, to increase Minsk's leverage vis-à-vis Moscow in order to obtain economic concessions from Russia (Portela [2011] 495–7; Pierson-Lyzhina [2021] 341). Brussels, for its part, sought to build a "ring of friends" (Ferrero-Waldner [2004]) on its borders by launching the Eastern Partnership initiative in 2009 and wanted Belarus to be part of it. Minsk was only interested in the financial benefits that this project could provide and paid only lip service to the Union's democratisation agenda.

Minsk's 2008–10 reconciliation with the West was not meant to last. In 2011, the EU and the United States imposed targeted restrictive measures and an arms embargo on the Belarusian regime in response to the fraudulent 2010 presidential elections and repression (Council Decision 2011/69/CFSP [2011]). The sanctions lists were further extended in response to the flawed 2012 parliamentary elections in Belarus. Nevertheless, Russia's annexation of Crimea and the destabilisation of Donbas in 2014 paved the way for a new turn in relations between Belarus and the West. Given the positive role that Belarus played as a platform for negotiations on Donbas in 2014–15 and the release of political prisoners in 2015, the EU and the United States reciprocated by first suspending sanctions in 2015 and then lifting them in 2016, despite remaining concerns about the human rights situation in the country (Miadzvetskaya and Challet [2022] 14). The EU and the United States were ready to tolerate an autocracy in Belarus and proceed with the premature lifting of sanctions, despite the fact that Belarus has never taken any serious steps towards democratisation.

II Belarus under unprecedented sanctions (post-2020): from domestic crisis to co-aggressor status

The fourth sanctions episode began in 2020 when Belarus held presidential elections marked by blatant disregard for electoral norms and the brutal repression of peaceful protesters. Over 33 000 people were sentenced to administrative detention and fines; the total number of individuals recognised as political prisoners has exceeded 3 945 over the past five years (Human Rights Centre "Viasna" website). The first packages of sanctions consisted of modest targeted measures enacted by the EU, the United States, the United Kingdom and Canada. The forced landing of a Ryanair flight from Athens to Vilnius and the instrumentalisation of migrants at Belarus–EU borders (Belarus encouraged and facilitated the movement of third-country nationals to its borders with the EU) led to a further escalation of sanctions against Belarus, which included a flight ban as well as a number of sectoral import (i.e. petroleum and potash products) and export restrictions (i.e. goods used for the production or manufacturing of tobacco products) (Miadzvetskaya and Challet [2022] 11; Council Decision (CFSP) 2021/908 [2021] Article 2a; Council Decision (CFSP) 2021/1031 [2021] Articles 2e, 2f, 2g).

The number of sanctioning countries has also gradually increased: Iceland, Liechtenstein, Norway, Albania, Bosnia and Herzegovina, Montenegro, North Macedonia and Ukraine aligned themselves with the EU sanctions against Belarus (Statement by the High Representative on behalf of the EU on the alignment of certain countries concerning restrictive measures in view of the situation in Belarus and the involvement of Belarus in the Russian aggression against Ukraine [2023]), while Switzerland joined the EU sanctions regime.

In the aftermath of the Russian aggression against Ukraine in 2022, the level of restrictions against Belarus reached a peak. Australia, Japan and New Zealand extended some of their Russia-related restrictions to Belarus given its role as a co-aggressor and supporter of the Russian invasion of Ukraine. In addition to the sanctions already in place, the EU, the United Kingdom, the United States and Canada imposed additional restrictions, including targeted and sectoral measures as well as financial restrictions (SWIFT ban and a prohibition on transactions with the Central Bank of Belarus) (Council Decision (CFSP) 2022/399 [2022]). The EU banned the import of wood, cement, iron, steel and rubber products that, along with previously targeted petroleum and potash products, account for 70 per cent of Belarus's exports to the EU (Council Decision (CFSP) 2022/356 [2022]; Guarascio [2022]).

Minsk responded to Western sanctions with asymmetric countermeasures. The Belarusian authorities banned a number of officials from the sanctioning states from entering Belarus and the Union State of Russia and Belarus (Statement by the Ministry of Foreign Affairs of the Republic of Belarus in connection with the decisions of the Council of the European Union [2020]), adopted an import ban on a number of goods originating from unfriendly states (The Council of Ministers of the Republic of Belarus Resolution No. 700 [2021]) and issued a list of states that take unfriendly actions against Belarus (The Council of Ministers of the Republic of Belarus Resolution No. 209 [2022]).

The EU, the United States and their allies are considering a closer alignment of their restrictions against Belarus and Russia in order to close existing loopholes in the sanctions regime against Russia and to prevent sanctions circumvention through Belarus (Gijs et al. [2024]). Such alignment is particularly relevant for highly sensitive goods and technologies in the aviation, space and defence industries, as well as for various IT services that could contribute to Russia's military and technological enhancement. While most Russia-specific restrictions were extended to Belarus (Council Decision (CFSP) 2024/1864 [2024]), there are also advocates (Italy, Portugal and Spain) for some easing of sanctions on Belarusian potash used in agricultural fertilisers in order to address growing food security concerns (Jozwiak [2024]). Questions also persist as to whether partial sanctions relief could be offered in exchange for the release of political prisoners in Belarus. While the re-engagement with the Belarusian authorities is generally discouraged, there is also recognition that the sanctions pressure contributes to the broader isolation of the country and its population from the West.

Against this backdrop, sanctioning States are caught in a delicate balancing act: they must exert pressure on the Belarusian authorities without compromising their ability to shape developments in the country in the future. The sanctions regime against Belarus, thus, remains subject to constant changes, updates and legal creativity, which are worthy of further study.

Bibliography

Literature

Miadzvetskaya Y and Challet C, 'Are EU Restrictive Measures really Targeted, Temporary and Preventive? The Case of Belarus' (2022) 6(1) *Europe and the World: A Law Review* 1.

Pierson-Lyzhina E, 'Belarus's Oscillating Foreign Policy toward the EU: From Engagement to Retrenchment (1994–2021)' (2021) 63(3–4) *Canadian Slavonic Papers* 338.

Portela C, 'The European Union and Belarus: Sanctions and Partnership?' (2011) 9(4) *Comparative European Politics* 486.

Silitski V, 'Preempting Democracy: The Case of Belarus' (2005) 16(4) *Journal of Democracy* 83.

Van Elsuwege P, 'The European Union and the Belarus Dilemma: Between Conditionality and Constructive Engagement' (2010) *Proceedings of the Institute for European Studies* 7–20.

Documents

Belarus Democracy Act (20 October 2004).

Council Common Position 2004/661/CFSP concerning restrictive measures against certain officials of Belarus (24 September 2004) OJ L301/67.

Council Common Position 2004/848/CFSP amending Common Position 2004/661/CFSP concerning restrictive measures against certain officials of Belarus (13 December 2004) OJ L367/35.

Council Common Position 2006/362/CFSP amending Common Position 2006/276/CFSP concerning restrictive measures against certain officials of Belarus (18 May 2006) OJ L134/45.

Council Decision (CFSP) 2021/1031 amending Council Decision 2012/642/CFSP concerning restrictive measures in view of the situation in Belarus (24 June 2021) OJ L224/15.

Council Decision (CFSP) 2022/356 amending Decision 2012/642/CFSP concerning restrictive measures in view of the situation in Belarus (2 March 2022) OJ L67/103.

Council Decision (CFSP) 2022/399 amending Decision 2012/642/CFSP concerning restrictive measures in view of the situation in Belarus and the involvement of Belarus in the Russian aggression against Ukraine (9 March 2022) OJ L82/9.

Council Decision (CFSP) 2024/1864 amending Decision 2012/642/CFSP concerning restrictive measures in view of the situation in Belarus and the involvement of Belarus in the Russian aggression against Ukraine (29 June 2024) OJ L.

Council Decision (CFSP) 2021/908 amending Decision 2012/642/CFSP concerning restrictive measures in view of the situation in Belarus (4 June 2021) OJ L197/3.

Council Decision 2011/69/CFSP amending Council Decision 2010/639/CFSP concerning restrictive measures against certain officials of Belarus (31 January 2011) OJ L28/40.

Executive Order 13405 Blocking Property of Certain Persons Undermining Democratic Processes or Institutions in Belarus (16 June 2006) Federal Register Vol 71, No. 118.

Ferrero-Waldner B, Speaking note, Press Conference to launch first seven Action Plans under the European Neighbourhood Policy (9 December 2004) <https://ec.europa.eu/commission/presscorner/detail/en/SPEECH_04_529> accessed 26 June 2024.

Gijs C, Zimmermann A and Verhelst K, 'Germany, France Fight for Putin's Oligarchs to Get Their BMWs and Mercedes' *Politico* (6 June 2024) <https://www.politico.eu/article/bmw-mercedes-vladimir-putin-russia-germany-france/> accessed 26 June 2024.

Guarascio F, 'EU Bans 70% of Belarus Exports to Bloc with New Sanctions over Ukraine Invasion' *Reuters* (2 March 2022) <https://www.reuters.com/world/europe/eu-approves-new-sanctions-against-belarus-over-ukraine-invasion-source-2022-03-02/> accessed 31 July 2024.

Human Rights Centre 'Viasna' website <https://spring96.org/en/news/101223> accessed 25 June 2024.

Jozwiak R, 'Wider Europe Briefing: The EU's Latest Attempt to Hit Russia (and Belarus)

Yuliya Miadzvetskaya

with Sanctions' *Radio Free Europe* (13 May 2024) <https://www.rferl.org/a/wider-europe-rikard-jozwiak-eu-sanctions-russia-belarus/32944303.html> accessed 25 June 2024.

OFAC, Additional Designations of Entities Pursuant to Executive Order 13405 (19 November 2007) Federal Register Vol 72 No. 222.

Statement by the High Representative on behalf of the EU on the alignment of certain countries concerning restrictive measures in view of the situation in Belarus and the involvement of Belarus in the Russian aggression against Ukraine (21 August 2023).

Statement by the Ministry of Foreign Affairs of the Republic of Belarus in connection with the decisions of the Council of the European Union of 2 October 2020 (2 October 2020).

The Council of Ministers of the Republic of Belarus Resolution No. 700 "On the application of special measures in relation to certain types of goods" (6 December 2021).

The Council of Ministers of the Republic of Belarus Resolution No 209 "On the list of foreign states committing unfriendly actions towards Belarusian legal entities and (or) individuals" (6 April 2022).

The US Department of the Treasury, Press Releases 'Treasury Targets Lukashenko-controlled Petrochemical Conglomerate' (13 November 2007) <https://home.treasury.gov/news/press-releases/hp676> accessed 27 June 2024.

33. Cuba

SUSANNE GRATIUS

I Introduction

US unilateral embargo and extraterritorial sanctions against Cuba, aimed at the regime's breakdown, are the second oldest and least successful sanctions system in the world. It was imposed in 1962, as a reaction to the nationalization of former US properties on the island by the Cuban Revolution in 1959. Diplomatic relations were also suspended. The bilateral conflict forced the revolutionary regime, governed until 2006 by Fidel Castro, to establish relations with the Soviet Union and other socialist countries to compensate for the economic losses caused by the US sanctions system and to replace its asymmetric relationship with Washington by its accession to the Council for Mutual Economic Assistance (COMECON) in 1972.

In the post–Cold War, when Cuba lost its main partners in the former socialist bloc COMECON and was about to collapse (its gross domestic product [GDP] dropped by one-third), the US administration established two laws that imposed extraterritorial sanctions to increase pressure and provoke an economic collapse of the Castro regime: the so-called Torricelli Law in 1992 and the Helms–Burton Law, approved in 1996. Both generated a conflict with the European Union (EU) and European companies whose investments in Cuba were threatened by both laws (Roy [2000]). The Helms–Burton Law codified the embargo, which can only be lifted by the US Congress.

The unilateral US sanctions regime against Cuba clearly failed to accomplish its main goal: the breakdown of the revolutionary regime that has governed the island since 1959. Its second goal, to isolate Cuba, has been equally unsuccessful: the island holds diplomatic relations with Canada, the EU, China and many other countries, including its Latin American and Caribbean neighbors and, since 2014, even the United States (see Adler-Nissen [2014]).

II The ongoing purposes of the US embargo

Thus, the key question is why the US embargo against Cuba has not been lifted, despite all evidence of its negative or even counterproductive effects. In fact, the US embargo against the island has contributed to stabilizing the revolutionary regime and the single-party system since the Cuban Revolution of 1959. For more than six decades, academics and politicians have written countless papers on the negative economic and political effects of coercion, and a clear majority of US citizens reject it, but the embargo and extraterritorial sanctions are still in place.

There are several explanations for the maintenance of unilateral sanctions:

- Firstly, the United States and Cuba are still trapped in the Cold War dynamics of a bilateral realist political power struggle.
- Secondly, the Cuban-American lobby of Republican hardliners, such as Secretary of State Marco Rubio, defines US Cuban policy.
- Thirdly, in an era of populist and emotional politics, anger, hate and mistrust dominate. Sanctions serve as a form of revenge.
- Finally, sanctions benefit both the US and the Cuban governments: from Washington's viewpoint, they serve as a protective shield against a massive immigration flow, and the Cuban regime uses the discourse of the *blockade* as a scapegoat for economic misery and an argument for the political unity of the Cuban Communist Party (CCP) against a powerful external enemy.

Several attempts have been made to undermine or lift some of the restrictive measures through a soft policy of engagement. Both coercion and engagement coexist in US-Cuba policy (Gratius [2023]). In 1994, after the so-called 'Balsero crisis', when 35 000 Cubans left the island in self-made boats towards the US coast, the United States and Cuba finally agreed on a visa regime of 20 000 people per year and migration flows are regulated today. In 2000, the Democratic administration of President Bill Clinton decided to allow the export of food and medicines to Cuba for cash payments. Since then, remittances and people-to-people contacts, including travel permits and postal communications are allowed under certain circumstances, depending on the respective US administration. In response to these measures of engagement, bilateral trade relations increased, and in 2023, the United States ranked fifth in Cuban imports.

In addition, the United States and Cuba re-established bilateral diplomatic relations in 2014, in parallel discourses by then presidents Barack Obama and Raúl Castro. Obama's official visit to the island in 2016 confirmed a change of policy from coercion to constructive engagement, but the embargo and extraterritorial sanctions remained in place and were not affected by the short bilateral 'honeymoon'. The first Trump administration reimposed – as a concession to the powerful Cuban-American hardliners in Florida – several restrictions on people-to-people contacts, and qualified the Castro regime as a communist threat. Some of these restrictions were lifted by President Joseph Biden (2021–25), but US-Cuba policy remained practically the same.

III The ineffectiveness of the US sanctions regime

For nearly six decades, US sanctions and hostility have offered the revolutionary regime an excuse for economic hardship and the maintenance of the single-party system as a protective shield against the external enemy, the United States. After the end of the Cold War, the nationalist discourse against US imperialism and the potential threat of military intervention, following the example of the failed attempt in the Cuban Bay of Pigs in 1962, replaced the former Marxist-Leninist rhetoric under the strategic alliance with the Soviet Union. The revitalization of the national myths of Liberator José Martí and the Cuban Revolution served to maintain a highly centralized civil-military regime based on the Revolutionary Armed Forces and the CCP.

The failure of the sanctions system, reinforced in the 1990s by the United States to provoke the end of the Castro regime, is evident, as well as its rally-around-the-flag effects and anti-US sentiments in Cuba. Apart from reinforcing the legitimation of the revolutionary regime, the embargo and other sanctions also served to gain new international allies: each year, the Cuban government wins with an overwhelming majority the vote at the UN General Assembly against the US embargo, whereas the United States has only been supported by its loyal ally Israel and minor allies. Another negative side effect of unilateral US sanctions is the replacement of economic ties by alternative partners such as Canada, Brazil, China, Mexico, Russia and the EU. Particularly, the latter has replaced Cuba's historically close relations with the United States: in 2016, the EU signed a bilateral Cooperation and Political Dialogue Agreement with Cuba and ranked first in 2023 in the country's trade exchanges, investment and development cooperation flows (Gratius [2023]).

The unequal struggle against the superpower United States also attracted many countries of the Global South to express their solidarity with the Cuban regime, augmenting its global legitimacy and international recognition. The group of friends of Cuba is an example of this counterproductive effect of unilateral US sanctions by encouraging the creation of anti-imperialist alliances in the South. In 2024, Cuba was accepted as an associate member in the powerful BRICS group (Mongan [2024]).

IV Conclusion

Why are sanctions still in place if they are highly ineffective? The main reason for their maintenance is the powerful Cuban American lobby in US exile that still defends the embargo (Florida International University [2024]) and dominates politics in the swing state of Florida and in the US Congress. Consequently, the logic of the sanctions regime is a domestic one, while foreign policy objectives have long lost their appeal and sense.

Bibliography

Literature

Adler-Nissen R, 'Stigma Management in International Relations: Transgressive Identities, Norms, and Order in International Society' (2014) 68 *International Organization* 143.

Domingo E and Barrera S, 'La conformación de la política de Estados Unidos hacia Cuba: las sanciones como política pública' (2020) 8 *Estudios del Desarrollo Social: Cuba y América Latina* 172.

Domínguez J and others (eds), *Debating US-Cuban Relations: How Shall We Now Play Ball?* (Routledge 2017).

Drezner DX, 'Sanctions Sometimes Smart: Targeted Sanctions in Theory and Practice' (2011) 13 *International Studies Review* 96.

Gratius S and Mongan M (eds), *El futuro de la Cuba postrevolucionaria* (Tecnos 2023).
Leogrande V, 'A Policy Long Past its Expiration Date: US Economic Sanctions against Cuba' (2015) 82 *Social Research* 939.
Leogrande V, 'Normalizing US-Cuba Relations: Escaping the Shackles of the Past' (2015) 91 *International Affairs* 473.
López-Levy A, 'Sanciones secundarias en el triángulo Estados Unidos-Unión Europea-Cuba' (2020) 9 *Revista CIDOB d'Afers Internacionals* 87.
Roy J, *Cuba, the United States and the Helms-Burton Doctrine: International Reactions* (University Press of Florida 2000).
Vidal P, 'El impacto económico de las sanciones estadounidense a Cuba, 1994–2020' (2022) Documento de Trabajo 1, Real Instituto Elcano, Madrid.
Zimbalist A, 'Failed on All Counts: El embargo de Estados Unidos a Cuba' in Santamaría García A and Azcona JM (eds), *0 millas: Relaciones Económicas Cuba-Estados Unidos, 1898–2020* (Dykinson 2021) 217.

Documents

Cuban Liberty & Democratic Solidarity Act of 1996, Pub. L. No. 104–114, 110 Stat. 785 (1996), Washington DC.
Florida International University, *The 2022 FIU Cuba Poll. How Cuban Americans in South Florida View US Policies towards Cuba, Critical National Issues and the Upcoming Election* (FIU 2022).
Obama B, Statement by the President on Cuba Policy Changes, The White House, Office of the Press Secretary, 17 December 2014<https://obamawhitehouse.archives.gov/the-press-office/2014/12/17/statement-president-cuba-policy-changes>.

SUSANNE GRATIUS

34. Democratic People's Republic of Korea

Laura Di Gianfrancesco

I Introduction

The United Nations Security Council (UNSC) has adopted numerous resolutions imposing and strengthening sanctions on the Democratic People's Republic of Korea (DPRK) in response to its nuclear and missile activities (see chapter on Sanctions for nuclear non-proliferation). Between 2006 and 2017, the country conducted six nuclear tests and significantly increased its ballistic missile testing. Each resolution condemned these actions, demanding that North Korea cease its unlawful conduct in violation of previous UNSC decisions. The UNSC also required that North Korea return to the 1968 Treaty on the Non-Proliferation of Nuclear Weapons (NPT). Although North Korea acceded to the treaty in 1985, it withdrew in 2003 following allegations of pursuing a nuclear weapons programme. The adoption of sanctions is closely tied to a shift in China's attitude towards North Korea: the missile and nuclear tests conducted in 2006 were perceived as a challenge to a negotiated resolution of the crisis via the Six-Party Talks, which were hosted and chaired by Beijing. The UN sanctions regime against North Korea combines targeted and comprehensive measures affecting the country as a whole. In recent years, as the UNSC has become increasingly paralysed, a group of states has independently imposed autonomous sanctions on the DPRK. These sanctions not only address the nuclear programme but also other threats, including cyber activities.

II The evolution of the UN regime

The expansion of the UN sanctions regime against the DPRK reflects an action–reaction dynamic in response to its nuclear and missile testing episodes. The initiatives taken by the UNSC can be divided into two distinct phases. The first phase, spanning from Resolution 1718 (2006) to Resolution 2094 (2013), essentially focused on targeted measures aimed at individuals. The second phase, initiated with Resolutions 2270 (2016) and 2321 (2016), marked a transition towards a more comprehensive sanctions regime. During the first phase, the UNSC – apart from the arms embargo on North Korea – primarily targeted its measures (including trade controls, travel bans, and asset freezes) at persons and entities directly involved in the nuclear programme, and on senior government officials. A notable feature of Resolution 1718 was its explicit prohibition on the supply of "luxury goods" to the DPRK, a measure implicitly directed at members of the ruling elite (Joyner [2017] 109; see chapter on Commodity sanctions).

The second phase has been marked by a substantial escalation in the severity of the measures aimed at exercising significant pressure on the Kim regime by targeting specific sectors key to the North Korean economy (Borlini [2017] 333). In addition to the previous measures, the current UN sanctions regime, following the adoption of Resolution 2397 (2017), includes a ban on imports from North Korea of electrical equipment, coal, minerals, seafood and other food, and agricultural products, wood, textiles, and stones (see chapter on Trade embargoes); a ban on exports to the DPRK of goods necessary for military and industrial development (industrial machinery, transportation vehicles, and all metals); bans and restrictions on the DPRK's access to energy sources such as condensates and natural gas liquids, crude oil, and refined petroleum products (see chapter on Energy embargo); a ban on providing work authorisations for DPRK nationals overseas, and a requirement to repatriate DPRK nationals earning income; and financial sanctions (see chapter), such as an obligation to close existing branches, subsidiaries, or representative offices of DPRK banks.

Given the key role that DPRK diplomats play in the country's prohibited programmes (UN Panel of Experts [2018] 4), the UNSC has also imposed diplomatic sanctions (see chapter) to prevent North Korea's abuse of privileges and immunities. These measures include the duty to expel DPRK diplomats who act on behalf of or under the direction of designated individuals or entities, as well as financial restrictions, limiting each DPRK diplomatic mission or consular post, along with accredited staff members, to a single bank account. Significantly, the relevant UNSC resolutions also provided for measures specifically aimed at combating sanctions evasion and illicit shipping activities, such as an obligation on member states to inspect cargo, including personal luggage, transiting through their territory to or from North Korea. Maritime interdiction, conducted in accordance with international law, is also regarded as a crucial enforcement mechanism. The UNSC has called upon member states to inspect vessels on the high seas, with the consent of the flag state, when there are reasonable grounds to believe that they are transporting illicit cargo (Kraska [2019]).

III Supplementary and autonomous measures

In 2022, an attempt to adopt a new UNSC resolution aimed at expanding the sanctions regime was blocked by vetoes from China and Russia. Both countries criticised the proposed measures, labelling them as counterproductive and inhumane. The draft decision sponsored by the United States (UNSC Verbatim Record UN Doc. S/PV.9048 [2022]; for the text of the draft see UN Doc. S/2022/431) introduced language on the DPRK's malicious cyber activities, calling upon member states to take appropriate measures within their jurisdiction "to prevent the DPRK and its nationals from using their territories to conduct or facilitate" such malicious activity. Although the UNSC has been unable to tackle cyber activities, these have been addressed by states' autonomous sanctions, which have increasingly complemented UNSC measures against the DPRK.

Notably, the United States has over the years applied a comprehensive package of autonomous measures (Han [2021]), including secondary sanctions in consideration of the central role of the US dollar in international trade and finance, to address not only the nuclear weapons programme but also human rights violations, malicious cyber activities, and, more recently, the DPRK's military and financial cooperation with the Russian Federation.

Various other states, such as Japan (see chapter) have imposed their own autonomous sanctions against the DPRK that go beyond the measures required by UNSC resolutions. The European Union (EU) (see chapter) has adopted additional measures that are intended to complement and reinforce the UN regime in two directions: by creating its own autonomous list of designated individuals and entities subject to sanctions, and by introducing more stringent measures, including a ban on North Korean vessels and aircraft entering EU ports or airports; a total ban on EU investment in the DPRK in all sectors; and a total ban on the sale of refined petroleum products and crude oil to the DPRK (Council Decision (CFSP) 2016/849 and subsequent modifications; Esteban and Portela [2021]).

IV Conclusion

Analysts widely agree that while sanctions have succeeded in isolating the North Korean regime, they have failed to pressure the DPRK into abandoning its nuclear weapons programme (Preble and Willis [2024]). In March 2024, the UNSC failed to adopt a resolution extending the mandate of the UN Expert Panel (see chapter) assisting the Sanctions Committee on the DPRK (see UNSC Verbatim Record UN Doc. S/PV.9591 [2024]), due to a veto by the Russian Federation, which subsequently launched military cooperation with Pyongyang. After 15 years of work, the Panel's Final Report addressed the continuing challenges to the effective implementation of this UN sanctions regime. On the one hand, the Panel focused on the combination of obfuscation methods to evade maritime sanctions, including the fraudulent registration of ships and elaborate techniques of vessel identity laundering. On the other hand, it recognised that the sanctions and their implementation "have unintentionally affected the humanitarian situation and some aspects of aid operations, exacerbating the problems caused by the country's inefficient and ineffective economic policies" (UN Panel of Experts [2024] para. 203).

Bibliography

Literature

Borlini L, 'The North Korea's Gauntlet, International Law and the New Sanctions Imposed by the Security Council' (2017) 26 *Italian Yearbook of International Law* 319.

Esteban M and Portela C, 'EU Sanctions against North Korea: Making a Stringent UN Sanctions Regime Even Tougher' in Casarini N et al. (eds), *The Routledge Handbook of Europe–Korea Relations* (Routledge 2021) 382.

Han B, 'Secondary Sanctions Mechanism Revisited: The Case of US Sanctions against North Korea' in van Bergeijk PAG (ed.), *Research Handbook on Economic Sanctions* (Edward Elgar 2021) 223.

Laura Di Gianfrancesco

Joyner DH, 'UN Counter-Proliferation Sanctions and International Law' in van den Herik (ed.), *Research Handbook on UN Sanctions and International Law* (Edward Elgar 2017) 105.

Kraska J, 'Maritime Interdiction of North Korean Ships under UN Sanctions' (2019) 46 *Ecology Law Quarterly* 215.

Preble KA and Willis CN, 'Trading with Pariahs: North Korean Sanctions and the Challenge of Weaponized Interdependence' (2024) 4 *Global Studies Quarterly*.

Documents

EU Council Decision (CFSP) 2016/849 of 27 May 2016 concerning restrictive measures against the Democratic People's Republic of Korea and repealing Decision 2013/183/ CFSP [2016] OJ L141/79.

UNSC, Final Report of the Panel of Experts Submitted Pursuant to Resolution 2345 (2017) (5 March 2018) S/2018/171.

UNSC, Final Report of the Panel of Experts Submitted Pursuant to Resolution 2680 (2023) (7 March 2024) UN Doc. S/2024/215.

UNSC Res 1718 (14 October 2006) UN Doc. S/RES/1718.

UNSC Res 2094 (7 March 2013) UN Doc. S/ RES/2094.

UNSC Res 2270 (2 March 2016) UN Doc. S/ RES/2270.

UNSC Res 2321 (30 November 2016) UN Doc. S/RES/2321.

UNSC Res 2397 (22 December 2017) UN Doc. S/RES/2397.

LAURA DI GIANFRANCESCO

35. Haiti

Francesco Giumelli

I Introduction

Haiti has faced repeated international sanctions due to political instability, military coups, and human rights abuses. Two major sanctions cases have been imposed on Haiti by the United Nations Security Council (UNSC) (see chapter) primarily since the end of the Cold War: the first began in response to the 1991 military coup and lasted from 1993 to 1994, while the second started in 2022 due to escalating gang violence and political instability. These sanctions were primarily imposed by the Organization of American States (OAS) and the United Nations (UN) to address regime changes, human rights violations, and humanitarian crises.

II Protecting the new world order: 1993–94, the military coup d'etat

In 1991, a military coup overthrew Haiti's first democratically elected government. A military junta took power led by General Raoul Cédras, and the elected President Jean-Bertrand Aristide was forced into exile. Being at the onset of the new world order as defined by President George Herbert Walker Bush, the international community began to play a role in the crisis in defence of the legitimate government. The OAS imposed a voluntary trade embargo, and the United States (see chapter) implemented unilateral measures, such as visa restrictions on supporters of the Cédras regime. In November 1992, the UN General Assembly voted in favour of Aristide's return, and diplomatic efforts intensified. A UN and OAS civilian mission (MICIVIH) was deployed in March 1993, followed by the first UN targeted sanctions, adopted by UNSC Resolution 841 in June 1993.

In August 1993, UN sanctions were suspended following the Governor's Island Agreement, which stipulated conditions for Aristide's return. However, key elements of the agreement were not implemented. In October 1993, the UN Mission in Haiti (UNMIH) was prevented from deployment. On 8 October 1993, as the *USS Harlan County* approached the Port international de Port-au-Prince to participate in training exercises with Haitian authorities, the Haitian Army prevented the ship from docking, and Cédras announced that he would not comply with the previously signed accord, further destabilizing the situation.

Consequently, the UN reinstated oil and arms embargoes with UNSC Resolution 873 (1993), and Resolution 875 (1993) authorized the inspection of cargoes to facilitate the implementation of the measures. The Haitian Parliament attempted to negotiate a resolution in early 1994 without success. Simultaneously, tensions rose between the Clinton administration and US domestic political groups advocating for stronger action against the Cédras regime.

In May 1994, the UN imposed comprehensive sanctions (UNSC Res 917 [1994]) due to worsening human rights violations, extrajudicial killings, and repression under the military regime. Shortly after, Emile Jonassaint was installed as president by the ruling military junta, who immediately intensified crackdowns on political opposition. In July 1994, the OAS and the UN pushed for stronger measures as the humanitarian crisis deepened. At the time, these were some of the most restrictive measures applied against one of the poorest countries in the world, forcing the P5 to pen a note to the president of the UNSC to consider the unintended consequences of sanctions for all future cases (S/300/1995).

With the Cédras regime refusing to comply with international demands and the situation deteriorating, the UN authorized military intervention (UNSC Res 940 [1994]) in July 1994. In mid-September, the United States announced the imminent deployment of a multinational force. However, a last-minute diplomatic effort led by former US President Jimmy Carter secured an agreement for the military junta's departure. Aristide returned to Haiti on 15 October 1994, and the sanctions were lifted the following day.

III The Security Council at the crossroads: the return to sanctions

The deteriorating situation in Haiti in the 2020s provided the opportunity for the Security Council to work together, despite geopolitical tensions, and apply UN sanctions against Haiti for the second time in almost 20 years since the measures were lifted following Aristide's return to Port-au-Prince.

Haiti's prolonged instability worsened following the 2021 assassination of President Jovenel Moïse. Delayed elections, political deadlock, and increasing gang violence, as well as natural disasters, led to an institutional collapse that caused a humanitarian crisis. In July 2022, the UN extended the mandate of its political mission, called the United Nations Integrated Office in Haiti (BINUH), and signalled its readiness to impose sanctions on individuals supporting criminal activities, which were rampant given the breakdown of formal governance. On 21 October 2022, the UNSC unanimously adopted Resolution 2653, imposing travel bans, asset freezes, and an arms embargo on individuals and groups engaged in gang violence and other criminal activities. The resolution marked the first time that the UN recognized criminal networks as a threat to international peace and security (see chapter on Sanctions against organised crime). Gang leader Jimmy Chérizier ("Barbecue") was specifically sanctioned for orchestrating attacks that contributed to economic paralysis and human rights violations.

By November 2022, the Haitian authorities had regained control of vital infrastructure, but gang activity persisted. The humanitarian crisis deepened, with cholera cases surpassing 24 000 by early 2023. A transitional political agreement was reached in December 2022, but internal divisions had re-emerged by mid-2023, and violence escalated further. Despite multiple appeals for an international security force, Haiti's history with UN peacekeeping missions led to a reluctance among potential contributors (most notably the spread of cholera beginning in 2010 with its origins traced to UN peacekeepers: see WHO [2022]). In July 2023, BINUH's mandate was renewed for another year. Kenya offered to deploy police forces in August 2023, but opposition from Haitian civil society and divisions within the UNSC complicated the process. Reports indicated that by late 2023, 80 per cent of Port-au-Prince was under gang control, highlighting the ongoing instability leading to further decisions by the Security Council.

On 2 October 2023, UNSC Resolution 2699 imposed a broader arms embargo on Haiti, addressing illicit arms smuggling fuelling gang violence, and it authorized a Multinational Security Support (MSS) mission to aid Haiti's overwhelmed police. On 19 October, UNSC Resolution 2700 extended sanctions, emphasized the inspection of shipments, and aimed to reinforce arms embargo enforcement. Despite these efforts, gang violence continued to intensify into early 2024. Political transitions also struggled, with protests demanding action and limited progress in the electoral process. In March 2024, a political breakthrough led to the formation of a Transitional Presidential Council (TPC) to manage elections. However, the deployment of the MSS mission was delayed, with the first contingent only arriving in June 2024 due to logistical and political issues. Despite a decrease in gang violence, Haiti's security and humanitarian conditions remained critical in 2024.

IV Reflecting on the effectiveness of sanctions in Haiti

Sanctions can serve three primary functions: coercion, which forces a change in behaviour; constraint, which limits the ability of targets to act; and signalling, which sends a political message or reinforces norms (see chapter on Measuring sanctions effectiveness). The two major cases of sanctions in Haiti – those imposed in the early 1990s and those initiated in 2022 – demonstrate varying degrees of effectiveness across these three dimensions as reported by the UN Sanctions Database.

During the 1993–94 sanctions period, the early measures were effective in coercing Haiti's military leaders to enter negotiations, demonstrating that even the threat of sanctions could influence decision-making. These measures also constrained political manoeuvring and reinforced international norms supporting democratic governance. However, the temporary suspension of sanctions that followed was ineffective, allowing the Cédras regime to regroup and stockpile resources while failing to secure meaningful compliance with democratic commitments. When sanctions were reimposed, they significantly constrained the regime's ability to govern and reinforced diplomatic efforts, but they did not directly coerce Cédras into stepping down. As sanctions intensified, the economic and political costs increased for the regime, but repression also escalated, suggesting that sanctions alone were not sufficient to force change. Their main effect was as a signalling tool, reinforcing the legitimacy of Aristide's government. In the final phase before intervention, sanctions contributed to weakening the de facto regime but were ultimately not decisive. Cédras left power only after the credible threat of military intervention and US-led negotiations, showing that sanctions work best when combined with other policy instruments.

The 2022 sanctions case has so far been largely ineffective in coercing or constraining criminal groups, but its signalling dimension is key to the evaluation. The UN's decision to impose sanctions against gang leaders, particularly Jimmy Chérizier, had minimal impact on security dynamics. The criminal gangs adjusted to sanctions and adapted their activities. The security and humanitarian situations remained dire, with armed gangs allegedly controlling over 80 per cent of Port-au-Prince. Constraints on gangs remain weak also because only one leader has been designated under sanctions, leaving much of Haiti's criminal network untouched. Despite sanctions, gangs continue to grow stronger, diversify their revenue sources, and remain largely unconstrained. However, the primary role of sanctions has been signalling, reinforcing international condemnation of gang violence, and supporting political negotiations. Certainly, weak enforcement, such as the lack of awareness among Haitian authorities about the embargo, undermined the credibility of sanctions, but the decision of the Security Council to adopt sanctions in a novel way sent an important message to both local and international constituencies. Ultimately, if sanctions are designed to have a light impact, then the expectations of their impact on the political and security dynamics in the country should be limited.

V Conclusion

Sanctions on Haiti have been a recurring international response to political crises, human rights abuses, and security threats. Haiti serves as a case study for sanctions in two crucial decades between the twentieth and the twenty-first centuries, from the end of the Cold War to one characterized by a divided UNSC. The two cases are different, yet they serve well the aim of showing both the similarities and novelties of sanctions across time. On the one hand, there are key similarities that demonstrate how studying the case of Haiti can still be relevant today. This refers, for instance, to the need for actors willing to enforce the measures to increase the likelihood of impact and the challenges emerging from dealing with non-cooperative targets. On the other hand, these are measures that define criminal organizations as a threat to international peace and security for the first time, marking an important difference with the past practice of the Security Council. Yet, effectiveness remains questionable. Both coercion and constraint do not seem to have been achieved by sanctions, even though there are mixed assessments when it comes to signalling.

Haiti, however, also reminds us of two truths when it comes to the effectiveness of sanctions. First, the lack of apparent success is not evidence to suggest that a lack of sanctions would lead to a better outcome for Haiti. Second, resorting to sanctions, if embedded in a broader foreign policy strategy, suggests that signalling may work not only towards targets in the crisis, but also as a form of political communication to an international audience. This form of communication is essential to the holding together of an international society and, ultimately, resorting to sanctions also serves that purpose.

Bibliography

Literature

Benton L and Ware G, 'Haiti: A Case Study of the International Response and the Efficacy of Nongovernmental Organizations in the Crisis' (2001) *Small Wars Journal*.

Biersteker T, Hudakova Z and Tourinho M, 'UNSanctionsApp: An Interactive Database of UN Sanctions' (*UNSanctionsApp*, August 2023) <https://unsanctionsapp.com>.

Cortright D and Lopez GA, *The Sanctions Decade: Assessing UN Strategies in the 1990s* (Lynne Reiner Publishers 2000).

Gibbons DE, *Sanctions in Haiti: Human Rights and Democracy Under Assault* (Praeger 1999).

Kreps SE, 'The 1994 Haiti Intervention: A Unilateral Operation in Multilateral Clothes' (2007) 30(7) *Journal of Strategic Studies* 449.

Malone D, 'Haiti and the International Community: A Case Study' (1997) 39(2) *Survival* 126.

Martin I, 'Haiti: International Force or National Compromise?' (1999) 31(3) *Journal of Latin American Studies* 711.

Francesco Giumelli

Morris J, 'Force and Democracy: UN/US Intervention in Haiti' (1995) 3(2) *International Peacekeeping* 391.
Swindells F, 'UN Sanctions in Haiti: A Contradiction Under Articles 41 and 55 of the UN Charter' (1996–1997) 20 *Fordham International Law Journal* 1878.
von Hippel K, *Democracy by Force: US Intervention in the Post-Cold War World* (Cambridge University Press 2000).
Werleigh C, 'The Use of Sanctions in Haiti' in Cortright D and Lopez GA (eds), *Economic Sanctions: Panacea or Peacebuilding* (Westview Press 1995) 162.
World Health Organization. 'Cholera- Haiti' (WHO, 13 December 2022) <https://www.who.int/emergencies/disease-outbreak-news/item/2022-DON427> accessed 10 February 2025.
Zagaris B, 'Transnational Organized Crime' (2022) 38 *International Enforcement Law Reporter* 450.
Zaidi S, 'Humanitarian Effects of the Coup and Sanctions in Haiti' in Weiss T, Minear L, Cortright D and Lopez GA (eds), *Political Gain and Civilian Pain: The Humanitarian Impacts of Economic Sanctions* (Rowman & Littlefield 1997) 189.

Documents

UNSC Res 841 (16 June 1993) UN Doc. S/RES/841.
UNSC Res 873 (13 October 1993) UN Doc. S/RES/873.
UNSC Res 875 (16 October 1993) UN Doc. S/RES/875.
UNSC Res 917 (6 May 1994) UN Doc. S/RES/917.
UNSC Res 940 (31 July 1994) UN Doc. S/RES/940.
UNSC Res 2653 (21 October 2022) UN Doc. S/RES/2653.
UNSC Res 2699 (2 October 2023) UN Doc. S/RES/2699.
UNSC Res 2700 (19 October 2023) UN Doc. S/RES/2700.
Letter dated 13 April 1995 from the Permanent Representatives of China, France, the Russian Federation, the United Kingdom of Great Britain and Northern Ireland and the United States of America to the United Nations Addressed to the President of the Security Council (13 April 1995) UN Doc S/300/1995.

FRANCESCO GIUMELLI

36. Iran

MANUEL HERRERA

I Introduction

Modern sanctions against Iran began with the Tehran embassy hostage crisis, leading to US economic actions that were reimposed and expanded in 1987 due to Iran's conduct during the Iran–Iraq war and its support for terrorism (Hewitt and Nephew [2019]; Clawson [2010]).

On the other hand, sanctions linked to its nuclear programme date back to the 1995 Iran and Libya Sanctions Act adopted by the US Congress. However, it was not until 2006 that the first multilateral sanctions package against Iran was adopted. These were the United Nations (UN)-mandated sanctions under Resolution 1737, introduced in December 2006 following Iran's non-compliance with Resolution 1696 regarding uranium enrichment (UNSC Res 1737 [2006]).

Over the following years, at least until 2013, this package of multilateral sanctions imposed by the UN was expanded and/or reaffirmed seven times. In turn, other actors, such as the European Union (EU) and third countries, imposed their own sanctions packages and measures with greater or lesser scope. The Joint Comprehensive Plan of Action (JCPOA), finalised in Vienna on 14 July 2015, constituted a landmark political agreement between Iran, the P5+1 (the five permanent members of the United Nations Security Council [UNSC] – China, France, Russia, the United Kingdom, the United States – plus Germany), and the EU. The deal, which was later endorsed by the UNSC (UNSC Res 2231 [2015]), was based on reciprocal commitments with agreed limits on Iran's nuclear programme and the lifting of most sanctions (Robinson [2023]). However, the US withdrawal from the JCPOA in 2018 reignited tensions, reinstating and broadening economic restrictions (Landler [2018]).

II US sanctions

The historical evolution of US sanctions against Iran spans several decades, shaped by geopolitical shifts and diplomatic strategies. Originating in November 1979 after the Tehran embassy hostage crisis, sanctions froze $8.1 billion of Iranian assets under Executive Order 12170 (Office of the Historian [2019]).

Subsequent sanctions in 1984 during the Iran–Iraq war prohibited arms sales and cut off aid to Iran, aligning with Tehran's adversaries (Takeyh and Maloney [2011]). Comprehensive sanctions in 1995 targeted Iran's nuclear programme and support for designated groups (Iran and Libya Sanctions Act [1996]). Over time, these measures expanded to cover various sectors, including bans on imports and restrictions on financial transactions. They aimed not only at economic pressure but also at human rights concerns and information access.

Sanctions intensified in the early 2010s due to Iran's nuclear activities, leading to a multinational framework targeting Iran's nuclear, missile, energy, and financial sectors (United States Institute of Peace [2011]). While some sanctions were lifted under the JCPOA in 2015–18, the United States withdrew in 2018, imposing additional measures (International Crisis Group [2020]). While there remains much controversy regarding the reasons why the United States abandoned the JCPOA, they could be summarised as the Iranians' reluctance to open a discussion regarding their ballistic missile programme, the Iranians' unwillingness to discuss issues related to the stability and security of the Middle East (i.e. US relations with Saudi Arabia and Israel), and the Israeli government's pressure on the US administration. Thereafter, the Biden administration continued targeted sanctions on Iranian entities, reflecting ongoing security concerns (US Department of the Treasury [2023]).

III The UN sanctions regime

The UNSC has imposed numerous sanctions on Iran due to its non-compliance with nuclear safeguards, as highlighted by the International Atomic Energy Agency (IAEA). These sanctions were triggered by Iran's refusal to suspend enrichment and reprocessing activities, leading to resolutions such as Resolution 1696 in 2006, demanding suspension and threatening sanctions (UNSC Res 1696 [2006]). Subsequent resolutions like Resolution 1737 (2006) compelled Iran to cooperate with the IAEA and imposed sanctions on nuclear-related activities (UNSC Res 1737 [2006]). Other resolutions, like Resolution 1747 (2007) and Resolution 1803 (2008), expanded asset freezes and imposed an arms embargo (UNSC Res 1747 [2007]; UNSC Res 1803 [2008]).

Resolution 2231 (2015) established a timeline for lifting sanctions under the JCPOA (UNSC Res 2231 [2015]). However, efforts to extend the arms embargo on Iran faced challenges, and the embargo expired in 2020 (Plazas [2020]). Despite attempts to expand UN sanctions under a JCPOA "snapback" provision, opposition from UNSC members hindered such efforts (Karimi [2020]). These events illustrate the complex diplomatic landscape surrounding Iran's nuclear programme and the challenges in maintaining international consensus on sanctions and arms control measures.

IV The EU measures

The EU's response to human rights violations in Iran and concerns over its nuclear programme have led to a series of significant sanctions and diplomatic actions. Council Regulation (EU) No. 359/2011, amended by Council Regulation (EU) No. 264/2012, targeted equipment used for internal repression and internet surveillance (Council Regulation (EU) 264/2012 [2012]).

The EU's focus on Iran's nuclear programme intensified in the early 2010s. A report by the EU Council in January 2012 expressed concerns about Iran's nuclear activities (Council of the European Union [2012]), leading to measures restricting trade, financial services, energy industries, and technology collaborations. The EU also froze the assets of Iran's Central Bank and banned trade in precious metals and petrochemical products. Council Decision 2012/635/CFSP reinforced these measures, targeting Iran's nuclear and ballistic programmes (Council Decision (CFSP) 2012/635 [2012]). Notably, the EU compelled the Society for Worldwide Interbank Financial Telecommunication (SWIFT) to disconnect Iranian banks violating sanctions, highlighting the severity of these measures (SWIFT [2012]).

Iran downplayed the impact of these sanctions on its oil revenues but signalled a readiness for drastic measures like closing the Strait of Hormuz (Khalaj [2012]). Iran suspended oil sales to certain EU countries, emphasising tensions amid EU–Iran relations (Reuters [2012]). Despite the lifting of certain sanctions following the JCPOA, recent sanctions against Iranian officials for human rights violations and ongoing restrictions by France, Germany, and the United Kingdom underscore the persistent complexities in EU–Iran relations.

V UK sanctions

In July 2023, following the UK's withdrawal from the EU, British Foreign Secretary James Cleverly announced the introduction of a new sanctions regime specifically tailored to Iran, which would increase the UK's ability to target key decision-makers in Tehran (Reuters [2023]). The Iran Regulations of 2023 came into force on 14 December 2023, with dual objectives: deterring Iran and affiliated groups from hostile actions towards the United Kingdom or other nations and urging Iran to uphold international human rights standards (The Iran (Sanctions) Regulations 2023 SI 2023/1314 [2023]). These regulations replaced the EU-based Iran (Sanctions) (Human Rights) (EU Exit) Regulations 2019 post-Brexit (Houses of Parliament [2019]).

Separately, the United Kingdom maintains a sanctions framework targeting Iran's nuclear capabilities. The Iran Regulations of 2019 were fully enacted on 31 December 2020, ensuring the continuity of sanctions post-Brexit (The Iran (Sanctions) (Nuclear) (EU Exit) Regulations 2019 SI 2019/461 [2019]). Legislative adjustments were made, aligning with the UK's post-EU political landscape. The nuclear-related sanctions aim to compel Iran to fulfil UN mandates and abandon nuclear weapons programmes, in line with Resolution 2231 (UNSC Res 2231 [2015]). Additionally, the United Kingdom enforces a sanctions regime focusing on Iran's human rights practices to encourage compliance with international norms (The Iran (Sanctions) (Human Rights) (EU Exit) Regulations SI 2019/134 [2019]). These frameworks, while replacing EU legislation, reflect the United Kingdom's evolving responsibilities in post-Brexit sanctions targeting Iran.

VI Other third-party sanctions

During the period from 2012 to 2015, many countries implemented significant restrictive measures in alignment with UNSC Resolution 1929 (UNSC Res 1929 [2010]). These actions were coordinated with the United States and the EU to enforce sanctions and address concerns related to Iran's nuclear programme. For instance, China adopted a cautious stance regarding the rapid expansion of its trade and investment relations with Iran, opting to adjust transactional flows to renminbi. This approach helped the Obama administration avoid sanctioning Chinese banks (Voice of America [2010]).

Meanwhile, Australia implemented financial sanctions, travel bans, and an arms embargo on individuals and entities connected to Iran's nuclear and missile programmes (Australian Government – Department of Foreign Affairs and Trade, n.d.). In Canada, the government imposed a ban on trading goods with designated Iranian nationals, established an arms embargo, and restricted various activities related to Iran's oil and gas sectors (Global Affairs Canada [2015]). India, although it banned the export of items that could contribute to Iran's nuclear programme, was reluctant to expand sanctions due to its heavy reliance on Iranian oil imports (Soltaninejad [2017]; Verma and Fabi [2012]). Israel adopted strict measures, prohibiting business and travel to Iran, penalising companies that violated international sanctions, and creating regulations to prevent any trade with Iran (Government of Israel [2020]). In East Asia, both Japan and South Korea imposed sanctions on Iranian banks, investments in Iran's energy sector, and froze assets related to the Iranian nuclear programme (Sang-Hun [2010]). Finally, Switzerland imposed bans on arms sales, dual-use items, and goods related to Iran's oil and gas sector, alongside restrictions on financial services (Geiser [2012]). These measures collectively demonstrate global efforts to enforce sanctions and address proliferation concerns related to Iran's nuclear activities.

VII Effects of sanctions

The impact of sanctions on Iran has been multifaceted, affecting various aspects of its economy, politics, and humanitarian conditions. Economically, sanctions significantly hampered Iran's oil-dominated economy, leading to a decline in exports of petroleum products and hindering the acquisition of materials necessary for its nuclear programme (Yousefi [2020]). This resulted in reduced access to products vital for the oil and energy sectors, causing oil companies to withdraw and impacting oil production (Krause-Jackson [2010]). The sanctions also disrupted Iran's ability to repatriate oil revenues, leading to budget deficits (Iran International [2024]). The Iranian rial faced sharp depreciation and economic volatility, affecting public confidence and necessitating government interventions (Dehghan and Borger [2012]). The political landscape was also shaped by sanctions, with internal effects leading to attempts to impeach President Ahmadinejad (Borszik [2015]). The sanctions contributed to public discontent, leading to violent unrest and protests against economic hardships (Foumani [2022]). The harsh economic conditions, worsened by sanctions, fuelled political tensions and influenced electoral outcomes (Geranmayeh [2020]).

Humanitarian impacts were notable, with shortages of essential medicines due to banking restrictions despite exemptions in sanction regimes (Radio Free Europe [2012]). Cancer treatments, blood clotting medications, and HIV/AIDS treatments became scarce, affecting thousands of patients (Borger and Dehghan [2013]). The sanctions also hindered Iran's response to the COVID-19 pandemic, limiting access to vaccines and essential medical resources (Human Rights Watch [2020]).

The imposition of sanctions on Iran also had notable effects on global oil prices and regional economies. Regarding global oil prices, there have been contrasting viewpoints. The United States projected that Iran's entry into the global oil market could potentially reduce crude oil prices by 10 per cent, leading to significant savings for oil-importing nations such as the United States (De Rosa and Hufbauer [2008]). However, Iranian officials have also warned about oil price fluctuations due to geopolitical tensions, highlighting the interconnectedness of oil markets and regional stability. Iranian Oil Minister Javad Owji emphasised Iran's potential to address the global energy crisis of 2021 if sanctions on its oil and gas industry were lifted (Hafezi [2021]). Energy analysts anticipate a tight oil market amid ongoing economic sanctions against Iran, with differing perspectives between the United States and European countries on Iran's role in stabilising global oil prices (S&P Global Ratings [2022]).

Regionally, the impact of sanctions has been significant. Iran's trade relations with neighbouring countries such as Afghanistan and Iraq, which had seen growth before 2016, faced challenges after the reimposition of secondary sanctions in 2018 (Dehghanpisheh and

Shalizi [2019]). The devaluation of Iran's currency and intensified financial sanctions led to economic hardships, fuelling protests and clashes in major Iranian cities (BBC [2018]). Border regions like Zahedan felt pronounced economic impacts, with increased import costs and reduced export values affecting local economies (BBC [2018]). Iraq, heavily reliant on Iranian wheat exports, experienced rising food prices due to ongoing sanctions (World Food Programme [n.d.]). To mitigate regional economic disruptions, exemptions and extensions were granted for imports of essential goods such as refined fuels and electricity from Iran (Lee [2023]).

Bibliography

Literature

BBC, 'Iran Sanctions: How Iranians are Feeling the Impact' (*BBC*, 5 November 2018) <https://www.bbc.com/news/world-middle-east-46102017> accessed 29 March 2024.

Borger J and Dehghan SK, 'Iran Unable to Get Life-Saving Drugs due to International Sanctions' (*The Guardian*, 13 January 2013) <https://www.theguardian.com/world/2013/jan/13/iran-lifesaving-drugs-international-sanctions> accessed 29 March 2024.

Borszik O, 'International Sanctions against Iran and Tehran's Responses: Political Effects on the Targeted Regime' (2015) 22(1) *Contemporary Politics* 20.

Clawson P, 'U.S. Sanctions' (*United States Institute of Peace*, 11 October 2010) <https://iranprimer.usip.org/resource/us-sanctions> accessed 11 September 2024.

De Rosa DA and Hufbauer GC, 'Normalization of Economic Relations Consequences for Iran's Economy and the United States' (2008) National Foreign Trade Council <https://www.nftc.org/archive/trade/NFTC%20Iran%20Normalizaton%20Book.pdf> accessed 11 September 2024.

Dehghan SK and Borger J, 'Iran's Currency Hits All-Time Low as Western Sanctions Take Their Toll' (*The Guardian*, 1 October 2012) <https://www.theguardian.com/world/2012/oct/01/iran-currency-rial-all-time-low> accessed 28 March 2024.

Dehghanpisheh B and Shalizi H, 'Afghanistan Feels Impact of Iran's Economic Isolation' (*Reuters*, 25 April 2019) <https://www.reuters.com/article/us-iran-afghanistan-returnees/afghanistan-feels-impact-of-irans-economic-isolation-idUSKCN1S10HO/> accessed 29 March 2024.

Foumani M, 'Rage against the Regime: How Iran Erupted after the Death of Mahsa Amini' (*The Guardian*, 23 September 2022) <https://www.theguardian.com/global-development/2022/sep/23/how-iran-erupted-after-mahsa-amini-death-protests> accessed 29 March 2024.

Geiser U, 'Swiss Stop Short of Ban on Trading Iranian Oil' (*Swiss Info*, 5 July 2012) <https://www.swissinfo.ch/eng/swiss-politics/swiss-stop-short-of-ban-on-trading-iranian-oil/33051240> accessed 28 March 2024.

Geranmayeh E, 'Reviving the Revolutionaries: How Trump's Maximum Pressure is Shifting Iran's Domestic Politics – European Council on Foreign Relations' (European Council on Foreign Relations [ECFR], 23 June 2020) <https://ecfr.eu/publication/reviving_the_revolutionaries_how_trumps_maximum_pressure_is_shifting_irans> accessed 29 March 2024.

Hafezi P, 'Iran Determined to Increase its Oil Exports Despite U.S. Sanctions –Oil Minister' (*Reuters*, 1 September 2021) <https://www.reuters.com/world/middle-east/iran-determined-increase-its-oil-exports-despite-us-sanctions-oil-minister-2021-09-01/> accessed 11 September 2024.

Hewitt K and Nephew R, 'How the Iran Hostage Crisis Shaped the US Approach to Sanctions' (*Brookings*, 12 March 2019) <https://www.brookings.edu/articles/how-the-iran-hostage-crisis-shaped-the-us-approach-to-sanctions/> accessed 11 September 2024.

Iran International, 'A $500 Billion Economic Deficit Pushes Iran Toward "Catastrophe"' (*Iran International*, 15 January 2024) <https://www.iranintl.com/en/202401153993> accessed 11 September 2024.

Khalaj M, 'Iran Accuses West of Seeking "Tension"' (*Financial Times*, 2012) <https://www.ft.com/content/147beb06-c35f-11e1-966e-00144feabdc0> accessed 27 March 2024.

Krause-Jackson F, 'Sanctions Cost Iran $60 Billion in Oil Investments, Burns Says' (*Bloomberg*, 1 December 2010) <https://www.bloomberg.com/news/articles/2010-12-01/sanctions-cost-iran-60-billion-in-oil-investments-burns-says> accessed 9 October 2023.

Landler M, 'Trump Abandons Iran Nuclear Deal He Long Scorned' (*The New York Times*, 8 May 2018) <https://www.nytimes.com/2018/05/08/world/middleeast/trump-iran-nuclear-deal.html> accessed 11 September 2024.

Lee M, 'US Extends Sanctions Waiver Allowing Iraq to Buy Electricity from Iran' (*AP News*, 14 November 2023) <https://apnews.com/article/iran-iraq-sanctions-waiver-816c2ba3f8eae10553ed07304c02db0f> accessed 29 March 2024.

Plazas N, 'La ONU rechaza la demanda de EE. UU. de extender el embargo de armas a Irán' (*France 24*, 15 August 2020) <https://www.france24.com/es/20200815-acuerdo-nuclear-iran-eeuu-onu> accessed 11 September 2024.

Radio Free Europe, 'Iran Sanctions Result In Shortages of Cancer Drugs, Heart Medicine' (*Radio Free Europe/Radio Liberty*, 6 May 2012) <https://www.rferl.org/a/iran_sanctions_medicine_shortages/24571398.html> accessed 29 March 2024.

Reuters, 'Britain to Target Iranian Decision Makers with New Sanctions Regime' (*Reuters*, 6 July 2023) <https://www.reuters.com/world/uk/britain-target-iranian-decision-makers-with-new-sanctions-regime-2023-07-06/> accessed 27 March 2024.

Reuters, 'Iran Stops Oil Sales to British and French Firms' (*Reuters*, 19 February 2012) <https://www.reuters.com/article/us-iran-oil-europe-idUSTRE81I07W20120219/> accessed 27 March 2024.

Robinson K, 'What Is the Iran Nuclear Deal?' (*Council on Foreign Relations*, 27 October 2023) <https://www.cfr.org/backgrounder/what-iran-nuclear-deal> accessed 29 March 2024.

S&P Global Ratings, 'Iran's Potential Return to the Oil Market' (*S&PGlobal*, 2022) <https://www.spglobal.com/en/research-insights/featured/markets-in-motion/iran-s-potential-return-to-the-oil-market> accessed 29 March 2024.

Sang-Hun C, 'South Korea Aims Sanctions at Iran' (*The New York Times*, 8 September 2010) <https://www.nytimes.com/2010/09/09/world/asia/09korea.html> accessed 28 March 2024.

Soltaninejad M, 'Iran–India Relations: The Unfulfilled Strategic Partnership' (2017) 73(1) *India Quarterly: A Journal of International Affairs* 21.

Takeyh R and Maloney S, 'The Self-Limiting Success of Iran Sanctions' (2011) 87(6) *International Affairs* 1297.

United States Institute of Peace, 'New U.S. Sanctions on Iran Air and Others – The Iran Primer' (United States Institute of Peace, 23 June 2011) <https://iranprimer.usip.org/blog/2011/jun/23/new-us-sanctions-iran-air-and-others> accessed 11 September 2024.

Verma N and Fabi R, 'Indian Shipping Firms to Carry Iran Crude Despite Reduced Insurance' (*Reuters*, 24 April 2012) <https://www.reuters.com/article/india-oil-iran/exclusive-indian-shipping-firms-to-carry-iran-crude-despite-reduced-insurance-idINDEE83N08H20120424/> accessed 11 September 2024.

Voice of America, 'China Rejects US Concerns About Deals with Iran' (*Voice of America*, 4 August 2010) <https://www.voanews.com/a/china-rejects-us-concerns-about-deals-with-iran-100016424/123307.html> accessed 11 September 2024.

Yousefi Y, 'Oil Market Efficiency: A Case Study for Iranian Economic Prosperity' (*The Sustainable Development Watch*, 9 March 2020) <https://sdwatch.eu/2020/03/oil-market-efficiency-a-case-study-for-iranian-economic-prosperity/> accessed 28 March 2024.

Documents

Australian Government Department of Foreign Affairs and Trade, 'Iran Sanctions Regime' (Australian Government Department of Foreign Affairs and Trade, n.d.) <https://www.dfat.gov.au/international-relations/security/sanctions/sanctions-regimes/iran-sanctions-regime> accessed 11 September 2024.

Council Decision (CFSP) n. 2012/635 of 15 October 2012 amending Decision 2010/413/CFSP concerning restrictive measures against Iran [2012] OJ L282/58.

Council of the European Union, '3142nd Council Meeting Foreign Affairs Brussels' (European Commission, 23 January 2012) <https://ec.europa.eu/commission

/presscorner/detail/en/PRES_12_18> accessed 27 March 2024.

Council Regulation (EU) 264/2012 of 23 March 2012 on amending Regulation (EU) No. 359/2011 concerning restrictive measures directed against certain persons, entities and bodies in view of the situation in Iran [2012] OJ L87/26.

Global Affairs Canada, 'Canadian Sanctions Related to Iran' (Government of Canada, July 15 2024) <https://www.international.gc.ca/world-monde/international_relations-relations_internationales/sanctions/iran.aspx?lang=eng> accessed 11 September 2024.

Government of Israel, 'About the Sanctions Bureau' (Government of Israel, 2020) <https://www.gov.il/en/departments/general/about_sanctions_headquarters> accessed 11 September 2024.

Human Rights Watch, 'US: Ease Sanctions on Iran in COVID-19 Crisis' (Human Rights Watch, 6 April 2020) <https://www.hrw.org/news/2020/04/06/us-ease-sanctions-iran-covid-19-crisis> accessed 11 September 2024.

International Crisis Group, 'The Iran Nuclear Deal at Four: A Requiem?' (2020) International Crisis Group <https://www.crisisgroup.org/middle-east-north-africa/gulf-and-arabian-peninsula/iran/210-iran-nuclear-deal-four-requiem> accessed 11 September 2024.

Iran and Libya Sanctions Act of 1996, Public Law No. 104-172 110 Stat 1541 (1996) <https://www.govinfo.gov/content/pkg/STATUTE-110/pdf/STATUTE-110-Pg1541.pdf> accessed 11 September 2024.

Office of the Historian, 'The Iranian Hostage Crisis – Short History – Department History – Office of the Historian' (State Gov, 2019) <https://history.state.gov/departmenthistory/short-history/iraniancrises> accessed 11 September 2024.

SWIFT, 'Swift Instructed to Disconnect Sanctioned Iranian Banks Following EU Council Decision' (SWIFT, 15 March 2012) <https://www.swift.com/es/node/2891> accessed 11 September 2024.

The Iran (Sanctions) (Human Rights) (EU Exit) Regulations 2019, SI 2019/134.

The Iran (Sanctions) (Nuclear) (EU Exit) Regulations 2019, SI 2019/461.

The Iran (Sanctions) Regulations 2023, SI 2023/1314.

The Sanctions (EU Exit) (Miscellaneous Amendments) (No. 3) Regulations 2020, SI 2020/950.

The Sanctions (EU Exit) (Miscellaneous Amendments) Regulations 2019, SI 2019/843.

The Sanctions (EU Exit) (Miscellaneous Amendments) Regulations 2020, SI 2020/591.

US Department of the Treasury, 'Treasury Designates Iranian Regime Operatives Involved in Assassination Plots in the United States and Abroad' (US Department of the Treasury, 1 June 2023) <https://home.treasury.gov/news/press-releases/jy1513> accessed 11 September 2024.

US Department of the Treasury – Office of Foreign Assets Control, '824. What is the Swiss Humanitarian Agreement' (US Department of the Treasury, 27 February 2020) <https://ofac.treasury.gov/faqs/824> accessed 11 September 2024.

US Department of the Treasury, 'Treasury Sanctions Two Senior Iranian Officials for Serious Human Rights Abuses' (US Department of the Treasury, 13 December 2011) <https://home.treasury.gov/news/press-releases/tg1383> accessed 11 September 2024.

UNSC Res 1385 (27 September 2008) UN Doc. S/RES/1385.

UNSC Res 1696 (31 July 2006) UN Doc. S/RES/1696.

UNSC Res 1737 (23 December 2006) UN Doc. S/RES/1737.

UNSC Res 1747 (24 March 2007) UN Doc. S/RES/1747.

UNSC Res 1803 (3 March 2008) UN Doc. S/RES/1803.

UNSC Res 1929 (9 June 2010) UN Doc. S/RES/1929.

UNSC Res 1984 (9 June 2011) UN Doc. S/RES/1984.

UNSC Res 2049 (7 June 2012) UN Doc. S/RES/2049.

UNSC Res 2231 (20 July 2015) UN Doc. S/RES/2231.

World Food Programme, 'Iraq – Food Prices – Humanitarian Data Exchange' (*HDX*, n.d.) <https://data.humdata.org/dataset/wfp-food-prices-for-iraq> accessed 29 March 2024.

37. Iraq

Clara Portela

I Introduction

With the end of the Cold War in 1989 and the cessation of antagonism between the world's superpowers, members of the United Nations Security Council (UNSC) found themselves able to cooperate on a range of issues, greatly increasing their activity. As a result, UN action to address peace and security experienced its apex, playing a key role in the termination of protracted conflicts through mediation and the dispatch of peacekeeping missions worldwide. It also imposed new sanctions regimes in response to various international security threats. The first sanctions regime imposed in the early days of the post–Cold War period, the embargo on Iraq, was the subject of harsh criticism to the point that the legitimacy of the measures applied was openly questioned.

II Sanctions against Iraq

In 1990, Iraq, under Saddam Hussein, invaded the neighbouring state of Kuwait, which prompted the UNSC to impose sanctions on Iraq under UNSC Res 661. Under the terms of this resolution, all trade with Iraq was banned. Iraq's failure to leave Kuwait forced the UNSC to authorise a military operation, which was conducted by a US-led coalition, to compel the withdrawal of Iraqi forces. On completion of this operation, named 'Desert Storm', and the departure of Iraq from Kuwait, the comprehensive trade embargo against Iraq was left in place in order to compel Baghdad to comply with a broader list of demands. Some of these demands were disarmament requirements motivated by the uncovering of an advanced clandestine nuclear weapons programme during the military operation, which Iraq had been building in defiance of its obligations under the Treaty on the Non-proliferation of Nuclear Weapons. Although the Iraqi leadership complied with most demands, it fell short of fulfilling all of them (Cortright and Lopez [2000]). As a result, the trade embargo was left in place and was not lifted until the 2003 invasion of Iraq by the United States and the United Kingdom (UNSC Res 1483 [2003]).

III The Oil-for-Food programme

Between 1990 and 1993, the severe humanitarian effects of the comprehensive trade embargo, such as high levels of child morbidity and mortality, provoked an international outcry against the sanctions (Zaidi and Fawzi [1995]). Furthermore, public contestation of the measures led to a major crisis of legitimacy for the UN (see chapter on Legality and legitimacy). However, any easing of the embargoes required a UNSC decision with at least nine yes votes in the Security Council as well as the absence of a veto by any of the permanent members. In response to the continuation of sanctions, Council members, such as France and Russia, publicly advocated a relaxation of the embargo. Washington and London, however, announced that they would veto any such modification (Jones [2015]). The UNSC was able to compromise by setting up the Oil-for-Food programme in 1995 under Resolution 986, as a temporary measure that permitted the sale of Iraqi oil in exchange for funds that would be used exclusively for the purchase of medicine and food under UN supervision, with a view to alleviating the humanitarian hardship inflicted on the Iraqi civilian population while keeping the embargo in place.

Despite initially rejecting the terms of the resolution, Iraq agreed to conclude a memorandum of understanding with the UN to implement the programme, which led to the establishment of the UN Office of the Iraq Programme to administer it. Over the seven-year life of the programme (1996–2003), oil sales amounted to $65 billion, while the value of humanitarian goods purchased totalled $46 billion (Liddick [2007]). However, the operation of the programme was marred by large-scale corruption and mismanagement, the magnitude of which was confirmed by an independent enquiry commissioned by the United States, called the Volcker Report (Independent Inquiry Committee [2005]).

IV Consequences of the Iraq embargo

The UN trade embargo on Iraq had several far-reaching effects. The most important consequence was the de-legitimisation of comprehensive sanctions on account of the humanitarian hardship they brought to the civilian population (Gordon [2006]). The backlash against the measures was such that it was believed that any new trade embargoes imposed ran the risk of not being implemented by UN members, despite their obligatory nature (Portela and Nair [2021]). Such outcry is the single most important reason accounting for the development of targeted sanctions, which became UN practice and the global standard thereafter. Among lawyers, the debate centred on how sanctions could be limited based on human rights and humanitarian law standards, including the principle of the proportionality of sanctions (see chapter) (O'Connell [2002]). The unpopularity of embargoes and the belief in their scarce political viability persist today even though mortality and morbidity figures released at the time were found to be exaggerated upon review. A return to the enactment of comprehensive sanctions (involving total embargoes of a state) by the UNSC has never been contemplated, even though it has been claimed that they made a covert comeback in the shape of financial sanctions (see chapter) (Gordon [2019]). Frustration with the impossibility of lifting or at least easing embargoes once imposed led to the adoption of sunset clauses providing for an expiry date for measures that require a positive decision for their renewal, a feature that has also become standard in multilateral sanctions practice (Weschler [2010]). Lastly, the severe mismanagement of the Oil-for-Food programme had two repercussions: firstly, it undermined confidence in the UN's ability to manage any mechanism geared towards mitigating humanitarian consequences, resulting in a preference for humanitarian exceptions to limit hardship (see chapter on humanitarian carveouts); secondly, it accentuated the distrust of the US political elite in the organisation, leading to reduced financial contributions to the UN by its erstwhile main funder (Paschke [2000]).

V Conclusion

The history of UNSC sanctions cannot be told without reference to the Iraq sanctions regime of the early 1990s, undoubtedly the most important episode as it precipitated the demise of comprehensive trade embargoes (see chapter). As an export-dependent economy, Iraq was severely impacted by the embargoes, an effect that was exacerbated by the underdevelopment of humanitarian exemptions and exceptions, the rigidity of UNSC sanctions decision-making, and the mismanagement to which the Oil-for-Food programme was subject. The impact of the negative experience with this sanctions regime lasts to this day, most notably in the form of targeted sanctions, sunset clauses, and increased oversight of the UN system.

Bibliography

Literature

Cortright D and Lopez G, *The Sanctions Decade: Assessing UN Strategies in the 1990s* (Lynne Rienner 2000).

Gordon J, 'The Accusations against the Oil-for-Food Program: The Volcker Report' (2006) 28(3) *Arab Studies Quarterly* 19.

Gordon J, 'The Hidden Power of the New Economic Sanctions' (2019) 118 *Current History* 3.

Jones L, *Societies under Siege* (Oxford University Press 2015).

Liddick D, 'The United Nations Oil-for-Food Program: Corruption, Bribery and International Relations in the Serious Crime Community' in Bovenkerk F and Levi M (eds), *The Organized Crime Community* (Springer 2007) 59.

Zaidi S and Fawzi MC, 'Health of Bagdad's Children' (1995) 346 *The Lancet* 1485.

O'Connell ME, 'Debating the Law of Sanctions' (2002) 13 *European Journal of International Law* 63.

Portela C and Nair D, 'The UN "Oil-for-Food" Programme: Good Intentions that Went Awry?' (SMU Centre for Management Practice 2021).

Paschke KT, 'Accountability and the Role of Internal Oversight in the United Nations' in Carter W (ed.), *Government Ethics and Law Enforcement* (Praeger 2000) 3.

Weschler J, 'The Evolution of Security Council Innovations in Sanctions' (2010) 65(1) *International Journal* 31.

Documents

Independent Inquiry Committee into the Oil-for-Food Programme report (the Volcker Report), <https://www.files.ethz.ch/isn/10495/doc_10525_290_en.pdf>.

UNSC Res 986 (1995) (14 April 1995) UN Doc. S/RES/986 (2003).

UNSC Res 1483 (2003) (22 May 2003) UN Doc. S/RES/1483 (2003).

38. Libya

THOMAS KRUIPER

I International sanctions in response to state-sponsored terrorism (1986–2004)

The Libyan Arab Jamahiriya (Libya) has been intermittently subjected to international sanctions since the mid-1980s. During the reign of Muammar Gaddafi (1969–2011), a revolutionary leader of anti-imperialist movements across Africa and the Arab world, Libya supported various national liberation movements, communist movements, and terrorist organizations, including the African National Congress (ANC) in apartheid South Africa, the Palestine Liberation Organization (PLO), Euskadi Ta Askatasuna (ETA) in Spain, and the Sandinista movement in Nicaragua. After partly nationalizing the oil industry, Libya experienced continuous political and military tensions with the United States, including an attack on the US embassy in Tripoli (1979) and military confrontations in the Gulf of Sidra in 1986.

Washington imposed unilateral sanctions against the Gaddafi regime in that same year, including trade sanctions (most notably oil), a travel ban, credit restrictions, an employment ban, and asset freezes. According to Hufbauer et al. ([2008]), the sanctions were supported by an aerial bombing campaign against Tripoli and Benghazi, while the European Community imposed diplomatic sanctions.

United Nations (UN) sanctions were only imposed in March 1992 (UNSC Res 748 [1992]) in response to the notorious aircraft bombings of Pan Am flight 103 over the Scottish town of Lockerbie (1988), and UTA flight 772 over Niger (1989). The attacks killed 440 people, including 197 American and 57 French citizens, whose governments were the target of the attacks. The sanctions included an arms embargo, travel restrictions, and diplomatic restrictions. The resolution demanded that Libya cease all forms of terrorist action and that it cooperate fully in establishing responsibility for the attacks. The United Nations Security Council (UNSC) vote saw ten votes in favour, with abstentions from China, India, Morocco, Zimbabwe, and Cape Verde. In November 1993, when the Gaddafi regime refused to comply with the demand to extradite two suspects in the attacks, the sanctions were expanded with asset freezes and a halt to the transfer of oil technology.

Between 1993 and 1998, Libya successfully mobilized support from the Arab League and the Organization of African Unity (OAU) to threaten to stop implementing the UN sanctions (Cortright and Lopez [2000] 107; Niblock [2001] 47). They did so not only to mitigate the humanitarian consequences on Libyan citizens and to convince London and Washington to organize a trial on neutral territory, but also to challenge the legitimacy of the sanctions and the Council itself (Hurd [2005] 495). European companies doing business in Libya's oil sector also increasingly complained about indirect US sanctions through the Iran and Libya Sanctions Act of 1996 (McCurdy [1997] 399). Eventually, the parties agreed that the two suspects in the Lockerbie bombing would be handed over for trial in the Netherlands under Scottish law, leading the UN to announce the lifting of the sanctions in 1998 (UNSC Res 1192 [1998]). In 2000, one of the suspects was convicted and sentenced to life in prison because of his involvement in the Lockerbie bombing; the other suspect was found not guilty. The UN formally lifted sanctions in 2003 (UNSC Res 1506 [2003]), followed by the United States in 2004.

II International sanctions in response to Libya's civil war (2011–ongoing)

The second phase of international sanctions against Libya began amid the Arab Spring uprisings that had already affected Libya's direct neighbours, Tunisia and Egypt. In February 2011, following Gaddafi's violent crackdown on popular anti-regime protests in Benghazi, the situation escalated into a nationwide rebellion and the start of a civil war. In response, the UNSC imposed Resolution 1970 on 26 February 2011, expressing grave concern at the situation and imposing an arms embargo to prohibit both the import and export of weapons, along with a travel ban for 16 key regime individuals and asset freezes for Gaddafi and 5 family members. The European Union (EU) followed suit two days later with Council Decision 2011/137/CFSP. The League of Arab States suspended Libya's membership, while the African Union engaged Gaddafi diplomatically to step down without opening "Libya's Pandora's Box" (De Waal [2003] 370).

On 17 March 2011, Gaddafi announced in a call-in radio programme that a large-scale attack on Benghazi was imminent. This prompted the UNSC to operationalize, for the first time, the Responsibility to Protect (R2P) doctrine in Resolution 1973 (2011). The resolution also expanded the sanctions regime with a ban on flights and additional asset freezes of key financial and economic institutions under the regime's control, including the Libyan Central Bank, the Libyan Investment Authority, and the National Oil Corporation. Crucially, the resolution also authorized a request from the League of Arab States to allow regional organizations to take all necessary measures to protect civilians and to enforce compliance with sanctions. In the Security Council, just as in 1992, only ten states voted in favour; Brazil, China, Germany, India, and Russia abstained. Five days later, a coalition led by the North Atlantic Treaty Organization (NATO) began Operation Unified Protector to implement a no-fly zone and to cut off the flow of weapons and mercenaries through the Mediterranean.

Although the mission's objective was not to overthrow Gaddafi's regime, the intervention did swing the military balance in favour of the National Transitional Council (NTC), a coalition of rebel groups that captured and killed Gaddafi in Sirte on 20 October 2011. The death of Gaddafi further divided the Council, after which sanctions became less stringent. The aviation ban and some asset freezes on entities were lifted, while the arms embargo was relaxed to support disarmament assistance under the new authorities in collaboration with the United Nations Support Mission in Libya (UNSMIL).

Violence in Libya resurged after the 2014 elections, which split the country into two opposing political factions. The internationally recognized Government of National Accord (GNA) controlled most of Western Libya, including Tripoli, while the House of Representatives, based in Tobruk, controlled the East. Simultaneously, between 2014 and 2020, the conflict also involved not only a range of armed Islamist groups, most notably Ansar Al-Sharia and the Islamic State (Libya Province), but also a range of armed groups from Sudan and Chad, fractionalizing the battlefield and entangling tribal politics with criminal networks. This exacerbated the power vacuum and facilitated the illicit export of crude oil by actors outside of government control.

Starting in 2014, international sanctions aimed to support the GNA in gaining and retaining control over the National Oil Corporation, the Central Bank of Libya, and the Libyan Investment Authority. In March 2014, Resolution 2146 (2014) appointed a focal point to inform the sanctions committee of any vessels transporting crude oil illicitly exported from Libya and authorizing member states to inspect suspected vessels on the high seas. The EU buttressed the sanctions with Council Decision 2015/1333/CFSP ([2015]), going well beyond the UNSC mandate by designating harbours and additional individuals. US sanctions also expanded its asset freezes and travel bans in 2016 with Executive Order 13726 ([2016]).

Since 2018, the UN sanctions regime in Libya also targets people involved in organized criminal networks, most notably human trafficking, drug trafficking, and illicit oil transactions. Although this novel approach was unprecedented in signalling that non-political actors can also be targeted by UN sanctions, setting a precedent for the UN sanctions regime in Haiti (UNSC Res 2653 [2022]), an atmosphere of impunity remains (Haenlein and Kadlec [2022]). Reports by panels of experts mention the continued presence of foreign armed groups and mercenaries in Southern Libya (UNSC Report [2019]), the control of armed groups over detention centres, and the involvement of government officials in illicit narcotics markets (UNSC Final Report [2023]). As of July 2024, the UN consolidated sanctions list includes 2 entities and 29 individuals, 5 of whom are designated as leaders of international trafficking networks. As long as Libya remains a failed state and Libyan politics remain entrenched (UNSC Briefing [2024]), spoilers will continue to evade sanctions without repercussions.

Bibliography

Literature

Cortright D and Lopez GA, 'Taming Terrorism: Sanctions Against Libya, Sudan, and Afghanistan' in Cortright D and Lopez GA (eds), *The Sanctions Decade: Assessing UN Strategies in the 1990s* (Lynne Rienner Publishers 2000).

THOMAS KRUIPER

De Waal A, 'African Roles in the Libyan Conflict of 2011' (2013) 89 *International Affairs* 365.

Haenlein C and Kadlec A, 'An Unprecedented Failure? UN Sanctions Against Human Traffickers in Libya' (*Royal United Services Institute*, 20 December 2022) <https://www.rusi.org/explore-our-research/publications/commentary/unprecedented-failure-un-sanctions-against-human-traffickers-libya> accessed 25 July 2024.

Hufbauer GC et al., 'Case 78-8 and 92-12: United States v. Libya (1978–2004: Gaddafi, Terrorism); United Nations v. Libya (1992–99: Pan Am 103)' (*Peterson Institute for International Economics*, 1 May 2008) <https://www.piie.com/commentary/speeches-papers/case-78-8-and-92-12> accessed 15 January 2025.

Hurd I, 'The Strategic Use of Liberal Internationalism: Libya and the UN Sanctions, 1992–2003' (2005) 59 *International Organization* 495.

McCurdy M, 'Unilateral Sanctions with a Twist: The Iran and Libya Sanctions Act of 1996' (1997) 13 *American University International Law Review* 397.

Niblock T, *Pariah States and Sanctions in the Middle East: Iraq, Libya, Sudan* (Lynne Rienner Publishers 2001).

Documents

Council Decision 2015/1333/CFSP of 31 July 2015 concerning restrictive measures in view of the situation in Libya, and repealing Decision 2011/137/CFSP [2015] OJ L206/34.

Executive Order 13726, 82 Fed. Reg. 18533 (19 April 2017) (USA).

UNSC Verbatim Record: 'Briefing on UNSMIL' (16 April 2024) UN Doc. S/PV.9605.

UNSC 'Final Report from the Panel of Experts on Libya' (14 September 2023) UN Doc. S/2023/673.

UNSC, 'Report from the Panel of Experts on Libya' (29 November 2019) UN Doc. S/2019/914.

UNSC Res 748 (31 March 1992) UN Doc. S/RES/748.

UNSC Res 1192 (27 August 1998) UN Doc. S/RES/1192.

UNSC Res 1506 (12 September 2003) UN Doc. S/RES/1506.

UNSC Res 1973 (17 March 2011) UN Doc. S/RES/1973.

UNSC Res 2146 (19 March 2014) UN Doc. S/RES/2146.

UNSC Res 2653 (21 October 2022) UN Doc. S/RES/2653.

THOMAS KRUIPER

39. Mali

Tiziana Corda

I Introduction

The United Nations (UN) sanctions regime in Mali, established in September 2017 and terminated in August 2023, was one of the measures the international community took in response to the continued hostilities occurring in the West African country in breach of the Agreement on Peace and Reconciliation. This agreement, which emanated from the Algiers Process, was signed in 2015 by the Malian government and a coalition of armed groups from Northern Mali to improve the security situation of the country. The sanctions regime was unanimously imposed by the United Nations Security Council (UNSC) (see chapter) through Resolution 2374 [2017] against individuals and entities obstructing the implementation of that agreement. Other designation criteria entailed abuses and violations of human rights and international humanitarian law in the country. The measures set out in paragraphs 1–7 of the resolution included a travel ban and asset freeze on individuals and entities who, according to the Sanctions Committee established by the resolution itself, met such designation criteria. The resolution also set out the creation of a Panel of Experts (see chapter), tasked with assisting the Sanctions Committee in monitoring the implementation of those measures, and requested the United Nations Multidimensional Integrated Stabilization Mission in Mali (MINUSMA), which had been established through Resolution 2100 [2013], to assist the panel in this endeavour.

II Implementation challenges

This sanctions regime was renewed every year until August 2023, when the UNSC failed to secure another renewal due to a Russian veto. Russia was specifically opposed to the renewal of the mandate of the Panel of Experts after they criticized recent actions by the Malian armed forces and their foreign security partners, primarily Russian since late 2021 [S/2023/638]. The transitional military-led Malian government, established in 2021 after the second military coup d'état the country registered in just two years, went even further and called for the lifting of the entire UN sanctions regime on the alleged grounds that the hostilities between the signatory movements had come to an end and that the Panel of Experts exceeded its mandate by focusing on regions that were not within the scope of the agreement.

Throughout the six years of its implementation, only eight individuals were designated by the Sanctions Committee and most parts of the agreement remained unimplemented. The final report of the Panel of Experts published in August 2023 acknowledged a "substantial impasse" and the limited implementation of sanctions measures (S/2023/578 [2023] at 2–3). In 2023, some of the signatory armed groups from Northern Mali even suspended their participation in the peace process to protest the junta's lack of political commitment to it, and the first direct clashes between the two sides since 2015 were recorded. Overall, the limited application of sanctions in terms of the number of designees (only eight over six years), the measures imposed (only five of the designees were supplemented with asset freezes; the others remained only under travel ban restrictions), and the actions to secure their implementation in the face of circumvention attempts failed to coerce the signatory parties into fully implementing the agreement and, more broadly, to prevent violations of human rights and international humanitarian law in the country.

The targeted nature of the few UN designations ensured this sanctions regime did not directly produce major unintended effects on the Malian population at large. However, the lack of progress in the implementation of the agreement facilitated the proliferation of criminal activities and jihadist groups, which worsened the humanitarian situation in large swathes of the country. These factors, in turn, fuelled domestic political instability that led to the two military coups Colonel Assimi Goita executed in 2020 and 2021, which triggered new sanctions regimes by the Economic Community of West African States (ECOWAS), the African Union (AU), and the European Union (EU), aimed at restoring the constitutional order. These sanctions regimes had a more detrimental impact on the population and the humanitarian situation in the country because they were less targeted. A case in point was ECOWAS's economic sanctions, which suspended all commercial and financial transactions between ECOWAS members and Mali, with the exception of basic and essential goods, inflicting hardship on the whole Malian population.

III Conclusion

The termination of the UN sanctions regime in Mali raised concerns about Mali's security as well as the future of multilateralism. Although security had already worsened in the final years of the UN sanctions regime, its termination put an end to the only remaining tool of UN oversight of Malian security, given the withdrawal of the UN mission MINUSMA between June and December 2023. It also opened up space for more direct attacks between the agreement signatory groups that the UN sanctions regime had largely prevented, eventually paving the way for the gradual abandonment of the agreement itself, which formally occurred in January 2024 following the Malian ruling junta's decision to immediately withdraw from it. Moreover, the inability to secure a renewal in spite of a large cross-regional UNSC majority, inclusive of its three non-permanent African members Gabon, Ghana, and Mozambique (A3), revealed once again the limits of the multilateral system. Sanctions adoption and renewal remain vulnerable to the veto powers of UNSC permanent members. The UN sanctions regime in Mali was the only new sanctions regime of two (the other being against Haiti in 2022; see chapter on Sanctions against organized crime) that the UNSC managed to initiate over the previous eight years, in spite of similar situations in the region and worldwide on which multilateral sanctions could have been used. It also confirmed the limited voice of regional actors, in this regard African countries and organizations. They were the most affected by the cross-border consequences of the Malian instability and, in vain, supported the renewal and better implementation of the UN sanctions regime, which proved unable to change the security situation for them.

Bibliography

Literature

Charbonneau B, 'Intervention in Mali: Building Peace between Peacekeeping and Counterterrorism' (2017) 35(4) *Journal of Contemporary African Studies* 415. <https://doi.org/10.1080/02589001.2017.1363383>.

Charron A and Portela C, 'The UN, Regional Sanctions and Africa' (2015) 91(6) *International Affairs* 1369. <https://doi.org/10.1111/1468-2346.12452>.

Sabrow S, 'Local Perceptions of the Legitimacy of Peace Operations by the UN, Regional Organizations and Individual States: A Case Study of the Mali Conflict' (2016) 24(1) *International Peacekeeping* 159. <https://doi.org/10.1080/13533312.2016.1249365>.

Raleigh C, Nsaibia H and Dowd C, 'The Sahel Crisis since 2012' (2021) 120(478) *African Affairs* 123. <https://doi.org/10.1093/afraf/adaa022>.

Documents

UNSC Res 2100 (25 April 2013) UN Doc. S/RES/2100.

UNSC Res 2374 (5 September 2017) UN Doc. S/RES/2374.

UNSC 'Draft resolution on renewal of sanctions imposed by Security Council resolution 2374 (2017) and extension of the mandate of the Panel of Experts concerning Mali until 30 Sept. 2024' (30 August 2023) S/2023/638.

UNSC 'Letter from the Panel of Experts on Mali' (3 August 2023) S/2023/578.

TIZIANA CORDA

40. Myanmar

Marco Bünte and Loren Bustos

I Introduction

Situated at a strategic location between China, India, and Southeast Asia, Myanmar has been subject to a series of sanctions (multilateral and autonomous) since the late 1980s. These were phased out during the country's decade of democratic reforms from 2011 to 2021, but reapplied after the coup in 2021. In 1988, the United States and Canada imposed an arms embargo in response to the military's brutal crackdown on peaceful demonstrations. Driven by widespread economic mismanagement, chronic corruption, and a lack of political freedoms under the sclerotic Ne Win regime, students, monks, and ordinary citizens took to the streets to demand political reforms. The military stepped in to restore law and order, killing more than 1000 protestors and arresting many more (Lintner [1990]). In 1990, the new military junta – the State Law and Order Restoration Council (SLORC, led by Senior General Than Shwe since 1992 and renamed the State Peace and Development Council [SPDC] in 1997) – allowed relatively free elections but refused to hand over power to the winning National League of Democracy (NLD). Instead, it remained in full control until 2010, imprisoning NLD leader Aung San Suu Kyi and many of her supporters. During the 1990s, the number of political prisoners remained constantly high; between 1989 and 2010, Aung San Suu Kyi spent 15 years under house arrest. Due to the lack of democratic progress, repression of the opposition, and severe human rights abuses in the areas of ethnic minorities, Western countries incrementally increased their sanctions in range and scope.

II International sanctions against Myanmar

Encouraged by the (apparent) success of multilateral and autonomous sanctions against South Africa (Petersen [2008] 49–50), Australia, Canada, the United States, and the European Union (EU) employed a number of smart sanctions, such as a visa ban, against senior government officials, junta members, and their families, as well as an asset freeze on government officials and senior members of the military regime. The EU also targeted military companies, banned investments in the country, and adopted an arms embargo in 1990. US sanctions were broader in scope: In 1997, the US administration enacted an investment ban for US citizens; in 2003, the US Burmese Freedom and Democracy Act prohibited imports from Myanmar. The 2008 JADE (Junta's Anti-democratic Efforts) Act placed restrictions on the import of jadeite, rubies, and other jewellery. In addition to the sanctions adopted under the EU's Common Foreign and Security Policy (CFSP), Myanmar had its trade privileges under the Generalized System of Preferences cut off in March 1997 in response to Myanmar's practice of forced labour (Jones [2015]). The United States and Canada had already initiated similar steps in 1989 (see Table 40.1). Sanctions were primarily a tool of Western countries, although Japan also enacted an arms embargo in 1988, suspended non-humanitarian aid, and imposed visa restrictions on senior members of the regime. Myanmar did not face multilateral sanctions, though: the United Nations Security Council (UNSC) debated the situation in Myanmar several times. After the violent suppression of the Saffron Revolution in 2007, a series of peaceful demonstrations of monks against the military regime, the United States and the United Kingdom tabled Resolution 5619 in the Security Council, which condemned the military's violence and proposed an arms embargo and a travel ban. The resolution was vetoed by China and Russia, who argued that the situation in Myanmar was an internal matter and did not endanger international security (UN Draft Resolution [2007]).

In 2010, Myanmar held its first election since 1990, and junta leader Senior General Than Shwe retired. The new President Thein Sein (2011–15), a former general and member of the SPDC, embarked on political and economic reforms, including the release of political prisoners. The quasi-civilian regime entered into dialogue with the opposition and started a new peace initiative with ethnic rebel groups, some of whom had been fighting the regime for decades. Although the reforms were a top-down affair, Aung San Suu Kyi was able to win a parliamentary seat in the 2012 by-elections. In the elections held in 2015, the NLD won by a landslide and took over the government. Due to these reforms, Western countries slowly began to ease their sanctions. In 2013, the EU suspended all sanctions while

Table 40.1 Sanctions against Myanmar (1988–2012)

Sanction Type	EU	United States	Canada	Australia	Japan
Arms embargo	X (1990)	X (1988)	X (1988)	X (1990)	X (1988)
Generalized System of Preferences cut	X (1997)	X (1989)	X (1989)	–	–
Suspension of non-humanitarian aid	X (1990)	X (1994)	X (1988)	X (1988)	X (1988)
Visa ban for senior government officials, junta members, and families	X (1996)	X (1996)	X (2003)	X (1991)	X (1991)
Asset freeze for junta members and families	X (1998)*	X (2000)*	X (2007)	X (2008)	–
Ban on imports of timber	X (2007)	–	–	X (2007)	–
Ban on imports of rubies and jade	X (2008)	X (2008)	–	X (2007)	–
Ban on investments in Myanmar	X (2003)	X (2003)	X (2007)	X (2007)	–
Ban on all imports	–	X (2003)	X (2007)	–	–

Note: * Extended several times.

maintaining an arms embargo (Bünte and Portela [2012]), and under President Obama, the United States lifted many sanctions in 2016.

III Impact of sanctions

Some commentators ascribe the reforms to the sanctions imposed: Giumelli ([2013] 31) asserts that 'the ruling class after 20 years of isolation may have realized that they would be in a better position by opening up the country'. However, other scholars are more sceptical: Petersen ([2008]) argues that the sanctions only brought hardship to the population and hardened the generals' resistance. Restrictions on aid hampered the development of alternative governance structures for the army and constrained the development of non-governmental organizations (NGOs) (Jones [2015]). Smart sanctions directed at senior regime leaders and state officials had little impact since Myanmar elites could acquire and access all the financial, medical, educational, and recreational services they needed in Asia and the Middle East. In addition, the arms embargo failed since the military was able to find other suppliers (from China and Russia) (Portela [2014]; Jones [2015]). Bünte ([2014]) highlights that the reforms were only introduced *after* the generals managed to strengthen their coercive apparatus and ensure the military's role as a guardian of the 'disciplined democracy', which also gave them complete control over security issues. In 2017, it reacted to attacks on army outposts by a Rohingya armed group, the Arakan Rohingya Salvation Army (ARSA), with a brutal crackdown on Rohingya villagers across northern Rakhine state, which the United Nations (UN) called a textbook example of 'ethnic cleansing'. Canada, the EU, and the United States enacted targeted sanctions against military leaders and visa bans for those involved in human rights abuses. The UNSC discussed the situation again but failed to pass a resolution due to the veto of China and Russia.

IV Post-2021 military coup

After a decade of power-sharing between civilians and military forces, the military seized back control in February 2021 (Bünte [2021]). The coup and the military's violent suppression of peaceful resistance – leading to an increased civil war inside the country – triggered another round of Western sanctions. Learning from past episodes, both the EU and the United States have tried to avoid broader sanctions, which affect the entire Myanmar economy (such as the textile and garment sector), and used more targeted and sector-specific sanctions against individual military leaders, military companies, and their supporters than in the period from 1988 to 2016. Based on better knowledge about the military's involvement in Myanmar's economy, the EU and the United States imposed restrictions on military-owned companies such as Myanmar Economic Holding (MEH) and Myanmar Economic Corporations (MEC). However, though Asian states have condemned the coup, they have refrained from sanctioning the regime. Thus, the effects of the sanctions remain limited. Freezing the accounts of Myanmar's state-owned banks has limited the junta's ability to access foreign currency reserves (Marston [2023]). At the same time, Russia and China have helped to evade the sanctions. The military junta continues to rely on the political, military, and economic support of these authoritarian partners.

Bibliography

Literature

Bünte M and Portela C, *Myanmar: The Beginning of Reforms and the End of Sanctions* (GIGA Focus International n 3, 2012).

Bünte M, 'Myanmar's Transition to Quasi-Military Rule: from Rulers to Guardians' (2014) 40 *Armed Forces and Society* 742>.

Bünte M, 'Myanmar: Civil-Military Relations in a Tutelary Regime' (2021) *Oxford Research Encyclopedias of Politics* <https://doi.org/10.1093/acrefore/9780190228637.013.1887> accessed 11 June 2024.

Giumelli F, *How EU Sanctions Work. A New Narrative* (Chaillot Papers N 129, Paris 2013) <https://www.files.ethz.ch/isn/182217/Chaillot_129.pdf> accessed 11 June 2024.

Jones L, *Societies under Siege. Exploring How International Economic Sanctions (Do Not) Work* (Oxford University Press 2015).

Lintner B, *Outrage. Burma's Struggle for Democracy* (White Lotus 1990).

Marston H, 'Many Sanctions, Few Friends: Junta Grapples with its Grip on Power' (*Stimson Center, Commentary*, 11 October 2023) <https://www.stimson.org/2023/many-sanctions-few-friends-junta-grapples-with-its-grip-on-power/> accessed 11 June 2024.

Petersen M, *Promoting Human Rights in Burma. A Critique of Western Sanction Policy* (Rowman & Littlefield 2008).

Portela C, *The EU's Use of Targeted Sanctions. Evaluating Effectiveness* (CEPS Working Document n 391, March 2014) <https://cdn.ceps.eu/wpcontent/uploads/2014/03/WD391%20Portela%20EU%20Targeted%20Sanctions.pdf> accessed 11 June 2024.

Document

UNSC Draft Resolution (12 January 2007) UN Doc. S/2007/14.

41. Russian Federation (sanctions episode)

Iikka Korhonen

I Introduction

Initial sanctions in 2014 after the illegal annexation of Crimea and Russia's incursions into eastern Ukraine were relatively mild and mostly targeted financial flows to Russia. The sanctions lowered Russia's foreign indebtedness, providing Russia with the impetus to create its own internal payment system. Russia entered a recession, but its real gross domestic product (GDP) recovered to the level of mid-2014 in mid-2017. Somewhat paradoxically, Russia's actions and policy adjustments in response to these sanctions made it more resilient to the sanctions introduced after the invasion of February 2022.

When Russia launched its illegal, full-scale invasion of Ukraine on 24 February 2022, Western countries responded with widespread condemnation and a wide variety of economic sanctions. As before, various sanctions packages targeted individuals, but there were also wide export bans on various goods to Russia and, perhaps surprisingly, freezing of the central bank assets held in the sender countries. The onset of the war and sanctions combined to produce a significant drop in Russia's GDP, but since then it has climbed above pre-invasion levels. However, this has required the Russian government to increase public spending significantly as it has channeled resources to military use. In mid-2024, economic growth seemed to stall as an increasing number of sectors were hitting capacity constraints.

According to several analysts, post-invasion sanctions have had success in many of their stated aims (Itskhoki and Ribakova [2024]; Simola [2024]). They have reduced Russia's access to critical components and dual-use goods. The oil price cap, another sanctions innovation introduced by the G7 countries, had initial success in lowering Russia's export and tax revenue from its crude oil exports. Over time, Russian operators learned to circumvent the initial oil price stipulations, as often happens. While sanctions help in retarding Russia's ability to wage war in Ukraine, they do not stop the aggression. For that purpose, other tools and means of assistance to Ukraine are needed.

II Sanctions in 2014

In winter 2013–2014, Ukraine experienced a prolonged period of political instability and mass demonstrations, when President Viktor Yanukovych rejected signing an association agreement with the EU and opted for a trade deal with Russia instead. The demonstrations culminated in Yanukovych fleeing from Ukraine to Russia. At the same time, Russian soldiers took over most of Crimea and entered many eastern parts of Ukraine. On 17 March 2014, Crimea's authorities declared independence and requested to join Russia. Russia incorporated Crimea officially the next day (Kalb [2015]).

After Russia's annexation of Crimea and Sevastopol, along with its military actions in eastern Ukraine, sanctions were imposed on Russian individuals and organizations by the EU, the United States, Canada, Australia, and other nations.

The sanctions against Russian entities in 2014 were implemented in two main waves. The first wave followed Crimea's annexation in the spring of 2014 and involved travel bans and asset freezes targeting Russian individuals and organizations. However, this initial round of sanctions was relatively limited, as it did not affect major state-owned companies or the Russian government itself. The second wave of sanctions, introduced after the downing of Malaysia Airlines flight MH-17 by Russia in July 2014, was more extensive. They included a ban on the sale of military equipment and dual-use goods with military applications. However, the most effective sanctions tool was prohibiting long-term financing for many large Russian-owned companies, especially in banking but also in the energy sector. For example, the state-owned banks Sberbank and VTB, as well as oil giant Rosneft, were added to the list of sanctioned companies.

It should be noted that these sanctions were introduced only after fighting between Ukrainian troops and purported insurgents, led and armed by the Russian military, had been going on for months in the Donetsk and Luhansk regions.

The consensus is that sanctions have been effective in reducing Russia's GDP and partially decoupling Russia's capital markets from the global markets (Korhonen [2019]).

The International Monetary Fund ([2019]) concluded that sanctions reduced Russia's growth rate by 0.2 percentage points every year during 2014–2018. Pestova and Mamonov

([2019]) determine that the cumulative effect of sanctions in 2014 and 2015 decreased the Russian GDP by 1.2 per cent. They argue that sanctions have worked via reduced investment by Russian companies. Ahn and Ludema ([2020]) find that Western sanctions against individual companies have been successful in reducing their revenue, asset values, and employment. However, Russia has been able to shield strategically important companies from the effects of sanctions, although with a fiscal cost.

An important channel of influence against Russia has been finance. More specifically, foreign investors have not been able to renew their lending to sanctioned Russian entities and, moreover, they have refused to lend money to non-sanctioned Russian entities. Russia's foreign debt peaked in March 2014 and has been on a broadly declining trend ever since. Interestingly enough, Russia has not been able to tap into Chinese or any other Asian financing in any meaningful volumes.

This weaponization of international finance has had some unforeseen consequences: Russian authorities began to see foreign indebtedness as a source of vulnerability, and therefore many steps were taken to reduce Russian banks' and large corporations' foreign exposure. Furthermore, Russia took many measures to ensure its domestic payment system could work even if many or all Russian banks were disconnected from the Society for Worldwide Interbank Financial Telecommunication (SWIFT), the global payment messaging system, headquartered in Belgium. The expulsion of Iranian financial institutions, including the central bank, in 2006 was the obvious precedent. In late 2017, Russia introduced the System for Transfer of Financial Messages (SPFS) as an alternative to SWIFT. In addition, the mir payment card system was introduced in May 2017 as a potential alternative to Western payment cards. These measures made the Russian financial system more resilient to the sanctions that were introduced after the full-scale invasion of Ukraine in February 2022.

III Sanctions in 2022 and beyond

Since Russia's invasion of Ukraine on 24 February 2022, it has been the target of several rounds of sanctions by the EU, the United States, the United Kingdom, and other allies both in Europe and Asia. Some of the sanctions have been "merely" a continuation of sanctions introduced in 2014. Many individuals and entities have been sanctioned (asset freezes and travel bans) for their role in Russia's illegal war. Over time, a growing number of goods have been added to the export ban lists of the EU and other allies. Financial sanctions have been greatly expanded, and a very large number of Russian financial institutions have been cut off from SWIFT, which makes their international payments more expensive and cumbersome, if not impossible. The EU has moved towards banning imports of more Russian goods, including crude oil shipments.

Senders have also introduced sanctions that have rarely been used in recent years. The Bank of Russia had approximately half of its international reserves (some $300 billion) invested in EU area government securities. These assets are now frozen, as no Western financial institution is allowed to enter into transactions with the Russian Central Bank. Central bank asset freezes and seizures have happened before, but the size of the frozen Russian assets is probably unique (Krahnke et al. [2024]). Now the accrued interest from the frozen assets will be used to service debt taken on by Ukraine's Western allies, another novel innovation in sanctions and financial engineering.

The G7 countries introduced a price cap of $60 per barrel for Russia's crude oil exports. The price cap allows Western shipping and insurance companies to handle, ship, and insure Russian crude oil shipments, provided the barrel price remains below $60. With this innovative approach, the sanctioning countries sought to reach two potentially clashing objectives: to keep the physical flow of crude oil in the global markets constant and to reduce Russia's tax revenue from the sale of that oil. For many sanctioning countries, a possible oil price hike following the removal of even some part of Russian crude oil from the global market would have been politically very difficult. This illustrates one recurring theme in the design of various sanctions: how to minimize one's own costs while making sure the sanctions hurt the intended target. The oil price cap was apparently relatively successful in limiting Russia's oil revenue in the first half of 2023 and, to some extent, also after it. However, over time, Russian companies and other global oil market operators have learned how to circumvent the oil price cap, at least partly. This illustrates another factor common to many sanctions: over time, their efficacy declines if no changes are made to their implementation.

One should also note the establishment of the multilateral Russian Elites, Proxies, and Oligarchs (REPO) Task Force, which has coordinated various sanctions measures between the G7 countries, the European Commission, and Australia. This institutional innovation has made it easier to coordinate sanctions across various jurisdictions and may also be a blueprint for similar coordinated actions in the future.

Notwithstanding the availability of some studies on the effects of sanctions implemented in 2022 and thereafter, identifying the effects of sanctions is hampered by many factors. The EU and other partners have coordinated their sanctions, but not perfectly. At least, the timing of various measures has often been different. Many measures have included possibilities for long grace periods or exemptions.

As noted before, by mid-2024, Russia's official GDP had surpassed its pre-invasion peak by some 4 per cent. However, Russia's GDP in 2024 is very different from its GDP in 2021. The shares of public consumption and investment have risen, especially in sectors related to the military. The same applies to manufacturing, where growth has been very strong in those sub-sectors that are directly supplying the Russian military. Simola ([2023]) finds that war-related manufacturing sectors have contributed significantly to Russia's economic recovery, while other sectors are stagnant. Itskhoki and Ribakova ([2024]) document how Russia's foreign trade has been completely reorientated towards the East, and China is now by far Russia's biggest trading partner. At the same time, sanctions have been effective in reducing the value of sanctioned goods flowing to Russia. Simola ([2024]) reports that Russian companies have been unable to replace lost imported goods with domestic production. Moreover, the unit prices of many imported goods in the sanctioned categories have risen.

IV Conclusion

Sanctions and Russia's own actions have decoupled it from a large part of the global economy. Yet, Russia has been able to increase its GDP and at least its production in the war-related industries. This illustrates the difficulty of sanctioning a large economy that also has a sizeable current account surplus and low initial public debt. As long as Russia is able to sell its oil and other raw materials in the global markets, it can most likely maintain the current level of tax revenue. Sanctions have clearly limited Russia's access to critical high-technology goods and have made them more expensive. Yet, Russia has been able to maintain production in the military-related sectors at the current level for quite some time. Sanctions help Ukraine in its fight, but they will not decide the war in the absence of both financial and military assistance.

Iikka Korhonen

Bibliography

Literature

Ahn DP and Ludema R, 'The Sword and the Shield: The Economics of Targeted Sanctions' (2020) 130 *European Economic Review* 1.

Kalb M, *Imperial Gamble: Putin, Ukraine, and the New Cold War* (Brookings Institution Press 2015).

Krahnke T, Ferrari Minesso M, Mehl A and Vansteenkiste I, 'Seizing Central Bank Assets? Mimeo' (CEPR Discussion Paper No 19186, 2024) <https://www.riksbank.se/globalassets/media/konferenser/2024/monetary-and-financial-history-lessons-for-the-21st-century-21-22-november-2024/session-5-p2-seizing-central-bank-assets.pdf> accessed 4 December 2024.

International Monetary Fund, 'Russian Federation: 2019 Article IV Consultation-Press Release; Staff Report' (*International Monetary Fund*, 9 August 2019) <https://www.imf.org/en/Publications/CR/Issues/2019/08/01/Russian-Federation-2019-Article-IV-Consultation-Press-Release-Staff-Report-48549#:~:text=Summary,tax%20rate%20on%20private%20consumption> accessed 4 December 2024.

Itskhoki O and Ribakova E, 'The Economics of Sanctions: From Theory Into Practice' (2024) Brookings Papers on Economic Activity <https://www.brookings.edu/wp-content/uploads/2024/09/6_ItskhokiRibakova.pdf> accessed 4 December 2024.

Korhonen I, 'Sanctions and Counter-Sanctions – What are Their Economic Effects in Russia and Elsewhere?' (BOFIT

Policy Brief 2019) <https://ideas.repec.org/p/zbw/bofitb/22019.html> accessed 4 December 2024.

Pestova A and Mamonov M, 'Should We Care? The Economic Effects of Financial Sanctions on the Russian Economy' (BOFIT Discussion Papers No. 13/2019) <https://EconPapers.repec.org/RePEc:zbw:bofitp:bdp2019_013>.

Simola H, 'The Role of War-Related Industries in Russia's Recent Economic Recovery' (BOFIT Policy Brief 2023) <https://publications.bof.fi/bitstream/handle/10024/53201/bpb1623.pdf> accessed 4 December 2024.

Simola H, 'Recent Trends in Russia's Import Substitution of Technology Products' (BOFIT Policy Brief 2024) <https://publications.bof.fi/bitstream/handle/10024/53402/bpb524.v2.pdf?sequence=5&isAllowed=y> accessed 4 December 2024.

IIKKA KORHONEN

42. Sierra Leone

Alix J. Boucher

I Introduction

The Sierra Leone sanctions regime, which was in force between 1997 and 2010, became a model for how targeted sanctions should be designed and implemented in the two decades that followed. Sanctions became an instrument for enforcing democratic governance and transparency norms, not just across government institutions but also in key economic sectors.

II Overview of the Sierra Leone sanctions regime: 1997–2010

President Ahmad Kabbah, who had negotiated a peace agreement between the Revolutionary United Front (RUF) and the government after a civil war, was deposed in a military coup on 25 May 1997. In response, the Economic Community of West African States (ECOWAS) demanded that he be reinstated and imposed an embargo on petroleum and arms exports to Sierra Leone on 26 June 1997. ECOWAS had deployed a peacekeeping operation, ECOMOG, in 1995, tasking the mission with enforcing the embargo. On 8 October 1997, the United Nations Security Council (UNSC) imposed a travel ban on members of the junta and oil and arms embargoes (UNSC Res 1132 [1997]). The UNSC demanded that the junta relinquish power and restore Kabbah and constitutional order. The Conakry Agreement (23 October 1997) led to Kabbah's reinstatement on 10 March 1998.

The UNSC lifted the petroleum embargo (UNSC Res 1156 [1998]), then authorized the deployment of a small military observer mission (subsequent resolutions saw the mission's mandate expanded to peacekeeping and the troop ceiling increased to more than 17 000 troops by March 2001). The UNSC also modified the travel ban and arms embargo so that they no longer applied to the government. But ECOWAS and United Nations (UN) forces were unable to fully control the country, leaving rebel RUF forces in control of lucrative resources, particularly diamonds. On 5 July 2000, the UNSC imposed a diamonds export ban on Sierra Leone (UNSC Res 1306 [2000]) and appointed a UN panel of experts to monitor the implementation of the sanctions. The expert panel found that neighboring Liberia was violating sanctions by providing the RUF with support (UN Panel of Experts Report, December 2021), leading the UNSC to impose secondary sanctions on Liberia, the first such instance for the UNSC (UNSC Res 1346 [2001]).

After the war ended in January 2002, Kabbah won re-election in May 2002, and the sanctions were gradually phased out, with diamond sanctions lapsing in June 2003. The arms embargo and other measures, however, were maintained as an incentive to continue the peace process, including a demobilization, disarmament, and reintegration program for combatants, and the rebuilding of the Sierra Leonean armed forces. Sanctions were terminated in September 2010 (UNSC Res 1940 [2010]).

III Impact of Sierra Leone sanctions on structuring of multilateral sanctions and their uses

The initial rationale for imposing sanctions on Sierra Leone was to force the junta that had deposed President Kabbah to reinstate him and hold democratic elections. The UNSC, when imposing sanctions, increasingly recognized the link between autocracy and threats to peace and security (Charron and Portela [2015] 1384), and, thus, set requirements for lifting the measures that explicitly required countries to support democracy by holding free and fair elections and adopting transparent governance mechanisms, particularly for commodities thought to fund conflict (Charron and Portela [2015] 1373).

A second impact of sanctions on Sierra Leone was that they reinforced international efforts to adopt a trade certification scheme for diamonds, an effort that had been promoted by non-governmental organizations (NGOs), but whose implementation benefited from the attention of the UNSC on the matter (Vines and Cargill [2009] 52). The Panel of Experts on Angola, chaired by Ambassador Robert Fowler, similarly drew the attention of the UNSC, not only by documenting how the illicit exploitation of oil and diamonds was funding belligerents in Angola, but also by detailing the role of neighboring states and their leaders in fueling the war. Moreover, by making transparent governance of a key economic sector a requirement for lifting the sanctions, the norm of ensuring the transparent exploitation of key resources provided a rationale for imposing sanctions in the first place. The diamond embargo on Sierra Leone had a particularly important impact on raising awareness of the role of diamonds in funding conflict, and in turn, on prompting the creation of a diamond certification scheme and eventually better regulation of the diamond trade in general. The Sierra Leone certification of origin system, whose creation was required by the Security Council as a condition for removing the diamonds sanctions, was developed between July and October 2000 (Report of the Panel of Experts on Sierra Leone [2000] paras 99–109).

Sierra Leone's experience also emphasized the need to address unofficial (i.e., illegally smuggled) diamond exporting, since the bulk of the diamonds produced in Sierra Leone transited through Liberia. The Sierra Leone sanctions, along with simultaneous measures for Angola, therefore contributed to the adoption of the global international certification scheme for rough diamonds, which eventually became known as the Kimberley Process Certification Scheme (KPCS [2024]). With Sierra Leone meeting that condition, the Council allowed the diamonds sanctions to lapse in June 2003. More generally, the Kimberley Process Certification Scheme was soon followed by other similar mechanisms, including the Extractive Industries Transparency Initiative (EITI [2024]) and the OECD Due Diligence Guidance for Responsible Business Conduct ([2018]).

The arms embargo, travel ban, and asset freeze served as the final incentive for rebuilding a democratic and accountable security force. The remaining sanctions were lifted only once Sierra Leone had completely revamped its security force in 2010 (Albrecht and Jackson [2009]). Indicative of the adoption of using sanctions to enforce democratic governance norms, the United States, Canada, and the European Union (EU) briefly imposed targeted sanctions on Sierra Leone after international observers found that the 24 June 2023 general elections had been marred by fraud.

Finally, the model of using small expert panels, first adopted in Angola and Sierra Leone, was then replicated for sanctions regimes mostly in Africa, but also in other contexts. These panels took on the task not just of monitoring potential violations, but also of assessing progress toward conditions for lifting the sanctions and, as the Sierra Leone panel had done, providing recommendations for helping the targeted countries meet those conditions and allow for sanctions to be terminated.

Bibliography

Literature

Albrecht P and Jackson P, *Security System Transformation in Sierra Leone, 1997–2007* (University of Birmingham 2009).

Amaral J, 'UN Sanctions and Mediation in Sierra Leone: Opportunities and Pitfalls When Managing Veto Players' (2022) 28 *Global Governance* 274.

Boucher AJ and Holt VK, *Targeting Spoilers: The Role of United Nations Panels of Experts* (Stimson Center 2009).

Charron A and Portela C, 'The UN, Regional Sanctions and Africa' (2015) 91(6) *International Affairs* 1369.

Hellquist E, 'Regional Sanctions and the Struggle for Democracy: Introduction to the Special Issue' (2021) 91(6) *International Political Science Review* 437.

Vines A and Cargill T, 'The Impact of UN Sanctions and their Panels of Experts: Sierra Leone and Liberia' (2009) 65(1) *International Journal* 45.

Documents

Extractive Industries Transparency Initiative (2024) <https://eiti.org/> accessed 16 July 2024.

Kimberley Process (2024) <https://www.kimberleyprocess.com/> accessed 16 July 2024.

OECD, 'OECD Due Diligence Guidance for Responsible Business Conduct' (2018) <https://mneguidelines.oecd.org/OECD-Due-Diligence-Guidance-for-Responsible-Business-Conduct.pdf>.

UNSC Res 1132 (8 October 1997) UN Doc. S/RES/1132.

UNSC Res 1156 (16 March 1998) UN Doc. S/RES/1156.

UNSC Res 1306 (5 July 2000) UN Doc. S/RES/1306.

UNSC Res 1346 (30 March 2001) UN Doc. S/RES/1346.

UNSC Res 1940 (29 September 2010) UN Doc. S/RES/1940.

UNSC 'Report of the Panel of Experts Established by Resolution 1306 (2000) to the Security Council Committee Established Pursuant to Resolution 1132 (1997) Concerning Sierra Leone' (20 December 2000) UN Doc. S/2000/1195.

Alix J. Boucher

43. South Africa

JO-ANSIE VAN WYK

I Introduction

The National Party (NP) assumed political power in South Africa in 1948. The party legalised and enforced apartheid (apart-ness) as a racially based political system to keep a white minority in power, while Black South Africans suffered the consequences of social injustice, political exclusion, violent control and social isolation. International punitive measures to persuade South Africa to terminate apartheid and its regional effects (such as restrictions on labour movements from the region to South African gold mines and bans on South African exports to the region) followed; however, over time, these measures hardened as a survival strategy for South Africa's white regime. The historical international sanctions episode (1963–94) against apartheid South Africa remains a case study in states that defy international law and the consequences thereof.

II Prelude to sanctions and the criminalisation of apartheid

The international response to South Africa's racial policies predated 1948. Barely a year into the existence of the United Nations (UN), in 1946, India lodged a complaint about the treatment of people of Indian origin in South Africa at the UN. The United Nations General Assembly (UNGA) responded with a resolution stating that the treatment of Indians in South Africa should comply with the bilateral agreements between India and South Africa on persons of Indian origin, and the UN Charter (UNGA [1946] para. 2).

After 1948, the UN repeatedly appealed to South Africa to terminate apartheid and install democratic rights. The Sharpeville Massacre (21 March 1960) was a turning point at home and abroad: more than 250 people were killed or injured by police during a peaceful protest. Consequently, the banned African National Congress (ANC) intensified its liberation struggle through the internationalisation of its struggle, repeatedly calling for comprehensive and mandatory sanctions against South Africa, while the organisation also established anti-apartheid organisations in several countries (Tambo [1982]; Konieczna and Skinner [2019]).

UN sanctions against South Africa became one of the most comprehensive actions against any UN member and escalated from a voluntary arms embargo (UNSC [1963]) to a comprehensive mandatory arms embargo and more sanctions against South Africa (UNSC [1977]; UNSC [1985]). The UNGA led the charge, calling for extensive economic sanctions against South Africa, requesting states to terminate diplomatic relations, close ports to South African flag vessels and prohibit their ships from entering South African ports, boycotting South African goods, arms and ammunition sales, and refusing landing and passenger facilities (UNGA [1962]). The UNGA called on the UN Security Council (UNSC) to 'take appropriate measures, including sanctions', to secure South Africa's compliance with the UN Charter and established a Special Committee against Apartheid to review South Africa's racial policies and report to the UNGA (UNGA [1962] paras 4, 5 and 8). The Special Committee became a significant actor in the global isolation of and the imposition of extensive punitive actions against the apartheid regime as it provided evidence of the injustices of apartheid and the regime's behaviour.

On 7 August 1963, the UNSC imposed a voluntary arms embargo against South Africa (UNSC [1963] para. 3), but the five permanent members of the Council (the P5) disagreed on the need for wider economic sanctions against Pretoria. A further blow to the apartheid regime's economic and ideological foundation came in the form of the UN oil embargo on 13 November 1963, the Organisation of Petroleum Exporting Countries' (OPEC) oil embargo in 1973 and the UNGA's adoption of the International Convention on the Suppression and Punishment of the Crime of Apartheid in 1973. However, the UN and the ANC published evidence of some Western states' continued and uninterrupted military collaboration with apartheid South Africa despite the voluntary arms embargo against the country; effectively defying the arms embargo (UN [1973]; ANC [1975] 12; ANC [1976] 32–9). Following the discovery of South Africa's nuclear weapons test site in September 1977, the UNSC imposed a mandatory arms embargo against South Africa on 4 November 1977 (UNSC [1977]). However, some states continued to support South Africa, and it took almost another decade to change this. In 1985, the UN imposed new sanctions that required member states that had not introduced sanctions against South Africa to do so. For the UNSC, 'only the total elimination of apartheid and the establishment in South Africa of a free, united and democratic society on the basis of universal suffrage can lead to a solution' (UNSC [1985] para. 5). Italy, Denmark, Sweden, France, Portugal, Spain, the Netherlands, Austria and Ireland, acting individually, strengthened their restrictions against South Africa. In comparison, the United States implemented the most comprehensive measures against South Africa, the Comprehensive Anti-Apartheid Act (CAAA), albeit in 1986, to 'end apartheid in South Africa and lead to the establishment of a non-racial, democratic form of government' and included a comprehensive list of measures 'to undermine apartheid' banning imports of Krugerrands, military articles, products from parastatal organisations, uranium, coal, sugar, agricultural products and food, iron and steel (Comprehensive Anti-Apartheid Act of 1986 [1986]). The Act also prohibited exports of computers, munitions, crude oil and petroleum products, loans and accounts to the South African government, air transportation, nuclear trade, new investment, US government procurement, US tourism, US government assistance to, investment in, or subsidy for trade with South Africa, and cooperation with the South African armed forces (Comprehensive Anti-Apartheid Act of 1986 [1986]).

The European Economic Community (EEC) and the Commonwealth also imposed sanctions following UNSC Resolution 566 (1985). The EEC imposed a comprehensive set of mandatory sanctions against South Africa on 16 September 1986, banning imports of iron, steel and gold coins from and new investments in South Africa but excluded coal, diamonds or other forms of gold. Commonwealth action against South Africa also escalated over time even though the country withdrew from it in 1961. On 5 August 1986, Commonwealth Heads of Government adopted 'further substantial economic measures' against South Africa to dismantle apartheid and establish a non-racial and representative democracy, banning air links, investment in agricultural products, government procurement and contracts, tourism, new public and private bank loans and uranium, coal, iron and steel imports (Commonwealth [1986] 292). The Commonwealth also terminated double taxation agreements, government assistance to invest in, and trade with, South Africa, and decided to withdraw all consular facilities in South Africa. In contrast to these measures, the UK government, albeit a member of the Commonwealth, led by Margaret Thatcher, declined to support these measures, opting for a voluntary ban on new investment in South Africa and on the promotion of tourism to South Africa, and accepting and implementing 'any EEC decision' to ban the import of coal, iron and steel, and of gold coins from South Africa (Commonwealth [1986] 292–3). Therefore, compared to the Commonwealth, the United Kingdom took a less stringent approach to sanctions against South Africa, including 'a voluntary ban' rather than the Commonwealth's 'substantial' measures.

III Impact and regime survival

Sanctions as coercive diplomatic instruments have produced mixed results, as target states do not always change their domestic and foreign policies, turn to status-seeking behaviour, escalate aggression and/or seek alternative markets via third-party states (so-called 'black knights') (Borozna and Kochtcheeva [2024] 13). Despite instances of the circumvention of sanctions against South Africa and the long time it took to erode the apartheid regime's ideological and moral (apartheid as a crime against humanity and a threat to global peace), sociocultural (through sports and cultural boycotts) and economic foundations, the South African sanctions episode had contributed to the intended regime and social change in the country.

The diplomatic consequences of sanctions against South Africa included the loss of diplomatic status. Although only a few states officially terminated diplomatic ties with South Africa, as called for by the UNGA in 1961, South Africa lost its seat on the International Atomic Energy Agency (IAEA) board of governors, was not allowed to maintain an embassy in some countries, diplomats' credentials were denied, bilateral visa agreements were suspended and, South Africa, under international pressure or out of deviance, withdrew its membership from multilateral organisations such as the Commonwealth (1986).

The economic impact of sanctions on South Africa could be described as a success. By 1982, South Africa's international trade was limited to six states, namely, the United States, the United Kingdom, West Germany, France, Italy and Japan. Prior to the CAAA, the United States led a disinvestment campaign against South Africa that, by 1984, had resulted in 162 US companies disinvesting from the country, a trend that continued after the CAAA. By 1987, US and UK trade with South Africa had decreased, with US sanctions against South African exports costing the latter about $417 million (Mendelowitz [1988] 3–5, 9). The refusal of Western banks in 1985 to extend existing or provide new loans to South Africa was another blow. In retaliation, South Africa declared a moratorium on the repayment of $24 billion owed to these banks, forcing them to negotiate with South Africa on the rescheduling of its debt. Additionally, once the CAAA was enacted, generous loans from the United States also declined significantly (Mendelowitz [1988] 7–8).

Whereas voluntary punitive measures against South Africa's international engagements regarding sports and cultural matters were successful in isolating the apartheid government, the UNSC mandatory arms embargo was not as effective as several states continued to trade and collaborate with South Africa. Some unintended consequences of sanctions enabled regime survival. The United States designated ten minerals as strategic and essential for its economy or defence industry, and exempted them from the CAAA. Between 1983 and 1987, US imports of South African platinum group metals increased significantly, while West Germany and Portugal refused to support the EEC ban on South African coal (Mendelowitz [1988] 13).

The apartheid regime was astute in circumventing sanctions through new trade channels, secret bilateral agreements and 'black knights' (Borozna and Kochtcheeva [2024] 27). South Africa signed secret agreements with, for example, Israel and Iran, the latter to circumvent the oil embargoes against South Africa.

The mid-1980s were a turning point in this sanctions episode. Besides the UN, Commonwealth, EEC and OPEC sanctions, the country's main bilateral trading partners, most notably the United States, increased economic pressure on the regime. The mid-1980s thus also saw the first of a series of talks between the apartheid regime and the exiled ANC, essentially a strategy to extend regime survival on the regime's terms.

IV Conclusion

The United States lifted sanctions on 10 July 1991, with the EEC following on 4 October 1993 and the UN on 25 May 1994, after the inauguration of a newly elected government headed by Nelson Mandela – a black man.

Sanctions against apartheid South Africa remain significant. They represent an attempt at global normative convergence against apartheid. Although it took more than 50 years to address racism in South Africa, these sanctions contributed to regime change, the end of apartheid and democracy in South Africa. It was also one of the most comprehensive international sanctions regimes against any country at the time, superseding, at times, Cold War tensions. A notable aspect is the role played by the ANC and its efforts to establish a global anti-apartheid movement and to work through UN structures. The South African case remains significant for understanding the long-term economic consequences of sanctions. Whereas post-apartheid South Africa could rejoin the diplomatic community as a paragon of conflict resolutions and reconciliation, the same cannot be said about its international economic rehabilitation. The country lost its historical trade partners, and its public and private industrial base collapsed, opening the door for emerging geo-political actors such as China, globally renowned for its poor human rights record. In post-apartheid South Africa, these international sanctions are regarded as one of the outcomes of the ANC's internationalisation of the anti-apartheid struggle and a contributing factor to the end of apartheid despite its lasting economic impact on the country as South Africa lost investment and export opportunities during the sanctions period.

Bibliography

Literature

Borozna A and Kochtcheeva LV, *War by Other Means Western. Sanctions on Russia and Moscow's Response* (Palgrave Macmillan/Springer 2024).

Konieczna A and Skinner R (eds), *A Global History of Anti-Apartheid. 'Forward to Freedom' in South Africa* (Oxford Palgrave Macmillan 2019).

Tambo O, 'Statement at the Meeting of the Special Committee against Apartheid' (*South African History Online*, 12 January 1982) <https://www.sahistory.org.za/archive/statement-oliver-tambo-meeting-special-committee-against-apartheid-12-january-1982> accessed 2 September 2024.

Documents

African National Congress, 'Introduction' (Sechaba, Vol. 9, Nos. 11/12, 1975) 12.

African National Congress, 'International Nuclear Conspiracy with Racist South Africa' (Sechaba, Vol. 10, 1976) 32–9.

Commonwealth, *Commonwealth Heads of Government Review Meeting Communiqué* (3–5 August 1986) 291–4. <https://www.thecommonwealth-ilibrary.org/index.php/comsec/catalog/download/886/886/7472?inline=1> accessed 2 September 2024.

Mendelowitz AI, 'U.S. Sanctions Against South Africa' (Statement of the Senior Associate Director, National Security and International Affairs Division, U.S. General Accounting Office before the Committee on Foreign Relations of the United States Senate, GAO/T-NSIAD-38-34, 24 June 1988) <https://www.gao.gov/assets/t-nsiad-88-34.pdf> accessed 2 September 2024.

Legislation

Comprehensive Anti-Apartheid Act of 1986 (Public Law 99-440, 1986) <https://www.congress.gov/99/statute/STATUTE-100/STATUTE-100-Pg1086.pdf> accessed 2 September 2024.

UN Documents

UNGA, 'Treatment of Indians in the Union of South Africa' UNGA Res 44(1) (8 December 1946) UN Doc. A/RES/44 (1) (1946).

UNGA, 'The Policies of Apartheid of the Government of the Republic of South Africa' UNGA Res 1761/1962 (6 November 1962) UN Doc. A/RES/1761(XVIII).

UNSC, 'Questions Relating to the Policies of Apartheid of the Government of the Republic of South Africa' UNSC Res 181/1963 (7 August 1963) UN Doc. S/RES/181 (1963).

UNGA, 'Question of South West Africa' UNGA Res 1899 (XVIII)/1963 (13 November 1963) UN Doc. A/RES/1900(XVIII) (1963).

UN, 'International Convention on the Suppression and Punishment of the Crime of Apartheid' Vol. 1015, 1-14861 (30 November 1973).

UNSC, 'The Question of South Africa' UNSC Res 419/1977 (4 November 1977) UN Doc. S/RES/418 (1977).

UNSC, 'The Question of South Africa' UNSC Res 569/1985 (26 July 1985) UN Doc. S/RES/569 (1985).

Jo-Ansie van Wyk

44. Syria

Peter Seeberg

I Introduction

Since March 1963, the Syrian Arab Socialist Ba'ath Party, offering a secular Arab nationalist ideology, has been the only officially recognized Syrian political party. An internal power struggle within the party ended with victory in 1970 for Hafez al-Asad, who was an extremely authoritarian leader of Syria until his death in 2000. During this period, the Sunni Muslim majority, reluctantly, learned to live with the Syrian regime dominated by the Alawite elite (an originally Shia Muslim minority), and a hardcore anti-Israel and anti-Western foreign policy. With the weakening of the Soviet Union in the late 1980s, al-Asad manoeuvred Syria away from the influence of Iraq's Saddam Hussein and strengthened its relations with the Islamic Republic of Iran. Attempting to prevent the disintegration of Lebanon, Syria invaded in 1976 and came to play a dominant role there for three decades. In 1979, the United States designated Syria a state sponsor of terrorism – due to Syrian relations with radical leftist non-state actors (the Popular Front for the Liberation of Palestine, the Democratic Front for the Liberation of Palestine, etc., and Islamist groups like Hezbollah, Hamas, and Islamic Jihad) – and imposed sanctions on Syria.

II International sanctions on Syria before the civil war

In November 1986, the European Community (EC) imposed sanctions on Syria, including a ban on arms sales, a suspension of exchange visits by high-level officials, a review of the activities of Syrian diplomatic missions, and tighter surveillance of the operations of Syrian Arab Airlines. The measures were imposed because Syria was responsible for an attempted bombing of an Israeli aircraft in London; the measures were lifted in 1994. Hafez al-Asad died in 2000, passing his dictatorship on to his son, Bashar al-Asad. However, despite promises of reform and modernization, the regime and its policies did not change substantially.

The sanctions episodes imposed by the United States were extended in 2004, based on Executive Order (13338), aiming to affect Syrian policies "supporting terrorism, continuing its occupation of Lebanon, pursuing weapons of mass destruction (WMDs) and missile programs, and undermining U.S. and international efforts to stabilize Iraq" (Executive Order 13338 [2004] 26751). The US sanctions were followed in 2006 and 2008 by new measures because the Syrian regime continued to engage in conduct that earlier sanctions had targeted. For these reasons, a permanent diplomatic crisis characterized the relationship between Syria and the United States in these years. Still, the US sanctions imposed on Syria, most of them measures aimed at blocking the property of persons within the Syrian regime, did not affect the regime significantly (Alalwani and Shaar [2021]).

In the mid-1980s, US reports indicated that Syria was developing chemical weapons. This was, as mentioned, reflected in the US sanctions. However, the toxic attacks in the years after the Arab Spring resulted in further sanctions, for instance by the European Union (EU), which added names to the lists of persons and entities who were subject to restrictive measures because they had assisted in the production and development of chemical weapons for the Syrian regime or shared responsibility for organizing chemical weapons attacks (Council Decision 2013/255).

III Sanctioning Syria following the Arab Spring

The Arab Spring changed the political climate for Syria in 2011. Aiming to avoid a regime change like in Egypt and Tunisia, the Syrian regime decided to clamp down harshly on demonstrations and protests. The situation escalated and led to an extremely violent civil war fought by the Syrian army, secret services, and regime-loyal militias against uncoordinated groups of anti-regime fighters, causing significant human loss, millions of Syrian refugees fleeing to neighbouring countries, in particular Turkey, Lebanon, and Jordan, and huge numbers of internally displaced persons in Syria.

The conflict and the resulting humanitarian crises in Syria led to comprehensive sanctions episodes applied by the United States and the EU, with the intentions of weakening the regime considered by the senders to be a rogue state. The US sanctions were applied via Executive Order 13572 of 29 April 2011, which referred to the human rights abuses in connection with the violent repression of the

Syrian opposition. The measures blocked all property in the United States owned by Maher al-Asad (commander of the Syrian Army's Fourth Armoured Division, and a younger brother of the Syrian President) and the assets of two other persons and two specific entities (the Syrian General Intelligence Directorate and the Islamic Revolutionary Guard Corps) involved in the violent repression of the Syrian opposition. These measures were later extended to cover hundreds of other persons and entities involved in the atrocities against the Syrian opposition and the population in general.

EU sanctions related to the Syrian crisis were applied in May 2011. As in the American case, a few persons were subject to restrictive measures (and again, the first person mentioned was Maher al-Asad) aiming to stop the violence and put political pressure on the regime. In the following months, the sanctions list continued to expand and, from September 2011, an EU import ban on oil products was added to the sanctions, leading to a drastic fall in EU imports from Syria. However, in April 2013, a ban was lifted on exports from the opposition-controlled areas of Syria in order to help the civilian population and support the opposition. A month later, this was followed by new names and entities being added to the sanctions list in order to signal a more active EU policy (Seeberg [2015] 70). Furthermore, the EU invited states with close relations to the EU, among which were Bosnia and Herzegovina, Iceland, Norway, and Serbia, to align with the EU sanctions – a practice that, by 2020, had been adopted by 14 countries (Cardwell and Moret [2023] 7–8).

Pointing to what EU sources describe as the world's largest humanitarian disaster and refugee crisis with 7.2 million internally displaced, 5.2 million registered Syrian refugees, and 7 out of 10 Syrians in need of humanitarian assistance, the EU had expanded its list of individuals and entities sanctioned to 316 individuals and 86 entities by June 2025 (Council of the EU Press release [2024]; see also Boogaerts et al. [2016] 217; Seeberg [2016]).

In May 2011, Canada applied targeted sanctions against the Assad regime that were similar to the US and the EU sanctions (SOR/2011-113 to 116). Canada also extended and expanded measures in the following years, including the freezing of assets belonging to individuals and entities associated with the Syrian government. Other states, like Australia and Switzerland, also imposed targeted individual and sectoral restrictive measures. Furthermore, regional actors imposed sanctions on Syria: the League of Arab States (Arab League) (see chapter) in 2011 imposed different forms of sanctions on Syria and expelled the country from the organization (BBC News [27 November 2011]). Turkey also, in 2011, imposed its own sanctions on Bashar al-Asad's regime, freezing financial assets and cutting strategic links with Syria. In May 2023, the Arab League, based on certain concessions from Syria, readmitted the regime into the organization. A Jordanian plan suggesting that Syria should take steps to reduce Iranian influence in Syria, restrict drugs and weapons smuggling, and prepare for the safe return of Syrian refugees abroad formed the basis for the agreement on readmission and a gradual reduction of the sanctions (Loft [2023] 21).

The international and regional sanctions have had negative consequences for the targeted Syrian individuals and entities, and the impact of the sanctions on the humanitarian situation in Syria has been significant (Leclerc [2023] 6). Nevertheless, for a long while the survival of the Syrian regime as such was not in jeopardy. Very much due to military and financial support from Russia and Iran/Hezbollah, Bashar al-Asad and the elite around him were able to muddle through and secure the survival of the regime without being seriously affected by the sanctions. However, in December 2024, the regime collapsed under pressure from oppositional forces and Bashar al-Assad left, hiding in Moscow. The new regime was during 2025 met by a gradual lifting of the US and EU sanctions.

Bibliography

Literature

Alalwani W and Shaar K, 'A Comprehensive Review of the Effectiveness of US and EU Sanctions on Syria' (6 August 2021) Middle East Institute.

BBC News, 'Syria Unrest: Arab League Adopts Sanctions in Cairo' (27 November 2011).

Boogaerts A, Portela C and Drieskens E, 'One Swallow Does Not Make Spring: A Critical Juncture Perspective on the EU

PETER SEEBERG

Sanctions in Response to the Arab Spring' (2016) 21(2) *Mediterranean Politics* 205.
Cardwell PJ and Moret E, 'The EU, Sanctions and Regional Leadership' (2023) 32(1) *European Security* 1.
Leclerc G, 'Impact of Sanctions on the Humanitarian Situation in Syria' (2023) European Parliamentary Research Service.
Loft P, 'Syria's Civil War in 2023. Assad Back in the Arab League' (2023) House of Commons Library.
Seeberg P, 'The Crisis in Syria, International and Regional Sanctions, and the Transformation of the Political Order' in Beck M, Jung D and Seeberg P (eds), *The Levant in Turmoil. Syria, Palestine, and the Transformation of Middle Eastern Politics* (Palgrave Macmillan 2016) 101.
Seeberg P, 'The Limits of the Sanctions Regime Against Syria' in Dreyer I and Luengo-Cabrera J (eds), *On Target? EU Sanctions as Security Policy Tools* (ISSEU Report, No. 25, September 2015) 67.

Documents

Canada Gazette, Statutory Instruments. SOR/2011-113 to 116 (8 June 2011).
Council of the EU Press release: 'Syria: Council Renews Restrictive Measures and Extends Humanitarian Exemption for Another Year' (28 May 2024).
Council Decision 2013/255/CFSP of 31 May 2013 concerning restrictive measures against Syria OJ L147/14.
Federal Register, The President, Executive Order 13338 (13 May 2004).
Federal Register, The President, Executive Order 13572 (29 April 2011).

45. Venezuela

Stefano Palestini and Luciano Quispe

I Introduction

Since 2014, Venezuela has experienced a clear democratic deterioration (Rosales and Jiménez [2021]; Corrales [2023]). According to V-Dem or Freedom House, Venezuela is a dictatorship due to the extent of the power concentration vested in the president, the control of several state institutions, and the erosion of constitutional checks and balances. Furthermore, the political opposition has been systematically persecuted, arrested, and exiled. Venezuelan civil society, in constant mobilization since the election of Maduro in 2013, suffered severe episodes of state violence and repression in 2014, 2018, and 2024. Moreover, freedom of the press has been significantly reduced. Together with the political crisis, an economic debacle has generated a massive exodus of around 7.7 million Venezuelans, according to the Interagency Coordination Platform for Refugees and Migrants (2023).

II The US and EU sanctions

International sanctions are one of the key instruments that have been used by states and regional intergovernmental organizations to force a change in policy and, arguably, to facilitate a possible change of regime in Venezuela. Hitherto, all sanctions imposed against Venezuela have been autonomous from the United Nations. Western governments have sought to impose specific costs on members of the ruling elite through targeted sanctions. These measures include travel bans and asset freezes. Starting in 2014, after the irregular elections that brought Maduro to power and the government crackdown on the opposition, the United States imposed visa restrictions and asset freezes on key members of the ruling coalition (Visa Restrictions against human rights abuses in Venezuela and Defense of Human Rights and Civil Society Act of 2014). Among the targeted individuals were President Maduro, the former president of the Constituent National Assembly Diosdado Cabello, the prosecutor general of Venezuela Tarek William Saab, and the Minister of Defense Vladimir Padrino. These first packages of targeted sanctions were followed by measures broader in scope on institutions central to the economy of the regime, such as the state-owned company Petróleos de Venezuela (PDVSA) and the Central Bank of Venezuela. Executive Orders 13808, 13827, 13835, and 13857 imposed by the government of Donald Trump between 2017 and 2020 sought to limit the access of these institutions to international credit or prohibit transactions (Palestini and Villarroel [2024]).

In parallel, Canada and the European Union (EU) began to impose sanctions in 2017, including asset freezes and prohibitions on economic activities in the case of the former, and travel bans, asset freezes, and arms and goods bans in the case of the latter. Specifically, in 2017, Canada sanctioned 19 members of the Venezuelan elite, including President Maduro, under the Justice for Victims of Corrupt Foreign Officials Act (or Magnitsky Act). Following the line set by the EU, Switzerland in 2018 and the United Kingdom in 2019 also imposed bans on arms and military goods, in addition to travel bans and asset freezes, following common patterns of alignment.

III Regional sanctions in Latin America

In addition to Western countries, Latin American states and regional organizations have played an active role in different phases of the political crisis and autocratization process in Venezuela. Some countries, such as Panama, have imposed sanctions on specific personalities, such as the asset freeze of several critical actors of the regime, like the above-mentioned Diosdado Cabello, Vice-President Delcy Rodríguez, and First Lady Cilia Flores (Resolution No. 02-018). Likewise, the Lima Group, a coalition of Latin American states, urged the international community to continue adopting sanctions against Maduro's regime and authorized its members to do so in January 2019. In a similar manner, members of the Inter-American Treaty of Reciprocal Assistance in 2019 advocated for the imposition of financial sanctions on members of Maduro's regime.

Finally, the Common Market of the South (Mercosur) suspended the membership of Venezuela on two occasions. In December 2016, Venezuela was suspended for violation of the Protocol of Accession to the organization, following the contemporary practice of regional international organizations to impose sanctions against members that breach treaty commitments (von Borzyskowski and Portela [2023]). In August 2017, Venezuela was indefinitely suspended on the basis of Mercosur's democracy clause, the Protocol of Ushuaia (Palestini and Villarroel [2024]). Other regional organizations such as the Organization of American States were close to suspending Venezuela, but the initiative did not pass the two-thirds voting threshold due to the ability of Maduro's government to build a support coalition within the organization. This is an indication of the level of polarization that the Venezuelan crisis has brought about in the region.

IV The impact of sanctions

In 2022, the administration of US President Joe Biden initiated direct talks with Maduro's government, offering to lift specific sanctions if Maduro's government resumed in good faith a negotiation process with the opposition. These talks led to the Barbados Agreement of 2023, in which the government committed to hold free and fair presidential elections in 2024. As a result of the agreement, the US Department of the Treasury lifted a group of sanctions on the oil and gas industry, arguing that the sanctions would be reimposed if the Maduro government did not comply with the agreement (AJIL [2024]). However, in 2024, the Venezuelan government vetoed Maria Corina Machado's presidential candidacy, arrested several members of the opposition, and denied the participation of the EU in election monitoring, forcing the United States to reimpose sanctions against the Venezuelan oil industry in April and impose new sanctions on 16 individuals in September after the 28 July elections.

Undoubtedly, the sanctions have had a severe impact on the Venezuelan economy by directly affecting the most important export industry: the oil sector. Although several oil-exporting countries saw an increase in their revenues due to the increase in oil prices in 2017, Venezuela did not experience such growth, coinciding with the sanctions imposed on PDVSA, as Executive Orders 13808 and 13857 by the United States. From that year onwards, oil production contracts for the following years coincided with the sanctions imposed by the United States on PDVSA in 2019 and the sanctions imposed on partners of PDVSA, such as the Russian company Rosneft in 2020. Even though the collapse of the Venezuelan economy started in 2014 with the drop in international oil prices and the government's economic mismanagement, it is likely that the many layers of sanctions on the Venezuelan economy have curtailed its capacity to recover.

Furthermore, sanctions may also explain the government's reliance on alternative sources of financing. Venezuela has become China's largest debtor in the region. After the first package of US sanctions in 2014, there have been at least 11 publicly announced deliveries of financial assistance from China to Venezuela, consisting of loans, grants, and debt restructuring. On the other hand, Venezuela has increased its relations with other autocracies at the international level, such as Cuba and Russia, which offer security and intelligence support, important for hampering elite defection and the rise of an alternative leadership (Gratius [2022]). Arguably, this international support has undercut the impact of the sanctions.

V Conclusion

Despite their scope, international sanctions have not been effective to date in generating either a significant shift in policy or a transition to a democratic regime. Maduro's regime has survived internal and external pressure and has been able to weather the storm, even radicalizing authoritarian practices. On the other hand, international actions – including the imposition and lifting of sanctions – have suffered from weak coordination, falling short of a coherent multilateral approach, despite existing multilateral instruments and frameworks in the region, such as the Inter-American Democratic Charter (Palestini and Martinelli [2023]). In this scenario, international sanctions have not led to concrete changes in the behavior of Maduro's government, which has been able to withstand the material and reputational costs derived from sanctions. Following the 2024 presidential elections, the crisis is still ongoing despite the restitution of previous and the imposition of new unilateral sanctions.

STEFANO PALESTINI AND LUCIANO QUISPE

Bibliography

Literature

Corrales J, *Autocracy Rising: How Venezuela Transitioned to Authoritarianism* (Brookings Institution Press 2023).

Gratius S, 'The West against the Rest? Democracy versus Autocracy Promotion in Venezuela' (2022) 41(1) *Bulletin of Latin American Research* 141.

Palestini S and Martinelli E, 'Enforcing Peoples' Right to Democracy: Transnational Activism and Regional Powers in Contemporary Inter-American Relations' (2023) 29(3) *European Journal of International Relations* 780.

Palestini S and Villarroel Y, '"What Gives You the Right?" Foreign Policymakers' Perceptions of the Legitimacy of Sanctions against Democratic Breakdown in Venezuela (2014–2019)' (2024) 37 *Cambridge Review of International Affairs* 1.

Rosales A and Jiménez M, 'Venezuela: Autocratic Consolidation and Splintered Economic Liberalization' (2021) 41(2) *Revista de Ciencia Política* 425.

'The US Provides and Then Rescinds Sanctions Relief for Venezuela' (2024) 118 *American Journal of International Law* 344.

von Borzyskowski I and Portela C, 'Global Governance from Below: Regional Sanctions as Drivers of UN Sanctions' (2023) 67(10) *Journal of Conflict Resolution* 1930.

Documents

Canada, Justice for Victims of Corrupt Foreign Officials Act (S.C. 2017, c. 21) (6 November 2017).

EU, Council Decision (CFSP) 2017/2074 of 13 November 2017 concerning restrictive measures in view of the situation in Venezuela [2017] OJ L 295/60.

Interagency Coordination Platform for Refugees and Migrants (2023) <https://www.r4v.info/en#:~:text=The%20Inter%2Dagency%20Coordination%20Platform,17%20countries%20in%20Latin%20America> accessed 15 january 2025.

Lima Group Declaration (4 January 2019) <https://www.international.gc.ca/world-monde/international_relations-relations_internationales/latin_america-amerique_latine/2019-01-04-lima_group-groupe_lima.aspx?lang=eng> accessed 15 January 2025.

Panama's Ministry of Economy and Finance, 'Resolución No. 02-018 por la cual se dispone la publicación de la lista de personas expuestas políticamente de la República Bolivariana de Venezuela' (27 March 2018).

UK, The Venezuela (Sanctions) (EU Exit) Regulations 2019 (31 January 2019).

US, The Venezuela Defense of Human Rights and Civil Society Act of 2014 (S. 2142).

US, Executive Order 13692 (8 March 2015).

US, Executive Order 13808 (24 August 2017).

US, Executive Order 13827 (19 March 2018).

US, Executive Order 13835 (21 May 2018).

US, Executive Order 13850 (1 November 2018).

US, Executive Order 13857 (25 January 2019).

US, Executive Order 13884 (5 August 2019).

Ushuaia Protocol on democratic commitment in the Mercosur, the Republic of Bolivia and the Republic of Chile (24 July 1998) 2177 UNTS 373.

STEFANO PALESTINI AND LUCIANO QUISPE

46. Yemen

Zuzana Hudáková

I Introduction

The United Nations Security Council (UNSC) adopted sanctions on Yemen in February 2014 to support the political transition that followed the ouster of former President Ali Abdullah Saleh. They consist of an asset freeze, a travel ban and, since April 2015, a targeted arms import embargo on specific individuals and entities (UNSC Res 2140 [2014]; Res 2216 [2015]).

II Threats of sanctions

The UNSC first discussed the possibility of imposing sanctions on Yemen in October 2011, in the context of Resolution 2014 (2011) and the ongoing 'Arab Spring' protests calling for the resignation of President Saleh. Saleh, who had been in power since 1978, stepped down the following month amid United Nations (UN) mediation efforts and significant domestic and international pressure. The negotiated political transition, laid out in the Gulf Cooperation Council Initiative and the accompanying UN-mediated implementation mechanism, included the formation of a government of national unity, the holding of early presidential elections, the formal transfer of power from former President Saleh, the convening of a Conference for National Dialogue, the adoption of a new constitution and the organization of parliamentary and presidential elections under the new constitution (Office of the Special Adviser to the UN Secretary-General on Yemen [2011]).

The use of sanctions was formally threatened on 12 June 2012 in Resolution 2051 to address 'actions aimed at undermining the Government of National Unity and the political transition' led by the newly elected President Abd Rabbuh Mansour Hadi (UNSC Res 2051 [2012]). The UNSC reiterated its readiness to impose sanctions in its press statements on 28 September 2012 (SC/10778 [2012]) and 27 November 2013 (SC/11195 [2013]), while the 15 February 2013 presidential statement explicitly named former President Saleh as interfering in Yemen's transition (UNSC Presidential Statement 3 [2013]; on the use and effectiveness of threats of sanctions in the country see Hudáková [2022]).

III The adoption of sanctions and initial designations

However, sanctions were not adopted until 26 February 2014, when the UNSC authorized the imposition of an asset freeze and a travel ban on those 'engaging in or providing support for acts that threaten the peace, security or stability of Yemen', without identifying any targets (UNSC Res 2140 [2014]). As specified in Resolution 2140, such acts include obstructing or undermining the successful completion of the political transition, impeding the implementation of outcomes of the National Dialogue Conference through violence, violating international human rights law or international humanitarian law and engaging in human rights abuses in Yemen.

No individuals or entities were subject to the UN sanctions until 7 November 2014, when the UN Sanctions Committee designated three individuals: former President Saleh and two Houthi military commanders (SC/11636 [2014]). The Houthis (Ansar Allah), a Zaydi Shi'a group from northern Yemen that had fought the Saleh regime in the 2000s, were making significant territorial gains. The group, which seized the capital, Sana'a, in September 2014, rapidly became the main spoiler of the Yemeni political transition and the focus of UNSC demands (SC/11470 [2014]; UNSC Presidential Statement 18 [2014]). Although a UN-brokered agreement was reached in September 2014 to keep the transitional process on track, the Houthis seized power in early 2015 when they placed President Hadi under house arrest and dissolved the parliament. Fighting started in March 2015 after President Hadi escaped to the South, and a coalition led by Saudi Arabia intervened militarily on Hadi's behalf on 26 March 2015, plunging Yemen into war.

IV The expansion of the regime

On 14 April 2015, the UNSC adopted Resolution 2216, which made several Houthi-specific demands, authorized a targeted arms import embargo and expanded the listing criteria to those violating the arms embargo, obstructing the delivery or distribution of humanitarian assistance and engaging in sexual violence or recruiting or using children in armed conflict (UNSC Res 2216 [2015]). The resolution also imposed sanctions on two additional designees – Houthi leader Abdulmalik al-Houthi and the son of former

President Saleh – bringing the total number of individuals sanctioned by the UN to five.

Seven additional Houthi officials were added to the UN sanctions list in 2021 and 2022 (UNSC Res 2564 [2021]; SC/14695 [2021]; SC/15040 [2022]; SC/15051 [2022]) and the Houthis as a group were made subject to a targeted arms embargo on 28 February 2022 (UNSC Res 2624 [2022]). In April 2022, President Hadi resigned in favour of a presidential council, and the UN brokered a six-month ceasefire. Although the conflict in Yemen has not terminated, hostilities have remained relatively low.

Former President Saleh, who was killed by the Houthis in December 2017 after ending their alliance, and his son, who played a key role in facilitating the Houthi military expansion but switched sides following the death of his father, were delisted on 31 July 2024 (SC/15781 [2024]). Their delisting refocused the UN sanctions regime on Yemen exclusively on the Houthis. The travel ban and asset freeze, which are renewed regularly, remain in place on ten Houthi-affiliated individuals, while the targeted arms import embargo, which is in place indefinitely, currently applies to the ten Houthi-affiliated individuals and one entity (the Houthis).

V Conclusion

Despite the efforts of multiple UN mediators, the conflict in Yemen continues. However, its intensity has diminished significantly since the UN-mediated ceasefire took effect in April 2022. While the political and economic divisions persist, the conflict in Yemen has remained low intensity despite the lapse of the ceasefire in October 2022.

Bibliography

Literature

Hudáková Z, '"Speak Softly and Carry a Big Stick": The Threat of Sanctions in the UN Mediation Process in Yemen' (2022) 28(2) *Global Governance a Review of Multilateralism and International Organizations* 203.

Documents

Office of the Special Adviser to the UN Secretary-General on Yemen, Agreement on the Implementation Mechanism for The Transition Process in Yemen in Accordance with the Initiative of the Gulf Cooperation Council (23 November 2011).

UNSC 'Security Council 2140 Sanctions Committee Adds One Entry to Its Sanctions List' (4 October 2022) Press Release SC/15051.

UNSC 'Security Council 2140 Sanctions Committee Adds Three Entries to Its Sanctions List' (9 November 2021) Press Release SC/14695.

UNSC 'Security Council 2140 Sanctions Committee Adds Two Entries to Its Sanctions List' (27 September 2022) Press Release SC/15040.

UNSC 'Security Council 2140 Sanctions Committee Designates Three Individuals as Subject to Assets Freeze, Travel Ban' (7 November 2014) Press Release SC/11636.

UNSC 'Security Council 2140 Sanctions Committee Removes Two Entries from Its Sanctions List' (31 July 2024) Press Release SC/15781.

UNSC 'Security Council Press Statement on Fighting in Yemen' (11 July 2014) Press Release SC/11470.

UNSC 'Security Council Press Statement on Friends of Yemen' (28 September 2012) Press Release SC/10778.

UNSC 'Security Council Press Statement on Yemen' (27 November 2013) Press Release SC/11195.

UNSC Presidential Statement 18 (29 August 2014) UN Doc. S/PRST/2014/18.

UNSC Presidential Statement 3 (15 February 2013) UN Doc. S/PRST/2013/3.

UNSC Res 2014 (21 October 2011) UN Doc. S/RES/2014.

UNSC Res 2051 (12 June 2012) UN Doc. S/RES/2051.

UNSC Res 2140 (26 February 2014) UN Doc. S/RES/2140.

UNSC Res 2216 (14 April 2015) UN Doc. S/RES/2216.

UNSC Res 2564 (25 February 2021) UN Doc. S/RES/2564.

UNSC Res 2624 (28 February 2022) UN Doc. S/RES/2624.

Zuzana Hudáková

47. Former Yugoslavia

ANTONIO BULTRINI

The first set of comprehensive economic sanctions in relation to former Yugoslavia was adopted by the United Nations Security Council (UNSC) on 30 May 1992 (UNSC Res 757 [1992]), soon after the eruption of all-out hostilities in Bosnia-Herzegovina. The war in Yugoslavia had actually begun the year before, when Slovenia and then Croatia declared independence in June 1991, which led to intense but brief fighting within the Slovenian entity and then to the lengthier and bloodier Serbo-Croatian war. The UNSC had already decided, on 25 September 1991, to impose a general arms embargo on Yugoslavia (UNSC Res 713 [1991]), actually at the request of the Yugoslav government. This proved to be a controversial decision, since the arms embargo ended up giving an initial advantage to the well-armed federal (and Belgrade-controlled) forces over the breakaway regions (an approach that Bosnia-Herzegovina then tried to challenge in front of the International Court of Justice [ICJ] in the *Genocide* case against Serbia). The cautious approach of the UNSC changed after the conflict extended to Bosnia-Herzegovina. While noting that "all parties bear some responsibility for the situation" (UNSC Res 757 [1992]), the UNSC nonetheless identified what was left of the Yugoslav Federation, meaning Serbia and Montenegro (forming a new state at that point), as the main "spoiler" (a role later assigned more specifically to the Bosnian Serbs: sanctions were extended to the territories under their control by UNSC Res 820/1993). The first set of blanket trade sanctions consisted of an export ban on commodities and products, a ban on financial resources, and an aviation ban (including spare parts and maintenance services). United Nations (UN) member states were also requested to reduce diplomatic personnel, prevent participation in sporting events by persons representing the Yugoslav Federation, and suspend scientific and technical cooperation. A number of exceptions were nevertheless foreseen, namely with regard to medical supplies, foodstuffs, and humanitarian flights. These exemptions had to be notified to and approved by a committee that had already been set up in relation to the arms embargo, and which was then going to operate as a proper "Sanctions Committee".

Additional subsequent sanctions included a ban on the transshipment of petroleum and other energy products (UN member states were authorised to halt maritime shipping and to inspect cargoes; UNSC Res 787 [1992]); a ban on all commercial maritime traffic and the requirement that states detain and impound (in case of a determination of sanction violation) majority-owned Yugoslav vessels, freight vehicles, and aircraft (UNSC Res 820 [1993]); and a ban on riverine traffic on the Danube and in Bosnian Serb–held territory (UNSC Res 820 [1993]; UNSC Res 942 [1994]). The refusal of the UNSC to consider the Yugoslav Federation as a successor state to Yugoslavia (UNSC Res 777 [1992]), entailing the loss of UN membership, can be added to the list.

Sanctions against the Yugoslav Federation are among the broadest in scope in the history of the UN. They were also accompanied by non-UN restrictive measures by the European Union (EU) and the United States. The EU arms embargo – one of the few at the time – actually preceded the UN arms embargo.

A series of military measures were adopted in parallel to the economic sanctions: the early launching of a peacekeeping operation, the UN Protection Force (UNPROFOR I); the creation of six safe areas (including Srebrenica); a reinforced peacekeeping mandate (UNPROFOR II) tasked with protecting the safe areas; and a no-fly zone. Furthermore, the UNSC set up the International Criminal Tribunal for the Former Yugoslavia (ICTY) (UNSC Res 808 [1993]).

Civilian passenger flights and ferry services, plus participation in sporting events and cultural exchanges, were allowed to resume (to and from Serbia and Montenegro) as of September 1994 (UNSC Res 943 [1994]), after Serbia had agreed to break with the Bosnian Serbs. All other sanctions (including the arms embargo) were progressively suspended as of November 1995, i.e. after the Srebrenica genocide and the North Atlantic Treaty Organization's (NATO) military operation ("Deliberate Force", based on UNSC Res 836 ([1993])), which had led to the lifting of the siege of Sarajevo, a ceasefire (October 1995), and the negotiation of the Dayton Peace Agreement. UNSC Resolution 1074 ([1996]) of 1 October 1996 terminated all sanctions and the Sanctions Committee. Yet, a new arms embargo was adopted in 1998 (until 2001) against Serbia and Montenegro in the context of the crisis in Kosovo. This was likewise accompanied by non-UN restrictive measures (by the EU, the United States, the United Kingdom, and others).

The setting up of the ICTY greatly contributed to revitalising international criminal justice, ensured some degree of accountability, and offered satisfaction to the victims (although it had failed to produce any meaningful impact in terms of deterrence). On the other hand, the military action that unfolded in August–September 1995 was critical for breaking the deadlock, putting an end to the siege of Sarajevo, avoiding any further acts of genocide, and fostering the conditions for negotiating a ceasefire. The Yugoslav case is indeed a much-debated one. Notwithstanding its multilateral character, the actual impact of the (tough) sanctioning policy is disputed. Some (including US Chief Negotiator Holbrooke and human rights groups in former Yugoslavia) considered that economic sanctions did contribute to pushing Serbia to negotiate, since Milosevič appeared to be more interested in the lifting of sanctions than in stopping the NATO air campaign. Others argued that military pressure (and especially the August–September 1995 military developments) played a critical role. Sanctions against former Yugoslavia were, in any case, not carefully calibrated from the start, led to a general economic depression (outweighing the negative economic effects inherent to the war and to the disintegration of Yugoslavia), and adversely affected healthcare despite humanitarian exemptions. The regime in Belgrade benefited from black-marketeering, through which it reallocated resources in favour of supporters and friends and which incidentally favoured the rise of organised crime. The regime could also exploit a "rally-around-the-flag" effect by blaming economic difficulties on sanctions. At the same time, the dire economic situation weakened the opposition and led to an exodus from Serbia of middle-class professionals and youth. It may be that sanctions (but also the setting up of the ICTY, for that matter) were used as a substitute for serious conflict-management involvement, or were at best a common denominator for diverging positions within the international community. Yet, the very military intervention that states had been reluctant to envisage eventually became inevitable, and this after a very high human toll. The Yugoslav case thus illustrates that the impact of sanctions is maximised when they are part of a clear and comprehensive strategy, flexible (therefore including incentives), targeted (as opposed to unqualified/blanket sanctioning regimes), and combined with other instruments, especially (in the circumstances) effective conflict mediation/management tools supported by credible and carefully designed military options, including the sort of multilateral peace enforcement action that was – belatedly – resorted to in Bosnia. Both Iraq and former Yugoslavia critically influenced the subsequent evolution towards targeted sanctions.

Bibliography

Literature

Akrivoulis DE, 'Memory, Forgiveness and Unfinished Justice in the Former Yugoslavia' (2017) 19 *Journal of Balkan and Near Eastern Studies* 366.

Beardsley K, Cunningham DE and White PB, 'Resolving Civil Wars before They Start: The UN Security Council and Conflict Prevention in Self-Determination Disputes' (2015) 47 *British Journal of Political Science* 675.

Garfield R, 'Economic Sanctions on Yugoslavia' (2001) 358 *The Lancet* 580.

Heine-Ellison S, 'The Impact and Effectiveness of Multilateral Economic Sanctions: A Comparative Study' (2001) 5 *The International Journal of Human Rights* 81.

Kerr R, 'International Judicial Intervention: The International Criminal Tribunal for the Former Yugoslavia' (2000) 15 *International Relations* 17.

Kerr R, *The International Criminal Tribunal for the Former Yugoslavia: An Exercise in Law Politics and Diplomacy* (Oxford University Press 2004).

Lopez AG and Cortright D, 'The Sanctions Era: An Alternative to Military Intervention' (1995) 19 *The Fletcher Forum of World Affairs* 4.

Meron T, 'Closing the Accountability Gap: Concrete Steps Toward Ending Impunity for Atrocity Crimes' (2018) 112 *The American Journal of International Law* 433.

Popovski V, 'The UN Security Council Approach to the Conflicts in Former Yugoslavia' (2002) 3 *Southeast European and Black Sea Studies* 39.

ANTONIO BULTRINI

Weiss TG, 'Sanctions as a Foreign Policy Tool: Weighing Humanitarian Impulses' (1999) 36 *Journal of Peace Research* 499.

Williams J, 'The Ethical Basis of Humanitarian Intervention, the Security Council and Yugoslavia' (1999) 6 *International Peacekeeping* 1.

Documents

UNSC Res 713 (25 September 1991) UN Doc. S/RES/713.

UNSC Res 757 (30 May 1992) UN Doc. S/RES/757.

UNSC Res 777 (19 September 1992) UN Doc. S/RES/777.

UNSC Res 787 (16 November 1992) UN Doc. S/RES/787.

UNSC Res 808 (22 February 1993) UN Doc. S/RES/808.

UNSC Res 820 (17 April 1993) UN Doc. S/RES/820.

UNSC Res 836 (4 June 1993) UN Doc. S/RES/836.

UNSC Res 942 (23 September 1994) UN Doc. S/RES/942.

UNSC Res 943 (23 September 1994) UN Doc. S/RES/943.

UNSC Res 1074 (1 October 1996) UN Doc. S/RES/1074.

ANTONIO BULTRINI

PART IV

CROSS-CUTTING ISSUES

48. Blocking statutes

Daniel Ventura

I Introduction

A blocking statute is a national law or regulation aimed at protecting domestic entities, businesses, administrations or citizens from foreign behaviours that target them by enforcing foreign legislation, judicial decisions or administrative orders. Blocking statutes have historically adapted to these behaviours, the increasing frequency of which affects domestic operators (Section II). Since the 1990s, blocking statutes have flourished in the specific context of international sanctions, notably US sanctions regimes (Section III). The concrete effects of blocking statutes remain highly debatable, considering the collateral effects they may produce on the persons they are supposed to protect (Section IV).

II *In genere*: a tool against (perceived) wrongful and/or unreasonable extraterritorial norms

Blocking mechanisms emerged after World War II in reaction to US ambitions to extend the reach of its antitrust laws abroad, including issuing injunctions to foreign companies that impacted their domestic markets (e.g. *United States v Alcoa*, 2nd Circuit, 1945). Interestingly, the closest allies of the United States were the first to denounce the extraterritorial application of US laws. After decades of diplomatic protests and judicial activism, the United Kingdom (Protection of Trading Interests Act [1980]) and Canada (Foreign Extraterritorial Measures Act [1985]) were among the first countries to implement genuine blocking statutes forbidding domestic actors from complying with foreign legal demands that conflicted with their sovereignty. However, blocking statutes did not prevent the United States from gradually extending its jurisdiction abroad into other domains, such as corruption (Foreign Corrupt Practices Act), tax compliance (US Foreign Account Tax Compliance Act) or digital data matters (US Clarifying Lawful Overseas Use of Data Act), and in contravention of the regular diplomatic or judicial channels.

From a legal standpoint, blocking statutes amount to compulsory rules designed to deconflict the concurrent application of domestic and foreign laws. To that end, a blocking statute compels the receiving domestic entities to act in accordance with domestic laws and denies the applicability of any injunctions based on foreign extraterritorial law. In other words, blocking statutes impose the application of the *lex fori* (the law of the country in which an action is brought) on the grounds that the 'long-arm jurisdiction' of the foreign state violates both international law and domestic law, whether this assertion proves to be justified or not. Indeed, one of the (many) legal challenges of blocking statutes is that they operate in the grey areas of international law surrounding the lawful display of a state's competencies.

III *In specie*: a shield against foreign unilateral sanctions regimes

Blocking laws have found a privileged field of application in the context of certain extraterritorial sanctions regimes (see also chapter on Secondary sanctions and the extraterritorial effects of sanctions). In this case, blocking laws seek to neutralise foreign injunctions on domestic operators to apply a foreign sanction regime on third states. Therefore, the impugned extraterritorial conduct lies in the alleged disproportionate scope of enforcement of the foreign unilateral sanctions regime. The 'blocking statute' adopted in 1996 by the European Union (EU) (see chapter) is the most notorious. It was adopted in response to two American sanctions regimes against Cuba (Helms–Burton Act) and Iran (d'Amato–Kennedy Act) to forbid actors located within the EU from enforcing them. A consolidated version entered into force on 7 August 2018 following the withdrawal of the United States from the Joint Comprehensive Plan of Action (JCPOA), the 'Iran nuclear deal', and the resumption of strong extraterritorial sanctions (see also chapter on Iran). In response to the US extraterritorial sanctions in the 1990s, Australia and Canada updated their pre-existing 'blocking laws', followed by Mexico and Argentina. More recently, Russia and China have developed their own mechanisms to block 'unfriendly' (in the case of

Russia) or 'unjustified' (in the case of China) applications of foreign sanction regimes.

IV *In concreto*: specific features (or inherent flaws) of enforcement of blocking statutes

Blocking statutes face an inherent dilemma stemming from a paradoxical situation: prohibiting domestic operators from complying with extraterritorial sanctions is not necessarily in their best interest. As such, beneficiaries of the blocking statute may naturally apply extraterritorial sanctions if they have substantially more to lose in complying with the former rather than the latter. Moreover, considering the relative weaknesses of the penalties incurred for non-observance of blocking statutes, compared with multibillion US dollar fines or a temporary or complete ban from the US market, the balance of interests may naturally favour compliance with US extraterritorial sanctions. Therefore, the dilemma for the state enacting a blocking statute is whether to stand guard and raise the shield against extraterritorial sanctions or let its guard down to favour domestic operators at the expense of the efficacy of the blocking law.

In a landmark decision, the Court of Justice of the EU has had the opportunity to confirm that the freedom to exercise an economic or commercial activity entails that compliance with the blocking statute is to be weighed against the potential substantial economic losses that such compliance may provoke for the domestic operator (*Bank Melli Iran v Telekom Deutschland GmbH* [2021] paras 78–95). In other words, the Court has given precedence to domestic actors' interests on the grounds of protecting their economic and social rights.

Recently, the EU's attempts at finding a way out of this dilemma seem to have taken a new direction, less focused on protecting domestic actors than retaliating to any 'measure' of 'economic coercion' adopted by a third state. In this respect, the 'anti-coercion instrument' adopted in 2023 by the EU has been described as a 'weapon' rather than a 'shield', providing it with a new legal ground for taking direct countermeasures against recalcitrant states. In this renewed context, the usefulness of blocking statutes should not be called into question. Despite their limited practical effects on domestic operators, they convey a legal stance against extraterritoriality that may very well be invoked before an international court someday.

V Conclusion

Third-country laws and blocking statutes are two sides of the same coin. Their simultaneous development in the international order is particularly relevant from the standpoint of the sociology of law. Both initiatives illustrate the shortcomings of an international 'self-ordering society' (Allott [1990]) subject to growing antagonistic forces. As extraterritorial behaviours flourish in a context of profound divisions over the content of international rules on jurisdiction, it must be recalled that blocking statutes are just as much unilateral as the ills they seek to address. In this context, measuring their effectiveness eventually proves to be a delicate matter. While blocking statutes are always justified by the need to protect domestic operators, they are also – or perhaps primarily – a communication tool that demonstrates power, with stakes that far outweigh the legal justifications provided.

Bibliography

Literature

Allott P, *Eunomia: New Order for a New World* (Oxford University Press 1990).

Bismuth R, 'The European Union Experience of Extraterritoriality: When a (Willing) Victim has become a (Soft) Perpetrator' in Parrish A and Ryngaert C (eds), *Research Handbook on Extraterritoriality in International Law* (Edward Elgar 2023) 118.

Ireland-Piper D, 'Extraterritoriality in the Commonwealth: Case Studies from Australia, New Zealand and the United Kingdom' in Parrish A and Ryngaert C (eds), *Research Handbook on Extraterritoriality in International Law* (Edward Elgar 2023) 146.

Ventura D, 'Contemporary Blocking Statutes and Regulations in the Face of Unilateral and Extraterritorial Sanctions' in Beaucillon C (ed.), *Research Handbook on Unilateral and Extraterritorial Sanctions* (Edward Elgar 2021) 221.

DANIEL VENTURA

Documents

Bank Melli Iran v. Telekom Deutschland GmbH Case (C-124/20) [2021] ECLI:EU:C:2021:1035 (21 December 2021).

EU, Council Regulation (EC) No. 2271/96 protecting against the effects of the extra-territorial application of legislation adopted by a third country, and actions based thereon or resulting therefrom [1996] OJ L309/1.

Council Regulation (EU) 2023/2675 on the protection of the Union and its Member States from economic coercion by third countries [2023] OJ L.

Federal Law No. 127-FZ, 4 June 2018, 'On Measures of Impact (Countermeasures) on the Unfriendly Actions of the United States of America and Other Foreign States' (Russia).

Foreign Extraterritorial Measures Act 1985 (Canada).

Foreign Proceedings (Excess of Jurisdiction) Act 1984 (Australia).

IFIC Holding v. Commission (Case T-8/21) [2023] ECLI:EU:T:2023:429 (12 July 2023).

Ley de Protección al Comercio y la Inversión de Normas Extranjeras que Contravengan el Derecho Internacional (Mexico).

Ley No. 24.871 Establécese el marco normativo referido a los alcances de las leyes extranjeras en el Territorio Nacional (Argentina).

Order No. 1/2021 on the Rules on Counteracting Unjustified Extraterritorial Applications of Foreign Legislation and Other Measures (China).

Protection of Trading Interests Act 1980 (United Kingdom).

49. Confiscation

CEDRIC RYNGAERT

I Introduction

Confiscation or seizure is a judicial or administrative measure that results in the loss of property for the benefit of the state. It may consist of forfeiture of property or deprivation of illegally obtained benefits. In the field of sanctions, the question has arisen whether assets that have been frozen or blocked pursuant to (targeted) sanctions legislation could also be confiscated. Such confiscation may serve the purpose of repairing the damage caused by the sanctioned person or state to the victim or the victim state.

A distinction should be made between confiscating assets belonging to private persons and confiscating assets belonging to foreign states, as they are governed by different legal regimes. Also, a distinction should be made between unilateral confiscation by states and confiscation mandated by the United Nations (UN).

II Private property

Confiscation of assets belonging to private persons is governed by the regime protecting the human right to property. Under human rights law, natural and legal persons are entitled to the peaceful enjoyment of their possessions (e.g., Article 1(1) of Protocol No. 1 to the European Convention on Human Rights). The right to property does not, however, impair the right of the state to enforce laws to control the use of property in accordance with the general interest, e.g., through confiscation of the instruments and proceeds of a crime. States may unilaterally confiscate such assets after obtaining a criminal conviction, e.g., on the grounds of sanctions evasion. Some states also allow for forms of (preventive) non-conviction-based confiscation if it can be demonstrated that the property originates from criminal activity.

The confiscating state can either keep the proceeds of confiscation or transfer them to the victims of the crime, including a foreign state victim of an international crime, such as aggression. The United States, for instance, has authorized the transfer to Ukraine of the frozen assets of a Russian oligarch, which were seized after his indictment on charges of sanctions evasion (Reuters [2023]). Other countries, like Germany, have also confiscated Russian oligarchs' assets on the grounds of sanctions evasion, but have so far remained silent on the eventual use of the assets (Marsh [2023]).

III State property

Unilateral confiscation of state assets is governed by the legal regimes of state (sovereign) immunity and countermeasures. Pursuant to international immunity law, states cannot take measures of constraint against the property of another state, unless such property serves a commercial purpose (see Articles 18–21 of the UN Convention on Jurisdictional Immunities of States and Their Property, not yet in force, but largely representing customary international law). It has been argued that immunity rules only apply to court proceedings and not to administrative confiscation by the executive branch (e.g., Brunk [2023]). In most states, however, confiscation will tend to be under judicial control (e.g., under Canada's Special Economic Measures (Ukraine) Regulations, SOR/2014-60). Accordingly, confiscation of a foreign state's assets will, in principle, be internationally unlawful.

While confiscation at first sight violates international law regarding immunity, its wrongfulness could be precluded under the international law of countermeasures (see chapter). This is a body of law that allows a state to suspend its own international law obligations in response to another's prior violation of international law (ARSIWA [2001] Articles 49–54). Thus, where a state has committed a serious violation of international law, another state would arguably be entitled to respond to this violation by, for instance, no longer upholding the international protection granted to the former state's property under immunity law.

It is contested, however, whether confiscation could legally qualify as a countermeasure (Hathaway et al. [2024]). First, countermeasures are not a means of punishing another state, but a means of inducing it to comply with its international obligations. This is why the law requires countermeasures to be temporary and reversible. Confiscating a foreign state's assets by way of sanction appears to be permanent and irreversible, however. Second, it is not clear whether states that are not directly injured by the foreign state's violation of international law are entitled to take countermeasures. It has been argued that such third-party countermeasures have, in the meantime, risen to the level of customary international law (Dawidowicz [2017]), but the exact legal contours remain uncertain.

IV UN authorization

Asset confiscation is legally less problematic if it is not done by states on a unilateral basis, but pursuant to a mandate given by the UN. In particular, the United Nations Security Council (UNSC) (see chapter), acting under Chapter VII of the UN Charter, can adopt a resolution that mandates UN member states to confiscate the assets of a state that poses a threat to the peace, has breached the peace, or has committed an act of aggression. However, the UNSC has not yet adopted such a resolution. In 1991 (UNSC Res 687 [1991]; Res 692 [1991]), the UNSC established a UN Compensation Commission (UNCC), mandated to process claims and pay compensation for losses and damage suffered as a direct result of Iraq's unlawful invasion and occupation of Kuwait. Compensation was paid using funds from frozen assets and the oil revenues of Iraq. The UNCC had fulfilled its mandate by 2022 (UNSC Res 2621 [2022]).

Alternatively, the UN General Assembly (UNGA) could adopt a country-specific or general resolution allowing or mandating states to confiscate assets belonging to states that have committed a serious violation of international law. While, as such, the UNGA lacks the power to bind UN member states, a UNGA resolution, if supported by a large majority of states, could provide the impetus for the formation of a new customary norm that allows for the sanction of asset confiscation in cases of serious violations of international law.

V Conclusion

States can unilaterally confiscate a private person's assets if such assets demonstrably originate from criminal activity, e.g., the evasion of sanctions (see chapter on Evasion and circumvention). It is less clear whether states can also unilaterally confiscate a foreign state's assets by way of sanction. Such assets are, in principle, protected by sovereign immunity. Also, confiscation may not satisfy the requirements for countermeasures, given its permanent character. A new international norm may crystallize that allows for the confiscation of the assets of a state that has committed a serious violation of international law. It is most uncertain, however, whether a sufficient number of states would support such a norm.

Bibliography

Literature

Brunk I, 'Central Bank Immunity, Sanctions, and Sovereign Wealth Funds' (2023) *George Washington Law Review* 1616.

Dawidowicz M, *Third-Party Countermeasures in International Law* (Cambridge University Press 2017).

Hathaway O et al., 'War Reparations: The Case for Countermeasures' (2024) 76 *Stanford Law Review* 971.

Marsh S, 'Germany to Seize More than $790 Mln from Russian Financial Group' (*Reuters*, 20 December 2023) <https://www.reuters.com/business/finance/germany-seize-more-than-790-mln-russian-financial-group-2023-12-20/> accessed 9 November 2024.

Reuters, 'U.S. Attorney General OKs Transfer of Forfeited Funds from Russia Oligarch for Use in Ukraine' (*Reuters*, 10 May 2023) <https://www.reuters.com/world/europe/us-attorney-general-oks-transfer-forfeited-funds-russia-oligarch-use-ukraine-2023-05-10/> accessed 9 November 2024.

Documents

Canada, Special Economic Measures (Ukraine) Regulations, SOR/2014-60.

Protocol No. 1 to the European Convention on Human Rights (adopted 20 March 1952, entered into force 18 May 1954) ETS 009.

UN General Assembly, United Nations Convention on Jurisdictional Immunities of States and Their Property (2 December 2004) A/RES/59/38.

UNGA Res 56/83, 'Articles on Responsibility of States for Internationally Wrongful Acts' (12 December 2001) UN Doc. A/56/10.

UNSC Res 2621 (22 February 2022) UN Doc. S/RES/2621.

UNSC Res 687 (3 April 1991) UN Doc. S/RES/687.

UNSC Res 692 (20 May 1991) UN Doc. S/RES/692.

50. Contracts

Paschalis Paschalidis and Björn ten Seldam

I Introduction

Sanctions can significantly impact contractual obligations, particularly when applied to pre-existing agreements. In the absence of specific clauses in their contracts, operators often rely on the general force majeure doctrine to avoid liability for non-performance due to sanctions. To enhance legal certainty, operators often insert sanctions-specific clauses in their contracts to limit or avoid liability when the performance of contracts is affected by sanctions.

More recently, legislators have taken action to require operators to include clauses preventing the circumvention of sanctions by effectively requiring counterparties to commit not to provide exported goods or services to the target of the sanctions.

Finally, the performance of international contracts may be affected by a variety of legal systems that may have diverging or even conflicting approaches to sanctions. Thus, sanctions imposed by a country may affect the performance of a contract, even when the contract is governed by the law of another country. The performance of the contract may conflict with the public policy of the country imposing sanctions but not with the public policy of other countries. At the same time, non-performance due to sanctions can violate the law governing the contract, especially if it is the law of the country targeted by the sanctions (Ninth Arbitrazh Court of Appeal of the Russian Federation No. 09AP-9815/2018 [2018]).

II Non-performance of contractual obligations due to sanctions

Certain legal systems have a general doctrine of force majeure that may justify the non-performance of contractual obligations due to the effect of sanctions. For example, under French law, an event will generally qualify as force majeure if it is irresistible, unpredictable, and external to the debtor (Gréau [2024]). Accordingly, the French Court of Cassation rejected the claim of an Iranian bank alleging that the freezing of its assets constituted force majeure, preventing payment of its debt, and excusing it from the consequences of non-performance. The Court held that the freezing of the bank's assets resulted from its direct involvement in the Iranian nuclear programme and, therefore, did not arise from circumstances external to the bank's activities to justify force majeure (French Court of Cassation No. 18-18542 and 18-21.814 [2020]).

By contrast, when the contract affected by sanctions is governed by English law, the courts will examine whether non-performance due to sanctions can be justified on the basis of a force majeure clause contained in the contract. In *RTI Ltd v MUR Shipping BV* [2024], the UK Supreme Court held that, absent clear wording to the contrary effect, a "reasonable endeavours" provision in a force majeure clause did not require a party to accept payment under the contract in euros when the contract specifically provided for payment in US dollars, even if it were highly probable that it would be difficult to make timely payment in dollars due to US sanctions.

In the absence of a force majeure clause, the matter is examined under the doctrine of frustration or supervening illegality. In the case of supervening illegality under English law, UK statutes may provide broader defences than the common law (Sanctions and Anti-Money Laundering Act 2018, s 4). In the case of foreign law supervening illegality, non-performance may be excused only if performance becomes illegal under the law of the jurisdiction where the contract is to be performed (*Ralli Brothers v Campania Naviera Sota Y Aznar* [1920] 2 KB 287). Thus, in a case where a bank refused to allow a Libyan client to withdraw US dollars from its account, citing US sanctions, the High Court held that the violation of the contract was not excused because payment in cash or some forms of bank transfer in London did not necessarily involve any performance in the United States (*Libyan Arab Foreign Bank v Bankers Trust Co* [1989] QB 728). In the same vein, the French courts will give effect to foreign sanctions in force at the place of a contract's performance (French Court of Cassation No. 08-21.511 [2010]). However, they may refuse to give effect to such sanctions in French territory and uphold arbitral awards rendered in France even if they are incompatible with US sanctions (Paris Court of Appeal No. 19/07261 [2020]; French Court of Cassation No. 20-20.376 [2022]). The effect of foreign sanctions on contract performance may be limited by blocking regulations, which can prohibit an operator from complying with such sanctions and may require the operator to perform the contract (e.g., Council Regulation (EU) No. 2271/96). However, the effect of such prohibitions may be limited if an operator faces significant economic losses due to a breach of the foreign sanctions (Azeredo da Silveira [2018]).

Finally, sanctions may not excuse non-performance where the defaulting party could have mitigated the impact of the sanctions by seeking a licence that would enable it to perform its obligation (*Melli Bank plc v Holbud Ltd* [2013] EWHC 1506 (Comm)).

III Contractual provisions to address risks arising from sanctions

To enhance legal certainty, parties often include force majeure clauses in contracts to deal specifically with cases where the contract's performance will be frustrated or become extremely difficult due to international or unilateral sanctions. These clauses normally limit the liability of the defaulting party, unless failure to perform is due to gross negligence or wilful misconduct.

Beyond the risk of non-performance of contractual obligations, operators also need to address the risk of becoming liable, through the performance of a contract, for involvement in a breach or circumvention of sanctions. Under the so-called *best-efforts* obligations, regulators require operators to take all suitable and necessary actions to prevent the circumvention of sanctions (Council Regulation (EU) 2024/1745 recital 30).

The European Commission has previously recommended that EU operators include clauses in their contracts imposing liability on third-country counterparties that re-export goods to Russia (Commission Consolidated FAQs [2022] Export-Related Restrictions for Dual-Use Goods and Advanced Technologies, question 46). Operators are expected to ensure compliance with sanctions, despite the absence of EU legislation outlining specific measures required to achieve this (Commission Consolidated FAQs [2022] Circumvention and due diligence, question 1). To address concerns that certain operators would not take adequate measures regarding certain export restrictions, the EU legislator decided to resort to a binding provision. Thus, the twelfth EU package of sanctions against Russia introduced an obligation for traders of certain goods to insert so-called "Russia clauses" in their contracts preventing the buyers of these goods from reselling them to the Russian market (Council Regulation (EU) No. 833/2014 Art. 12g). This obligation has since been expanded for contracts related to certain intellectual property rights or trade secrets (Council Regulation (EU) No. 833/2014 Art. 12ga), as the EU Commission monitors the impact of such clauses on deterring circumvention (Council Regulation (EU) 2024/1745 recital 32). Meanwhile, these clauses continue to operate alongside the broader contractual provisions addressing sanctions risks.

IV Conclusion

Navigating the intersection of sanctions and contractual obligations requires careful consideration. Operators must draft contracts that address the contract-specific risks posed by sanctions, including incorporating force majeure and sanctions-specific clauses to limit potential liabilities. Additionally, due diligence and compliance with evolving regulatory frameworks, such as the inclusion of clauses to prevent circumvention of sanctions, are critical for reducing the risk of liability. As sanctions continue to evolve, parties engaged in cross-border transactions must ensure that their contracts remain adaptable to such changes.

Bibliography

Literature

Azeredo da Silveira M, 'Economic Sanctions, Force Majeure and Hardship' in Bortolotti F and Ufo D (eds) *Hardship and Force Majeure in International Commercial Contracts – Institute Dossier XVII* (International Chamber of Commerce 2018).

Gréau F, 'Force majeure' *Répertoire de droit civil* (Dalloz, June 2017, updated October 2024).

de Verneuil Smith P, Kramer A, Day W and Scott G, 'COVID-19, Brexit, and Russia Sanctions: Force Majeure, Frustration and Illegality in English Law: A Detailed Guide' *Practical Law UK PLC* (30 November 2023).

Szabados T, *Economic Sanctions in EU Private International Law* (Bloomsbury Publishing 2020).

Documents

Council Regulation (EU) No. 269/2014 of 17 March 2014 concerning restrictive measures in respect of actions undermining or threatening the territorial integrity, sovereignty and independence of Ukraine, as amended [2014] OJ L78/6.

Council Regulation (EU) No. 833/2014 of 31 July 2014 concerning restrictive measures in view of Russia's actions destabilising the situation in Ukraine, as amended [2014] OJ L229/1.

Commission Consolidated FAQs on the implementation of Council Regulation No. 833/2014 and Council Regulation No. 269/2014, as amended.

French Court of Cassation, Full Court, 10 July 2020, No. 18-18.542 and 18-21.814.

French Court of Cassation, 16 March 2010, No. 08-21.511.

French Court of Cassation, 9 February 2022, No. 20-20.376.

Libyan Arab Foreign Bank v Bankers Trust Co (1989) QB 728.

Melli Bank plc v Holbud Ltd (2013) EWHC 1506 (Comm).

Ninth Arbitrazh Court of Appeal of the Russian Federation, 10 April 2018, No. 09AP-9815/2018, Case No. A40-171207/2017.

Paris Court of Appeal, 3 June 2020, No. 19/07261.

Ralli Brothers v Campania Naviera Sota Y Aznar (1920) 2 KB 287.

RTI Ltd v MUR Shipping BV (2024) UKSC 18.

Paschalis Paschalidis and Björn ten Seldam

51. Criminalisation of sanctions violation

Jacob Öberg

I Introduction

This entry examines the criminalisation of sanctions violations, which can be defined as the process of establishing breaches of international sanctions as criminal offences under domestic law. One of the key ideas behind the criminalisation of sanctions violations is to deter individuals and companies contemplating breaching the existing international sanctioning regimes (Genocide Network [2021]). Criminalisation in this field also includes circumvention offences that prohibit knowing and intentionally participating in activities that seek to circumvent the restrictive measures at issue (*Afrasiabi and Others* [2011]).

States across the world adopt very divergent approaches in relation to the extent to which they criminalise breaches of restrictive measures. Since the Russian invasion of Ukraine, the European Union (EU) has become an important international actor in the area of sanctions violations, primarily by adopting a comprehensive sanctioning regime against Russia (Council of the European Union [2024], and also Directive 2024/1226/EU, which criminalises the violation of EU restrictive measures). While this entry intends to generally discuss the criminalisation of restrictive measures, the new EU directive is the central case study for outlining the key issues pertaining to criminalisation in this field.

II Domestic enforcement of sanctions violations

There are different models for the enforcement of sanctions violations. Some countries categorise sanctions violations as a criminal offence, while others consider them as just an administrative offence, whereas a third category of states envisages the possibility of sanctions violations being categorised either as criminal or administrative offences, on their gravity or the frequency of violations. If we take the example of the EU, there is substantive divergence. Twelve member states ensure that the violation of EU restrictive measures is a criminal offence, while the violation of these measures can amount to an administrative or a criminal offence in 13 member states. In two member states (Spain and Slovakia), the violation of EU restrictive measures is considered merely an administrative offence (Genocide Network [2021]).

The criteria according to which the conduct falls within a category of measures commonly pertain to its gravity, determined in either qualitative (intent, serious negligence) or quantitative (damage) terms, but they differ in each state. Penalty systems also differ substantially across EU member states: in 14 member states, the maximum length of imprisonment is between two and five years, while maximum sentences of between 8 and 12 years are possible in eight member states. Fourteen member states provide for the criminal liability of legal persons for the violation of EU restrictive measures, whereas 12 member states provide for administrative penalties, notably fines, which may be imposed on legal persons when their employees or management violate restrictive measures (Genocide Network [2021] 22–4).

III EU harmonisation of criminal offences and penalties in the area of restrictive measures

The most significant action at the international level pertaining to sanctions violations is the EU directive on the criminalisation of restrictive measures. The political rationale behind the directive is that restrictive measures are inconsistently enforced, undermining the EU's ability to speak with one voice, which is particularly urgent within the context of Russia's military aggression against Ukraine. The effective enforcement of restrictive measures, including through criminal law measures addressing the violation of restrictive measures, is envisaged to support this policy (Peers [2022]; Öberg [2024] chapter 3; European Commission [2022] 2).

In the absence of law enforcement having effective tools available to prevent, detect, investigate and prosecute the violation of EU restrictive measures, designated individuals and legal persons whose assets are frozen may continue to be able to support regimes that are targeted by EU restrictive measures, thus frustrating the objectives of those restrictive measures. Moreover, member states have very different definitions of, and disparate penalties for, the violation of EU restrictive measures, entailing that the same infringement might be punished with different penalties. This may lead to forum shopping by offenders and to their (quasi)-impunity in case they choose to conduct their activities in a member state(s) that has a more lenient sanctioning regime, thereby risking frustrating the EU objectives to safeguard international peace and security and uphold EU common values (European Commission [2022] 4–6).

Based on these rationales, the Commission went on to propose to the Council the criminalisation of violations of EU restrictive measures as a new area of EU crime according to the legal basis of Article 83(1) of the Treaty on the Functioning of the European Union. Pursuant to this provision, the European Parliament and the Council may, by means of directives, establish minimum rules concerning the definition of criminal offences and sanctions in the areas of *particularly serious crime* with a *cross-border dimension* resulting from *the nature or impact of such offences* or from a *special need* to combat them on a common basis.

Following the procedure in this provision for adding new crimes to the list, the Council unanimously decided in 2022 (Council Decision 2022/2332) to extend the list of Eurocrimes to violations of EU restrictive measures as another area of crime meeting those criteria (Oberg [2024]). Subsequent to this and basing its legislation on the legal basis of Article 83(1) in the Treaty on the Functioning of the European Union (TFEU), the Council adopted – upon a proposal by the Commission – EU Directive 2024/1226/EU harmonising the member states' criminal laws in respect of those criminal offences.

IV The EU directive on criminal offences and penalties for violation of Union restrictive measures

The new EU directive has a fairly far-reaching and comprehensive scope covering a number of offences, including requirements to impose several types of criminal penalties for natural and legal persons. The agreed directive will require member states to criminalise nine types of breaches of EU sanctions, which can be summarised in two categories:

(1) *direct violations*: (a) making funds available to sanctioned persons; (b) failing to freeze the funds of sanctioned persons; (c) enabling the entry or transit of a person covered by an entry ban deriving from EU sanctions; (d) entering into transactions with sanctioned entities; (e) trading in goods or services covered by EU sanctions; (f) providing services banned by sanctions law; and (2) *Circumvention offences*: (a) circumvention of sanctions or (b) abusing exceptions to the sanctions laws (Directive 2024/1226 Art. 3(1) A–H).

In terms of the *type* of sanctions covered, the directive suggests that this is a broad power, applying not only to economic sanctions such as restrictions on trade or financial relations but also to bans on entry into the territory and to arms embargoes (Directive 2024/1226 Art. 3). In every case, an intentional breach will have to be criminalised; and in one case (trade in arms or dual-use goods subject to sanctions), 'serious negligence' resulting in the breach will have to be criminalised as well. The Commission had proposed that 'serious negligence' should be criminalised in most cases (Commission [2022B] Art. 3(3)), but this was dropped in the final version of the directive.

As for penalties, member states must provide for a maximum possible penalty of at least five years for most offences and one year for the remaining offences (subject to a threshold of €100 000 being involved). No financial threshold will apply in two cases: breaches of entry bans and trade in sanctioned arms or dual-use goods. Furthermore, a three-year maximum possible penalty applies to breaches of entry bans. Otherwise, member states are obliged to provide at least for the possibility of some imprisonment and, in all cases to provide for additional penalties such as fines (Directive 2024/1226 Art. 5). Legal persons are subject to liability, too (Directive 2024/1226 Art. 6) and must be subject to penalties such as shutting down the business, closure, disqualification, exclusion from entitlement to public funding or withdrawal of their licences (Directive 2024/1226 Art. 7). The directive is very detailed in specifying the extent of possible fines, including basing them on annual turnover (Directive 2024/1226 Art. 7(2)), which is a method commonly used in the area of EU competition law.

V A legal analysis of the EU's exercise of competence to criminalise violations of EU restrictive measures

In order for the EU legislator to justify the adoption of a directive under Article 83(1) TFEU, any proposed legislation must satisfy two substantive criteria: the 'particularly serious offence' criterion and the 'cross-border' criterion (see Öberg [2024] chapter 3). The EU legislator claims that the violation of EU restrictive measures (European Commission [2022] 8) is a 'particularly serious crime' since it can perpetuate threats to international peace and security, undermine support for democracy and human rights, and result in significant economic, societal, and environmental damage. It also argues that because of such violations, individuals and entities whose assets are frozen continue to be able to access their assets or continue to access state funds that were misappropriated and use them to purchase arms with which they commit their crimes (European Commission [2022] 8). The broad experience with sanctions evasions since the commencement of the war launched by Russia against Ukraine suggests that there is a plausible argument for suggesting that this might be a 'particularly serious crime'.

In respect of the cross-border criterion, there is a good argument for claiming that violations of EU restrictive measures have an inherently cross-border dimension. Not only are they usually committed by natural persons and legal entities operating on a global scale, but, in some cases, EU restrictive measures (e.g. restrictions on banking services) even forbid cross-border operations (European Commission [2022] 4, 8). Furthermore, these are typically situations where the underlying restrictive measure itself is of a cross-border character.

VI Conclusion

In general, it is very difficult to ascertain the impact that the criminalisation of violations of restrictive measures has in practice without more detail on what changes states undertake to ensure conformity with international sanctioning regimes. One issue with criminal law is the resources and expertise necessary to investigate and bring prosecutions.

On this point, there is an argument for claiming that the EU response to date provides for the most effective enforcement sanctioning regime, having recently adopted a seminal legislative framework for the criminalisation of breaches of EU sanctions. The prospect of extending competence to the European Public Prosecutor's Office to include breaches of EU foreign policy sanctions has been raised by some member states, and such a development would clearly entail much stronger enforcement (Le Monde [2022]). Whereas many member states have legislation in place to enforce violations of this legislation, it appears that the EU is better placed to enforce this type of legislation.

The politics associated with the criminalisation of international sanctions is also worth reflecting on. On this point, the EU's extension of the competence and proliferation of initiatives in this field is closely related to the Russian invasion of Ukraine. While the extension of EU competence and the use of those criminal law powers will not end the invasion, they may make some contribution to the effective implementation of those sanctions that have been established to oppose the invasion, and in any event, it sends a political message that the EU is stepping up enforcement (Peers [2022]). This suggests that – if viewed more in terms of its symbolic and communicative dimension – the criminalisation of restrictive measures may be an effective tool to achieve the specific foreign policy objectives of states or international organisations.

Bibliography

Literature

Genocide Network, *Prosecution of Sanctions (Restrictive Measures) Violations in National Jurisdictions: a Comparative Analysis* (2021) <www.eurojust.europa.eu/sites/default/files/assets/genocide_network_report_on_prosecution_of_sanctions_restrictive_measures_violations_23_11_2021.pdf> accessed 5 August 2024.

Immenkamp B, 'Directive on the Violation of Union Restrictive Measures' (European Parliament Research Service, July 2024) <https://www.europarl.europa.eu/RegData/etudes/BRIE/2023/751409/EPRS_BRI(2023)751409_EN.pdf>.

'L'appel des ministres français et allemand de la justice: "Nous souhaitons l'extension

de la compétence du parquet européen aux violations des sanctions prises par l'UE"' (*Le Monde*, 29 November 2022).
Öberg J, *Normative Foundations of EU Criminal Law: Powers, Limits and Justifications* (Hart Publishing 2024).
Peers S, 'EU Foreign Policy Sanctions: Extending and Using EU Criminal Law Powers to Enforce Them' (*EU Law Analysis*, 18 January 2024) <https://eulawanalysis.blogspot.com/2024/01/foreign-policy-sanctions-and-criminal.html> accessed 6 January 2025.

Documents

European Commission, 'Communication from the Commission to the European Parliament and the Council – Towards a Directive on criminal penalties for the violation of Union restrictive measures' [2022] COM 249 final.
Council Decision (EU) 2022/2332 on identifying the violation of Union restrictive measures as an area of crime that meets the criteria specified in Article 83(1) of the Treaty on the Functioning of the European Union [2022] OJ L308/18.
Council Directive (EU) 2024/1226 on the definition of criminal offences and penalties for the violation of Union restrictive measures and amending Directive (EU) 2018/1673 [2024] OJ L series.
Council of the European Union, 'EU Sanctions against Russia Explained', <https://www.consilium.europa.eu/en/policies/sanctions-against-russia-explained/> last review 18 December 2024.
Case C-72/11 *Afrasiabi and Others* [2011] ECLI:EU:C:2011:874.
Council of the European Union, 'General Approach: Proposal for a Directive of the European Parliament and of the Council on the definition of criminal offences and penalties for the violation of Union restrictive measures' [2023] Council Doc. 9312/23.
European Commission, 'Proposal for a Council Decision on adding the violation of Union restrictive measures to the areas of crime laid down in Article 83(1) of the Treaty on the Functioning of the European Union' [2022] COM 247 final.
European Commission, 'Proposal for a Directive of the European Parliament and of the Council on the definition of criminal offences and penalties for the violation of Union restrictive measures' [2022] COM 684 final.

52. Domestic implementation

Radka Druláková and Štěpánka Zemanová

I Introduction

International organisations predominantly use international sanctions following the objectives and competencies outlined in their foundational treaties. In these treaties, the member states also pledge to implement the respective sanctions decisions, such as those delineated in the United Nations Security Council (UNSC) (see chapter) resolutions or the European Union (EU) (see chapter) Common Foreign and Security Policy positions. Consequently, the authorities within member states are expected to establish the necessary frameworks to facilitate the implementation and enforcement of various types of sanctions within their domestic jurisdictions.

Nevertheless, member states' sanctions commitments differ from other international law obligations due to their delayed practical effects. International sanctions are only activated by an international organisation issuing a binding secondary act (e.g., a UNSC resolution) that specifies their parameters, including objectives, targets, content, duration, and exemptions for an individual sanctions episode.

Therefore, the member states should proactively prepare for the implementation as soon as a commitment to general sanctions is made. The preparation includes developing relevant legislation, control and enforcement mechanisms, and adapting to the dynamic nature of sanctions processes – tightening, easing, modifying sanctions lists, etc. However, in practice, especially within the United Nations (UN) context, states often neglect these obligations or fail to fulfil them sufficiently. Such omissions complicate the use of international sanctions and diminish their overall effectiveness.

II Legal framework for effective domestic implementation

From a legal perspective, the domestic implementation of international sanctions involves several steps. The precise configuration of these steps depends on the sending organisation, the state's approach to the relationship between international and domestic law, and the development of its national sanctions legislation. Implementation begins with the incorporation of international decisions into the national legal framework. With the exception of EU regulations, which are directly applicable in all member states without the need for domestic implementing legislation, the manner of incorporation is not specified in international law, leaving states free to choose their specific method.

In some countries, sanctions decisions directly apply within the national legal system without further legislative action. Direct application primarily concerns the state's recognition of international law as an integral part of its domestic legal system, such as in Article 144 of the Namibian Constitution (Gowlland-Debbas [2004] 4; Tzanakopoulos [2011] 1). However, in most cases, the sanctions decision must first be transposed into the domestic legal order. Theoretically, this can be achieved through a general incorporation clause, but in practice occurs either through individual incorporation or a general empowering (or enabling) act.

Through individual (or ad hoc) incorporation, a state (e.g., Iraq, United Arab Emirates) responds to each sanctions decision separately, translating it into national law through an individual bill. This method requires extensive legislative procedures, as the drafting of such bills is subject to strict procedural rules in national legal systems. Sometimes, it also becomes a complex political process that may deviate from the original (international) sanctions decision or be blocked by the domestic institutions with veto power without implementing a sanctions decision. This method, therefore, presents significant practical difficulties and frequently results in implementation delays or failure.

Therefore, it is more appropriate to create a legal basis for the implementation of all subsequent sanctions decisions (Druláková and Zemanová [2020]) by transferring the implementing powers from a legislative to an executive body with a general enabling act (United Kingdom and Japan). Nevertheless, even with these approaches, the use of an individual sanctions bill may sometimes be necessary, especially when the sending international organisation employs a new sanctions tool that is not yet covered by the existing enabling legislation.

III Practical implementation

While the incorporation of international sanctions into domestic law is a necessary precondition for their practical implementation, it is not sufficient to ensure full compliance with individual sanctions decisions. To ensure, e.g., that prohibited goods are not exported to areas under sanctions or that financial transactions with sanctioned entities do not take place, further legislative, control, and enforcement measures need to be introduced. Several such measures were identified as part of the Stockholm Process, an integral part of the UN sanctions reforms at the turn of the millennium.

According to the Stockholm Process final report (Wallensteen et al. [2003]), these measures include:

a) the development of administrative capacities within the delegated authorities;
b) the establishment of coordination mechanisms to ensure cooperation between these authorities;
c) informing the private sector about the obligation to respect sanctions measures and identifying contact points that can advise or assist in the correct implementation of the sanctions in the private sector;
d) creating monitoring mechanisms to follow up on the implementation of sanctions by national bodies;
e) introducing administrative and criminal law sanctions for national actors whose behaviour constitutes serious breaches of sanction regimes.

Beyond the Stockholm Process recommendations, many states have developed additional tools to ensure the proper implementation of each sanctions regime, often in sophisticated and detailed ways. These include, for example, procedures for locating, seizing, and managing frozen accounts from financial sanctions (including details such as securing the crediting of interest to accounts and deducting bank charges from accounts) or the introduction of licensing procedures and the certification of goods subject to arms embargoes (see chapter) (Biersteker et al. [2005] at 60–2).

Despite these measures, new challenges and unforeseen situations continue to arise in practice. In the past, these have included problems with the transcriptions of names in financial sanctions lists or the implementation of sanctions in the education sector in relation to the Iranian and North Korean nuclear regimes. Additional challenges regularly emerge in dealing with the seized assets of sanctioned persons, especially when entire companies are involved, and the welfare of their (not targeted) employees needs to be considered, or when live animals are seized and require care.

IV International support for compliance

The domestic implementation of certain sanctions measures benefits from other international regimes in related areas. For example, the enforcement of arms embargoes in more than 40 states has improved due to their involvement in the 1995 Wassenaar Arrangement on Export Controls for Conventional Arms and Dual-Use Goods and Technologies (see chapter on Coalitions of the willing). Similarly, measures to implement financial sanctions were enhanced thanks to their connection to international anti-money laundering duties (see chapter on Financial Action Task Force Recommendations). Additionally, international organisations without autonomous sanctions practices, such as the International Criminal Police Organisation (INTERPOL) which investigates arms smuggling, money laundering, and support for terrorism, or the International Civil Aviation Organization (ICAO), which helps prevent the circumvention of flight bans, provide substantial support to states in improving domestic implementation.

Practical experience also shows that the standardisation of sanctions measures, consistent use of terminology in individual sanctions decisions, and coherent and consistent interpretation reduce complexities and enhance domestic implementation processes (Cortright and Lopez [2002] at 173). International organisations authorised to impose sanctions also contribute significantly by providing legal expertise, facilitating information exchange, identifying best national practices, developing model domestic legislation and model procedures for monitoring, and enforcing compliance with international sanctions by national authorities (see e.g., Security Council Counter-Terrorism Committee 2019 and UNSC Res 1624 [2005]).

Radka Druláková and Štěpánka Zemanová

V Conclusion

The domestic implementation of international sanctions is a complex process that involves legal frameworks, practical measures, and international support mechanisms. States must incorporate sanctions into their national legal systems, facing challenges in ensuring effective enforcement. The process begins with the incorporation of international decisions into domestic law, which may be done directly or require transposition through legislative acts. Effective implementation often necessitates general reception clauses or enabling acts to streamline the process. Practical implementation also demands robust administrative capacity, coordination mechanisms, private sector engagement, monitoring systems, and enforcement measures in case of violations (see chapter on Criminalisation of sanctions violation). International regimes, organisations, and initiatives such as the Wassenaar Arrangement, INTERPOL, ICAO, and the Stockholm Process provide crucial support through expertise, standardisation, and the promotion of best practices, thereby enhancing the capacity of states to comply effectively. By adopting best practices and leveraging international cooperation, states can address the challenges of implementing sanctions and achieve better compliance.

Bibliography

Literature

Biersteker TJ, Eckert SE, Halegua A and Romaniuk P, 'Targeted Sanctions and State Capacity: Towards a Framework for National Level Implementation' in Wallensteen P and Staibano C (eds), *International Sanctions. Between Words and Wars in the Global System* (Frank Cass 2005) 57.

Cortrigh D and Lopez GA, *Sanctions and the Search for Security. Challenges to UN Action* (Lynne Rienner Publishers 2002).

Druláková R and Zemanová Š, 'Why the Implementation of Multilateral Sanctions Does (not) Work: Lessons Learned From the Czech Republic' (2020) 29(4) *European Security* 524.

Gowlland-Debbas V (ed.), *National Implementation of United Nations Sanctions: A Comparative Study* (Martinus Nijhoff 2004).

Tzanakopoulos A, *Disobeying the Security Council. Countermeasures against Wrongful Sanctions* (Oxford University Press 2011).

Wallensteen P, Staibano C and Eriksson M (eds) *Making Targeted Sanctions Effective: Guidelines for the Implementation of UN Policy Options* (Department of Peace and Conflict Research, Uppsala University 2003).

Documents

UNSC Counter-Terrorism Committee, 'Security Council Guiding Principles on Foreign Terrorist Fighters: The Madrid 2015 Principles and 2018 Addendum' (2019) UN Doc. S/2015/939 and S/2018/1177 <https://www.un.org/securitycouncil/ctc/sites/www.un.org.securitycouncil.ctc/files/security-council-guiding-principles-on-foreign-terrorist-fighters.pdf>

UNSC Resolution 1624 (adopted on 14 September 2005) UNS/RES/1624.

53. Evasion and circumvention

KEITH A. PREBLE

I Introduction: evasion and circumvention – two sides of the same coin

Evasion and circumvention of economic sanctions undermine their effectiveness and represent a challenge to implementation. While reference to evasion and circumvention of sanctions appears interchangeably across legal, regulatory, policy, and academic discussions, sanctions evasion and circumvention are not synonymous; they are best understood as different sides of the same coin. What distinguishes evasion from circumvention are the qualitative differences between the actors carrying out licit and illicit economic activities that undermine economic sanctions and the ability of sanction senders to deter and punish in their respective legal systems. Because the actions taken by evaders and circumventors to undermine economic sanctions are frequently similar, complicating the challenge of effectively conceptualizing sanctions evasion and circumvention, it is important to situate evasion and circumvention by differentiating the actors involved. Importantly, however, evaders and circumventors frequently rely on each other – wittingly or unwittingly – to facilitate customary trade and finance.

Sanctions evasion refers to activities that actors – persons and entities – in sanctioned states engage in to maintain customary trade and economic activities by weakening or eliminating the effects of a state's sanctions policies. These actors can be states but more frequently are persons or entities blacklisted by the sender. Evasion often involves obscuring activities and obfuscating ownership by sanctions firms and individuals. For example, Russian entities placed on blacklists can evade sanctions in a jurisdiction by exploiting ownership loopholes by transferring control of entities to non-listed individuals in the targeted jurisdiction or to individuals or businesses in jurisdictions friendly to the sender.

Sanctions circumvention, on the other hand, refers to the methods that actors or networks of actors utilize to avoid or bypass their jurisdictions' implementation and enforcement of economic sanctions or jurisdictions where they engage in economic activity. Actors engaged in circumvention may or may not be coordinating with targeted persons or entities, or may be unwittingly undermining economic sanctions and unaware of the true nature of trade and financial transactions. Financial institutions are an example of this unwitting form of sanctions circumvention through the processing of wire transfers or the provision of financial services. The oil price cap is another prominent example where sanctions circumvention has occurred. When Western countries imposed an oil price cap on Russian oil exports, Russian exporters sought the means to sell oil above the price cap. Firms exporting Russian oil *evade* sanctions by working with firms willing *to circumvent* economic sanctions by using flagged tankers from jurisdictions that operate under the rules where the oil price cap may not be observed (Parliament [2024]; Reuters [2024]).

Sanctions evasion and circumvention are challenges inherent to the implementation and enforcement of economic sanctions that fall under the larger rubric of "sanctions busting" (Early [2015]). Because evasion and circumvention employ similar activities that facilitate sanctions busting, the design of economic sanctions must consider not only those activities that evade economic sanctions but also anticipate how actors operating in less restrictive jurisdictions or even in the very jurisdiction "sending" the sanctions might work to circumvent economic sanctions. The lack of conceptual clarity in policy, law, and regulations underscores the challenges of combating evasion and circumvention. Furthermore, it reinforces the need to approach sanctions implementation and enforcement by ensuring that a state's own constituents obey laws and regulations while simultaneously limiting the ability of targeted persons and entities outside a state's jurisdiction from taking advantage of arbitrage and legal and regulatory loopholes.

II Sanctions evasion

Sanctions evasion consists of a typology of activities, some that originate within the target state while others are facilitated by third-party states. From a policy perspective, evasion and circumvention, while supporting one another, involve similar processes by different actors. Sanctions evasion is best understood as activities that actors targeted by sanctions engage in to weaken or eliminate the effects of economic sanctions on sanctioned economic activities. However, in many cases, actors engaged in sanctions evasion require assistance from actors in either sender and third-party states to circumvent sanctions.

Depending on the sanctioning jurisdiction, evaders often seek to exploit loopholes in legislation, regulations, and rules. Actors may exploit loopholes by changing the ownership structure of a sanctioned entity or reducing the controlling stake by actors targeted by economic sanctions. Bank Rossiya, a Russian bank with ties to key individuals in the Russian government, sought to evade sanctions by exploiting such loopholes to protect its subsidiaries from US regulators. Blacklisted individuals may also sell their controlling stakes and ownership to non-listed individuals, especially individuals in jurisdictions that may be friendlier with the sending state (Johnston [2024]).

The use of diplomatic cover has emerged as a means of evading economic sanctions, a practice that North Korean diplomats have utilized. Not only do diplomats typically enjoy immunity, which imposes procedural bars on enforcement and adjudicative jurisdiction and is itself a custom of international law, embassies, too, are often shielded from searches and monitoring by jurisdictions. This form of sanctions evasion turns embassies from diplomatic missions into quasi-financial institutions, allowing sanctioned entities to facilitate in financial and economic activities in jurisdictions through the veil of diplomatic protection (Salisbury [2021]).

Front companies and shell companies are also common means of evading economic sanctions, especially if legitimate companies have been added to blacklists. When an Iranian dissident group revealed Iran's nuclear weapons program in 2003, their presentation to the media in Washington, DC highlighted a sophisticated network of procurement agents operating through a myriad of front and shell companies to obscure and evade US sanctions (Jacobson [2008]).

III Sanctions circumvention

Because the imposition of economic sanctions is said to generate network effects that make sanctions evasion activities profitable, developing effective tools for circumventing economic sanctions is critical for the evader of economic sanctions as it seeks to partner with actors in sanctioning jurisdictions to facilitate customary trade and finance. Very often, the tools used to circumvent economic sanctions are those used for legitimate trade and commerce, which not only makes sanctions enforcement more challenging but also creates conceptual (and legal) challenges. Sanctions circumvention refers to the methods by which the exchange and trade of goods and services are structured to avoid jurisidction implementing and enforcing economic sanctioins.

The financial services sector is extremely vulnerable to both sanctions evasion and sanctions circumvention, which means increased scrutiny by regulators. Sanctioned entities may utilize alternative means of financial settlement – eschewing the US dollar for local currencies – or employing cryptocurrencies to avoid commercial banks, which are required to report suspicious activities. The use of cryptocurrencies allow buyers and sellers to transfer virtual currencies from their respective virtual wallets without the involvement of a third party to facilitate and broker the transaction (Reinsch and Palazzi [2022]).

Actors engaged in activities to circumvent economic sanctions may also utilize vessels flying one of the many "flags of convenience", especially flags of states where the implementation and enforcement of economic sanctions are spotty or non-existent. An Iranian-owned or affiliated tanker or container vessel, for example, might employ a flag of convenience that would limit the ability of law enforcement to distinguish legitimate and illegitimate trade (Braw [2023]). Reports have highlighted the ease and frequency that sanctioned entities are able to flag and re-flag their vessels with some ships moving across as many as five registries per month. (The Economist [2025]). Thus, states and shipping firms wittingly and unwittingly contribute to the activities of sanctions evaders by employing tactics to circumvent sanctions and other regulatory requirements.

The exchange of goods outside the guise of customs officials through ship-to-ship transfers is a frequent tactic of targets and third parties. In the case of North Korea, exports of crude oil to North Korea often involve one vessel transferring crude oil to another on the high seas, where states have no jurisdiction. The deactivation of ship tracking transponders allows vessels to hide their locations and obscure their sanctions circumvention activities (Perlangeli [2018]). While the United

Nations Panel of Expert Reports have provided satellite imagery showing these transfers, most of these post hoc discoveries do little to stop the evading activity but can help identify circumventors within the sanction sender's jurisdiction. North Korean actors are the evaders, but the actors participating in the economic sanctions are circumventing sanctions as their vessels, firms, and actors involved in the transactions are not likely to be targeted.

IV Conclusion

Combatting circumvention and evasion should not only focus on the repression of problematic economic and financial activity but also strive preventative such activities. Laws and regulations are adept at punishing criminally and civilly such violations, but governments imposing sanctions must also work across jurisdictions by sharing information, coordinating data collection, and publishing clear guidance (European Commission [n.d.]). Also, more frequent and consistent enforcement across jurisdictions would also help to curtail sanctions circumvention and evasion. Identifying the pathways of circumvention can minimize the ability of targeted states, persons, and firms to evade sanctions while also providing the means to not only punish and repress illegal activity but also prevent future occurrences of circumvention.

Because sanctions evasion and circumvention involve complex networks of actors engaged in the export, import, financing, payment, logistics, and transport across sanctioned, sanctioning, and third-party jurisdictions, it is critical that states understand the likelihood and impacts of sanctions evasion and circumvention across the myriad of actors engaged in these activities. A focus only on the methods employed fails to account for the variation in actors engaged in undermining the effectiveness and implementation of economic sanctions. Lastly, a singular focus on the tools obscures the coordination needed by both evaders and circumventors, as well as the often-complementary role that each plays in undermining the effectiveness, implementation, and enforcement of economic sanctions.

Bibliography

Literature

Braw E, 'Ships are Flying False Flags to Dodge Sanctions' (*Foreign Policy*, 30 January 2023) <https://foreignpolicy.com/2023/01/30/ships-false-flags-convenience-sanctions/> accessed 19 September 2024.

Early BR and Preble KA, 'Going Fishing versus Hunting Whales: Explaining Changes in How the US Enforces Economic Sanctions' (2020) 29(2) *Security Studies* 231.

Early BR, *Busted Sanctions: Explaining Why Economic Sanctions Fail* (Sanford University Press 2015).

Jacobson M, 'Sanctions against Iran: A Promising Struggle' (2008) 31(3) *The Washington Quarterly* 71.

Johnston C, 'Sanctions against Russia: Evasion, Compensation, and Overcompliance' (EU Institute for Security Studies 2024).

Perlangeli S, 'Flagging Down North Korea on the High Seas' (*RUSI Commentary*, 29 March 2018) <https://rusi.org/explore-our-research/publications/commentary/flagging-down-north-korea-high-seas> accessed 19 September 2024.

Reinsch WA and Palazzi AL, 'Cryptocurrencies and U.S. Sanctions Evasion: Implications for Russia' (*Center for Strategic & International Studies*, 20 December 2022) <https://www.csis.org/analysis/cryptocurrencies-and-us-sanctions-evasion-implications-russia> accessed 19 September 2024.

Reuters, 'Western Insurers Say Russian Oil Price Cap Doesn't Work' (*Reuters*, 30 April 2024) <https://www.reuters.com/business/energy/western-insurers-say-russian-oil-price-cap-doesnt-work-2024-04-30> accessed 19 September 2024.

Salisbury D, 'Spies, Diplomats, and Deceit: Exploring the Persistent Role of Diplomatic Missions in North Korea's WMD Proliferation and Arms Trafficking Networks' (2021) 17(3) *Asian Security* 313.

The Economist, 'The flashing red threat from Russia's dark fleet' (*The Economist*, 30 September 2025) <https://www.economist.com/international/2025/09/30/the-flashing-red-threat-from-russias-dark-fleet> accessed 15 October 2025.

Keith A. Preble

Documents

European Commission, 'Making Sanctions Effective', <https://commission.europa.eu/topics/eu-solidarity-ukraine/eu-sanctions-against-russia-following-invasion-ukraine/making-sanctions-effective_en> accessed 28 December 2024.

Parliament of the United Kingdom, 'Written Evidence Submitted by International Group of P&I Clubs' (*Parliament Committees*, 2024) <https://committees.parliament.uk/writtenevidence/129266/pdf/> accessed 19 September 2024.

54. Gendered effects of sanctions

Loraine Rickard-Martin

I Introduction

Sanctions, whether comprehensive or targeted, imposed by an individual state, a regional organisation, or a multilateral organisation such as those of the United Nations Security Council, can hurt vulnerable or marginalised groups. While the threads of sanctions imposed by various senders are difficult to untangle, and deprivation may be experienced by an entire society, a common thread is that women and girls are predisposed to suffer disproportionately from sanctions, as they are subject to discrimination as a traditionally disadvantaged group.

It is important to note at the outset that it is difficult to discern the effects of sanctions as different from the impact of national defense spending prioritised over social welfare. Further, given that autocratic leaders are adept at deflecting the pain of sanctions onto their populations, who in turn tend to have little influence on the leadership, the ability of sanctions to change behavior is severely limited. Therefore, it is important to note that sanctions have multiple purposes, of which behavioral change is only one. Other purposes are to signal disapproval of norm-breaking and to limit the flow of resources available for norm-breaking. One must note as well that deterrence, one of the purposes of sanctions, is difficult, if not impossible, to quantify.

Prior to the early 1990s, most sanctions regimes were designed as total sector bans, which could include categories of goods related to manufacturing, agriculture, and health. Since then, targeted sanctions, which are more discriminating, such as asset freezes and travel bans directed at individual norm breakers, have been instituted to mitigate the impact of sanctions on entire civilian populations. Most sanctions cases today are targeted. However, some cases (such as sanctions on North Korea) include prohibitions on so many economic sectors that they approach the comprehensive model.

Both comprehensive and targeted sanctions have traditionally included humanitarian exemptions, e.g., for medicines and foodstuffs, as in the case of Iraq targeted because of its invasion of Kuwait. While the sanctions were imposed as of 1990, the exemptions were not applied until 1992. Corruption also goes hand in hand with sanctions and their exempted products (as was the case in Iraq), which can result in goods and medicines being sold on the black market instead of being distributed to the needy population. In addition, bureaucratic approval procedures and politics can get in the way of the timely approval of exemptions. Furthermore, humanitarian organisations working in and with sanctioned states may be constrained in their activities because banks and donors may not authorise financial transactions due to a fear of sanctions violations, termed overcompliance or derisking.

II Iraq

In the case of comprehensive sanctions against Iraq from 1990 to 2003, women suffered the effects of deprivations (food, medicine, and fuel, for example) disproportionately because of discrimination and patriarchy. Women were the first to lose their jobs to ensure that men kept their jobs. Their nutrition and reproductive health suffered. Sexual and other types of exploitation increased, and girls were likely to be kept out of school and forced into early marriages or into work to supplement the family income.

In Iraq, prior to sanctions, women depended on state-sponsored programmes for education and employment. When the state was unable to supply those services, Iraqi women suffered from a lack of access to food, employment, and health services. Because of their primary role as caretakers, Iraqi women were more vulnerable in times of scarcity. Women's employment was considered secondary to the employment of men, and women came increasingly under men's control. Their relegation to informal economic activities (such as selling food or household goods) made them increasingly vulnerable to exploitation and abuse. Single, divorced, and widowed women suffered the most from patriarchal control and domination. Girls were pulled out of school to work in the informal employment sector, often in hazardous conditions, or were pressured into early or polygamous marriage, or into begging on the streets.

Because of the deteriorating quality of food, health, water, and sanitary conditions, there was high malnutrition among women and increased maternal and infant mortality. Increased domestic, public, and state violence against women resulted in Iraqi women and girls leaving jobs and employment to avoid heightened risks of harassment and aggression. While there were few changes in legal rights for women, sanctions resulted in women's impoverishment and a lessening of their social and economic rights.

III North Korea

Current United Nations (UN) sanctions on North Korea began in 2006 and range from trade bans, including luxury goods, embargoes against conventional and non-conventional weapons, asset freezes, and travel bans. Many of the gendered impacts seen in the Iraq sanctions case are also present in North Korea. Women suffer a diminishment of their socioeconomic and human rights. A breakdown in social order has produced increased violence against women. Women in North Korea have long enjoyed legal protections under the state and employment in many areas such as health, fisheries, and textiles that are particularly impacted by sanctions. Women's role as primary caretakers in charge of the household and food security means that they are particularly impacted during times of scarcity and crisis.

While market trading is seen as women's domain, also in order to keep men in their state jobs, the impact of sanctions on market activities has increased women's job insecurity. Economic pressures on women result in increased pressures to pay bribes and to suffer sexual violence and sex trafficking. Lack of access to adequate food, and unsafe drinking water and sanitation contribute to malnutrition and negative impacts on women's reproductive and maternal health.

IV Iran

Since the late 1970s, Iran has been under unilateral, regional, and multilateral sanctions that include prohibitions against arms, trade, financial sanctions, assets, and travel bans. Women's participation in the labor market in Iran was 25 per cent at its highest in 2005, and 16 per cent in 2022, lower than the average of 19 per cent in the Middle East and North Africa. The reasons include increased conservative policies, pressures from economic sanctions, and the effects of the Covid-19 pandemic. The poverty rate doubled between 2012 and 2019, with the brunt borne by households in rural areas and those headed by women.

Sanctions on Iran have resulted in the disempowerment of women in a number of ways: by decreasing opportunities for employment in more progressive environments offered by foreign firms that left because of sanctions; when women entrepreneurs had to close their shops and hair salons due to lower revenues and higher rents, as families cut back on leisure spending.

V Conclusion

Besides an accumulation of experience and evidence on issues of overcompliance and derisking that impact financial transactions in sanctions cases, there is a dearth of research on the gendered effects of targeted sanctions in the form of travel bans and asset freezes on individuals, which form a significant part of UN and unilateral sanctions cases. Most persons on UN and other sanctions lists subject to asset freezes and asset bans are men. It is reasonable to believe, but unverified, that, as in the cases of total trade bans, when economies suffer negative impacts from sanctions affecting employment levels and household incomes, financial and other resources available to women, and girls' education are sacrificed in favor of the males in the family.

While technically a purpose rather than an effect, the use of sanctions by the UN to address sexual- and gender-based violence (S/GBV) and conflict-related sexual violence (CRSV) that began in 2008 with the case of the Democratic Republic of the Congo (DRC), was slow to take effect. The addition of perpetrators to the sanctions list has also been slow and sporadic. As of 2021, of 720 total listed individuals and entities, a mere 28 listings were for S/GBV offenses or human trafficking.

Even with increased attention to ensuring humanitarian exemptions, sanctions of any type involve unintended effects, particularly on vulnerable and disadvantaged groups, including women and girls, and can exacerbate the impacts of other economic factors in a target country. More study and mitigating measures are needed to address their disproportionate effects on women and girls and other disadvantaged groups.

LORAINE RICKARD-MARTIN

Bibliography

Literature

Hussein Al-Jawaheri Y, *Women in Iraq: The Gender Impact of International Sanctions* (Lynne Rienner 2008).

Korea Peace Now, 'The Human Costs and Gendered Impact of Sanctions on North Korea' (October 2019) <https://koreapeacenow.org/wp-content/uploads/2019/10/human-costs-and-gendered-impact-of-sanctions-on-north-korea.pdf> accessed 24 September 2024.

Rousdari BZ, 'Caught in the Crossfire: The Toll of Western Sanctions on Iran's Women's Rights Movement' (The Oxford Middle East Review, 12 July 2024) <https://omerjournal.com/2024/07/12/caught-in-the-crossfire-the-toll-of-western-sanctions-on-irans-womens-rights-movement/> accessed 25 November 2024.

International Crisis Group, 'U.S. "Maximum Pressure" on Iran Hurts the Women it Claims to Help' (International Crisis Group, 6 March 2020) <https://www.crisisgroup.org/middle-east-north-africa/gulf-and-arabian-peninsula/iran/us-maximum-pressure-iran-hurts-women-it-claims-help> accessed 24 September 2024.

Rickard-Martin L, 'United Nations Sanctions: Through a Gender Lens' in Charron A and Portela C (eds), *Multilateral Sanctions Revisited: Lessons Learned from Margaret Doxey* (McGill-Queens University Press 2022) 163.

LORAINE RICKARD-MARTIN

55. Humanitarian carveouts

Erica Moret

I Introduction

Sanctions – particularly those that are broad and sectoral in nature, or in instances where multiple sanctions regimes overlap with one another – can have unintended humanitarian consequences on a variety of levels. These can include barriers to payments, supply chains of essential goods, or remittances (Moret [2023a]). They can also involve restrictions on specific types of interactions with certain groups or individuals, which can complicate the work of humanitarian organisations. Humanitarian exceptions are necessary to prevent such impacts and to uphold international humanitarian principles, in line with international humanitarian law (IHL) (Ferraro [2022]). All sanctions regimes, including those of a multilateral or autonomous nature, tend to include some form of humanitarian provision, which seeks to ensure that humanitarian assistance and other trades and services vital for the well-being of civilians are not impacted by measures in place.

II UNSC Resolution 2664 (2022)

The United Nations Security Council (UNSC) Resolution 2664 (2022) is a landmark resolution that introduced a humanitarian exception across all United Nations (UN) asset freezes. Co-penned by Ireland and the United States, UNSC Resolution 2664 was adopted on 9 December (the UN's anti-corruption day), following extensive advocacy by humanitarian organisations and member states. Its adoption represented a major achievement of collective action across the UNSC's permanent and temporary members and stakeholders. The resolution provides a comprehensive framework for ensuring that humanitarian activities are not impeded by UN sanctions, including provisions for the delivery of food, medical supplies, and other essential goods (IPI [2023]). It also establishes mechanisms for monitoring and reporting on the implementation of humanitarian exceptions, helping to ensure that they are effectively enforced (Lewis et al. [2022]). The resolution is significant as it sets a precedent for incorporating humanitarian considerations into the design and implementation of sanctions across other regimes.

Before the creation of UNSC Resolution 2664, private and not-for-profit organisations needed to seek ad-hoc permissions (such as specific licences in the United States and the United Kingdom, derogations in the EU, or exceptions in the UN) if their activities in sanctioned jurisdictions did not fall under existing standing exceptions (called general licences [GL] in the United States and the United Kingdom or exemptions in the EU and the UN). These ad-hoc permissions were widely criticised as being insufficient, too broad in scope, with costly and time-consuming processes for application and confusion over the nature of permissible activities. Furthermore, certain humanitarian organisations, such as the International Committee for the Red Cross (ICRC), view derogations as incompatible with the humanitarian principles of independence and neutrality enshrined in IHL, fearing that engaging in such mechanisms could tarnish their reputation and pose security risks to staff.

III Carveouts under autonomous sanctions

Following a consultative review by the US Department of the Treasury into the future of US sanctions practice (US Department of the Treasury [2021]), alongside the implementation of UNSC Resolution 2664 into domestic law, the United States quickly followed suit in announcing similar measures (GLs) across all its autonomous sanctions regimes; a move that has been followed by other sanctioning powers (albeit still only partially by some).[2] The US Treasury went on to publish its *2023 De-Risking Strategy* and also stepped up outreach efforts to curtail derisking and overcompliance. Other sanctioning powers are yet to publish similar strategies of their own.

IV Terminology and harmonisation

The language used to refer to humanitarian provisions varies across sanctioning authorities, and a great deal of confusion exists across sectors (and even within governments) over related terminology and application. As noted in one recent UNU-CPR report:

> There is considerable confusion around these terms, both procedurally and substantially. The Security Council, the European Union, States and even the academic sector all employ the terms differently. Indeed, inconsistencies were even noted between the terms employed in the English and French text of some Security Council sanctions resolutions. This inconsistency is problematic as it impedes effective advocacy, leads to confusion among humanitarian actors, and frustrates sanctions communities, who receive many different briefings and recommendations from humanitarians. Clarity on terms and substance is essential for sanctions and impartial humanitarian actors to enter a productive and international humanitarian law (IHL)-compliant dialogue on humanitarian safeguards in sanctions regimes. (Huvé and Brubaker [2022])

Stakeholders regularly call for the harmonisation of language across humanitarian provisions. Table 55.1 provides a brief overview of the main types of humanitarian provisions used by the principal sanctioning actors (subject to change).

V Ongoing challenges

Despite the existence of humanitarian exceptions, several challenges persist. One is the reluctance of financial institutions to process transactions related to humanitarian aid due to the fear of violating sanctions, or reticence linked to resourcing burdens, reputational concerns, and steep costs. This phenomenon, known as "derisking", can severely restrict the flow of aid and can also have negative impacts on the sending of remittances and legitimate economic activities.

Overcompliance (see chapter) in the wider private sector also poses significant challenges in the implementation of humanitarian exceptions, which can impact supply chains of essential goods to sanctioned jurisdictions, including in relation to shipping, insurance, and technology (Moret [2023a]). Another ongoing challenge is the lack of standing exemptions under related regulations, such as in relation to humanitarian goods that are impacted by US export controls (falling under the Department of Commerce). In parallel, a plethora of other regulations may also exist alongside sanctions regimes, further compounding pressures on private and public sector actors in sanctioned jurisdictions. These might include counterterrorism listings, export controls, measures to counter money laundering and terrorist financing, criminal laws and the Financial Action Task Force (FATF) listings relating to corruption risks.

VI Best practices

To enhance the effectiveness of humanitarian exceptions, several best practices can be adopted (Moret [2024]). These include:

- **Clear guidance**: By providing detailed and specific guidance to financial institutions and humanitarian organisations, it is possible to reduce the risk of derisking and overcompliance and ensure that aid can be delivered without unnecessary delays. These guidelines should include information on the types of activities that are exempt from sanctions, the processes for obtaining necessary approvals, and the mechanisms for reporting and monitoring compliance.
- **Monitoring and evaluation**: Establishing mechanisms to monitor the implementation of exceptions and evaluate their impact on humanitarian efforts. By establishing mechanisms to monitor the implementation of exceptions and evaluate their impact on humanitarian efforts, it is possible to identify and address any challenges or gaps in the system. This can include regular reporting and assessment, feedback from humanitarian organisations and affected populations, and the use of data and evidence to inform policy and practice.
- **Multistakeholder coordination**: Multistakeholder groupings that include sanctions units, regulators, civil society, and financial institutions can be useful to allow for troubleshooting and sharing of best practice. By fostering collaboration between sanctioning bodies, humanitarian organisations, and financial institutions, it is possible to streamline processes and ensure that aid can be delivered efficiently. This can include regular communication and information sharing, joint training and capacity building initiatives, and the establishment of dedicated coordination mechanisms.
- **Innovation**: Technology can be harnessed, with the right safeguards in place, to help support governments and other

Table 55.1 Carveouts and corresponding terminology by organisations and states

Type of carveout	Definition	UN terminology	US terminology	EU[i] terminology	UK terminology	Switzerland terminology	Canada terminology[ii]
Standing provision	A legal provision that carves out space for humanitarian and related activities and goods does not require prior authorisation from a competent authority and will automatically apply if the activity is in the scope of the parameters of the licence	Exemption[iii]	General licence	Exemption[iv] (one form of EU exception)	Usually an exception (in UK legislation) but sometimes implemented through general licences	Exemption	Usually an exception (in Canadian legislation) but sometimes implemented through certificates[v]

Type of carveout	Definition	UN terminology	US terminology	EU[i] terminology	UK terminology	Switzerland terminology	Canada terminology[ii]
Use	-	There are exemptions for all UN financial sanctions. The UN Security Council (UNSC) Res 2664 (2022) introduced a cross-cutting exemption for all sanctions regimes with the exception of Afghanistan, which had a tailored exemption under 2615 (2021)	The United States has a "baseline" set of humanitarian GLs across both its UN and autonomous financial sanctions. These authorise the activities of four categories: US government, international organisations, NGOs, agriculture and medical organisations	The EU has implemented UNSC Res 2664 for UN financial sanctions and introduced exemptions across some of the financial sanctions under all its "hybrid" (UN/autonomous) regimes and over half of its autonomous regimes. Prior to 2664, it also made use of exemptions in cases that include Syria and Somalia	The United Kingdom has implemented UNSC Res 2664 for UN financial sanctions and has introduced a similar standardised exception for financial sanctions under autonomous regimes. It has also used GLs to respond to crises and has issued them for its Russia, Syria, and CT regimes, among others	The Swiss Federal Council implemented UNSC Res 2664 and adopted a humanitarian exemption for Afghanistan provided for in Resolution 2615 (2021) as well as exemptions relating to the Syria earthquake of February 2023	Canada has implemented UNSC Res 2664 for UN financial sanctions

Type of carveout	Definition	UN terminology	US terminology	EU[i] terminology	UK terminology	Switzerland terminology	Canada terminology[ii]
Ad-hoc provision	A legal provision allowing humanitarian (and other related) actors to seek permission to conduct specific activities on an ad-hoc basis	Exception	Specific licence	Derogation[vi] (another form of EU exception)	Specific/individual licence	Derogation[vii]	Permit[viii]
Use	–	Used in particular for the DPRK regime	Supplements humanitarian GLs. Can be for financial and/or trade measures	Formerly used regularly by NGOs across a range of sanctions regimes in instances where exemptions are absent or not sufficient	Supplements humanitarian GLs and exceptions and can be for financial and/or trade measures. Humanitarian applications are prioritised by the licensing bodies	–	–

Type of carveout	Definition	UN terminology	US terminology	EU[i] terminology	UK terminology	Switzerland terminology	Canada terminology[ii]
Granting authority	–	UN sanctions committees	Office of Foreign Assets Control (OFAC) in the US Treasury[ix]	Member state competent authorities[x]	Office of Financial Sanctions Implementation (OFSI) and Export Control Joint Unit (ECJU)[xi] the Foreign, Commonwealth and Development Office (FCDO) usually holds the pen on exceptions in legislation	State Secretariat for Economic Affairs (SECO)	Global Affairs Canada[xii]

[i] The EU defines an exception as "provisions that enable otherwise restricted actions to be carried out. Legal instruments on restrictive measures make provision for appropriate exceptions to take account of in particular basic needs of targeted persons, legal fees, extraordinary expenses, humanitarian needs or international obligations, with regard to the various restrictive measures taken".

[ii] Legislated exceptions for certain activities – found in individual sanctions regulations – are in place under Canadian sanctions regimes. Regulations typically also include mechanisms for issuing certificates or permits in order to authorise specified activities or transactions that would otherwise be prohibited. Government of Canada (2020). This authority is found in the related orders or acts. "Certificates and Permits" <https://www.international.gc.ca/world-monde/international_relations-relations_internationales/sanctions/certificates_permits-certificats_permis.aspx?lang=eng>.

[iii] Referred to as an exception once it is transcribed into UK law.

[iv] According to EU DG ECHO (2023) "An exemption is a provision carving out certain activities from the scope of application of the general prohibition. Exemptions mean that a restriction does not apply when the purpose of the action coincides with the scope of the exemption; as a result, persons falling within the purview of the exemption can carry out the action at hand without any delay. Whenever a humanitarian activity falls within the scope of an exemption, a humanitarian operator may carry out the exempted activity without any prior authorisation. However, in case of ex post verification, humanitarian operators must be able to demonstrate that the activity in question did comply with all the conditions required for the exemption to apply. Exemptions are generally phrased along the following lines: "(The prohibitions laid down in) Article... shall not apply to..." <https://www.dgecho-partners-helpdesk.eu/sanctions/humanitarian-exceptions>.

[v] Certificates "may be granted in exceptional circumstances when certain activities are prohibited under the United Nations Act", according to Government of Canada (2020). "Certificates and Permits" <https://www.international.gc.ca/world-monde/international_relations-relations_internationales/sanctions/certificates_permits-certificats_permis.aspx?lang=eng>.

[vi] According to EU DG ECHO (2023) "The prohibitions set in the sanctions regime can be derogated if the action falling under the scope of the sanctions regime is necessary for the purpose of providing humanitarian aid. Derogations mean that a restricted (prohibited) action can be carried out only after the National Competent Authority has granted authorisation. In such a scenario, humanitarian operators have to apply for prior authorisation to conduct their activities. Once authorised, the operator can engage in relevant activities. This authorisation has to be requested from a national competent authority (NCA) of one of the EU Member States.

It is for the humanitarian operator to prove to the relevant NCA that the conditions for granting an authorisation for derogation are fulfilled. NCAs can provide necessary guidance as to how to obtain humanitarian derogations. When there is a derogation mechanism in an EU sanctions regime, the NCAs of the EU Member States responsible for granting such an authorisation are listed in the Annex to the relevant legal text. The Commission has put in place an EU-level Contact Point channel to help humanitarian operators obtain information and preliminary guidance on the practicalities for requesting humanitarian derogations in the context of the COVID-19 pandemic. Derogations are generally phrased along the following lines: 'By way of derogation from the (prohibitions in) Article..., the competent authorities may authorise, under the conditions they deem appropriate...'" <https://www.dgecho-partners-helpdesk.eu/sanctions/humanitarian-exceptions>.

[vii] "Humanitarian derogations" are derogations for the provision of humanitarian aid under Council regulations establishing EU sanctions pursuant to Article 215 of the Treaty on the Functioning of the European Union. Such authorisations are a precondition for carrying out actions otherwise subject to prohibitions envisaged in EU sanctions regulations. They provide the humanitarian operators with a formal indication of the scope of the permitted activities. "EU Sanctions Regulations" <https://finance.ec.europa.eu/system/files/2022-04/eu-restrictive-measures-humanitarian-derogations-factsheet_en.pdf>.

[viii] Permits "may be granted on an exceptional basis in respect of activities that are prohibited under the Special Economic Measures Act and the Justice for Victims of Corrupt Foreign Officials Act" and may only be issued to persons in Canada and Canadians outside the country. Government of Canada (2020). This authority is found in the related orders or acts. "Certificates and Permits" <https://www.international.gc.ca/world-monde/international_relations-relations_internationales/sanctions/certificates_permits-certificats_permis.aspx?lang=eng>.

[ix] Export control licences fall under the Department of Commerce's (DoC) Bureau of Industry and Security (BIS).

[x] A variety of rules and procedures are in place in different member states and are applied by their national competent authorities (NCAs) when assessing requests and granting humanitarian derogations under EU sanctions regulations <https://finance.ec.europa.eu/system/files/2022-04/eu-restrictive-measures-humanitarian-derogations-factsheet_en.pdf>.

[xi] The OFSI has the power to issue GLs for country sanctions regimes under the Sanctions and Anti-Money Laundering Act 2018 ("the Sanctions Act"). Export control licences issued by the Export Control Joint Unit permit prohibited activity under trade sanctions and embargoes. Even where an export control licence has been granted, an OFSI licence may still be needed, and it is not guaranteed that an OFSI licence will be granted.

[xii] The application process for sanctions permits and certificates is separate from the permit process under the Export and Import Permits Act, which is related to the Export Control List, the Import Control List, and the Area Control List. Government of Canada (2020) "Certificates and Permits" <https://www.international.gc.ca/world-monde/international_relations-relations_internationales/sanctions/certificates_permits-certificats_permis.aspx?lang=eng>.

stakeholders to ensure effective sanctions compliance while mitigating some of the unintended implications of sanctions regimes, such as negative impacts on humanitarian payments (Moret [2023b]).

VII Conclusion

Humanitarian exceptions are vital in ensuring that sanctions do not exacerbate human suffering. While significant progress has been made, ongoing challenges highlight the need for continuous improvement in the design and implementation of these exceptions and phasing out the use of ad-hoc and time-bound exceptions. Such policy adaptations should also be accompanied by proactive outreach to the private and not-for-profit sectors to avoid insurmountable risks being placed on these stakeholders' shoulders and the adoption of innovative technologies and evidence-based research in support of the mitigation of negative, unintended humanitarian consequences associated with the complex global compliance environment.

Notes

1. UNSC Res 2664 <http://unscr.com/en/resolutions/2664>, introductions of general licences across US autonomous sanctions <https://home.treasury.gov/policy-issues/financial-sanctions/recent-actions/20221220>, with further details in FAQs 1105–1108 <https://home.treasury.gov/policy-issues/financial-sanctions/faqs/added/2022-12-20>.
2. <https://ofac.treasury.gov/recent-actions/20221220>.

Bibliography

Literature

Debarre A, 'One Year On: Where Do We Stand on the Milestone Humanitarian Carve-Out in UN Sanctions Regimes?' (*IPI Global Observatory*, 15 December 2023) <https://theglobalobservatory.org/2023/12/one-year-on-where-do-we-stand-on-the-milestone-humanitarian-carve-out-in-un-sanctions-regimes/>.

Ferraro T, 'International Humanitarian Law, Principled Humanitarian Action, Counterterrorism, and Sanctions' (2022) 103 *International Review of the Red Cross* 109.

Gillard E-C, 'Humanitarian Exceptions: A Turning Point in UN Sanctions' (*Chatham House*, 21 December 2022) <https://www.chathamhouse.org/2022/12/humanitarian-exceptions-turning-point-un-sanctions>.

Huvé S and Brubaker R, 'Humanitarian Exemptions in UN Sanctions Regimes' UN Sanctions and Humanitarian Action Policy Brief 3 (2022) <http://collections.unu.edu/eserv/UNU:8748/UNSHA-PolicyMemo3.pdf>.

International Peace Institute (IPI), 'Safeguarding Humanitarian Action in UN Sanctions and Counter terrorism Regimes: The Impact and Implementation of Resolution 2664' (December 2023) <https://www.ipinst.org/wp-content/uploads/2023/12/IPI-E-RPT-Safeguarding-Humanitarian-Action2023.pdf>.

Lewis DA, Kapoor R and Modirzadeh NK, 'UNSCR 2664 (2022) and Counterterrorism Measures: An Analytical Frame for States' Harvard Law School PILAC (March 2023) <https://hls.harvard.edu/wp-content/uploads/2024/03/Res.-2664-and-Counterterrorism-Measures.pdf>.

Moret E, 'The Developing Role of National Tri-Sector Groups in Addressing Financial Sector Derisking' Dialogue Series on Solutions to Bank Derisking (Norwegian Refugee Council, January 2024) <https://www.nrc.no/resources/reports/the-developing-role-of-national-tri-sector-groups-in-addressing-financial-sector-derisking/>.

Moret E, 'Effectiveness of Humanitarian Exceptions to Sanctions: Syria Earthquake Lessons' (The Carter Center, 11 July 2023a) <https://www.cartercenter.org/resources/pdfs/peace/conflict_resolution/syria-conflict/2023/effectiveness-of-humanitarian-exceptions-to-sanctions-syria-earthquake-lessons.pdf>.

Moret E, 'Mitigating Financial Sector Derisking through Innovation: The Role of Digital Technologies in Humanitarian Fund Transfers' Dialogue Series on Solutions to Bank Derisking' (Norwegian Refugee Council, October 2023b) <https://www.nrc.no/resources/reports/mitigating-financial-sector-derisking-through-innovation-the-role-of-digital-technologies-in-humanitarian-fund-transfers>.

Erica Moret

Document

US Department of the Treasury, *The Treasury 2021 Sanctions Review* (October 2021) <https://home.treasury.gov/system/files/136/Treasury-2021-sanctions-review.pdf>.

56. International criminal justice and sanctions

Alice Riccardi

I Introduction

The competence of the United Nations Security Council (UNSC) to enforce the peace may overlap with the purpose of enforcing the law, which is inherent to international criminal courts and tribunals (ICTs). In the past, it was thus proposed to formalise the relationship between multilateral targeted sanctions and ICTs with the aim of fostering cooperation and information exchange. These attempts so far have failed (e.g. ICC ASP, Draft Action Plan on arrest strategies [2015]). Currently, therefore, the two enforcement mechanisms often coexist but are rarely coordinated. They do intersect, yet mostly coincidentally (Birkett [2020]). This entry categorises the ways in which targeted sanctions and international criminal proceedings interact, in order to expose phenomena of convergence and – more often – of mere parallelism or even divergence. Proceeding in four steps, the entry maps interactions happening at the level of (Section II) arrest and transfer, (Section III) asset freeze, and (Section IV) information sharing. Although since the 1990s sanctions have interacted with most ICTs, including hybrid ones, this entry mainly focuses on the relationship between sanctions regimes and the International Criminal Court (ICC or the Court). Also, this entry only discusses interactions between ICTs and multilateral sanctions, although ICC officials have been despicably targeted with unilateral sanctions by the United States in connection with the Afghanistan situation in 2020 and the Palestine investigation in 2024–2025.

II Arrest and transfer

Individuals subjected to ICTs' arrest warrants are fairly frequently also sanctioned by the UNSC. As mentioned, however, the two mechanisms are often uncoordinated and merely operate in parallel. This applies to the respective mechanisms' activation, suspension, and termination phases.

First, arrest warrants and sanctions are not issued concertedly. ICTs lack a police force of their own and rely on the decentralised enforcement provided by states to execute arrests. However, states are often recalcitrant to cooperate with ICTs to this end. To address this 'arrest problem', it was proposed to use UNSC targeted sanctions as negative incentives to induce fugitives to surrender. This technique has been demonstrated to be effective in the context of the broader diplomatic efforts to arrest persons indicted by the International Criminal Tribunal for the Former Yugoslavia (ICTY) (Portela [2010] 122). In 2004, the Council of the European Union imposed an asset freeze against ICTY indictees yet to be transferred by Bosnia and Herzegovina, Montenegro, and Serbia (Council Regulation No. 1763/2004 [2004]). The regulation mentioned as legal bases UNSC Resolution 827 (1993) establishing the ICTY and UNSC Resolution 1503 (2003) calling on states to render all necessary assistance to the ICTY. Against this experience, the ICC prosecutor suggested automatic listing upon issuance of an arrest warrant (UNGA Report of the International Criminal Court on its Activities to the UN General Assembly [2015] para. 96). This contrasts, however, with the discretion with which the United Nations (UN) Charter endows the UNSC. Others advocated for discretionary listing (Ruiz Verduzco [2015] 61; van den Herik [2017] 257). However, this would entail, first, sanctioning individuals for acts independent of them, i.e. the failure of requested states to execute their arrest. Absent a legal basis in the ICC Statute or specific listing criteria, current regimes do not permit the sanctioning of fugitives solely for not surrendering to the Court. Additionally, sanctions would lose their preventative aim and turn into pre-trial tools of criminal law enforcement substantially connected to ICC proceedings, thereby accruing known issues relating to respecting the fundamental rights of listed individuals (Riccardi [2020] 66–70). In any case, practice shows that, apart from the Libya situation, sanctions have targeted ICC fugitives only coincidentally (Birkett [2020] 995–6; Bentall [2016] 98). In the Sudan situation, the UNSC attitude even undermined ICC proceedings (van den Herik [2017] 244): vis-à-vis states' non-compliance in arresting then President Al-Bashir, the UNSC never took action. Conclusively, the establishment of coordination for arrest purposes between the ICC and the UNSC seems unlikely today.

Second, although most regimes provide for an exemption to travel bans when 'necessary for the fulfilment of a judicial process' (see CAR regime, UNSC Res 2399 [2018] para. 14(b)), some do not (e.g. the Sudan regime). This, pursuant to Article 103 UN Charter, prevents the transfer to the Court of arrested individuals who are sanctioned. The inclusion of the mentioned exemption, therefore, should be streamlined by the UNSC. The very broad drafting of the exemption should also allow the transfer of convicted and acquitted individuals. However, it is not clear whether it would also apply to the travel of sanctioned witnesses and, potentially, victims.

Third, to the best of this author's knowledge, no sanction has ever been terminated following the acquittal or non-confirmation of charges by the ICC of a sanctioned individual. Although the two mechanisms are motivated by different aims, many sanctions regimes (particularly so-called civil-conflict ones) still include as listing criteria international humanitarian law or human rights violations constituting international crimes. Hence the reasons for listing and indicting a person may overlap (see recently ICC ASP, Resolution on Cooperation [2023] para. 27). This can lead to problems with the coherence of the legal system. *Inter alia*, the perpetuation of sanctions against acquitted individuals may raise questions concerning their arbitrariness.

III Asset freeze

Both the UNSC and the ICC may issue orders directed to states to freeze individuals' assets. ICC judges may issue requests to freeze proceeds, property, and assets, and instrumentalities of crimes, as protective measures for the purpose of forfeiture and for the ultimate benefit of victims, including reparation (ICC Statute [2002] Arts 57(3)(e) and 93(1)(k)). Although coordination could be crucial – especially to facilitate the ICC's capacity to locate assets – UNSC and ICC freezing actions are generally unconcerted. Whereas initially the ICC used to explicitly refer to accused individuals' listings when requesting states to freeze assets (e.g. *Prosecutor v Lubanga* [2006] 3), lately it has abandoned such practice due to UNSC disinterest (Birkett [2020] 998; Bentall [2016] 97–8).

Issues discussed in Section II concerning the initiation, suspension, and termination of sanctions also apply to asset freezing. Yet, further problems may arise in this specific context: above all, UNSC resolutions do not provide for exemptions in the event of reparation orders issued by the ICC (they usually admit exemptions for 'expenses associated with the provision of legal services', a rather different matter; see e.g. UNSC Res 1596 [2005] para. 16(a). See UNSC Res 1970 [2011] para. 18 as the only exception; Bertrand and Schauder [2016] 166–8).

IV Information sharing

Practice shows that a binary information-sharing channel is operating between UNSC sanction bodies and the ICC Office of the Prosecutor (OTP). Calls to typify such a relationship (*inter alia* Mancini [2016] 229–31; High-Level Review Compendium [2015] 68) have never concretised. Cooperation, which is based on the broadly worded Article 5 of the ICC–UN Relationship Agreement (2004), appears at present to be informal and episodic – at least according to public documentation. In any case, UNSC sanctions bodies' information may play only a limited role in ICC trials, as follows.

First, sanctions bodies' open-source information – e.g. reports of panels of experts – falls short of meeting criminal evidential standards: above all, sources are often unidentified, and information can hardly be verified. Although routinely submitted as evidence, practice shows that said information has no or very limited probative weight (e.g. *Prosecutor v Gbagbo* [2021] 36).

Second, these problems are even greater when it comes to sanctions bodies' confidential information (mostly intelligence material). Should the OTP be interested in this information, it must conclude confidentiality agreements with the UNSC under Article 54(3)(e) of the ICC Statute, which the ICC Appeals Chamber clarified can only be used exceptionally and to gather so-called 'springboard evidence'. In any case, trial chambers retain the right to review *ex parte* confidential information, an activity to which the UNSC would hardly agree (*Prosecutor v Lubanga* [2008] paras 51, 55). Conclusively, the sharing of classified information is highly unlikely (Riccardi [2020] 74–7).

V Conclusion

The aims of multilateral sanctions and international criminal justice may overlap. However, in practice, synchronisation happens only on a case-by-case basis (van den Herik [2017] 249): the two mechanisms mostly appear to work in parallel. This is not entirely negative. In the past, there were hopes that the ICC–UNSC relationship would be formalised. At the current juncture in international relations, however, the preservation of the Court's judicial independence from UNSC political power dynamics appears crucial to promoting the cause of international criminal justice. At the same time, UNSC sanctions resolutions should be designed in such a way as not to create conflicting obligations for states, preventing them from cooperating swiftly with the ICC.

Bibliography

Literature

'United States Imposes Economic Sanctions and Visa Restriction on International Criminal Court Officials' (2021) 115 *American Journal of International Law* 138.

Bentall P, 'United Nations Targeted Sanctions and Other Policy Tools: Diplomacy, Legal, Use of Force' in Biersteker TJ, Eckert SE and Tourinho M (eds), *Targeted Sanctions* (Cambridge University Press 2016) 79.

Bertrand AA and Schauder N, 'Practical Cooperation Challenges Faced by the Registry of the International Criminal Court' in Bekou O and Daley JB (eds), *Cooperation and the International Criminal Court* (Brill Nijhoff 2016) 152.

Birkett DJ, 'Coexistent but Uncoordinated: Asset Freezing Measures at the International Criminal Court and the UN Security Council' (2020) 20 *International Criminal Law Review* 983.

Mancini M, 'UN Sanctions Targeting Individuals and ICC Proceedings: How to Achieve a Mutually Reinforcing Interaction' in Ronzitti N (ed.), *Coercive Diplomacy, Sanctions and International Law* (Brill Nijhoff 2016) 228.

Portela C, *European Union Sanctions and Foreign Policy. When and Why Do They Work?* (Routledge 2010).

Riccardi A, 'The Use of UN Smart Sanctions in Connection with ICC Proceedings: A (Human Rights-Oriented) Rebuttal' (2018) 12 *Diritti umani e diritto internazionale* 77.

Riccardi A, 'UNSC Sanctions Regimes and the ICC: Arguments against Cooperation for Arrest and Investigative Purposes in Light of Defendants' Rights' in Pérez-León-Acevedo JP and Nicholson J (eds), *Defendants and Victims in International Criminal Justice* (Routledge 2020) 62.

Ruiz Verduzco D, 'The Relationship between the ICC and the United Nations Security Council' in Stahn C (ed.), *The Law and Practice of the International Criminal Court* (Oxford University Press 2015) 30.

van den Herik L, 'The Individualization of Enforcement in International Law' in Maluwa T, du Plessis M and Tladi D (eds), *The Pursuit of a Brave New World in International Law. Essays in Honour of John Dugard* (Brill Nijhoff 2017) 234.

Documents

Council Regulation (EC) 1763/2004 of 11 October 2004 imposing certain restrictive measures in support of effective implementation of the mandate of the International Criminal Tribunal for the former Yugoslavia (ICTY) [2004] OJ L315.

ICC ASP, 'Report of the Bureau on cooperation, Addendum, Annex VII, Report on arrest strategies by the Rapporteur' (21 November 2014) ICC-ASP/13/29/Add.1.

ICC ASP, 'Report on the Draft Action Plan on arrest strategies, submitted by the Prosecutor' (16 November 2015) ICC-ASP/14/26/Add.1.

ICC ASP, Resolution on Cooperation (14 December 2023) ICC-ASP/22/Res. 5.

ICC, 'Judge Philippe Kirsch, President of the International Criminal Court. Address to the United Nations General Assembly' (9 October 2006).

ICC, Financial investigations and recovery of assets (November 2017).

Negotiated Relationship Agreement between the International Criminal Court and the United Nations (adopted 4 October 2004, entered into force 4 October 2004) 2283 UNTS 196.

Prosecutor v Gbagbo (Eighth decision on the review of Mr Laurent Gbagbo's detention pursuant to Article 60(3) of the Statute) ICC-02/11-01/11 (11 March 2015).

Prosecutor v Lubanga (Decision on the appeal of the Prosecutor against the decision of Trial Chamber I entitled 'Decision on the Consequences of Non-Disclosure of

ALICE RICCARDI

Exculpatory Material Covered by Article 54(3)(e) Agreements and the Application to Stay the Prosecution of the Accused, Together with Certain Issues Raised at the Status Conference on 10 June 2008') ICC-01/04-01/06-1401 OA 13 (21 October 2008).

Prosecutor v Lubanga (Request to the Democratic Republic of the Congo for the purpose of obtaining the identification, tracing, freezing and seizure of property and assets belonging to Mr Thomas Lubanga Dyilo) ICC-01/04-01/06 (9 March 2006).

Prosecutor v Yekatom and Ngaïssona (Transcript of hearing) ICC-01/14-01/18-T-021-Red-ENG (25 March 2021).

Statute of the International Criminal Court (adopted 17 July 1998, entered into force 1 July 2002) 2187 UNTS 3.

UNGA, 'Report of the International Criminal Court on its Activities to the UN General Assembly' (28 August 2015) UN Doc. A/70/350.

UNGA, UNSC, 'Annex, Compendium of the High-level Review of United Nations Sanctions' (12 June 2015) UN Doc. A/69/941-S/2015/432.

UNSC Res 827 (25 May 1993) UN Doc. S/RES/827.

UNSC Res 1503 (28 August 2003) UN Doc. S/RES/1503 (2003).

UNSC Res 1596 (3 May 2005) UN Doc. S/RES/1596.

UNSC Res 1970 (27 February 2011) UN Doc. S/RES/1970.

UNSC Res 2399 (30 January 2018) UN Doc. S/RES/2399.

57. Investment protection

Javier García Olmedo

I Introduction

Sanctions are having a major impact on global trade and investment, especially in relation to commodities markets and related industries such as shipping, insurance and trade finance. Apart from their effects at the macroeconomic level, there is little doubt that European Union (EU) (see chapter) sanctions may substantially affect the activities of businesses run by investors who are directly or indirectly subject to the measures. This entry examines whether, and if so to what extent, the field of international investment law can serve as a shield against sanctions affecting the value and operation of foreign investments in the EU. When examining how sanctions can fall within the scope of international investment law, it is important to think broadly about the realm of possible claims. In this regard, sender states have undertaken obligations under international investment agreements (IIAs) signed with Russia in respect of investments made in their territory by Russian individuals and companies that have been targeted or affected by sanctions. Sender states have also concluded IIAs with other countries around the world that protect investments (e.g., shares or participations) held by non-Russian investors in companies that have been targeted or affected by sanctions.

II The protection of investors in the face of sanctions

Currently, over 2500 IIAs are in force around the world, which include bilateral investment treaties (BITs), free trade agreements (FTAs) and multilateral investment treaties (UNCTAD [2023]; for a historical account of the proliferation of IIAs see Salacuse [2021]). The most important feature of IIAs is that they allow investors (both private individuals and corporations) to sue states before an arbitral tribunal for measures that damage their investments – a mechanism known as investor–state dispute settlement (ISDS). In addition to ISDS, IIAs provide investors with an unprecedented level of substantive protections, generally requiring host states to pay compensation in the event of an expropriation and to provide fair and equitable treatment (FET) (for an analysis of investment protection standards in IIAs see Bonnitcha [2014]). To access IIAs, the investor must be a national 'of a contracting State other than the host State in which the investment is made' (McLachlan et al. [2017] 156).

Investors can rely on protections conferred under IIAs and seek compensation from states that have adopted policy measures (i.e., sanctions) that adversely affect the economic value of their investments. To give an example, in August 2024, Russian businessman Mikhail Fridman filed a claim against Luxembourg, alleging that sanctions levied against him in the wake of Russia's invasion of Ukraine are in breach of the Luxembourg–Russia BIT (Bohmer [2024]). Mr Fridman alleges, more particularly, that Luxembourg violated the BIT's expropriation and FET standards by freezing his assets located in the state in compliance with EU sanctions. It should be noted that Mr Fridman has also challenged EU sanctions before the Court of Justice of the European Union (CJEU). In April 2024, after he submitted the notice of dispute under the BIT, the CJEU ruled that the Council of the EU had not provided sufficient evidence to establish that Mr Fridman had been involved in efforts that "undermine or threaten the territorial integrity, sovereignty and independence of Ukraine" (*Fridman v Council* [2024]).

This is not the only case where sanctions-related claims have arisen under IIAs. It has been reported that Belgium has also been threatened with investment arbitration over the billions of pounds in Russian assets that have been frozen in the country since the beginning of the war. The government has received requests from Russian companies to "release frozen accounts", which have referred to the Belgium–Russia BIT (Fisher [2024]). Moreover, in August 2023, Volga-Dnepr Airlines, a Russian company, threatened to bring an investment treaty claim against Canada (see chapter) over the seizure of one of its Antonov AN-124 freighter aircraft. The aircraft was seized by the Canadian government as part of sanctions taken against Russia (Jones [2023]).

These examples illustrate how sanctions may fall within the scope of international investment protection. When examining the realm of possible claims, one should consider that sanctions may come into conflict not only with obligations undertaken by sender states under IIAs concluded with Russia in respect of investments made in their territory by

Russian investors that have been targeted or affected by sanctions. Sender states have also concluded IIAs with other countries around the world that protect investments (e.g., shares or participations) held by non-Russian investors in companies that have been targeted or affected by sanctions. Sender states should be aware of the protections afforded by their IIAs and be prepared to defend against potential arbitration.

III Defences invoked by sanctioning states in investment disputes

Sender states can invoke various defences. They may attempt to characterise a sanction as a lawful countermeasure (see chapter). Under Articles 20–25 of the International Law Commission (ILC) Draft Articles on the Responsibility of States for Internationally Wrongful Acts (ARSIWA), there are certain circumstances under which states may not be held responsible for breaches of their customary or treaty-based obligations (ARSIWA [2001]). These circumstances include the invocation of countermeasures, which are unilateral measures adopted by a state (the "injured" state) in response to the breach of its rights by the wrongful act of another state (the "wrongdoing" or "target" state). In this context, sender states can argue that, in order to induce Russia to comply with the rules of international law, i.e., the ban on the use of force against the territorial integrity or political independence of Ukraine (United Nations Charter [1945] Art. 2(4)), they can breach their obligations under IIAs by imposing sanctions that damage Russian investors. As Paparinskis notes, "in investment law, countermeasures could theoretically appear [...] as a shield used by the host State to excuse a breach of the primary obligations under investment protection law" (Paparinskis [2008] 49). Sender states should, however, justify the implementation of sanctions as a "third-party countermeasure" precluding wrongfulness since they are not the direct victims of Russia's actions and are thus not "injured" states.

A sender state may also rely on security exception provisions (see also chapter on Security exceptions). Under these provisions, states can argue that treaty commitments do not prevent them from taking measures necessary to protect public order or "essential security interests" (ESI). These provisions respond to the uncertainty faced by treaty drafters that hold open possibilities to react to changed circumstances, including domestic or external shocks (van Aaken [2009]; Pelc [2016]; Henckels [2024]). Case law on security exceptions covers different situations, none of which include state responses to claims arising from sanctions. Argentina invoked the security exception of Article XI of the United States–Argentina BIT to defend itself against claims based on the country's responses to its economic crisis of 2000 (see *CMS v Argentina* [2005]; *LG&E v Argentina* [2007]; *Enron v Argentina* [2007]). More recently, the tribunals in *Devas v India* ([2016]), *Deutsche Telekom v India* ([2017]) and *Seda v Colombia* ([2024]) applied the ESI provision in the Germany–India BIT, the India–Mauritius BIT and the Colombia–United States FTA, respectively. This jurisprudence will likely be discussed in a case where a sanctioning state invokes a security exception clause to exclude liability under an IIA for damage caused to an investment because of sanctions. A crucial question that a tribunal will examine here is whether the state is the only judge of the legality of the invocation of the security exception, or whether the invocation is subject to some form of judicial review. In examining this issue, tribunals have refused to accept that security exceptions are inherently self-judging unless the treaty uses "self-judging" language referring to measures the state "considers necessary" for the protection of its ESI. The security exceptions of the applicable BITs examined in the Argentine and Indian cases did not contain "self-judging" wording. In *Seda v Colombia*, however, the tribunal had "no doubt" that the BIT provision, which contained such wording, was "self-judging" and was further satisfied on the evidence put before it that the measures taken by Colombia were "connected to the interest of combating drug-trafficking" (*Seda v Colombia* [2024]; Colombia–United States FTA [2012] Art. 22.2; Fischer [2024]).

Lastly, sanctioning states may rely on denial of benefits (DOB) clauses. These clauses have different objectives, including the possibility for host states to deny treaty protection to investors investing in their territory whose home state does not maintain diplomatic relations with the host state. Several states that have imposed sanctions on Russia and Russian investors have invoked the DOB clause found in the Energy Charter Treaty (ECT [1996] Art. 17.2). On 27 March 2024, the European Commission issued a Proposal ([2024]) in accordance with Article 17 of the ECT seeking to withdraw the treaty's investment protections from shell corporations owned or controlled by Russian or Belarusian nationals, as well as investments that are found to belong to Russian or Belarusian investors in circumstances where sanctions apply. Ukraine, Germany and the United Kingdom have issued similar Article 17 declarations (Coop and Kortazar [2024]). If these states are taken to arbitration under the ECT, they will be called to show compliance with the requirements for the application of the DOB clause. In particular, they will have to show that the claimant-investor and its investment are "owned or controlled" by a Russian national. The ECT does not define these terms, leaving interpretive discretion to arbitral tribunals (see *Plama v Bulgaria* [2005]; *Ulysseas v Ecuador* [2010]; García Olmedo [2020]). Complex and opaque ownership chains across several jurisdictions, frequent changes in corporate structure, and lack of restrictions on share transfers, among other things, make it difficult to determine who is behind a corporation. One issue that is likely to prove particularly contentious is at which corporate layer a tribunal should stop when trying to establish the effective owner or controller of the investment. The logic of sanctions – in particular, the need to avoid circumvention by corporate restructuring (see also chapter on Evasion and circumvention) – seems to demand the application of a test of ownership or control that is neither formal nor shallow.

IV Conclusion

This entry has discussed how sanctions can fall within the scope of international investment law. EU sanctions can trigger the invocation of a different set of IIAs. These treaties include those signed not only between Russia and member states but also between member states and countries outside the EU. The entry has also examined different defences that a respondent state can invoke to avoid its international responsibility under IIAs. Member states should, at any rate, be mindful of their obligations under IIAs when adopting sanctions and the potential of the unilateral turn policy to trigger investment treaty claims.

Javier García Olmedo

Bibliography

Literature

Aaken AV, 'International Investment Law Between Commitment and Flexibility: A Contract Theory Analysis' (2009) 12 *Journal of International Economic Law* 507.

Bohmer L, 'Revealed: Russian Individual Submits Treaty-Based Notice of Dispute to Luxembourg, Impugning Sanctions Levied against Him and Claiming Billions in Damages' (*Investment Arbitration Reporter*, 20 May 2024) <https://www.iareporter.com/articles/revealed-russian-individual-submits-treaty-based-notice-of-dispute-to-luxembourg-impugning-sanctions-levied-against-him-and-claiming-billions-in-damages/> accessed 9 July 2024.

Bonnitcha J, *Substantive Protection Under Investment Treaties: A Legal and Economic Analysis* (Cambridge University Press 2014).

Coop G and Kortazar AR, 'Denial of Benefits under the Energy Charter Treaty to Investors Owned or Controlled from Russia and Belarus: A Proposal by the European Commission' (*Kluwer Arbitration Blog*, 28 June 2024) <https://arbitrationblog.kluwerarbitration.com/2024/06/28/denial-of-benefits-under-the-energy-charter-treaty-to-investors-owned-or-controlled-from-russia-and-belarus-a-proposal-by-the-european-commission/> accessed 9 July 2024.

Fisher T, 'Belgium Risks Treaty Claims over Russian Asset Freezes' (*Global Arbitration Review*, 18 January 2024) <https://globalarbitrationreview.com/article/belgium-risks-treaty-claims-over-russian-asset-freezes> accessed 9 July 2024.

Fisher T, 'Colombia Beats ICSID Claim with "Essential Security" Defence' (*Global Arbitration Review*, 28 June 2024) <https://globalarbitrationreview.com/article/colombia-beats-icsid-claim-essential-security-defence> accessed 9 July 2024.

Henckels C, 'Whither Security? The Concept of "Essential Security Interests" in Investment Treaties' Security Exceptions' (2024) 27(1) *Journal of International Economic Law* 114.

Jones T, 'Russian Airline Threatens Treaty Claim against Canada' (*Global Arbitration*

Review, 15 August 2023) <https://globalarbitrationreview.com/article/russian-airline-threatens-treaty-claim-against-canada> accessed 9 July 2024.

McLachlan C, Shore L and Weiniger M, *International Investment Arbitration, Substantive Principles* (Oxford University Press 2017).

Olmedo JG, 'Recalibrating the International Investment Regime Through Narrowed Jurisdiction' (2020) 69(2) *International and Comparative Law Quarterly* 301.

Paparinskis M, 'Investment Arbitration and the Law of Countermeasures' (2008) 79(1) *British Yearbook of International Law* 264.

Pelc KJ, *Making and Bending International Rules: The Design of Exceptions and Escape Clauses in Trade Law* (Cambridge University Press 2016).

Salacuse JW, *The Law of Investment Treaties* (Oxford University Press 2021).

Documents

Angel Samuel Seda and others v Republic of Colombia (2024) ICSID Case No. ARB/19/6.

Case T-304/22 Fridman v Council [2024] ECLI:EU:T:2024:215.

CC/Devas Ltd, Devas Employees Mauritius Private Ltd and Telecom Devas Mauritius Ltd. v India (2016) PCA Case No. 2013-09.

Charter of the United Nations (adopted 26 June 1945, entered into force 24 October 1945) XV UNCIO 335.

CMS Gas Transmission Co v Argentina (2005) ICSID Case No. ARB/01/8.

Council Regulation (EU) No. 269/2014 concerning restrictive measures in respect of actions undermining or threatening the territorial integrity, sovereignty and independence of Ukraine [2014] OJ L78/6.

Deutsche Telekom AG v India (2017) PCA Case No. 2014-10.

Energy Charter Treaty (signed 17 December 1994, entered into force 16 April 1998) 2080 UNTS 95.

Enron Corp. and Ponderosa Assets, L.P. v. Argentina (2007) ICSID Case No. ARB/01/3.

European Commission, 'Proposal for a Council Decision on the partial suspension of the application of the Energy Charter Treaty between the Union and any legal entity that is owned or controlled by citizens or nationals of the Russian Federation or of the Republic of Belarus, and any Investment within the meaning of the Energy Charter Treaty which is an Investment of an Investor of the Russian Federation or of the Republic of Belarus', Brussels COM (2024) 8416 final.

ILC, 'Draft Articles on Responsibility of States for Internationally Wrongful Acts, adopted by the Commission at its fifty-third session in 2001 (Final Outcome)' UN Doc. A/56/10.

LG&E Energy Corp, LG&E Capital Corp and LG&E International, Inc v Argentine Republic (2007) ICSID Case No. ARB/02/1.

Plama Consortium Limited v Bulgaria (2005) ICSID Case No. ARB/03/24, Decision on Jurisdiction 8 (February 2005).

Ulysseas Inc v The Republic of Ecuador (2010) UNCITRAL.

UNCTAD, 'IIA Navigator Update: New Treaties, In Force Dates and Terminations' (13 April 2023) <https://investmentpolicy.unctad.org/news/hub/1716/20230413-iia-navigator-update-new-treaties-in-force-dates-and-terminations#:~:text=This%20update%20covers%20new%20treaties,since%20the%20beginning%20of%202022> accessed 10 July 2024.

58. Judicial review (European Union)

Celia Challet

I Introduction: the role of the (EU) judge in the field of sanctions

The judicial review of sanctions, be they adopted by the United Nations Security Council (UNSC) (see chapter), the European Union (EU) (see chapter) or individual states, has undergone significant evolutions over the past decades. As an instrument of foreign policy, sanctions initially pertained to the realm of legal acts that ought to be sheltered from the judicial review of national courts and, most importantly, the Court of Justice of the EU ('the Court' or 'CJEU'). The latter's jurisdiction over sanctions adopted under the Common Foreign and Security Policy (CFSP) used to be almost non-existent. The Treaty of Maastricht (1992), which created the CFSP, made it explicit that the jurisdiction of the Court did not extend to that policy. Subsequent treaty revisions maintained the exclusion of the Court's jurisdiction, and it is only with the Treaty of Lisbon (2007) that the Court was granted explicit competence to adjudicate cases against restrictive measures adopted under the CFSP. This was due, in part, to the impact of sanctions on the targets' fundamental rights, which led the Court to review the legality of some restrictive measures even before the adoption of the Treaty of Lisbon (e.g. *Yusuf v Council and Commission* [2005]). Cases such as *Kadi*, in which the Court assessed whether a Community regulation implementing UN sanctions complied with the target's fundamental rights (*Kadi v Council and Commission* [2008]), demonstrated the growing impact of fundamental rights and the rule of law in case law and on the conduct of foreign policy (De Baere [2012] 354).

As a result of the Treaty of Lisbon, under the current EU treaties, the Court's jurisdiction over CFSP acts in general remains excluded. However, what is important is the exception to that rule. Pursuant to Articles 24(1) and 275 of the Treaty on the Functioning of the European Union (TFEU), the CJEU is competent to review the legality of CFSP decisions imposing restrictive measures against natural or legal persons in the context of actions for annulment. The Court also has jurisdiction to monitor compliance with Article 40 of the Treaty on the European Union (TEU), according to which the CFSP competence and other EU competences shall not affect each other. In other words, the Court may verify that an EU measure has been adopted under the correct legal basis. The litigation against EU restrictive measures before the CJEU has led it to expand on the legal remedies available to applicants and on the question of legal standing (Section II). The grounds for review have also been the subject of dynamic developments within case law (Section III).

II Legal avenues

1 Judicial remedies

The implementation of most EU restrictive measures requires the adoption of two legal acts by the Council of the EU: a CFSP decision that declares the EU's position with respect to the restrictive measures (Article 29 TEU), and a regulation that gives effect to those measures at EU level (Article 215 TFEU). This binary process bears implications for the judicial remedies that are available against EU sanctions. While the Court may interpret and review the legality of a regulation through any of the legal remedies established by EU treaties, the latter only provide for the review of the legality of CFSP decisions via an action for annulment based on Article 263 TFEU. As a matter of principle, therefore, applicants may challenge both legal instruments through an action for annulment if they have standing (see point [5]). However, in some judgments of 'constitutional significance' (Van Elsuwege [2022] 881), the Court interpreted its jurisdiction extensively. It did so on the grounds of teleological arguments based on the rule of law and the principle of effective judicial protection. The *Rosneft* judgment established the Court's competence to adjudicate requests for preliminary rulings on the validity of CFSP decisions (*PJSC Rosneft Oil Company v Her Majesty's Treasury and Others* [2017]). At present, it remains unclear if the Court may rule on requests to interpret CFSP decisions. In *Neves 77*, the Court interpreted the scope of a restrictive measure contained in the CFSP decision. However, it did so because the Council had failed to implement the measure through a regulation even though it was obliged to do so (*Neves 77 Solutions SRL v Agenţia Naţională de Administrare Fiscală – Direcţia Generală Antifraudă Fiscală* [2024] paras 35–53). In *Bank Refah Kargaran*, the Court extended its jurisdiction to actions for damages against CFSP decisions ([2020] paras 26–49).

2 Measures open for judicial review

Pursuant to Article 275 TFEU, only the CFSP decision's restrictive measures against natural or legal persons can be subject to judicial review. It is the individual nature of restrictive measures (notably through a listing in annex) that grants access to the Court (*Manufacturing Support & Procurement Kala Naft v Council* [2013] paras 37–50). As a result, measures of a general nature, such as the flight ban on Russian aircraft, remain outside the scope of judicial review as far as the CFSP decision is concerned (see *Islentyeva v Council* [2023] paras 20–8). Most of these measures are also contained in a regulation and may therefore be subject to judicial review. However, scholars have underlined the shortcomings of the distinction operated by the Court (Poli [2018] 295; Lonardo [2018] 554). It would overlook the fact that certain sanctions, such as arms embargoes (see chapter) or travel bans of a general nature, are only contained in CFSP decisions and thus escape judicial review (Van Elsuwege [2021] 1752–3). In addition, curtailing the Court's jurisdiction to the regulations may affect the uniform and consistent interpretation of CFSP provisions (Van Elsuwege [2021] 1759). However, the Court's position remains, to date, unaltered.

3 Legal standing and types of applicants

Actions for annulment against EU restrictive measures may only be admissible if applicants have standing in the meaning of Article 263 TFEU. As EU restrictive measures are adopted via non-legislative acts, applicants must establish that they are directly concerned by the sanctions and that the latter do not require implementing measures by the EU or its member states (*Gazprom v Council* [2018]; *Venezuela v Council* [2021]). The Court has recognised standing to challenge restrictive measures for targeted individuals (e.g. *Abramovich v Council* [2023]), current or former public office holders (*Malayeh v Council* [2014]; *Viktor Yanukovych v Council* [2019]) and state-owned companies (*Almaz-Antey v Council* [2017]). In *Venezuela*, the Court ruled that a third country is a legal person in the meaning of Article 263 TFEU and may have standing to challenge restrictive measures. Although they are less likely to fulfil Article 263 TFEU's criteria, it is not inconceivable that natural and legal persons that are not targeted by restrictive measures may have standing. For example, an organisation of Belgian barristers was able to launch an action for annulment against the ban on legal advisory services to Russian entities (*Ordre néerlandais des avocats du barreau de Bruxelles* [2024]).

III Grounds of review

1 Competence of the Council to adopt certain restrictive measures

As explained above, the Court is competent to verify whether the challenged restrictive measures comply with Article 40 TEU, i.e. whether they affect EU competences. However, due to the Council's broad competence in the field of CFSP, none of the claims based on Article 40 TEU have so far succeeded before the Court. In *Rosneft*, the undertaking argued that the CFSP decision that imposed restrictive measures against Russia used an excessively detailed wording with respect to certain measures. This allegedly encroached on the joint power of the High Representative of the Union for Foreign Affairs and Security Policy and the Commission to design the regulation that would implement the decision (*Rosneft* [2017] para. 84). The Court dismissed the argument: since the two types of acts pursue different functions (see point [3]), the fact that a CFSP decision uses detailed wording cannot be regarded as encroaching on the procedure for the adoption of the regulation. This is particularly so if the measures relate to fields that are clearly technical in nature, such as access to capital markets, defence, dual-use goods and sensitive technologies (*Rosneft* [2017] paras 87 and 90). In *RT France*, the Court ruled that the adoption of the broadcast ban against Russian media outlets complied with Article 40 TEU. The measure contributed to the CFSP aims and notwithstanding the member states' authorities' competence towards audiovisual media, only an EU broadcast ban could guarantee a uniform and immediate intervention throughout the EU's territory (*RT France v Council* [2022]). In *Timchenko*, the Court held that the Council was competent to introduce an obligation on individuals targeted by asset freezes to report their assets in the relevant member states. The obligation was adopted to fight the circumvention of asset freezes and, therefore, to ensure their effective implementation throughout the EU (*Timchenko v Council* [2024] paras 51–8).

2 Duty to state reasons

Pursuant to Article 296 TFEU, EU legal acts shall state the reasons on which they are based. Applied to restrictive measures against listed natural and legal persons, the statement of reasons must indicate the actual and specific reasons that justify listing a target under a given criterion (e.g. *Shuvalov v Council* [2024] para. 26). However, the Court has maintained a rather flexible approach to the Council's duty to state reasons. Its requirements depend on the circumstances of each case, and the degree of precision of a statement of reasons must be 'weighed against practical realities and the time and technical facilities available for taking the measure' (e.g. *Sberbank of Russia v Council* [2018]). Overall, a statement of reasons is considered sufficient if the restrictive measures were adopted in circumstances known to the targets, which enable them to understand the scope of the sanctions adopted against them. In *RT France*, the Court even considered that the Council was not required to include a specific motivation in support of RT France's listing under the broadcast ban: the recital of the legal acts contained sufficient explanations on the context that led to the listing (*RT France* paras 111–14).

3 Burden of proof

Restrictive measures that imply a listing in annex, particularly if they target natural persons, require a certain burden of proof from the Council. It must explain the reasons for which a target has been listed under a certain measure or listing criterion, and provide evidence in support of this assessment. In the event of a challenge against an asset freeze (see chapter on Financial sanctions), the Council must present a sufficiently specific, precise and consistent body of evidence to establish that there is a sufficient link between the asset freeze and the regime or situations being combated (e.g. *Abramovich v Council* [2023] para. 77). The Court verifies the material accuracy of the alleged facts in light of the information and evidence, the probative value of which depends on the circumstances of each case. If the facts and evidence are inaccurate or insufficient, the Court may find that the Council relied on an insufficiently solid factual basis or that it (manifestly) erred in its appraisal of that factual basis. In order to verify that the Council's evidence matches the listing criteria used against a target, the Court is often led to interpret these criteria and define key concepts. Examples include the notion of 'persons associated with' a listed target (e.g. *Prigozhina v Council* [2023]) or 'leading businesspersons involved in economic sectors providing a substantial source of revenue to Russia' (e.g. *OT v Council* [2023]). The Court has also paid increasing attention to the reliability of the evidence used by the Council, especially if it consists of press articles (e.g. *Haswani v Council* [2022]). Finally, the temporality of the evidence has been at the core of some recent judgments of the Court: an initial listing must be based on the factual situation at the time of the designation, and the supporting evidence must remain up to date (*Ovsyannikov v Council* [2022]; *Mazepin v Council* [2024]).

4 Compliance with fundamental rights

Restrictive measures must comply with fundamental rights as guaranteed by the Charter of Fundamental Rights. In numerous cases brought against their listing, applicants argue that their (initial) listing infringed their procedural rights, such as the right to be heard or to access the file. In *RT France*, the Court recalled that the surprise effect of asset freezes justifies limitations on these procedural rights. It also held that a context of extreme urgency may dictate the same limitations in the case of a broadcast ban (*RT France* paras 84–92). In its *Russian Direct Investment Fund* judgment, issued two years later, the Court seems to have abandoned the reference to a context of urgency. It held that because the measure at stake (a ban on investment) individually applied to the Russian fund, it also had to take advantage of a surprise effect (*Russian Direct Investment Fund v Council* [2024] para. 73). The Court may also review the compliance of restrictive measures with the applicants' material rights. In most cases, the Court has dismissed claims based on the right to property, the freedom to conduct business or the freedom of expression. While restrictive measures restricted (some of) these rights, they respected their essential content, pursued an objective of general interest and were proportionate (*RT France*; *OT v Council* [2023] paras 194–202). The Court also held that the ban on legal advisory services against Russian entities does not infringe the right to a lawyer: lawyers can always represent their clients for contentious matters (*Ordre néerlandais des avocats du barreau de Bruxelles* [2024]).

IV Conclusion

In spite of its limited jurisdiction in the field of CFSP and of certain remaining questions as to its competence over (certain) restrictive measures, the Court has developed a thorough review of their legality. Actions for annulment against an individual's listing are frequently successful before the Court, and the Council often adapts its sanctions practice to conform to the case law. More than ever, the Court plays an instrumental role in the design and effectiveness of EU sanctions.

Bibliography

Literature

De Baere G, 'European Integration and the Rule of Law in Foreign Policy' in Dickson J and Eleftheriadis P (eds), *Philosophical Foundations of European Union Law* (Oxford University Press 2012) 354.

Filpo F, 'Evidence Standards in the Judicial Review of Restrictive Measures' (2020) 20 ERA *Forum* 615.

Lonardo L, 'Challenging EU Sanctions against Russia: The Role of the Court, Judicial Protection, and Common Foreign and Security Policy' (2023) 25 *Cambridge Yearbook of European Legal Studies* 40.

Lonardo L, 'Law and Foreign Policy before the Court: Some Hidden Perils of Rosneft' (2018) *European Papers*.

Poli S, 'Effective Judicial Protection and Its Limits in the Case Law Concerning Individual Restrictive Measures in the European Union' in Neframi E and Gatti M (eds), *Constitutional Issues of EU External Relations Law* (Nomos 2018) 287.

Poli S, 'The Right to Effective Judicial Protection with Respect to Acts Imposing Restrictive Measures and its Transformative Force for the Common Foreign and Security Policy' (2022) 59(4) *Common Market Law Review* 1045.

Van Elsuwege P, 'Judicial Review and the Common Foreign and Security Policy: Limits to the Gap-Filling Role of the Court of Justice' (2021) 58(6) *Common Market Law Review* 1752.

Van Elsuwege P, 'Securing a Coherent System of Judicial Protection in Relation to Restrictive Measures: Rosneft' in Butler G and Wessel RA (eds), *EU External Relations Law: The Cases in Context* (Hart Publishing 2022) 881.

Documents

Case C-134/19 P *Bank Refah Kargaran v Council* [2020] ECLI:EU:C:2020:793 OJ C414/3.

Case C-348/12 P *Manufacturing Support & Procurement Kala Naft Co v Council* [2013] ELCI:EU:C:2013:776 OJ C39/6.

Case C-351/22 *Neves 77 Solutions SRL v Agenția Națională de Administrare Fiscală – Direcția Generală Antifraudă Fiscală* [2024] ECLI:EU:C:2024:723 OJ C C/2024/6221.

Case C-402/05 P and C-415/05 P *Kadi v Council and Commission* [2008] ECLI:EU:C:2008:461 OJ C285/2.

Case C-72/15 *PJSC Rosneft Oil Company v Her Majesty's Treasury and Others* [2017] ECLI:EU:C:2017:236 OJ C161/2.

Case C-872/19 P *Venezuela v Council* [2021] ECLI:EU:C:2021:507 OJ C320/7.

Case T-125/22 *RT France v Council* [2022] ECLI:EU:T:2022:483.

Case T-193/22 *OT v Council* [2023] ECLI:EU:T:2023:716 OJ C C/2024/729.

Case T-212/22 *Prigozhina v Council* [2023] ECLI:EU:T:2023:104 OJ C155/58.

Case T-233/22 *Islentyeva v Council* [2023] ECLI:EU:T:2023:828 OJ C C/2024/1691.

Case T-235/22 *Russian Direct Investment Fund v Council* [2024] ECLI:EU:T:2024:311 OJ C C/2024/3911.

Case T-244/16 and T-285/17 *Yanukovych v Council* [2019] ECLI:EU:T:2019:502 OJ C328/38.

Case T-255/15 *Almaz-Antey v Council* [2017] ECLI:EU:T:2017:25 OJ C78/23.

Case T-289/22 *Shuvalov v Council* [2024] ECLI:EU:T:2024:57 OJ C C/2024/2295.

Case T-306/01 *Yusuf and Al Barakaat International Foundation v Council and Commission* [2005] ECLI:EU:T:2005:331; 2005 II-03533.

Case T-313/22 *Abramovich* v Council [2023] ECLI:EU:T:2023:830 OJ C C/2024/1692.
Case T-479/21 *Haswani v Council* [2022] ECLI:EU:T:2022:383 OJ C303/42.
Case T-644/22 *Timchenko v Council* [2024] ECLI:EU:T:2024:621 OJ C C/2024/6432.
Case T-732/14 *Sberbank of Russia* v *Council* [2018]ECLI:EU:T:2018:541 OJ C392/14.
Case T-735/14 *Gazprom v Council* [2018] ECLU:EU:T:2018:548 OJ C392/16.
Case T-743/22 *Mazepin v Council* [2024] ECLI:EU:T:2024:180 OJ C C/2024/2947.
Case T-797/22 *Ordre néerlandais des avocats du barreau de Bruxelles* [2024] ECLI:EU:T:2024:670 OJ C C/2024/6934.
Joined Cases T-307/12 and T-408/13 *Malayeh v Council* [2014] ECLI:EU:T:2014:926 OJ C448/19.

Celia Challet

59. Legality and legitimacy

Alexandra Hofer

I Introduction

Lawyers are trained to separate legal arguments from issues of legitimacy, yet the two are closely linked, and the lines are especially blurred when it comes to international sanctions. If sanctions are perceived as illegitimate this gives rise to legal objections. The opposite is also true, the perceived legitimacy of sanctions shapes legal arguments about their legality. Similarly, because the legality of sanctions is often disputed, this provides ample room to question their legitimacy. This entry first addresses the legality of international sanctions (Section II) before turning to questions about their legitimacy (Section III).

II Legality

Because there is no overarching rule governing their use, the legality of sanctions depends very much on the circumstances of their adoption: who adopted the measures, who are they adopted against, for what reasons, what kind of measures, etc. Depending on the sender and the target, sanctions are either 'multilateral' or 'unilateral', and each is addressed in turn below. As secondary sanctions and their extraterritorial effects (see chapter on Secondary sanctions and the extraterritorial effects of sanctions) are covered elsewhere, this entry does not address their legal controversies.

Multilateral sanctions

International law primarily regulates multilateral sanctions that are adopted by international and regional organizations. These restrictions are based on the organization's constitutive act, which provides when it can sanction a member state. The most well-known multilateral sanctions are those adopted by the United Nations Security Council (UNSC) (see chapter) per Article 41 of the UN Charter. While the UNSC has broad sanctioning power, it is often argued that it is not unlimited and that it should take human rights into account. The comprehensive sanctions imposed on Haiti and Iraq (see chapter) demonstrated how harmful these measures can be to the civilian population, ushering in a reform to targeted sanctions. Despite this development, human rights issues remain, particularly questions of rights of defence, judicial review (see chapter), and due process guarantees, eventually leading to the creation of the UN Focal Points and UN Ombudsperson (see chapter).

Another common illustration is the measures implemented by the African Union and ECOWAS (see chapter) (per Article 23 of the AU Constitutive Act and under Article 45(1) of the ECOWAS Protocol on Democracy and Good Governance, respectively), in response to non-democratic changes of government. Matters are more complicated when an organization sanctions a member state even though it does not have the legal authority to do so, such as when the Arab League imposed sanctions against Syria (see chapter) from 2011 to 2023. It is debated whether a non-authorized organization has the implied powers to sanction its member states or whether such acts should be considered *ultra vires*, and hence invalid (Hofer [2024]).

Unilateral sanctions

Unilateral sanctions are adopted by states per their national legislation and/or executive powers against a foreign state or non-state actor. The most active sender of unilateral sanctions is the United States (see chapter), which is often supported by its 'like-minded' partners and allies, the United Kingdom (see chapter), Canada (see chapter), Australia, New Zealand, and especially the European Union (EU) (see chapter), which together form a coalition of the willing (see chapter). While the EU's restrictive measures are adopted by an international organization, they are unilateral because, as a tool of the EU's Common Foreign and Security Policy, they are exclusively implemented against non-member states.

Unilateral sanctions are notorious for falling under a 'grey area' of international law, which essentially means that it is unclear when such measures are legal (Ruys [2017]). This is because, as mentioned, there is no overarching legal framework that governs their adoption. As international law is prohibitive, the general rule is that unilateral sanctions are permitted unless they are explicitly proscribed. To put it differently, unilateral sanctions are lawful unless they cause the sender to breach an obligation it owes the target. These policy tools can cause states to breach multilateral agreements. The most common examples are the General Agreement on Tariffs and Trade (GATT) and the General Agreement on Trade in Services (GATS). Sanctions can also fall foul of bilateral treaties that are applicable between the sender and the target. In *Military and Paramilitary Activities in and against Nicaragua* (1986), the International Court of Justice found that the US trade embargo against Nicaragua breached the Treaty of Amity between the two countries. Some treaties, notably GATT and GATS, contain security exceptions that permit states to adopt sanctions. There are also rules of customary international law that states must uphold in their international relations. It is often argued that unilateral sanctions are a breach of the prohibition of intervention, but this is heavily disputed (see also chapter on Sanctions and the use of force).

To the extent that a unilateral sanction is legally permitted, it is a retorsion. For example, aid cut-offs or diplomatic sanctions (see chapter) are generally considered to be lawful and thus constitute retorsions. If a sanction causes the sender to breach an obligation it owes the target, it constitutes an internationally wrongful act and the target can invoke the sender's responsibility.

If a sanction amounts to a breach of international law, depending on the conditions of the measures' adoption, the sender could try to justify the breach as a countermeasure (see chapter). The latter is known as a 'circumstance precluding wrongfulness': a breach of international law that is justified because it is a proportionate response to a prior wrongful act and aspires to induce compliance (as described under the International Law Commission's Articles on Responsibility of a State for Internationally Wrongful Acts, Article 22 and Chapter II). For instance, Qatar accused Bahrain, Egypt, Saudi Arabia, and the United Arab Emirates of violating the Chicago Convention and the International Air Services Transit Agreement through the adoption of airspace restrictions in 2017. However, these states argued that they had adopted lawful countermeasures in response to Qatar's breach of the Riyadh Agreements, which Qatar denied. The dispute was ultimately settled diplomatically in 2021 before the legal quagmires could be addressed (ICAO Annual Report [2021]).

It remains questionable whether states or international organizations can adopt so-called 'third-party countermeasures', also referred to as collective countermeasures. These are unilateral sanctions adopted by states not in their own interests but to defend community norms, such as human rights or the prohibition of the use of force. Because of the risks of abuse, their potentially destabilizing effects on interstate relations, and the difficulties surrounding their proper coordination (particularly whether they are compatible with UNSC sanctions), they are highly controversial. On the other hand, it is often argued that states should be able to act in response to grave violations of international law to protect shared values and interests. Currently, the debate is ongoing and uncertainty over their legality prevails (Hofer [2025]).

III Legitimacy

The adoption of sanctions, whether unilateral or multilateral, is often associated with human rights violations. After all, these measures entail a restriction, and oftentimes this limits the exercise of rights. An asset freeze, for instance, restricts the right to property. Problematically, when sanctions hurt national economies, they severely undermine a civilian population's access to basic necessities, such as food and medicine. Whereas from a legal standpoint it is challenging to argue that sanctions violate these human rights (it is often argued that senders do not have extraterritorial human rights obligations, see Prezas [2021] but see Djourabi-Asadabadi [2024]), their negative impact on the standard of living of civilian populations undermines the legitimacy of sanctions, especially when these are adopted to uphold fundamental norms. It is these issues that led the UNSC to reform targeted sanctions, but problems remain. Part of this is caused by overcompliance (see chapter) and derisking; to avoid violating sanctions, private actors prefer to overcomply and suspend any trade with a targeted economy, even if it involves goods that are not under sanctions (Moret [2022]). To mitigate this, senders adopt humanitarian derogations, but these are often ineffective (Demarais [2022]).

Furthermore, unilateral sanctions adopted by states and the EU are often perceived as illegitimate because they are tainted with double standards; like cases are not treated alike. There is also the concern that they are adopted to serve the political interests of the sender, even if the latter invokes international norms to justify their adoption. Targeted states frequently resent the sender for adopting a position of authority and imposing 'punishment' for wrongdoing, especially when the sender does not have a mandate to do so. Unilateral sanctions are historically a tool that was implemented by states to assert their hegemony against weaker states, and many states continue to perceive sanctions as a tool of political dominance, where the sanctioner only implements them when it serves their interests. When the purposes of sanctions are perceived as illegitimate, states are motivated to argue that they are unlawful. Additionally, if sanctions are not adopted in accordance with procedural rules (such as measures adopted by the UNSC or a mandated regional organization), this also triggers arguments challenging their legitimacy.

As such, an assessment of the legality and legitimacy of sanctions can only be carried out on a case-by-case basis, as these factors depend on the circumstances of their adoption.

Bibliography

Literature

Bogdanova I, *Unilateral Sanctions in International Law and the Enforcement of Human Rights: The Impact of the Principle of Common Concern of Humankind* (Brill Nijhoff 2022).

Djourabi-Asadabadi T, 'Unilateral Sanctions and Extraterritorial Obligations in the Area of Economic, Social and Cultural Rights' in Bultrini A, Giumelli F, Portela C and Sossai M (eds), *International Sanctions in Practice: An Interdisciplinary Perspective* (Taylor & Francis 2024) 107.

Demarais A, *Backfire: How Sanctions Reshape the World Against U.S. Interests* (Columbia University Press 2022).

Hofer A, 'The Developed/Developing Divide on Unilateral Coercive Measures: Legitimate Enforcement or Illegitimate Intervention?' (2017) 16 *Chinese Journal of International Law* 175.

Hofer A, 'Regional Organizations and the Non-Mandated Sanctioning of Member States: The Case of the League of Arab States Sanctions against Syria' in Adinolfi G, Lang A and Ragni C (eds), *Sanctions by and Against International Organizations* (Intersentia 2024) 111.

Hofer A, 'Third-Party Countermeasures: Making Custom out of Ambiguous Practice?' (2025) 74 *International and Comparative Law Quarterly* 287.

Moret E, 'More Civilian Pain Than Political Gain (Again?) The Demise of Targeted Sanctions and Associated Humanitarian Impacts' in Portela C and Charron C (eds), *Multilateral Sanctions Revisited: Lessons Learned from Margaret Doxey* (McGill-Queens University Press 2022) 177.

Prezas I, 'From Targeted States to Affected Populations: Exploring Accountability for the Negative Impact of Comprehensive Unilateral Sanctions on Human Rights' in Beaucillon C (ed.), *Handbook on Unilateral and Extraterritorial Sanctions* (Edward Elgar 2021) 385.

Ruys T, 'Sanctions, Retorsions and Countermeasures: Concepts and International Legal Framework' in van den Herik L (ed.), *Research Handbook on UN Sanctions and International Law* (Edward Elgar 2017) 19.

Subedi SP, *Unilateral Sanctions in International Law* (Hart 2021).

Documents

International Civil Aviation Organization, 'Annual Report of 2021 Legal and External Relations Services, Settlement of Differences' (ICAO 2021) <https://www.icao.int/annual-report-2021/Pages/supporting-strategies-legal-and-external-relations-services-settlement-of-differences.aspx> accessed 9 December 2024.

UNGA Res 56/83, 'Articles on Responsibility of a State for Internationally Wrongful Acts' (12 December 2001) UN Doc. A/RES/56/83.

Military and Paramilitary Activities in and against (Nicaragua v. United States of America) (Merits) [1986] ICJ Rep 14.

60. Measuring sanctions' effectiveness

Thomas Biersteker

I Introduction

"Do sanctions work?" This is probably the most frequently asked question about sanctions, a question that scholars of sanctions tend to abhor. The answer is relatively straightforward: it depends. Or put another way, sanctions sometimes work, but not very often. Sanctions' effectiveness always comes down to what one means by the word "work," how one identifies the different purposes of sanctions, when one makes the assessment, and how one measures "effectiveness."

II Literature review

The primary focus of leading scholarly analysts of the effectiveness of sanctions has long been on the ability of sanctions to coerce a change in target behaviour (Galtung [1967] 381; Wallensteen [1968] 249; Doxey [1972] 529; Hufbauer et al. [1990], [1997]; Morgan and Schwebach [1997]). However, a number of scholars have identified policy goals other than coercion when assessing the effectiveness of sanctions (Doxey [1972]; Barber [1979]; Lindsay [1986]). Francesco Giumelli introduced a typology that differentiates between three basic purposes of sanctions: to coerce, to constrain, and/or to signal a target (Giumelli [2011] 33–5). The Targeted Sanctions Consortium (TSC) Project on the effectiveness of United Nations (UN) targeted sanctions, discussed in more detail below, adopted Giumelli's categories in its research, but adapted them to allow for the possibility of senders simultaneously pursuing more than one purpose (Biersteker et al. [2016] 22).

While sanctions scholars are more likely to identify examples of sanctions' effectiveness than the general public (see, for example, Lopez and Cortright [2004]), most contend that sanctions are "effective" at most only about one-third of the time. Hufbauer et al.'s [2007] edition of *Economic Sanctions Reconsidered* (at 158) estimated that sanctions were at least partially successful in 34 per cent of the cases they studied. In their significantly larger sample of sanctions cases, Navin Bapat and Clifton Morgan concluded that sanctions are effective only about 23 per cent of the time (Bapat and Morgan [2009] 1082). The TSC Project concluded that sanctions are effective across different purposes about 22 per cent of the time, but only 11 per cent of the time in changing behaviour, 24 per cent in constraining targeted parties, and 29 per cent in sending an effective signal (Biersteker et al. [2018]; see also Biersteker et al. [2023]).

Like the popular and public discourse, much of the scholarly literature also assumes that sanctions will inevitably be less effective than the use of force. Many scholars also share with conventional wisdom the idea that sanctions exist on a continuum between words (diplomacy) and war (the use of force) (Wallensteen and Staibano [2005]). The scholarly literature generally shares most of the conventional wisdom with regard to the core purpose of sanctions (to coerce a change in behaviour), the effectiveness of sanctions (generally low), and the analytical focus of sanctions (with countries as a core unit of analysis). Most fail to distinguish systematically in their analysis of sanctions' effectiveness the multiple purposes of sanctions.

Most analyses also suffer from the problem of the contingent timing of evaluations in that the analysis of effectiveness is determined by what is ultimately an arbitrary decision (based on the time and context in which the country case regime is analyzed). Sanctions regimes between sender and target can change significantly over time. As years go by, sanctions regimes often change in terms of their purpose, context, target, and/or type of measure imposed (see chapter on Termination of sanctions). In a situation of ever-shifting political bargaining, an evaluation that considers effectiveness for the country's regime as a single unit of analysis cannot adequately incorporate these changes and ends up measuring the effectiveness of the entire regime based on what is often just the latest development in a long, continuing, and changing bargaining relationship between sender and target.

III Measuring sanctions' effectiveness

How should one best measure effectiveness? Qualitative case study analyses typically evaluate the consequences of the sanctions at the point in time when they conduct their analysis, balancing sanctions with the potential impacts of other policy interventions. Quantitative analyses typically have multiple coders assessing effectiveness on a linear scale and make a decision based on their aggregative assessment of inter-coder reliability. An alternative, one based on integrated qualitative and quantitative databases, is the method employed by the TSC Project, which attempts to make a systematic analysis of UN targeted sanctions.

The TSC Project breaks down UN sanctions regimes into case episodes and considers these its fundamental unit of analysis (this builds upon but adapts the method proposed by Eriksson [2011]). Each episode is defined as a period of time of varying duration within a larger sanctions regime in which the relationship between target and sender remains stable in terms of (a) the purposes of the sanctions; (b) their targets; and/or (c) the combination of sanctions measures imposed.

The TSC Project analyzes the multiple purposes of sanctions regimes separately, rather than focusing exclusively on the coercion of targets to change behaviour, including constraining and signalling as additional basic purposes of sanctions. Building on the general approach introduced by Hufbauer, Schott, and Elliott, who differentiated between policy outcomes and sanctions contributions to those outcomes using a four-point scale to assess effectiveness for each, the TSC Project also assessed sanctions' effectiveness as a function of those same two variables: the overall policy outcome for each purpose and the distinct contribution of UN targeted sanctions measures to that outcome.

For each episode, effectiveness is measured along a continuum ranging, for example in the case of coercion, from "complete intransigence/no change" in behaviour by the target to "all principal objectives of sanctions being met." A five-point scale is utilized, with 1 representing the least effective and 5 constituting the most effective. For constraint, 1 equates to "no discernible constraints experienced by the target" and 5 indicates "significant costs to the target resulting in a change of strategy or difficulties in engaging in proscribed activities." In the case of signalling, 1 constitutes "failure of international norms to be articulated and/or no stigmatization of the target" and 5 indicates "clearly articulated norms and full stigmatization/isolation of the target." The five-point scale enables a median outcome for each assessment, unlike the approach of Hufbauer, Schott, and Elliott, three of whose categories are arguably positive, creating a slight bias in favour of identifying effective outcomes.

Following the scoring of the policy outcome, the specific contribution of UN targeted sanctions to that outcome is assessed for each episode – often the most difficult analytical aspect of the exercise. Measurement of the sanctions' contribution considers all the other instruments simultaneously being utilized by the international community (such as diplomatic pressure, threats of or the use of force, legal referrals, unilateral or regional sanctions, etc.). In addition, an explicit counterfactual analysis is employed to consider what might have been the outcome had UN targeted sanctions never been imposed. A six-point scale is used in which 1 means "no discernible sanctions contribution," 5 indicates that UN sanctions are the "single most important factor" to the policy outcome, and 0 signifies that the sanctions' contribution is "negative" (the target is either strengthened or increases its proscribed activity).

The effectiveness of UN sanctions is determined for each relevant purpose by a combination of minimal threshold scores for both policy outcome and sanctions contribution to that outcome. To be considered effective, a high threshold score of 4 or 5 must be attained for policy outcome and a score of 3 or above must be attained for the UN sanctions contribution to that outcome (meaning that, at the very least, there should be evidence that sanctions reinforced other policy measures).

With the significant increase in the use of sanctions in recent years (Kirikakha et al. [2021]), the approach to measuring sanctions' effectiveness pioneered by the TSC Project could be extended to an analysis of the effectiveness of sanctions from other senders such as the European Union or the United States. While the approach has some advantages over alternative ways to measure sanctions' effectiveness (which tend to be overly aggregate, unidimensional, focused on behavioural change, and time contingent), it also has some limitations. By assessing effectiveness within specific episodes, it cannot distinguish between impacts within an episode that might be caused by measures applied in a previous episode. It also makes no effort to estimate the costs of the application of sanctions to the senders. While it tracks well the way policy practitioners design sanctions, the method of determining their effectiveness still contains aspects of subjective bias, particularly when estimating the counterfactual alternatives to sanctions.

IV Conclusion

While the frequency with which sanctions can be described as "effective" is relatively low, it is important to remember that sanctions are applied to some of the world's most difficult and intractable conflicts. Careful and systematic attention to how to measure sanctions' effectiveness across cases and episodes demonstrates the conditions under which an increasingly used policy instrument can achieve policy goals successfully.

Bibliography

Literature

Bapat NA and Morgan TC, 'Multilateral Versus Unilateral Sanctions Reconsidered: A Test Using New Data' (2009) 53 *International Studies Quarterly* 1075.

Barber J, 'Economic Sanctions as a Policy Instrument' (1979) 55(3) *International Affairs* 367–84.

Biersteker TJ, Eckert SE, Tourinho M and Hudáková Z, 'UN Targeted Sanctions Datasets (1991–2013)' (2018) 55 *Journal of Peace Research* 404.

Biersteker TJ, Hudáková Z and Tourinho M, 'UNSanctionsApp: An Interactive Database of UN Sanctions' (*UNSanctionsApp*, August 2023) <https://unsanctionsapp.com>.

Biersteker TJ, Tourinho M and Eckert SE, 'Thinking about United Nations Targeted Sanctions' in Biersteker TJ, Eckert SE and Tourinho M (eds), *Targeted Sanctions: The Impacts and Effectiveness of United Nations Action* (Cambridge University Press 2016) 11.

Doxey M, 'International Sanctions: A Framework for Analysis with Special Reference to the UN and Southern Africa' (1972) 26 *International Organization* 527.

Eriksson M, *Targeting Peace: Understanding UN and EU Targeted Sanctions* (Routledge 2011).

Galtung J, 'On the Effects of International Economic Sanctions: With Examples from the Case of Rhodesia' (1967) 19 *World Politics* 378.

Giumelli F, *Coercing, Constraining and Signalling: Explaining UN and EU Sanctions after the Cold War* (ECPR 2011).

Hufbauer GC, Schott JJ and Elliott KA, *Economic Sanctions Reconsidered: History and Current Policy* (2nd edn, Institute for International Economics 1990).

Hufbauer GC, Schott JJ, Elliott KA and Oegg B, *Economic Sanctions Reconsidered: History and Current Policy* (3rd edn, Peterson Institute for International Economics 2007).

Lindsay J, 'Trade Sanctions as Policy Instruments: A Re-Examination' (1986) 30(2) *International Studies Quarterly* 153–73.

Lopez GA and Cortright D, 'Containing Iraq: Sanctions Worked' (2004) 83(4) *Foreign Affairs* 90.

Kirikakha A, Felbermayr GJ, Syropoulos C, Yalcin E and Yotov YV, 'The Global Sanctions Data Base (GSDB): An Update that Includes the Years of the Trump Presidency' in van Bergeijk PAG (ed.), *Research Handbook on Economic Sanctions* (Edward Elgar 2021) 62.

Morgan TC and Schwebach WL, 'Fools Suffer Gladly: The Use of Economic Sanctions in International Crises' (1997) 41 *International Studies Quarterly* 27.

Wallensteen P, 'Characteristics of Economic Sanctions' (1968) 5 *Journal of Peace Research* 248.

Wallensteen P and Staibano C, *International Sanctions: Between Words and Wars in the Global System* (Routledge 2005).

Thomas Biersteker

61. Non-criminal penalties for sanctions violation

FRANCESCA FINELLI

I Introduction

The credibility and effectiveness of sanctions as a "smart" tool of foreign policy are highly dependent on the enforcement mechanisms established at the national level (see chapter on Domestic implementation). In fact, irrespective of whether sanctions are adopted in a multilateral or unilateral manner, it is national enforcement that ultimately ensures compliance with the adopted restrictions.

In this context, "enforcement" refers to the actions and measures taken by competent authorities, typically national agencies, bodies, or specialized offices, as well as criminal enforcement authorities, to ensure that sanctions are effectively implemented, and violations identified and penalized. Sanctions enforcement includes various activities such as monitoring commercial flows and financial transactions, tracking the movements of prohibited goods or sanctioned assets, reporting and sharing information with competent authorities, conducting investigations, and taking legal or punitive measures against those found to be in violation of sanctions. It requires a coordinated effort involving various stakeholders, fostering strong dialogue and collaboration, especially between public authorities and private entities within the economic and financial sector.

The ultimate goal of enforcement is to punish and deter actions that undermine the effectiveness of sanctions. In doing so, enforcement is key to protecting the credibility of sanctions and their intended political objectives. While much focus is placed on criminal penalties, *non-criminal* enforcement mechanisms play an equally vital role in addressing sanctions breaches. Unlike criminal penalties, which often involve higher evidentiary standards and lengthy legal procedures, non-criminal measures allow for swifter, cost-effective responses. These penalties are essential for the day-to-day enforcement of sanctions, fostering a culture of compliance among economic operators.

II Fragmentation in enforcement strategies

The enforcement of sanctions remains largely unregulated at the international level. In the absence of legal guidelines, the sanctioning actors, or "senders", design their domestic enforcement strategies unilaterally. They may decide to employ criminal penalties, such as imprisonment, or non-criminal penalties, such as monetary fines, or a combination of both, depending on the factual circumstances of the breach.

With regard to United Nations (UN) sanctions, the UN Charter provides that states "agree to accept and carry out the decisions of the Security Council" (UN Charter, Art. 25), including sanctions adopted by this organ. However, there is no further guidance on *how* to punish non-compliance with UN sanctions. States are tacitly asked to impose effective, proportionate, and dissuasive penalties under their domestic jurisdictions, but these penalties are not further regulated. Lacking international harmonization on the issue, states remain free to develop different enforcement mechanisms, either under their criminal or non-criminal laws. The only exception concerns terrorism, for which states are explicitly required to establish *criminal* offences for terrorism financing (see the 1999 International Convention for the Suppression of the Financing of Terrorism; FATF Recommendations [see chapter], No. 5; Sanctions in the fight against terrorism [see chapter]). With the exception of terrorism, the imposition of penalties for sanctions violations rests in the discretionary hands of states. Therefore, states may opt for criminal punishment for more serious (and wilful) violations (see chapter on Criminalisation of sanctions violation), but states may also use non-criminal penalties, particularly when non-compliance with sanctions is committed with no intent.

III Non-criminal enforcement

Senders usually establish specialized agencies to administer and enforce sanctions. These agencies, such as the Office of Foreign Assets Control (OFAC) in the United States (see chapter), or the Office of Financial Sanctions Implementation (OFSI) in the United Kingdom (see chapter), are mandated to ensure the correct implementation of sanctions in their respective jurisdictions and are equipped for the detection and punishment of non-compliance in a centralized manner. These agencies are not criminal prosecutors but are responsible for identifying the most appropriate response to sanctions violations in accordance with non-criminal liability rules. For instance, OFAC is responsible for detecting violations of US sanctions laws under a strict (civil) liability rule – with no requirement to demonstrate the wilfulness of the actors involved. The standard of proof for taking enforcement actions is low, and OFAC can simply rely on a "reason to believe" threshold. Similarly, OFSI has the power to impose penalties on a strict (civil) liability basis, relying on "the balance of probabilities".

These agencies are usually entitled to impose a variety of measures, ranging from warnings to monetary fines. To illustrate, OFAC maintains an indisputable record in the imposition of (draconian) monetary penalties. Over the years, its enforcement actions have generated significant revenues for the US government, amounting to millions, if not billions, of dollars each year (e.g., over $1.5 billion USD in 2023). This proves that non-criminal penalties can guarantee a swift, effective, and perhaps more beneficial enforcement system than criminal penalties. Monetary fines may, in fact, result from fast-track investigations governed by low evidentiary standards – rather than a beyond-any-reasonable-doubt test. The central role of specialized agencies, such as OFAC and OFSI, in ensuring the effectiveness of sanctions exemplifies the phenomenon of the *administratization* of sanctions, whereby policy decisions are translated into administrative tools, governed by *ad hoc* rules and enforcement procedures (Chachko [2019]). Moreover, the work of these specialized agencies is disseminated via official websites that offer publicly accessible guidelines on the correct application of sanctions and the interpretation of legal provisions. These websites foster a culture of compliance and serve to raise the awareness of economic operators in relation to the potential risks associated with non-compliance.

In contrast to the United States and the United Kingdom, the European Union (EU) (see chapter) lacks a centralized sanctions agency, and its efforts to counter non-compliance remain strongly decentralized. In fact, national competent authorities in the 27 member states are primarily responsible for the enforcement of EU restrictive measures (Portela and Olsen [2023]). Traditionally, sanctions violations in the EU have been addressed by criminal *and* administrative penalties, with significant variation across the member states. Yet, in 2022 and with the political momentum of Russia's war of aggression against Ukraine, the Union took steps towards harmonizing the definitions and penalties of sanctions breaches under common criminal rules. The Union aimed to approximate national criminal laws and strengthen the consistency and effectiveness of sanctions enforcement. In this unprecedented harmonization process, EU criminal law has gained a new role in the enforcement of sanctions. Yet, the recent criminalization process has a limited focus as it intends to regulate violations "committed *intentionally*" (see Directive (EU) 2024/1226, Art. 3). It does not regulate serious negligence, nor does it introduce strict (civil) liability. Therefore, it seems reasonable to believe that harmonized criminal penalties will be complemented by other-than-criminal penalties for EU sanctions breaches when committed *unintentionally*. These non-criminal measures will remain unharmonized among member states, which remain free to impose their unilateral set of penalties, such as fines, disqualifications, and exclusion from licences, grants, or concessions.

IV Conclusion

Effective enforcement mechanisms are essential to maintain the credibility of sanctions, deterring non-compliance and evasion schemes (see chapter on Evasion and circumvention). In this context, criminal and non-criminal penalties usually coexist. The former are typically imposed in the most egregious cases of (wilful) non-compliance and entail burdensome and costly procedures for the national authorities. On a general note, criminal enforcement entails strong procedural and substantive guarantees for the accused, including the rights to a defence as well as the presumption of innocence. The latter offer a flexible, cost-effective alternative, particularly for addressing unintentional breaches, avoiding lengthy and demanding procedures. Indeed, the burden of proof for the imposition of non-criminal penalties is lower and procedural safeguards for "suspects" are less demanding.

FRANCESCA FINELLI

The interplay between criminal and non-criminal penalties offers a nuanced response to non-compliance, but it remains largely unregulated. There is often a lack of clarity regarding the division of powers between criminal and non-criminal authorities: while it can be argued that criminal investigations strengthen non-criminal ones, there is no clear allocation of their respective roles.

The EU's recent shift towards the criminalization of sanctions breaches seems to overlook the dynamics between criminal and non-criminal penalties. The rationale behind the decision to exclusively rely on criminal enforcement, without concurrently reinforcing and aligning non-criminal penalties, remains unclear. It appears to be based on the presumption that criminal investigations guarantee a higher chance of detection, prosecution, and deterrence of sanctions violations. Nevertheless, national authorities may be better positioned to respond promptly and more cost-efficiently to sanctions violations using non-criminal means.

Bibliography

Literature

Early BR and Preble KA, 'Going Fishing versus Hunting Whales: Explaining Changes in How the US Enforces Economic Sanctions' (2020) 29 *Security Studies* 231.

Abely C, 'Causing a Sanctions Violation with US Dollars: Differences in Regulatory Language Across OFAC Sanctions Programs' (2019) 48 *Georgia Journal of International and Comparative Law* 29.

Portela C and Olsen K, *Implementation and Monitoring of the EU Sanctions' Regimes, Including Recommendations to Reinforce the EU's Capacities to Implement and Monitor Sanctions* (European Parliament 2023).

Chachko E, 'Administrative National Security' (2019) 108 *Georgetown Law Journal* 1063.

Giumelli F and others, 'United in Diversity? A Study on the Implementation of Sanctions in the European Union' (2022) 10 *Politics and Governance* 36.

Nielsen J, 'Considering the EU Commission's Proposal on Its Directive for Criminal Penalties for Violations of Restrictive Measures in the Context of a Comparative Analysis with US Sanctions Enforcement' (2022) <https://papers.ssrn.com/sol3/papers.cfm?abstract_id=4283807>.

Bernardini L and Finelli F, 'Violations of EU Sanctions and Criminal Penalties: Proportionality at Peril?' in Montaldo S, Mitsilegas V and Grossio L (eds), *Proportionality of Criminal Penalties in EU Law* (Hart 2025) 117.

62. Overcompliance

Pierre-Hugues Verdier

I Introduction

The proliferation of economic sanctions in recent years has raised concerns about overcompliance, a pattern of behaviour in which actors exceed legal requirements in complying with sanctions. More specifically, overcompliance has been defined as "a situation in which a market participant applies sanctions – that is, refrains from an otherwise desirable transaction or activity involving some connection with a sanctioned country or person – beyond what is legally mandated by the relevant regime" (Verdier [2023] 473; Breen [2022] 256; Douhan [2022] para. 17). While overcompliance with multilateral sanctions is possible, most attention to this phenomenon has focused on sanctions imposed outside of the United Nations (UN) Charter regime.

II Forms and causes of overcompliance

Overcompliance may take several forms. Market participants may apply sanctions to activities or transactions not covered, such as by avoiding any dealings with persons targeted by sanctions even though the sanctions regime only prohibits specific types of activities or transactions involving those persons. They may also apply sanctions to persons not formally targeted, such as by avoiding dealings with all nationals or residents of a state even though only certain persons from that state are legally subject to sanctions. A market participant may also choose to comply with sanctions even though it is not legally bound to do so. For example, non-US companies or banks may choose to avoid dealings with persons or countries targeted by US sanctions, even though neither they nor the activities they conduct fall within the sanctions' legal scope. All these forms of overcompliance appear to have been common in response to recent sanctions regimes, such as the sanctions imposed by the United States following Russia's full-scale invasion of Ukraine in 2022 (Verdier [2023] 475–6).

Although more empirical research on the causes of overcompliance is needed (see, e.g., Stępień et al. [2024]), several factors have been suggested. Market participants may overcomply due to uncertainty about the precise legal boundaries of sanctions regimes, uncertainty about how governments will interpret and enforce the sanctions in practice, anticipation that governments may expand the sanctions' scope in the future, overlaps and conflicts among sanctions regimes from multiple jurisdictions, high legal and compliance costs, the risk of secondary sanctions, and reputational concerns arising from association with sanctioned persons or states (see chapter on Secondary sanctions and the extraterritorial effects of sanctions; Verdier [2023] 477–88; Smith and Poplin [2023] 510–20; Abely [2024] 1340–44).

III Legal and policy criticisms

Although the notion of overcompliance did not gain widespread attention until recent rounds of targeted sanctions (including the Ukraine-related sanctions described above and the sanctions imposed on Iran), a debate has now arisen about its legal and policy implications. Two principal criticisms of overcompliance have emerged. First, commentators express concern that overcompliance might undermine the ability of policymakers to calibrate sanctions, effectively turning targeted (or "smart") sanctions into comprehensive (or "dumb") sanctions (Smith and Poplin [2023]). Others respond that, while overcompliance does make sanctions blunter, there is little reason to believe that policymakers cannot anticipate market participants' responses and calibrate sanctions accordingly (Verdier [2023] 491–4). Indeed, policymakers may welcome and even intentionally foster imprecision to deter evasion (Breen [2022] 263).

Second, overcompliance may exacerbate the humanitarian impact of sanctions. It may effectively nullify humanitarian exceptions to the sanctions regime, restricting food and medicine supplies to vulnerable populations (see also chapter on Humanitarian carveouts). It may also hinder non-governmental organisation (NGO) relief efforts that require operating in sanctioned countries or cooperating with sanctioned persons or organisations (Douhan [2022] 2, 5–6; Breen [2022] 266–8). "Derisking" by financial institutions, which involves terminating relationships with broad categories of customers linked to sanctioned countries or entities (such as all nationals of a sanctioned state), is a form of overcompliance that may violate equal treatment rights (Breen [2022] 257; European Banking Authority [2022]).

The legal implications of overcompliance under international human rights law have prompted controversy. The UN Special Rapporteur on the negative impact of unilateral coercive measures on the enjoyment of human rights has suggested that overcompliance can generate international human rights violations attributable to sanctioning states (Douhan [2022]; HRC Report of the Special Rapporteur [2023]). This position raises several unresolved legal questions, including the extraterritorial scope of the application of international human rights obligations and the rules governing attribution to states of violations mediated by decisions of non-state actors (Fellmeth [2023]). The causal link between sanctions overcompliance and human rights violations is also contested, especially in countries with poor human rights practices where government violations are common (Fellmeth [2023]).

Regardless of this legal debate, critics of the humanitarian costs of overcompliance appear to have attracted policymakers' attention. The United Nations Security Council, the United States, the European Union, and the United Kingdom recently adopted measures to broaden humanitarian exceptions or facilitate their use (Abely [2024] 1348–56). Because they are bare permissions, however, such exceptions may not suffice to induce market participants to process humanitarian transactions (Verdier [2023] 496–7).

Bibliography

Literature

Abely C, 'Facilitating Humanitarian Aid Amid Sanctions' (2024) 84 *Ohio State Law Journal* 1335.

Breen E, 'Corporations and U.S. Economic Sanctions: The Dangers of Overcompliance' in Beaucillon C (ed.), *Research Handbook on Unilateral and Extraterritorial Sanctions* (Edward Elgar 2022) 256.

Chachko E, 'Virtue Sanctioning' (2023) 84 *Ohio State Law Journal* 1435.

Douhan AF, 'Unilateral Coercive Measures: Effects and Legality Issues' (2023) *Yale Journal of International Law Online* <https://www.yjil.yale.edu/unilateral-coercive-measures-effects-and-legality-issues/> accessed 27 June 2024.

Fellmeth A, 'Unilateral Sanctions Under International Human Rights Law: Correcting the Record' (2023) *Yale Journal of International Law Online* <https://www.yjil.yale.edu/unilateral-sanctions-under-international-human-rights-law-correcting-the-record/> accessed 27 June 2024.

Smith AM and Poplin CM, 'Keeping Sanctions "Smart": Calibrating US Sanctions Policy to Overcome Overcompliance' (2023) 48 *North Carolina Journal of International Law* 499.

Stępień B et al., 'The Impact of External Pressure on Companies' Responses to Sanctions – An International Comparative Study' (2024) 30 *European Journal on Criminal Policy and Research* 301.

Verdier P-H, 'Sanctions Overcompliance: What, Why, and Does It Matter?' (2023) 48 *North Carolina Journal of International Law* 471.

Documents

European Banking Authority, 'Report on De-risking and its Impact on Access to Financial Services' EBA Doc. No. EBA/REP/2022/01 (2022).

HRC, 'Secondary sanctions, civil and criminal penalties for circumvention of sanctions regimes and overcompliance with sanctions – Report of the Special Rapporteur on the negative impact of unilateral coercive measures on the enjoyment of human rights, Alena F. Douhan' (15 July 2022) UN Doc. A/HRC/51/33.

63. Proportionality of sanctions

Nathanael Tilahun

I Introduction

In general international law, sanctions can be grouped into *retorsions* (unfriendly but not unlawful measures, such as aid restrictions) or *countermeasures* (unlawful but justified measures, such as trade restrictions). Retorsions are largely not governed by international law as they fall within states' sovereign prerogative. Consequently, there is no general proportionality requirement attached to the deployment of such sanctions.

Sanctions that can be characterised as countermeasures are subject to the requirement of proportionality under customary international law – although there is no uniform measurement of proportionality applicable across various types of countermeasures (Hofer [2019]; for an overview of types of countermeasures, see Frank [2008]). The general requirement of proportionality is articulated in the United Nations International Law Commission's (ILC) Articles on the Responsibility of States for Internationally Wrongful Acts (ARSIWA) as follows: 'Countermeasures must be commensurate with the injury suffered, taking into account the gravity of the internationally wrongful act and the rights in question' (ARSIWA [2001] Art. 51). A connected point is that countermeasures have to be temporary, and as much as possible reversible, measures (ARSIWA [2001] Art. 49(2) and (3)).

Countermeasures are also 'limited by the requirements of humanity' (*Naulilaa Arbitration* [1928] 1026). Specifically, such measures must not violate human rights obligations, constitute a retaliation against civilian populations, nor affect the fundamental norms of international law known as *jus cogens*, which include the prohibition of slavery, racial discrimination, torture, crimes against humanity, genocide, aggression, and the denial of self-determination (ARSIWA [2001] 131–3).

It must be noted, however, that proportionality, strictly speaking, is about the extent of injury that is permitted on the targeted wrongdoer itself. The protection of innocent third parties is technically a separate matter dealt with by the principle that countermeasures must only target the original wrongdoer (ARSIWA [2001] Art. 49(1)). Proportionality is relevant with respect to third parties inasmuch as it provides a safeguarding principle limiting the *unintended* negative consequences of countermeasures.

II Technique of assessment

The established view is that there must be 'some degree of equivalence' (*Air Services Agreement* case [1946] para. 83) between the injury a state suffers originally and the injury it inflicts by responding in countermeasures. However, this injury equivalence analysis must be qualified by two contextual factors: the *gravity* of the original wrongful act (i.e. the 'questions of principle' involved, see *Air Services Agreement* [1946] para. 83) and the *rights* that may be affected by the countermeasure (e.g. if the rights of third parties may be impacted; ILC Fourth Report [2001] 135). This means a straightforward an-eye-for-an-eye comparison is not a sufficient analysis of proportionality.

There is an academic view that regards the assessment of proportionality as dependent on the specific function of countermeasures. This view holds that countermeasures serve various functions (e.g. coercion, signalling, or simply retribution) and that their proportionality must be assessed based on their 'appropriateness and reasonableness' to attain the specific functions they serve (Cannizzaro [2001] 891). The law and policy of the most frequent sanctioning states and international organisations underscore this functionalist view of proportionality (Tilahun and Okafor [2024] 13; see, e.g. in EU *Ezz and others v Council* [2014] para. 175). This view, however, renders proportionality vulnerable to end-justifies-means reasoning. In particular, with regard to the coercive function of countermeasures, the functionalist view permits responses 'greatly exceeding the magnitude of the original breach' (Cannizzaro [2001] 892) in pursuit of inducing behavioural change in the target (ILC Fourth Report [2001] para. 65; Frank [2008] 717).

III Challenges to proportionality assessment

The assessment of proportionality becomes problematic in cases where (i) it is difficult to quantify the injury from the original wrongful conduct, (ii) multiple states adopt countermeasures in response to the same conduct, or (iii) countermeasures remain in place for protracted periods.

In cases where injury is difficult to quantify, e.g. with respect to human rights violations, the assessment of proportionality is done by approximation (*Air Services Agreement* [1946] para. 83). This might be easier said than done; there is an everpresent possibility that responses to non-quantifiable injuries could feel disproportionate. In this regard, it is pertinent to note that reciprocity between states could serve as a check on disproportionate countermeasures (Heath [2025]). International law is built on the presumption that self-help by states serves as a corrective mechanism for the abuse of rights: if a state adopts disproportionate countermeasures, the addressee state can also respond with its own countermeasures and 'restore equality' between the parties (*Air Services Agreement* [1946] para. 90).

Multiple states could adopt countermeasures against the same target in response to the same breach, either in solidarity with an injured state (i.e. collective countermeasures, see Jackson and Paddeu [2024]) or in defence of a general interest (see Davidowicz [2017]; Alland [2002]; for a critical appraisal, see Hofer [2019]). In such cases, there is a possibility that concurrent countermeasures could cumulatively become disproportionate to the original breach, but there is no clarity in international law on how to operationalise proportionality in an aggregated manner (Crawford [2001] 67).

Although countermeasures are expected to be temporary measures, often they remain in place for protracted periods. General international law does not require consideration of the duration of countermeasures in assessing their proportionality (Tilahun and Okafor [2024] 14). However, there are some judicial decisions indicating the importance of the temporal dimension of countermeasures. In the dispute between Hungary and Czechoslovaki (later Slovakia), the International Court of Justice hinted at the possibility of considering the longer-term effects of countermeasures in assessing their proportionality as it took into account 'the continuing effects' of the diversion of the Danube River by Slovakia 'on the ecology of the riparian area of the Szigetkoz [in Hungary]' (*Gabcikovo-Nagymaros* [1997] para. 85). The Court of Justice of the European Union (General Court) has also indicated that the length of time could be taken into account in assessing the proportionality of asset freeze countermeasures against individuals (*Sirine Ben Ali v Council* [2017] para. 175).

IV Proportionality of UN sanctions

At the global stage, the most important sanctioning body is the United Nations Security Council (UNSC). The United Nations Charter bestows upon the Council wide discretion in exercising its powers and does not expressly qualify it with a proportionality requirement. In practice, the Council has developed some restraints on itself in adopting sanctions, in particular by abandoning comprehensive sanctions and by introducing humanitarian exemptions into its sanctions regimes (Dam-de Jong [2020]; Angelet [2001]; UNSC Res 2264 [2022]).

The powers of the UNSC are not totally unchecked (Tzanakopoulos [2011]), and some suggest that proportionality binds the Council as a generally accepted principle of law (Peters [2017]). Scholars largely agree that the UNSC is bound by fundamental international human rights and humanitarian law obligations, and as such it must take into account possible adverse human rights and humanitarian consequences that arise from its sanctions (Ruys [2017] 16).

Bibliography

Literature

Alland D, 'Countermeasures of General Interest' (2002) 13(5) *European Journal of International Law* 1221.

Angelet N, 'International Law Limits to the Security Council' in Gowlland-Debbas V (ed.), *United Nations Sanctions and International Law* (Kluwer 2001) 71.

Cannizzaro E, 'The Role of Proportionality in the Law of International Countermeasures' (2001) 12(5) *European Journal of International Law* 889.

Crawford J, 'The Relationship between Sanctions and Countermeasures' in Gowlland-Debbas V (ed.), *United Nations Sanctions and International Law* (Kluwer 2001) 57.

Dam-de Jong D, 'Who is Targeted by the Council's Sanctions? The UN Security Council and the Principle of Proportionality' (2020) 89(3–4) *Nordic Journal of International Law* 383.

Dawidowicz M, *Third-Party Countermeasures in International Law* (Cambridge University Press 2017).

Franck TM, 'On Proportionality of Countermeasures in International Law' (2008) 102 *American Journal of International Law* 715.

Heath JB, 'Economic Sanctions as Legal Ordering' (2025) 46(2) *Michigan Journal of International Law* 219.

Hofer A, 'The Beliefs and Practice of Enforcing Collective Obligations through Unilateral Sanctions' (PhD thesis, University of Ghent 2019) <https://biblio.ugent.be/publication/8635353> accessed 06 October 2025.

Jackson M and Paddeu FI, 'The Countermeasures of Others: When Can States Collaborate in the Taking of Countermeasures?' (2024) 118(2) *American Journal of International Law* 231.

Peters A, 'Proportionality as a Global Constitutional Principle' in Lang AF and Wiener A (eds), *Handbook on Global Constitutionalism* (Edward Elgar 2017) 248.

Ruys T, 'Sanctions, Retortions and Countermeasures: Concepts and International Legal Framework' in van den Herik L (ed.), *Research Handbook on UN Sanctions and International Law* (Edward Elgar 2017) 19.

Tilahun N and Okafor O, '"Humanizing" Economic Sanctions? Lessons from International Humanitarian Law' (2024) *Yale Journal of International Law* <https://www.yjil.yale.edu/humanizing-economic-sanctions-lessons-from-international-humanitarian-law/> accessed 06 October 2025.

Tzanakopoulos A, *Disobeying the Security Council: Countermeasures against Wrongful Sanctions* (Oxford University Press 2011).

Documents

Air Service Agreement of 27 March 1946 (United States v France) [1978] 18 RIAA 1371.

Case T-149/15, Sirine Ben Ali v Council [2017] ECLI:EU:T:2017:693.

Case T-256/11, Ezz et al. v Council [2014] ECLI:EU:T:2014:93.

Gabcikovo-Nagymaros Project (Hungary/Slovakia) (Judgment) [1997] ICJ Rep 7.

ILC, 'Draft Articles on Responsibility of States for Internationally Wrongful Acts with commentaries' (2001) UN Doc. A/56/10.

ILC, 'Third Report on State Responsibility by Mr. James Crawford, Special Rapporteur' (15 March, 15 June and 18 July and 4 August 2000) UN Doc. A/CN.4/507/Add.1-4.

ILC, 'Fourth Report on State Responsibility by Mr. James Crawford, Special Rapporteur' (2 and 3 April 2001) UN Doc. A/CN.4/517/Add.1.

Naulilaa Incident Arbitration (Portugal v Germany) [1928] 2 RIAA 1011.

UNSC Res 2664 (9 December 2022) UN Doc. S/RES/2664.

64. Sanctions and the use of force

Yuleng Zeng

I Introduction

The relationship between economic sanctions and the use of military force has long been debated. There is no lack of prominent cases when economic sanctions failed to deter aggressors. For instance, Japan was hit with harsh oil embargoes and financial sanctions by the United States in 1941. But the economic warfare did not deter its aggression. Instead, Japan chose to attack Pearl Harbour and further escalated the conflict.

On the other hand, if sanctions do deter potential aggressors, then crises are not initiated in the first place. This means that the empirical data tends to under-report successful cases. Relatedly, some failures could be attributed to delayed decision-making or weak enforcement. For example, although the League of Nations' (see chapter) embargoes against Italy in 1935 did not stop its aggression against Ethiopia, one could argue that this was due to the half-hearted enforcement. Had the sanctions been forcefully implemented, Italy would probably have had to abandon its invasion plan.

These opposing views require one to carefully think through the possible relations between sanctions and the use of force. In theory, sanctions could play three possible roles.

II Economic sanctions as a substitute, a middle ground, or a complement

The first possibility is that economic sanctions could play an independent role in achieving important foreign policy objectives. In particular, sanctions may act as a substitute for military force. Indeed, one important role of the League of Nations was to enforce peace. Woodrow Wilson famously claimed that economic sanctions could be a 'deadly remedy' against aggressors and that when applied 'there would be no need for force' (Mulder [2022] 2). That is, economic coercion can act 'as a foreign policy substitute for military coercion' (Drezner [2003] 650).

A second possible role for sanctions is that they can strike a middle ground between inaction (or diplomatic protests) and military coercion. As such, economic sanctions can help states communicate and bargain in a non-violent manner (Stein [2003]). If states have the option of economic coercion, they will be less likely to escalate the disputes. Even if economic sanctions do not deter, they avoid the alternatives of inaction, which could embolden other revisionist states, or immediate military action, which can be riskier and more escalatory.

Third, some research views sanctions as part of the broader toolkits that states can employ. Economic sanctions do not simply succeed or fail. One should see them as being helpful for states in advancing their strategic goals or not (Nephew [2017] 4). In this regard, sanctions could serve as a complement to military force. If the measures of economic sanctions are backed up by military forces, they could be perceived as more credible, making it less necessary to escalate the conflict.

III Critiques of the usefulness of economic sanctions

The independent role of sanctions could be too optimistic. Pape ([1997] 93) argues that economic sanctions 'have little usefulness' for non-economic goals. This is because most modern states can tap into nationalism and use substitution or resource reallocation to mitigate or shift economic pain. As such, the 'deadly remedy' often ends up being too limited in overwhelming a state's commitment.

Scholars also question the 'costly signalling' logic of economic sanctions. Lektzian and Souva ([2007]) point out that states have a strong incentive to maximise economic pain on a target while minimising their own. As such, the target will question the determination of the sanctioning state and interpret the measure as a sign of weakness. This can embolden the target, leading to a higher likelihood of using military force for crisis resolution.

Some critique emphasises the context when states have to weigh between economic and military actions. In particular, economic sanctions are often used to compel rather than deter, i.e. to convince a state to walk back from an action already taken rather than to refrain from taking an action in the first place (Stein [2003] 124). In times of crisis, any policy options, including sanctions, would have a slim chance of success since deterrence has most likely already failed.

IV The real value of economic sanctions

If the above critiques stand, the true merits of sanctions are twofold: (1) they mitigate the intensity of an existing crisis where deterrence has likely failed anyway; and (2) they avoid the unfavourable situation where inaction (or mere diplomatic protests) embolden other potential revisionist states to act opportunistically, increasing the risk of militarised conflict in other areas.

First, stringent economic restrictions, dual-use export control and arms embargo in particular, could restrict aggressors' ability to maintain their military industrial base and sustain an existing military campaign. If so, the effectiveness of economic sanctions should be viewed from a broader and longer-term perspective. That is, to the extent that it can drain an aggressor's military capacity, it would lead to more effective military (or non-military) interventions further down the road (Zeng [2024]). Second, strong sanctions can transmit credible information to third-party states that are weighing the risks and benefits of military aggression. In particular, bystander countries that are worried about the costs of economic isolation are also more likely to postpone, change, or even forsake their military plans.

Finally, once we factor in states' strategic calculations over time, the exact impact of economic sanctions could be further complicated. If potential revisionist states are worried about economic coercion in the future, they would be more likely to turn towards self-reliance programmes (Mulder [2022]). This would render future economic sanctions less effective due to trade diversion (Stein [2003]). Worries about reliable access to markets and resources may even incentivise disadvantaged states to take pre-emptive militarised actions (Monteiro and Debs [2020]). This final point suggests that economic sanctions should not be applied lightly. Policymakers will often need to strike a good balance – imposing harsh economic costs on aggressors while keeping potential revisionist states sufficiently integrated in the global economy.

Bibliography

Literature

Drezner DW, 'The Hidden Hand of Economic Coercion' (2003) 57 *International Organization* 643.

Lektzian D and Souva M, 'Sanctions, Signals, and Militarized Conflict' (2007) *American Journal of Political Science* 415.

Monteiro NP and Debs A, 'An Economic Theory of War' (2020) *Journal of Politics* 255.

Mulder N, *The Economic Weapon: The Rise of Sanctions as a Tool of Modern War* (Yale University Press 2022).

Nephew R, *The Art of Sanctions: A View from the Field* (Columbia University Press 2017).

Pape RA, 'Why Economic Sanctions Do Not Work' (1997) *International Security* 90.

Stein AA, 'Trade and Conflict: Uncertainty, Strategic Signaling, and Interstate Disputes' in Mansfield ED and Pollins BM (eds), *Economic Interdependence and International Conflict: New Perspectives on an Enduring Debate* (University of Michigan Press 2003) 111.

Zeng Y, 'Microchips and Sneakers: Bilateral Trade, Shifting Power, and Interstate Conflict' (2024) *Journal of Peace Research* 659.

YULENG ZENG

65. Sanctions databases

Kerim Can Kavakli

I Introduction

Economic sanctions have grown in number and variety in recent decades. Consequently, the databases that catalogue these sanctions have also proliferated. This entry provides an overview of four widely used databases and introduces two newer ones that represent future research directions. Each database is described in terms of its coverage, scope, and its advantages and disadvantages. More detailed information can be found in their respective codebooks.

All the databases discussed here are created by academic researchers and are freely available online. They exclude official databases from government agencies (e.g., the United States Department of the Treasury) and international organizations, as well as proprietary databases from private companies. Although useful for building academic databases, these excluded sources often lack crucial details such as the political goals of a sanction episode and the extent to which these goals were achieved (Portela and Charron [2023]).

II The major databases

The first and most cited database is the one by Hufbauer, Schott, and Elliott (HSE) (1985), last updated in 2007. It aims to list all economic sanctions imposed between 1945 and 2000, detailing the target state, years of imposition, goal, and outcome. In addition to being the first comprehensive database, its main strength is the accompanying case summaries, which allow for deeper analysis. However, HSE has two major shortcomings: it excludes sanction threats and lacks detailed information on sanctioning coalitions. The omission of threats limits its usefulness in evaluating the political effectiveness of sanctions. The lack of a list of sanctioning states and organizations makes it difficult to study sanction coalition dynamics.

Despite its weaknesses, HSE was the most widely used sanction database for more than two decades. However, several new databases have been produced in the last two decades. The second key sanction database is TIES (Threat and Imposition of Economic Sanctions) (Morgan et al. [2009]), last updated in 2013. It aims to list all sanction threats and impositions from 1945 to 2005. TIES improves upon HSE by including sanction threats and providing detailed information on the participants in sanction episodes. This allows researchers to explore new questions, such as the conditions under which sanction threats are issued and the factors that influence the success of sanction coalitions.

Although TIES ends in 2005, two databases extend it for specific regions: EUSANCT (Webster and Schneider [2022]) and CES (Chinese Economic Sanctions) (Zhang and Shanks [2024]). EUSANCT, updated to 2015, includes sanctions initiated by the European Union (EU), the United States, and the United Nations (UN). CES, updated to 2020, focuses on sanctions initiated by China. Both are compatible with TIES and cover the largest economic actors in today's global economy. Future research could extend these updates to other significant regional players like Russia and India.

The third major database is the GSDB (Global Sanctions Database) (Felbermayr et al. [2020]), which aims to list all state pairs involved in sanctions each year since 1950. Its biggest advantage is its annual updates. However, the GSDB omits sanction threats, which, as discussed above, impede the study of sanction effectiveness. Moreover, the GSDB provides less information on the specifics of each sanction episode, such as when it began or which state was the sanction coalition leader. Therefore, the GSDB tells us when one state sanctions another but says little about how the two states got to that point.

An important development since the 1990s is the rise of 'targeted' (or 'smart') sanctions. These sanctions aim to minimize collateral damage in the target state by focusing on specific individuals or organizations responsible for undesirable policies. The databases discussed so far do not adequately capture this shift, as they mostly lack information on non-state targets and the specific actors targeted within a state.

The TSC (Targeted Sanctions Consortium) database aims to fill this gap (Biersteker et al. [2016]). The TSC includes only targeted sanctions by the UN and codes numerous variables not found in other datasets, detailing the measures taken. While the TSC paints a broad overview of the frequency and characteristics of UN targeted sanctions, its data is often too coarse for detailed statistical analysis.

For example, the TSC includes only a binary variable indicating whether 'key regime supporters' are targeted, but it cannot differentiate between cases where only a few or most regime supporters are targeted. If we had a similar dataset on Western targeted sanctions against Russia, this variable could not capture the massive increase in the number of Russians sanctioned after 2022 because a relatively small number were sanctioned even before the invasion of Ukraine. Because targeted sanctions' primary advantage for policymakers is their precision, the coarseness of the information in the TSC database limits its utility.

Given the proliferation of economic sanctions globally, it is perhaps unrealistic to expect a new database to combine and harmonize all types of information on all contemporary sanctions, like HSE or TIES did in the past. Luckily, technology has made it easier to compile specialized datasets for individual projects. I conclude by discussing two examples.

III The new research directions

When Russia invaded Ukraine on 24 February 2022, Western states quickly imposed new sanctions on Russia. Concurrently, many urged foreign investors to withdraw from Russia. To track which companies heeded these calls, within a week, Yale University researchers had created the 'Yale CELI List of Companies Leaving and Staying in Russia' (Yale [2023]), which has been regularly updated. This list includes over 1200 companies with significant investments in Russia at the time of the invasion, enabling the study of corporate behaviour in enhancing economic sanctions by either withdrawing or staying in the targeted state.

Finally, the SASCAT (Statements and Actions on Sanctions: Computer-Assisted Text Approach) (Elshehawy et al. [2023]) project uses advanced text analysis methods to examine large volumes of official documents and code the frequency and tone of statements made by policymakers in unprecedented detail. So far, the researchers have analyzed only American policymakers' statements on economic sanctions, but clearly the methodology is applicable to other states and international organizations involved in sanctions as well.

Kerim Can Kavakli

IV Conclusion

Over the past 40 years, several databases have allowed scholars to analyze economic sanctions using quantitative methodologies and produce policy-relevant research. However, the increasing complexity of economic sanctions necessitates new data collection methods. Fortunately, technological advancements like the internet and new text analysis methods enable researchers to meet this challenge.

Bibliography

Literature

Biersteker T, Eckert S and Tourinho M (eds), *Targeted Sanctions – The Impact and Effectiveness of United Nations Action* (Cambridge University Press 2016).

Elshehawy A, Marinov N, Nanni, F and Tama J, 'SASCAT: Natural Language Processing Approach to the Study of Economic Sanctions' (2023) 60(5) *Journal of Peace Research* 877.

Felbermayr G et al., 'The Global Sanctions Data Base' (2020) 129 *European Economic Review* 1.

Hufbauer G, Schott J, Elliot KA and Oegg B, *Economic Sanctions Reconsidered* (Institute for International Economics 1985).

Morgan C, Bapat N and Krustev V, 'The Threat and Imposition of Economic Sanctions, 1971–2000' (2009) 26(1) *Conflict Management and Peace Science* 92.

Morgan C et al., 'Threat and Imposition of Sanctions (TIES) Data 4.0' User's Manual, Case Level Data [2013].

Morgan TC, Bapat NA and Kobayashi Y, 'Threat and Imposition of Economic Sanctions 1945–2005: Updating the TIES Dataset' (2014) 31(5) *Conflict Management and Peace Science* 541.

Morgan TC, Bapat NA and Kobayashi Y, 'The Threat and Imposition of Economic Sanctions Project: A Retrospective' in Van Bergeijk P (ed.), *Research Handbook on Economic Sanctions* (Edward Elgar 2021).

Portela C and Charron A, 'Evolution of Databases in an Age of Targeted Sanctions' (2023) 25(1) *International Studies Review* <https://doi.org/10.1093/isr/viac061>.

Webster P and Schneider G, 'Post-Cold War Sanctioning by the EU, the UN, and the US: Introducing the EUSANCT Dataset'

(2022) 39(1) *Conflict Management and Peace Science* 97.

'Yale CELI List of Companies Leaving and Staying in Russia' (Yale School of Management, last updated July 2023) <https://www.yalerussianbusinessretreat.com/> accessed 23 July 2024.

Zhang JJ and Shanks S, 'Measuring Chinese Economic Sanctions 1949–2020: Introducing the China TIES Dataset' (2025) 42(3) *Conflict Management and Peace Science* 328 <https://journals.sagepub.com/doi/10.1177/07388942241248274>.

66. Sanction threats

T. Clifton Morgan

I Introduction

A long-standing conventional wisdom holds that economic sanctions seldom 'work' as an instrument of policy (Galtung [1967]; Hufbauer et al. [1990]). Although they incur economic costs on both targets and senders, they rarely lead targets to change their behaviour in accordance with the demands of the sender. In fact, depending on the data set used and one's definition of success, imposed sanctions produce outcomes desired by the states imposing them only 20–30 per cent of the time (Bapat et al. [2013]; Morgan et al. [2023]). This leads to an obvious question: why are sanctions used so frequently if they seldom work? A number of answers to this question have been offered; one of those suggests that the policy benefits of sanctions might often accrue before they are actually imposed.

II Sanction threats

States seldom impose sanctions out of the blue. Rather, they first threaten to impose sanctions if the target does not change its behaviour. The target can anticipate the cost of those sanctions and compare that to the cost of altering its policies. Some targets simply would not change their behaviour even if sanctions were imposed and stand firm in the face of threats. Other targets anticipate that they would capitulate if sanctions were imposed and would choose to do so at the threat stage, thereby avoiding the costs of even temporary sanctions. In such cases, sanctions would not be observed because the threat is successful (Smith [1996]; Drezner [2003]). However, some threats to sanctions might be bluffs. Sanctions are also costly to senders, so a sender might issue a threat it would not carry out in the hope that the target would back down. Targets who would capitulate if sanctions were imposed know this and would sometimes maintain their policies in the hope that the threat to sanction is a bluff. Because of this, senders cannot conclude that a failed threat means that the target will not back down. Moreover, if senders never carried out their threats to impose sanctions, those threats would not be credible or effective. Thus, we expect to observe that threats are often, but not always, successful; that some senders impose sanctions when threats fail and others do not; that a few targets back down when sanctions are imposed but most do not; and that senders maintain sanctions even when it becomes obvious that the target will not acquiesce. Even though it appears that *imposed* sanctions seldom produce policy benefits (and we can identify specific cases in which obviously failed sanctions endure), a policy of threatening, and sometimes imposing, sanctions can produce net gains over a large number of cases.

This argument suggests that empirical conclusions based only on the examination of cases in which sanctions have been imposed suffer from what is known as 'selection bias'. That occurs when the cases selected for study assume a single value on an important variable, which, in this case, is whether or not sanctions were imposed. Since the actors whose behaviour we want to explain make the choices that lead to this outcome, bias is introduced into our data. To address this issue, the 'Threat and Imposition of Economic Sanctions' (TIES) data set was created (Morgan et al. [2014]). It contains a total of 1412 cases in which sanctions were threatened and/or used, with 567 of these cases involving a threat without subsequent imposition. The data set covers the 1945–2005 period. It is state-centric in that all senders and targets must be states, or coalitions of states, but its coverage is global. Empirical tests using these data have shown that when we consider cases in which sanctions were threatened and/or imposed, the success rate increases to over 50 per cent (Bapat et al. [2013]; Morgan and Kobayashi [2021]).

Moreover, analyses using the TIES data have identified a number of factors associated with whether sanctions threats induce targets to alter their behaviour. Unsurprisingly, the greater the costs the target anticipates should sanctions be imposed, the greater the likelihood that the target will capitulate in the face of the threat, *ceteris paribus*. Similarly, if the sanctions were imposed by a coalition of senders, especially if coordinated through an existing international institution, the target is more likely to capitulate than if the threat came from a single state. In addition, the manner in which the threat is delivered affects the probability of success. Targets are more likely to change their behaviour when both the demands and the threatened sanctions are specific, precise, and unambiguous (Bapat et al. [2013]). Because these, and other, empirical results are consistent with our theoretical expectations, it seems safe to conclude that, in cases in which sanctions would be successful, the threat to impose them is often sufficient. It might be true that imposed sanctions do not typically lead the target to alter its behaviour. However, these 'failures' are an important component of an overall policy regarding sanctions use. Imposing, and maintaining, sanctions on recalcitrant targets enhance the credibility of threats.

It is also important to note that this argument and the supporting empirical evidence might still underestimate the value of sanctions as an instrument of policy. Our conclusions are based on cases in which we have observed explicit threats being made. Implicit threats to sanction are ubiquitous. For example, any state leader contemplating testing nuclear weapons has to expect that they will be the target of sanctions if such a test is conducted. We have no way of knowing how many nuclear tests have not been conducted, how many human rights have not been violated, or how many acts of aggression have been foregone because of the implicit threat of sanctions.

III Conclusion

It is natural that our attention is drawn more to things that happened than to things that did not happen. Research based on the TIES data has demonstrated that focusing only on sanctions that were imposed leads us to greatly underestimate the frequency with which sanctions policy does meet with success. Threats often induce targets to change their behaviour, but that would not be the case if senders were unwilling to carry out their threats. Sanctions processes are more complex than often assumed, and understanding them requires that we appreciate how threats are a part of that process.

Bibliography

Literature

Bapat N, Heinrich T, Kobayashi Y and Morgan TC, 'Determinants of Sanctions Effectiveness: Sensitivity Analysis Using New Data' (2013) 39(1) *International Interactions* 79.

Drezner DW, 'The Hidden Hand of Economic Coercion' (2003) 57 *International Organization* 643.

Galtung J, 'On the Effects of International Economic Sanctions, with Examples for the Case of Rhodesia' (1967) 19 *World Politics* 378.

Hufbauer G, Schott J and Elliott K, *Economic Sanctions Reconsidered: History and Current Policy* (2nd edn, Institute for International Economics 1990).

Morgan TC, Bapat N and Kobayashi Y, 'The Threat and Imposition of Economic Sanctions 1945–2005: Updating the TIES Dataset' (2014) 31(5) *Conflict Management and Peace Science* 541.

Morgan TC and Kobayashi Y, 'Talking to the Hand: Bargaining, Strategic Interaction, and Economic Sanctions' (2021) *European Economic Review* 134.

Morgan TC, Syropoulos C and Yotov YV, 'Economic Sanctions: Evolution, Consequences, and Challenges' (2023) 37(1) *Journal of Economic Perspectives* 1.

Smith A, 'The Success and Use of Economic Sanctions' (1996) 21 *International Interactions* 229.

T. CLIFTON MORGAN

67. Secondary sanctions and the extraterritorial effects of sanctions

Felipe Rodríguez Silvestre

I Introduction

The 1990s were widely described as the 'sanctions decade'. As the Cold War came to an end, the United Nations Security Council (UNSC) was able to operate without its usual deadlock, leading to a significant rise in the adoption of United Nations (UN) sanctions (Cortright and Lopez [2000]). Two decades later, as the initial momentum of the UNSC subsided, a new phase in the practice of international sanctions began. However, this new era is marked by a notable shift; states and international organizations have increasingly embraced unilateral sanctions at the expense of UN measures.

In the period following 2010, unilateral sanctions have consolidated as the main vehicle of economic statecraft, as evidenced by their significant increase. The current geopolitical landscape has provided fertile ground for these measures to thrive. The international economic order appears to be undergoing a reconfiguration, defined by a steady turn towards unilateralism and the weaponization of economic interdependence by major powers that previously advocated trade liberalization as a cornerstone of multilateral cooperation (Farrell and Newman [2019]).

In this context, secondary sanctions, designed to restrict economic or financial transactions between third states or third-state entities with the target, have raised significant concerns among states and scholars. This is due to their potential to infringe upon cornerstone principles and rules of international law, such as sovereign equality, the principle of non-intervention (Rodríguez Silvestre [2024]), and the rules governing the exercise of jurisdiction by states. Secondary sanctions are an accurate reflection of their era, an economic weapon reserved for powerful states, as their impact and reach are proportional to the economic or geopolitical leverage held by the sanctioning state.

Although not a new phenomenon, secondary sanctions have mainly been employed by the United States against its adversaries, including Cuba, Iran (see chapter), North Korea (see chapter), Venezuela (see chapter), Russia (see chapter), and China (see chapter). Once a thorn in the side of the transatlantic relationship between the United States and Europe, the aftermath of the Russian invasion of Ukraine in 2022 has prompted Europe to reassess its previous opposition to these measures (Ruys and Rodríguez Silvestre [2024]). Notable recent instances of secondary sanctions adopted by the United States include those imposed against the construction of the Nord Stream II pipeline project and the reimposition of sanctions on Iran following the US withdrawal from the Joint Comprehensive Plan of Action in 2018. In addition, the ongoing trade war between China and the United States, in which the latter has imposed secondary export controls on semiconductors, has underscored both the effectiveness and the challenges of secondary sanctions within the international legal order.

This entry addresses the controversial scope of secondary sanctions under international law, distinguishing between the extraterritorial effects of unilateral sanctions and their extraterritorial application from a jurisdictional perspective.

II The extraterritorial effects of sanctions

States and commentators generally agree that the controversial legal status of secondary sanctions stems from their extraterritorial nature (Ruys and Ryngaert [2020] 7). However, this characterization warrants clarification, as it may be reasonably argued that all unilateral sanctions are inherently extraterritorial (Meyer [2009] 935). More precisely, irrespective of their underlying motivations, i.e., regime change, human rights concerns, non-proliferation of nuclear weapons, etc., unilateral sanctions are invariably imposed to pressure or compel a foreign target located beyond the borders of the sanctioning state to alter its behaviour or policies. In this sense, unilateral sanctions are intrinsically designed to produce extraterritorial effects.

These effects, however, should not be conflated with extraterritorial jurisdiction. In other words, the extraterritorial effects of unilateral sanctions do not determine their scope of application, which is instead governed by the rules and principles regulating the exercise of jurisdiction by states (Kerbrat [2021] 166). Accordingly, the contentious nature of secondary sanctions does not arise from the effects they seek to produce on the target, but rather from their expansive jurisdictional reach.

III The extraterritorial application of sanctions

Unilateral sanctions emanate from the sovereign regulatory authority of states. Unlike UNSC sanctions, which are binding on all UN members and thus have a global reach, the scope of unilateral sanctions is limited and circumscribed to the jurisdictional authority of each sanctioning state (Beaucillon [2021] 4). Jurisdiction refers to the power a state holds under international law to regulate the conduct—and its consequences—of natural and legal persons. For unilateral economic sanctions, such as restrictions on trade, investment, or other financial activities with the target, to be effectively implemented domestically, the sanctioning state must enact laws or regulations binding on individuals, companies, or financial institutions within its jurisdiction. For instance, general embargoes or boycotts, such as those enforced by the United States against Cuba or Iran, typically require adopting legislation that restricts the sanctioning state's citizens and businesses from engaging in any transaction with the targeted country, under the threat of penalties for non-compliance. Without such domestic legislation, unilateral economic sanctions could hardly be set in motion, as economic activity is largely conducted by private actors rather than the state. This process constitutes an exercise of prescriptive jurisdiction.

There is broad consensus that states may only exercise jurisdiction when a valid jurisdictional basis exists, typically involving a genuine or substantial connection between the regulating state and the conduct or persons subject to regulation. Within this framework, the primary–secondary categorization distinguishes unilateral economic sanctions based on which conduct or transactions the sanctioning state seeks to regulate. Primary sanctions restrict a state's own economic or financial activity with the target. This includes transactions occurring within the sanctioning state's territory and those involving its nationals, regardless of their location, as jurisdiction based on a territorial or nationality connection is universally accepted under international law. The vast majority of unilateral sanctions fall under this category. The effectiveness of primary sanctions is limited due to their vulnerability to circumvention. Their success typically depends on the voluntary alignment of third states, given their autonomous nature and lack of institutional support. In a global economy, however, a target can easily relocate its trade or financial activities to alternative markets, thereby diminishing the impact of the measures imposed against it.

Secondary sanctions emerged to address the limitations of primary sanctions and exert additional pressure on the target. These measures restrict certain economic or financial transactions transpiring between third states or third-state entities (namely individuals, companies, or financial institutions) and the target of primary sanctions. Where the target is another country, such restrictions also extend to the transactions entered into with private entities operating under the jurisdiction of the target. The modus operandi of secondary sanctions is manifest in the choice they present to third states or third-state entities: either continue engaging with the target at the risk of monetary fines, loss of trade privileges, exclusion from the sender state's financial market, and even criminal prosecution, or comply with the restrictions imposed.

By imposing secondary sanctions, the sender state seeks to govern transactions conducted by foreign entities outside its territory, thereby exercising extraterritorial jurisdiction. Secondary sanctions have global aspirations as they aim to universalize a sanctions regime originating from the unilateral will of a single state or a coalition of states. When successful, they undermine the sovereign authority of third states to regulate the transactions within their territory or involving their nationals (Sossai [2020] 67). The impact of secondary sanctions has led several countries to enact legislation to counteract their extraterritorial application, such as the EU's blocking statute (see chapter) adopted in 1996 in response to US sanctions on Cuba, Iran, and Libya. The United Kingdom, Canada, and more recently China have also enacted similar legislation.

While secondary and extraterritorial sanctions are often used interchangeably (Ruys and Ryngaert [2020] 8), they are not identical concepts. Extraterritorial regulation is not exclusive to secondary sanctions; in fact, primary sanctions may also apply extraterritorially when the sender state regulates the transactions of its nationals abroad with the target. Thus, the defining feature of secondary sanctions lies instead in their absence of a territorial or nationality nexus with the sender state. Despite the foregoing, secondary sanctions do not inherently contravene jurisdictional rules, as they may be grounded on alternative bases of jurisdiction. The protective principle of jurisdiction, which allows states to regulate extraterritorial conduct threatening their national security or fundamental interests, is arguably the most plausible jurisdictional basis to potentially justify secondary sanctions. Although this principle is traditionally associated with serious crimes such as espionage, sedition, or terrorism, its boundaries remain vague. In practice, aside from US secondary sanctions against Iran, partially justified as measures to curb nuclear weapons development, few examples exist of states invoking the protective principle to substantiate extraterritorial jurisdiction in this context.

Whereas primary sanctions are generally regarded as less controversial than secondary sanctions from a jurisdictional standpoint (Lowenfeld [1996] 429), many measures labelled as primary, particularly those adopted by the United States in recent decades, rely on contentious wide-ranging interpretations of territory or nationality, blurring the line between primary and secondary sanctions. For example, the United States has persistently imposed sanctions on foreign actors based on transactions concluded abroad in US dollars, where the sole connection to the United States lies in the subsequent clearing of the transaction through the US financial system, or merely in the choice of currency itself (Emmenegger and Zuber [2022]). Similarly, foreign companies are threatened with sanctions for re-exporting US technology or goods to third countries, even if these have already been processed into different products abroad. While Europe has historically criticized this practice, it has recently revised its position, incorporating broad re-export prohibitions (including gold, steel, and iron) into Council Regulation (EU) 833/2014, concerning restrictive measures in view of Russia's actions destabilizing the situation in Ukraine. These tenuous links suggest that these measures in fact regulate extraterritorial conduct without a valid jurisdictional connection; thus, they could also be classified as secondary sanctions.

IV Conclusion

Although extraterritorial jurisdiction is generally viewed unfavourably by states, the contents and scope of the rules governing jurisdiction remain opaque. This ambiguity has fuelled the proliferation of unilateral sanctions with extraterritorial reach, including secondary sanctions, as states are generally able to invoke a jurisdictional nexus at their own discretion or simply interpret and bend the limits of territory or nationality as broadly as they choose.

Bibliography

Literature

Beaucillon C, 'An Introduction to Unilateral and Extraterritorial Sanctions: Definitions, State of Practice and Contemporary Challenges' in Beaucillon C (ed.), *Research Handbook on Unilateral and Extraterritorial Sanctions* (Edward Elgar 2021) 1.

Cortright D and Lopez G, *The Sanctions Decade: Assessing UN Strategies in the 1990s* (Lynne Rienner Publishers 2000).

Emmenegger S and Zuber F, 'To Infinity and Beyond: U.S. Dollar-Based Jurisdiction in the U.S. Sanctions Context' (2022) 2 *Swiss Review of Business and Financial Market Law* 114.

Farrell H and Newman AL, 'Weaponized Interdependence: How Global Economic Networks Shape State Coercion' (2019) 44 *International Security* 42.

Kerbrat Y, 'Unilateral/Extraterritorial Sanctions as a Challenge to the Theory of Jurisdiction' in Beaucillon C (ed.), *Research Handbook on Unilateral and Extraterritorial Sanctions* (Edward Elgar 2021) 165.

Lowenfeld AF, 'Congress and Cuba: The Helms–Burton Act' (1996) 90 *American Journal of International Law* 419.

Meyer JA, 'Second Thoughts on Secondary Sanctions' (2009) 30 *University of Pennsylvania Journal of International Law* 905.

Rodríguez Silvestre F, 'The Application of the Principle of Non-Intervention to Secondary Sanctions' in Ruys T, Ryngaert C and Rodríguez Silvestre F (eds), *The Cambridge Handbook of Secondary Sanctions and International Law* (Cambridge University Press 2024) 182.

Felipe Rodríguez Silvestre

Ruys T and Ryngaert C, 'Secondary Sanctions: A Weapon out of Control? The International Legality of, and European Responses to, US Secondary Sanctions' (2020) *British Yearbook of International Law* 1.

Ruys T and Rodríguez Silvestre F, 'Secondary Sanctions after Russia's Invasion of Ukraine: A Whole New World?' in Ruys T, Ryngaert C and Rodríguez Silvestre F (eds), *The Cambridge Handbook of Secondary Sanctions and International Law* (Cambridge University Press 2024) 463.

Sossai M, 'Legality of Extraterritorial Sanctions' in Asada M (ed.), *Economic Sanctions in International Law and Practice* (Routledge 2020) 62.

68. Security exceptions

Iryna Bogdanova

I Introduction

National security exceptions are common provisions in international trade and investment agreements allowing states to derogate from their obligations under such agreements, provided that the derogations are justified by national security considerations. As recent studies show, the nature of national security risks has dramatically changed over time, and now they encompass various types of threats that range from climate change to cybercrime (Heath [2020]).

In dispute settlement proceedings, these exceptions come to the forefront of the discussion on the possibility of justifying economic sanctions as permissible actions (Menkes [2019]; Ruys and Ryngaert [2020]). This has occurred in the context of judicial proceedings challenging the legality of economic sanctions before the International Court of Justice (ICJ) and the World Trade Organization's (WTO) panels. In the investor–state arbitrations recently initiated by sanctioned Russian businessmen and legal entities against Ukraine (*ABH Holdings v Ukraine*; *CTF Holdings S.A. v Ukraine*) and Luxembourg (*Mikhail Fridman v Luxembourg*), the respondent states would be deprived of the possibility to invoke such exceptions. This possibility is prevented while the bilateral investment treaties providing the legal grounds for such disputes do not explicitly stipulate national security exceptions, a common practice in international investment agreements (UNCTAD [2009]).

II International Court of Justice's approach to national security exceptions

In several disputes, the ICJ had to decide on whether national security exceptions could justify economic sanctions, which violate obligations under the Treaties of Friendship, Commerce, and Navigation. The most common and ambiguous formulation of such exceptions allows states to enact certain measures, including economic restrictions, if they are necessary "to protect its essential security interests" (e.g., the Treaty of Amity, Economic Relations, and Consular Rights between the United States of America and Iran [1955] Art. XX (1)(d)).

In the judgment of 30 March 2023 on *Certain Iranian Assets*, the ICJ reiterated its previous case law on the national security exceptions and their ambit. To begin with, the Court reiterated that the national security exception is not an objection to the Court's jurisdiction and that it only affords a possible defence on the merits (*Certain Iranian Assets* [2023] para. 94). Subsequently, the Court emphasized that the exact wording of an exception defines the ambit of a state's discretion in implementing national security measures and the benchmark for the Court's review of such measures. Relying upon such an approach, the Court ruled that the wording "necessary to protect its essential security interests" requires that "the measures taken must not merely be such as tend to protect the essential security interests of the party taking them, but must be 'necessary' for that purpose" and that "whether the measures taken were 'necessary' is 'not purely a question for the subjective judgment of the party' … and may thus be assessed by the Court" (*Certain Iranian Assets* [2023] para. 106). This conclusion echoes the Court's settled case law, for example, its findings in *Oil Platforms* ([2003]) and *Military and Paramilitary Activities in and against Nicaragua* ([1986]).

III WTO national security exceptions and their ambit

Article XXI of the General Agreement on Tariffs and Trade (GATT) 1994, and similar exceptions in the General Agreement on Trade in Services (GATS) and the Agreement on Trade-Related Aspects of Intellectual Property Rights (TRIPS), contemplate several national security exceptions. In particular, Article XXI(a) of the GATT 1994 allows a WTO member not to provide information "disclosure of which it considers contrary to its essential security interests", while Article XXI(b)(i) and XXI(b)(ii) allow certain trade restrictions that are directly related to fissionable materials and arms, ammunition, and other implements of war. Article XXI(c) of the GATT 1994 permits WTO members to implement United Nations Security Council resolutions imposing collective economic sanctions and binding under Articles 25, 48, and 103 of the UN Charter, without triggering members' responsibility for potential WTO law violations. As of this writing, WTO panels have not had an opportunity to interpret these provisions.

Article XXI(b)(iii) of the GATT 1994 allows a WTO member to take "any action which it considers necessary for the protection of its essential security interests", including economic sanctions if they are "taken in time of war or other emergency in international relations". The panel interpreted this clause for the first time in the WTO dispute initiated by Ukraine to question the legality of Russian transit restrictions on goods originating in Ukraine and goods transported through Ukraine (*Russia – Traffic in Transit*). In *Russia – Traffic in Transit* ([2019]), the panel introduced a framework to analyse the invocation of the national security exception. The panel distinguished between objective and subjective elements of the clause (Bogdanova [2019]). The prerequisite "taken in time of war or other emergency in international relations" was interpreted as an objective element that operates as a "limitative qualifying clause" (*Russia – Traffic in Transit* [2019] paras 7.101 and 7.65). The panel equated the term "war" with an armed conflict (*Russia – Traffic in Transit* [2019] para. 7.72), while defining "emergency in international relations" as "a situation of armed conflict, or of latent armed conflict, or of heightened tension or crisis, or of general instability engulfing or surrounding a state" (*Russia – Traffic in Transit* [2019] para. 7.76). This objective element not only requires an objectively established existence of "war" or "other emergency in international relations" but also chronological concurrence between trade-restrictive measures and such events (*Russia – Traffic in Transit* [2019] para. 7.70).

According to the panel, the WTO member's determination of the subjective elements of the national security exception – a determination of "essential security interests" and the necessity of such measures – should be reviewed against the background of the principle of good faith (*Russia – Traffic in Transit* [2019] paras 7.132 and 7.138). For this reason, a WTO member should articulate its essential security interests "sufficiently enough to demonstrate their veracity" (para. 7.134). Additionally, the element "necessary for the protection" requires a minimum degree of plausibility between trade-restrictive measures and their ability to contribute to the protection of declared security interests (para. 7.138).

In *Saudi Arabia – Intellectual Property Rights* ([2020]), the respondent argued that its restrictive measures, which were a part of the broader efforts to isolate Qatar economically instituted by its neighbouring countries in June 2017, were justified under the national security clause of Article 73(b)(iii) of the TRIPS. In this dispute, the WTO panel relied upon the analytical framework developed by the panel in *Russia – Traffic in Transit* (paras 7.241–7.242). In the most recent WTO disputes, panels reached similar conclusions on how Article XXI(b)(iii) of the GATT 1994 should be interpreted (e.g., *US – Origin Marking* [2022]).

In both disputes, *Russia – Traffic in Transit* and *Saudi Arabia – Intellectual Property Rights*, respondents were successful in justifying their economic sanctions by the invocation of the national security clause. That being said, not all economic sanctions might be justified by WTO national security clauses even when the panels' interpretation offers WTO members a wide margin of discretion (Bogdanova [2021]).

IV Conclusion

National security exceptions provide states with the flexibility to address their security concerns while being in compliance with their treaty obligations. The ICJ and the WTO, by interpreting national security clauses, have contributed to a more structured understanding of these provisions, ensuring that states' actions are justified and proportionate. It is expected that future disputes, including disputes over economic sanctions, will refine the balance between measures taken to protect security interests, e.g., economic sanctions, and states' obligations under international economic law.

Bibliography

Literature

Bogdanova I, 'Targeted Economic Sanctions and WTO Law: Examining the Adequacy of the National Security Exception' (2021) 48(2) *Legal Issues of Economic Integration* 171.

Bogdanova I, 'The WTO Panel Ruling on the National Security Exception: Has the Panel "Cut" the Baby in Half?' (*EJIL:Talk!*, 2019)

<https://www.ejiltalk.org/the-wto-panel-ruling-on-the-national-security-exception-has-the-panel-cut-the-baby-in-half/>.

Heath JB, 'The New National Security Challenge to the Economic Order' (2019–2020) 129 *Yale Law Journal* 1020.

Menkes MJ, 'The Legality of US Investment Sanctions against Iran before the ICJ: A Watershed Moment for the Essential Security and Necessity Exceptions' (2019) 56 *Canadian Yearbook of International Law* 328.

Ruys T and Ryngaert C, 'Secondary Sanctions: A Weapon Out of Control? The International Legality of, and European Responses to, US Secondary Sanctions' (2020) *British Yearbook of International Law* 1.

United Nations Conference on Trade and Development (UNCTAD), *The Protection of National Security in IIAs* (UNCTAD Series on International Investment Policies for Development 2009).

Documents

Certain Iranian Assets (Islamic Republic of Iran v. United States of America) (Judgement) [2023] ICJ Rep 51.

General Agreement on Tariffs and Trade (GATT) 1994 (adopted 15 April 1994, entered into force 1 January 1995) 1867 UNTS 190.

Military and Paramilitary Activities in and against Nicaragua (Nicaragua v. United States of America) (Merits) [1986] ICJ Rep 14.

Oil Platforms (Islamic Republic of Iran v. United States of America) (Merits) [2003] ICJ Rep 161.

Treaty of Amity, Economic Relations, and Consular Rights between the United States and Iran (adopted 15 August 1955, entered into force 16 June 1957) 284 UNTS 93.

WTO, Russia – Measures Concerning Traffic in Transit, Panel Report (5 April 2019) DS512.

WTO, Saudi Arabia – Measures Concerning the Protection of Intellectual Property Rights, Panel Report (16 June 2020) DS567.

WTO, United States – Origin Marking Requirement (Hong Kong, China), Panel Report (21 June 2022) DS597.

Iryna Bogdanova

69. Targeted sanctions and the sanctions reform process

George A. Lopez

The reform of United Nations (UN) economic sanctions emerged from the widely recognised negative humanitarian impact of the Security Council (UNSC) comprehensive trade sanctions on Iraq (1990). In responding to this tragedy, the Council defined and enacted targeted or 'smart sanctions' as more precise coercive measures against the leaders of sanctioned nations. Accordingly, every UNSC sanctions regime after 1994 involved targeted sanctions (Cortright and Lopez [2002] 1–3).

By the end of the decade, the Council had imposed financial and travel bans, as well as embargoes on arms and specific commodities in six new sanctions cases: Rwanda, Somalia, Liberia, Sudan, Sierra Leone and Afghanistan. There was wide recognition in the UN Secretariat and among member states that greater refinement of these measures, especially regarding shared definitions of items and greater clarity about means of implementing and enforcing sanctions, was badly needed (Biersteker et al. [2016] 2–4).

In 1998 and 1999, the Swiss government facilitated a wide-ranging set of meetings including staff of the Department of Political Affairs of the UN, diplomats from several nations, international bankers, financial analysts and academic experts. The first meeting addressed the definitional parameters of financial sanctions, tools that were successful in curtailing money laundering, and the legal and administrative challenges of implementing these measures. The second meeting addressed how sanctions implementation could succeed in a world with very different domestic economic systems and capacities. The agreed principles and practices were formalised in *Targeted Financial Sanctions: A Manual for Design and Implementation* (Watson Institute [2001]).

Building from this success, the German foreign office, the UN Secretariat and the Bonn International Centre for Conversion co-sponsored a series of expert seminars and working groups that focused on arms embargoes and varied travel and diplomatic sanctions. This Bonn–Berlin Process outlined model resolutions and provided wide-ranging guidance on arms export policies, air travel bans and monitoring and enforcement of arms embargoes (Brzoska [2001]).

Lastly, the Stockholm Process, sponsored by the Swedish Ministry for Foreign Affairs and Uppsala University, was a series of meetings during 2002. It involved over a hundred experts considering how to further institutionalise smart sanctions that were both effective and humane. The findings were presented to the Security Council in February 2003 and published (Wallensteen et al. [2005]).

Internally, the Secretariat and the Security Council developed an Informal Working Group on Sanctions (IWGS), which sharpened the practices developed in these reform conferences. The IWG gave special attention to the design of sanctions regimes, the use of expert panels and monitoring mechanisms (S/2006/997). In 2007, the Greek mission to the UN sponsored a summative symposium 'Best Practices and Recommendations for Improving the Effectiveness of United Nations Sanctions' (S/2007/734 [2007]), drawing from the IWG report.

Pressure for sanctions reform to address the lack of fair and due process for sanctioned individuals, especially those listed in the UNSC counterterrorism sanctions regimes, came from the Group of Like-Minded States on UN Targeted Sanctions (FDFA [nd]). Their efforts resulted in the creation within the Secretariat of the Focal Point for Delisting (UNSC Res 1730 [2006]) as a facilitating mechanism to receive delisting requests and aid individuals in learning the details about their designation.

Because the Focal Point was a small office overwhelmed with cases and had less authority than needed to have a fully transparent and fair process for individuals, the like-minded group led the creation of the Office of the Ombudsperson (UNSC Res 1904 [2009]) to receive and recommend action on requests for delisting from the ISIL (Da'esh) and Al-Qaida sanctions list.

Concern about the loss of focus on the design of sanctions and their implementation in a way that would return to the best use of targeted sanctions led the UN Secretariat and various member states to commission the High-Level Review of United Nations Sanctions (A/69/941-S/2015/432 [2015]). Their Compendium report contained 150 recommendations, some of which are yet to be addressed adequately by the Council (Watson Institute and Compliance and Capacity Skills International, LLC [2015]).

In a return to concern for 'the unintended humanitarian consequences of sanctions', the United States joined Ireland in spearheading UNSC Resolution 2664 ([2022]), which created an unprecedented humanitarian carveout for most UN asset freeze regimes.

Pressure for further attention to due process rights has been an ongoing, contentious issue within the Council. In UNSC Resolution 2734 ([2024]), the Council extended the mandate of the Ombudsperson for three years, but not with the wide range of authority on delisting that reform-minded states advocated. Similarly, in UNSC Resolution 2744 ([2024]), the Council strengthened the mandate of the Focal Point.

After much debate, in early December, the Security Council unanimously passed Resolution 2761 ([2024]), which reaffirms paragraph 1 of Resolution 2664 ([2022]) exempting humanitarian aid providers from asset freeze measures imposed by the 1267/1989/2253 ISIL (Da'esh) and Al-Qaida sanctions regime.

As the post-2017 UNSC controversies about targeted sanctions indicate, disagreements about the purpose and usage of such sanctions among the P5 Council members will make UN sanctions reforms less likely in the near future.

Bibliography

Literature

Biersteker TJ, Eckert S and Tourinho M (eds), *Targeted Sanctions: The Impacts and Effectiveness of United Nations Action* (Cambridge University Press 2016).

Brown University, Watson Institute for International Studies, *Targeted Financial Sanctions: A Manual for Design and Implementation. Contributions from the Interlaken Process* (Watson Institute for International Studies 2001).

Brzoska M (ed.), 'Design and Implementation of Arms Embargoes and Travel and Aviation Related Sanctions: Results of the "Bonn–Berlin Process"' (Bonn International Center for Conversion 2001).

Cortright D and Lopez GA (eds), *Towards Smart Sanctions: Targeting Economic Statecraft* (Rowman & Littlefield 2002).

Wallensteen P (ed.), *Between Words and War: The New Challenge of International Sanctions* (Frank Cass 2005).

Watson Institute and Compliance and Capacity Skills International, LLC Compendium of the High-Level Review of United Nations Sanctions (2015).

Documents

Compendium of the High-Level Review of United Nations Sanctions (12 June 2015) UN Doc. A/69/941-S/2015/432.

Switzerland, Federal Department of Foreign Affairs (FDFA), 'Due Process and Respect for Human Rights in UN Counter-Terrorism Sanctions' (*Federal Department of Foreign Affairs*, nd) <https://www.eda.admin.ch/eda/en/fdfa/foreign-policy/security-policy/new-challenges/countering-terrorism/protecting-human-rights.html>.

UNSC, 'Letter dated 12 December 2007 from the Permanent Representative of Greece to the United Nations addressed to the President of the Security Council' (13 December 2007) UN Doc. S/2007/734.

UNSC, 'Note by the President of the Security Council: Report of the Informal Working Group of the Security Council on General Issues of Sanctions' (22 December 2006) UN Doc. S/2006/997.

UNSC Res 1730 (19 December 2006) UN Doc. S/RES/1730.

UNSC Res 1904 (17 December 2009) UN Doc. S/RES/1904.

UNSC Res 2664 (9 December 2022) UN Doc. S/RES/2664.

UNSC Res 2734 (10 June 2024) UN Doc. S/RES/2734.

UNSC Res 2744 (19 July 2024) UN Doc. S/RES/2744.

UNSC Res 2761 (6 December 2024) UN Doc. S/RES/2761.

GEORGE A. LOPEZ

70. Termination of sanctions

Clara Portela

I Introduction

In contrast to sanctions imposition, the lifting of sanctions has traditionally received scarce attention. According to seminal large-N studies of sanctions conducted by Clifton Morgan and his team (Morgan et al. [2009]), sanctions episodes can end in sender victory, sender capitulation or accommodation between sender and target. While a large portion of sanctions episodes end in sender capitulation instead of accommodation or sender victory, little research has been conducted into the role that sanctions terminations play in accounting for these outcomes. This paucity of research is particularly relevant given that studies on sanctions effectiveness posit a decline as sanctions episodes drag on, making the success of protracted cases unlikely.

II Sunset clauses

The question of sanctions termination first acquired relevance with the legitimacy crisis surrounding the Iraq (see chapter) sanctions regime. The United Nations (UN) trade embargo resulted in humanitarian consequences of catastrophic dimensions that led to international outrage against sanctions as a tool of international enforcement. The lifting of the sanctions, however, proved impossible because a new resolution was required to that effect, and its adoption was blocked by the United Kingdom and the United States, which announced their intention to wield their vetoes. This led to the extension of the comprehensive trade embargoes against Iraq in unaltered form for over a decade between 1990 and 2000. In order to prevent such situations in which a sanctions regime could be held hostage by a member with veto power against a majority of UN Security Council (UNSC) members ready to ease the measures, sanctions resolutions were endowed with a date of expiration, called a 'sunset clause' (Weschler [2009]). This clause compelled members of the Council to review and renegotiate the sanctions regime, requiring a new positive decision to extend the measures, thereby reversing the previous dynamic. Sunset clauses have become standard in UN practice as well as in other composite decision-making settings such as the European Union (EU) (see chapter).

Sanctions-enacting documents detail information and reasons regarding the motivation and rationale for the imposition of sanctions, such as the circumstances giving rise to the sanctions, the international norms breached, and the identity of responsible individuals. However, indications about which actions are required for sanctions to be eased or rolled back rarely feature. Instead, standard formulations indicating that they will be 'kept under review', or that they 'may be renewed', or 'amended as appropriate' are used. On the one hand, the absence of stipulations concerning the easing of the measures reserves maximum flexibility to senders to relax sanctions whenever they are satisfied with progress towards compliance. On the other hand, the ambiguity associated with the absence of conditions for lifting can lead the target to believe that the sender will deny any progress they may accomplish and leave sanctions in place in perpetuity regardless of target concessions. Indeed, target leaders often express concern that senders will leave sanctions in place irrespective of their behaviour, viewing sanctions as a policy seeking to undermine the country's wealth and reputation rather than as a response to a specific norm violation.

An exception to the general pattern of ambiguity can be found in the US law setting up a global sanctions regime for the protection of human rights (see chapter on Sanctions for human rights and democracy). The Global Magnitsky Human Rights Accountability Act of 2016 stipulates that the application of sanctions may be terminated if it is determined that the designee:

(i) did not engage in the activity for which sanctions were imposed according to credible information;
(ii) was prosecuted appropriately for the activity for which sanctions were imposed;
(iii) credibly demonstrated a significant change in behaviour, paid an appropriate consequence for the activity for which sanctions were imposed, and credibly committed to not engage again in similar activity in the future.

In addition, ending sanctions is also contemplated 'in the national security interests of the United States' (Global Magnitsky Act,

§10102.g). Similar provisions are absent from the European equivalent legislation, the EU Global Human Rights Sanctions Regime (Decision 2020/1999 [2020]).

III Termination practices

Some practices by sender countries make the easing and phasing out of sanctions difficult to observe empirically and prevent the full termination of sanctions regimes. One such practice is leaving a residual measure in place after compliance has been achieved, the political dispute is over, and the sender has lifted most measures of the sanctions regime. After the UN lifted its sanctions on the former Yugoslavia (see chapter) following the signing of the Dayton Accords, the United States left an 'outer wall of sanctions' in place, which entailed an arms embargo (Portela [2010]). Similarly, the signature of the Joint Comprehensive Plan of Action (JCPOA) with Iran (see chapter) led to the removal of virtually all sanctions by the EU and the UN, but the United States left a number of its own restrictions in place. Significantly, UNSC Resolution 2231 (2015) contains a snapback mechanism for the reimposition of sanctions in case of significant non-performance by Iran of its commitments (Sossai [2020]). After sanctions on Myanmar (see chapter) were phased out following the political transition to a civilian government in 2011/12, the EU left an arms embargo in place after lifting all other measures in 2013. Thus, when new sanctions were imposed in response to the Rohingya crisis in 2018, they were added to an existing sanctions regime. The lifting of broader sanctions regimes against Zimbabwe and Burundi in 2022 did not result in their termination, given that a minimal number of designations remained in force: one entity in Zimbabwe and one in Burundi (Council Decision 2022/227[2022] and 2022/2051[2022]).

Several studies point to the promising effects of facilitating the termination of sanctions, especially in the form of exchanging sanctions relief for political concessions (Hudakova et al. [2021]). The phased easing and eventual termination of sanctions, often employed in the resumption of foreign assistance after political crises in recipient countries, showed an encouraging record; yet, the practice of other forms of assistance has not found application outside the realm of development cooperation (Portela [2023]). The realisation of such proposals requires a departure from standard termination practices.

IV Conclusion

While the introduction of sunset clauses represented a breakthrough in UNSC sanctions as it reversed the proclivity towards sanctions continuation, senders tend to follow a consistent policy for sanctions termination. These include the deliberate omission of clear conditions for lifting sanctions in the imposing legislation in order to maximise flexibility, or leaving a sanctions measure in place – normally an arms embargo or one designation – after the majority of restrictions have been lifted. Such practices have the effect of extending sanctions regimes beyond the political disputes they were designed to address, suggesting that they have a longer duration than they actually do, and by implication, generating an impression of inconclusiveness.

Bibliography

Literature

Hudakova Z, Biersteker T and Moret E, *Sanctions Relaxation and Conflict Resolution: Lessons from Past Sanctions Regimes* (The Carter Centre 2021).

Jones L and Portela C, 'Evaluating the Success of International Sanctions: A New Research Agenda' (2020) 125 *Afers Internacionals* 39.

Morgan TC, Bapat N and Krustev V, 'The Threat and Imposition of Economic Sanctions, 1971–2000' (2009) 26(1) *Conflict Management and Peace Science* 92.

Portela C, *European Union Sanctions and Foreign Policy* (Routledge 2010).

Portela C, 'Easing, Suspending and Phasing Out: The Untapped Potential of Sanctions Relief' (2023) Brief 16, EUISS: Paris.

Sossai M, 'The Dynamic of Action and Reaction and the Implementation of the Iran Nuclear Deal' (2020) *Questions of International Law* 1.

Weschler J, 'The Evolution of Security Council Innovations in Sanctions' (2010) 65(1) *International Journal* 31.

Clara Portela

Documents

Council Decision (CFSP) 2022/2051 of 24 October 2022 amending Decision (CFSP) 2015/1763 concerning restrictive measures in view of the situation in Burundi, OJ L 275, 25.10.2022, 72–3.

Council Decision (CFSP) 2022/227 of 17 February 2022 amending Decision 2011/101/CFSP concerning restrictive measures in view of the situation in Zimbabwe, OJ L 38, 18.2.2022, 5–7.

Council Decision (CFSP) 2020/1999 of 7 December 2020 concerning restrictive measures against serious human rights violations and abuses, OJ L 410I, 7.12.2020, 13–19.

Global Magnitski Human Rights Accountability Act, Public Law 114-328, 130 Stat, 2533, 2016.

UNSC Res 2231 (2015) S/RES/2231 (2015), adopted by the Council in its 7488th session, 20 July 2015.

71. The UN Focal Point and UN Office of the Ombudsperson

Gavin Sullivan

I Introduction

Economic sanctions provided for in the United Nations (UN) Charter were originally designed as state-centred and aimed at reducing the risk of interstate war by countering threats to international peace and security via non-military means. The key international human rights treaties adopted in the post-war period were similarly state-centred and "primarily designed to protect human beings against their own state", so they did not bind international organisations (IOs) like the UN (Tomuschat [2003] 84; Hovell [2016]). Until the early twenty-first century, "the UN had never thought of itself as actually capable of violating human rights" through sanctions, despite the profound "civilian pain" of the comprehensive sanctions inflicted upon the population of Iraq in the 1990s (Megret and Hoffman [2003] 314; Weiss et al. [1997]). But the rapid expansion of the grounds for UN sanctions throughout the 1990s and the development of UN targeted sanctions aimed at individuals and non-state entities complicated this state-centred focus and disturbed the presumptive disconnect between UN sanctions and human rights (Cortright and Lopez [2000]). As the UN began exercising quasi-governmental powers over ever larger numbers of people deemed threats to international peace and security in the post-9/11 period, imposing economic restrictions and global travel bans that profoundly interfered with their human rights, these individuals unsurprisingly came to expect access to the kinds of redress they would have ordinarily been entitled to if the sanctions had been issued by their own states or the European Union (EU), rather than IOs like the UN (Fassbender [2006]; Cohen [2012]). This due process problem has prompted a plethora of litigation in national and regional courts challenging the implementation of UN sanctions – including in the famous *Kadi* decisions by the EU courts between 2005 and 2013 (*Kadi and Al Barakaat v Council and Commission* [2008]; see also chapter on Judicial review (European Union)). It has also catalysed the development of two distinctive global administrative redress mechanisms that seek to provide "fair and clear procedures" for those affected by UN sanctions: the UN Focal Point (established in 2006) and the UN Office of the Ombudsperson (established in 2009) (Kingsbury et al. [2005]; UNGA Res 60/1 [2005]).

This entry briefly analyses the emergence of these UN sanction redress mechanisms and describes their key features. This emergence is often presented as an evolution and a sign of the UN's incremental movement towards greater respect for human rights norms (Heupel [2011]; Biersteker and Eckert [2012]). But I suggest that these measures are better understood as ad hoc procedural responses to crises provoked by the UN Security Council's (UNSC) extraordinary use of Chapter VII powers to target individuals as global security threats. In particular, the Ombudsperson mechanism was introduced to try to undermine the threat of EU judicial review following the Court of Justice of the European Union's (CJEU) groundbreaking 2008 *Kadi* decision and was designed to protect the Council's use of secret intelligence as evidence in UN counterterrorism sanctions. In other words, these forms of redress are less concerned with protecting due process and the rights of individuals affected by UN sanctions, and more concerned with bolstering the UNSC's exceptional global governance powers in the face of political and legal tension (Sullivan [2020]; True-Frost [2011]).

II The UN Focal Point

Originally, no procedural mechanism was available for individuals and entities subject to UN targeted sanctions to request that those measures be reviewed. In 2002, guidelines were introduced to the 1267 counterterrorism sanctions regime allowing those affected by UN sanctions to "petition the government of residence and/or citizenship to request review of the case". The petitioned government could (but need not) then approach the government that proposed the listing (the designating state) and ask for delisting, via a "redress" process that more closely resembled a bilateral diplomatic negotiation between states. The inadequacies of this diplomatic process was noted by the EU Court of First Instance (now General Court) in the first *Kadi* case (*Yassin Abdullah Kadi v Council of the European Union* [2005]). Mr Kadi's requests for Saudi Arabia to intervene and seek his delisting before the Sanctions Committee were ignored. The Court's decision confirmed that this diplomatic process was flawed in terms of protecting due process rights, as it gave no right to affected individuals to be heard or to defend themselves before the Sanctions Committee.

The following year, the UNSC established a new procedural mechanism known as the Focal Point within the UN Secretariat for receiving delisting requests from those subject to UN sanctions (UNSC Res 1730 [2006]). While it was justified as a means of providing "fair and clear procedures" for UN sanctions, it was designed as "more of a political message than anything else" (US Embassy Cable 06USUNNEWYORK917_a). The Focal Point receives delisting requests from petitioners, triages them to the designating state and government of the petitioner's citizenship or residence for their consideration, liaises with the relevant sanctions committee if needed, and then informs the petitioner of the outcome. It does not substantively consider the delisting request in any way, make any recommendations, or provide reasoning to the petitioner if the request is refused. It functions as little more than an administrative mailbox (Terlingen [2011]; van den Herik [2014]).

The Focal Point was proposed by France after considerable debate by the UNSC P5, and strong support from the highly influential Watson Institute Targeted Sanctions Project (Watson Institute [2006]). The United States had originally proposed that national states create their own mechanisms for administering delisting requests and argued that any delisting procedures should be strictly confined to the 1267 counterterrorism sanctions regime, where most sanctions litigation was arising (US Embassy Cables 06USUNNEWYORK917_a; 06USUNNEWYORK1078). France opposed this, arguing that having delisting requests considered at the UN level was important for European states concerned about due process because it would provide them with a degree of cover for their listing work and allow them to better "protect themselves" from listing-related controversy and litigation (US Embassy Cable 06USUNNEWYORK917_a). Concern for the rights of those adversely affected by UN sanctions, in other words, was hardly a consideration. The Focal Point was rather an ad hoc political compromise designed to offer a "visible change to procedures" across all sanctions regimes, without disturbing the status quo (US Embassy Cable 06USUNNEWYORK917_a). It has been widely discredited by UN member states and courts alike for its lack of independence, its wholly diplomatic and intergovernmental procedures, and its failure to afford those sanctioned by the UNSC with any meaningful right to be heard (UNSC [2007]; *Kadi and Al Barakaat v Council and Commission* [2008] para. 323).

The CJEU's 2008 *Kadi* decision was the primary catalyst for the next major round of UN procedural reforms. That decision sent shockwaves through world capitals for its potential to challenge and erode support for the Council's extraordinary post-9/11 extension of its Chapter VII powers (UNSC [2011] para. 30; Sullivan [2020] 206–20). P5 states were especially keen to introduce reforms that might placate the CJEU and "put off the courts" (US Embassy Cable 09LONDON452). As the former US Ambassador to the UN Susan Rice warned in a cable titled "*1267: Saving the Al-Qaeda/Taliban Sanctions Regime*": "Bold action is needed to salvage the UN's 1267 al-Qaeda … targeted sanctions regime … [which] has been seriously undermined by criticisms – and adverse European court rulings – asserting that procedures for listing and delisting … are not adequately fair and clear" (US Embassy Cable 09USUNNEWYORK818). As another cable from this period put it: "we cannot risk losing the use of one of our few non-military coercive tools because the EU courts believe that they are somehow illegitimate". To counter this risk, a "coordinated US interagency strategy" targeting EU leaders to "protect these policies from legal challenge" was needed, and further UN procedural reforms ought to be crafted (US Embassy Cable 09BRUSSELS616). It was these fractious conditions that led to the adoption of UNSC Resolution 1904 [(2009)] and its creation of a novel form of global administrative redress for the UN 1267 sanctions regime: the UN Office of the Ombudsperson. Again, the primary aim was to preserve the tool of UN targeted sanctions and the long-term credibility of the Council's novel post-9/11 use of global sanction powers by defusing political and legal critique, not the promotion of human rights or international due process.

III The UN Office of the Ombudsperson

The Ombudsperson procedure enabled targeted individuals for the first time to submit delisting applications to an independent legal expert requesting removal from the UN's 1267 counterterrorism sanctions list. It was first proposed by Denmark – a member of the so-called group of like-minded states that have long pushed for incremental due process procedural reforms to UN sanctions – and was strongly advocated for by an influential Transnational Policy Network (TPN) spearheaded by international relations scholars from the Watson Institute (Biersteker [2024]; Sullivan [2020] 153–77). After gathering information from listed persons and engaging in dialogue and undertaking "dialogue meetings" with petitioners, the Ombudsperson compiles a "comprehensive report" that recommends either retention of the sanctions or delisting. This report is then sent to the UN 1267 Sanctions Committee to assist it in taking its confidential decision. In 2011, a reverse consensus procedure was introduced to bolster the Ombudsperson's recommendation powers (UNSC Res 1989 [2011]). Under this procedure, the listings automatically terminate 60 days after an Ombudsperson delisting recommendation unless the UNSC decides by consensus that they should remain in place, or if there is no consensus, the Sanctions Committee can refer the matter to the UNSC with a view to overturning the Ombudsperson's recommendation. These procedures for overriding the Ombudsperson's delisting recommendations, however, have not been used to date. As of December 2024, the Office of the Ombudsperson had completed 103 delisting investigations – with 71 (69%) of these resulting in delisting, and 32 (31%) resulting in the continuation of the sanctions (UNSC Sanctions Committees [n.d.] Status of Cases).

These relative rates of success and respect for the Ombudsperson's delisting recommendations by the Sanctions Committee have led some scholars and policy practitioners to take a functionalist, outcome-orientated approach in their analysis of this novel global administrative redress mechanism. Some versions of this functionalist scholarship strongly argue in favour of the Ombudsperson procedure as a form of "de facto judicial review" that effectively resolves the UN's long-standing due process problem (Biersteker and Eckert [2012]) and criticise the non-recognition of the Ombudsperson mechanism by the EU courts as hegemonic interference with bona fide efforts to create greater international accountability for UN targeted sanctions (van den Herik [2014]). Other versions of this functionalist approach analyse the Ombudsperson as a "surprisingly effective review body" that makes an important incremental step in the right direction towards more responsive UN sanctions, even though there are still persistent legal flaws and "the entire process leaves much to be desired in terms of procedural fairness" (Lang [2023]).

Building on my practical experience of representing pro bono listed individuals in Ombudsperson delisting proceedings, my own research takes a less optimistic and more critical approach. I argue that the Office of the Ombudsperson is a quasi-legal procedure that performs important global security governance work, while leaving the structural inequalities and harms inflicted on individuals and groups by the Council's counterterrorism sanctions regime largely intact. It has helped to stabilise the UNSC's exceptional post-9/11 use of UN Charter powers and its unique global infrastructure for pre-emptively targeting individuals and groups from around the world as suspected terrorists by using intelligence-as-evidence and governing alleged terrorist "associations". The Ombudsperson procedure, in other words, is better understood as a quasi-legal extension of the UNSC's exceptional global security governance powers, rather than a human rights–inspired international redress mechanism that constrains these powers in any meaningful way or ameliorates their worst features (Sullivan and De Goede [2013]; Sullivan [2020]). For example, the Ombudsperson uses a so-called *de novo* approach that focuses on whether the petitioner poses a present security risk (UNSC Sanctions Committee [n.d. Approach and Standard]). But this approach deliberately leaves the original listing decision untouched, which protects the UNSC's unique prerogatives and authority in this area and allows states to use false intelligence, weak information, or indeed no information for listing individuals as potential terrorists without fear of it ever being challenged (Lang [2023] 54). It also means that individuals can be delisted – sometimes, as in the case of my clients, after more than a decade of being sanctioned – without having any real understanding of why they were targeted by UN sanctions in the first place.

IV Future challenges

So, despite the creation of these novel global administrative redress mechanisms, the due process problems effected through the Council's post-9/11 use of UN targeted sanctions powers persist today. In closing, I briefly highlight two challenges that will likely shape this global governance problem and related debates about the inequity of UN targeted sanctions regimes in the years ahead.

First, can the practical benefits of having access to an enhanced, individualised, and accelerated global delisting process be extended beyond UN counterterrorism sanctions to other UN sanctions regimes? Various efforts have been made throughout the years – particularly by the group of like-minded states and the targeted sanctions TPN assembled through the Watson Institute – to argue that the Office of the Ombudsperson mechanism ought to be extended to the other UN sanctions regimes. But these have all been firmly rebuffed by the P5. However, the UNSC recently adopted Resolution 2744 (2024), to strengthen the mandate of the UN Focal Point and transform it into "a robust framework that prioritises due process" (Sanctions Monitoring Board Malta [2024]). It seeks to do so by borrowing *some a*spects of the Ombudsperson process, while disregarding others. It gives the UN Focal Point new responsibilities for gathering substantive information, engaging in dialogue (including with petitioners), and producing comprehensive reports for Sanction Committee consideration. However, these reports will only summarise relevant information. The Focal Point will not make specific recommendations to list or delist, and so there are no equivalent reverse consensus procedures built in that could strengthen the mechanism or accelerate its delisting potential over time (UNSC Res 2744 [2024]). So, while this reform was celebrated by the UN as "the first major revision of delisting procedures in 18 years", it remains to be seen whether it will result in any meaningful improvements for those adversely affected by UN targeted sanctions. It is also possible that, in time, the Ombudsperson's powers will be whittled down even further to match the extremely limited powers of the new Focal Point mechanism, rather than the Focal Point mechanism progressively growing more procedurally robust over time as much of the functionalist sanctions scholarship on this issue is hoping for.

A second challenge concerns the potential for groups listed as "associated with" Al-Qaida (AQ) and ISIL to use the Ombudsperson delisting process to start challenging and disassembling the global AQ and ISIL network and related infrastructure created through the UN 1267 list in the post-9/11 period. Groups lumped together on the 1267 sanctions list as members of the global AQ and ISIL network may have no relation other than that drawn by the list itself (Sullivan [2020] 77). Some of those groups have since actively dissociated themselves from AQ and ISIL, but they nonetheless remain listed. Consider, for example, the case of Hayat Tahrir al-Sham (HTS). HTS were formerly affiliated with AQ and ISIL in Syria. But they appear to have since renounced those affiliations and have been in active conflict with both AQ and ISIL in Syria for some years. In December 2024, HTS spearheaded the successful insurgency in Syria that toppled the brutal authoritarian regime of Bashar al-Assad. They are now the key political actor within the new Syrian administration, evincing a practical and ideological shift "from jihad to politics" (Drevon [2024]). However, their ability to play a meaningful governance role in the newly liberated post-Assad Syria is severely constrained by the fact that they are still sanctioned by the UN as an alias of the Al-Nusrah Front and associated by the UN with AQ in Syria (The List established and maintained pursuant to Security Council Res 1267/1989/2253, List entry QDe.137). UN officials have intimated that sanctions might be lifted if HTS ensure an inclusive political transition process that is respectful of the rights of Syrian minorities (Wintour [2024]).

The profound impacts of UN terrorism listing and related national proscription regimes on conflict transformation processes have been well documented (Boon-Kuo et al. [2015]; Haspeslagh [2021]; Sentas [2020]; Dudouet [2010]). However, groups listed by the UN as associated with AQ, which have since shown "dissociation", have not yet brought delisting requests to the UN Office of the Ombudsperson to test the veracity of the Ombudsperson's *de novo* assessment standard. Such an intervention could potentially raise profound issues about the nature and purpose of UN counterterrorism sanctions. For example: is the UNSC capable of effectively differentiating armed Islamist insurgencies from "terrorism" in the Middle East in circumstances where listed groups can effectively show terrorist "dissociation" and behaviour change? Could such a case lead the UNSC to overturn the Ombudsperson's recommendations for the first time, and what are the political implications of such a scenario? Given the preponderance of stale listings, the lack of proactive delisting of dissociated groups by the Council since 9/11, and current transformative events unfolding in the Middle East, such delisting challenges - testing the limits of the Ombudsperson process and challenging the core assumptions of the post-9/11 global security architecture - will likely become both more pressing and prevalent in the years ahead.

Bibliography

Literature

Biersteker T and Eckert S, *Due Process and Targeted Sanctions: An Update of the 'Watson Report'* (Graduate Institute for the Study of International Governance and Watson Institute for International Studies 2012).

Biersteker T, 'The Role of Transnational Policy Networks in Informal Governance' in Abbott K and Biersteker T (eds), *Informal Governance in World Politics* (Cambridge University Press 2024) 215.

Boon-Kuo L, Hayes B, Sentas V and Sullivan G, *Building Peace in Permanent War: Terrorist Listing and Conflict Transformation* (International State Crime Initiative 2015).

Cohen JL, *Globalization and Sovereignty: Rethinking Legality, Legitimacy, and Constitutionalism* (Cambridge University Press 2012).

Cortright D and Lopez GA (eds), *The Sanctions Decade: Assessing UN Strategies in the 1990s* (Lynne Rienner 2000).

Drevon J, *From Jihad to Politics: How Syrian Jihadis Embraced Politics* (Oxford University Press 2024).

Dudouet V, *Mediating Peace with Proscribed Armed Groups* (US Institute of Peace 2010).

Fassbender B, 'Targeted Sanctions Imposed by the UN Security Council and Due Process Rights' (2006) 3 *International Organizations Law Review* 437.

Haspeslagh S, *Proscribing Peace: How Listing Armed Groups as Terrorists Hurts Negotiations* (Manchester University Press 2021).

Heupel M, 'With Power Comes Responsibility: Human Rights Protection in United Nations Sanctions Policy' (2011) 19(4) *European Journal of International Relations* 773.

Hovell D, 'Due Process in the United Nations' (2016) 110(1) *American Journal of International Law* 9.

Kingsbury B, Krisch N and Stewart RB, 'The Emergence of Global Administrative Law' (2005) 68(3/4) *Law and Contemporary Problems* 15.

Lang A, 'Alternatives to Adjudication in International Law: A Case Study of the Ombudsperson to the ISIL and Al-Qaida Sanctions Regime of the UN Security Council' (2023) 117(1) *American Journal of International Law* 48.

Megret F and Hoffman F, 'The UN as a Human Rights Violator? Some Reflections on the United Nations Changing Human Rights Responsibility' (2003) 25 *Human Rights Quarterly* 315.

Sanctions Monitoring Board Malta, 'The Adoption of Resolution 2744 (2024): Enhancing Transparency and Due Process in United Nations Sanctions' (smb.gov.mt 2 August 2024) <https://bit.ly/4gnugzC>.

Sentas V, 'Terrorist Organization Proscription as Counterinsurgency in the Kurdish Conflict' in Jarvis L and Legrand T (eds), *The Proscription of Terrorist Organisations: Modern Blacklisting in Global Perspective* (Routledge 2020) 98.

Sullivan G and De Goede M, 'Between Law and the Exception: The UN 1267 Ombudsperson as a Hybrid Model of Legal Expertise' (2013) 26(4) *Leiden Journal of International Law* 833.

Sullivan G, *The Law of the List: UN Counterterrorism Sanctions and the Politics of Global Security Law* (Cambridge University Press 2020).

Terlingen Y, 'The United States and the UN's Targeted Sanctions of Suspected Terrorists: What Role for Human Rights?' (2010) 24(2) *Ethics & International Affairs* 131.

Tomuschat C, *Human Rights: Between Idealism and Realism* (Oxford University Press 2003).

Gavin Sullivan

True-Frost C, 'The Development of Individual Standing in International Security' (2011) 32(4) *Cardozo Law Review* 1183.

Van Den Herik L, 'Peripheral Hegemony in the Quest to Ensure Security Council Accountability for Its Individualized UN Sanctions Regimes' (2014) 19(3) *Journal of Conflict and Security Law* 427.

Watson Institute, *Strengthening Targeted Sanctions through Fair and Clear Procedures: White Paper* (Watson Institute for International Studies 2006).

Weiss T, Cortright D, Lopez GA and Minear L (eds), *Political Gain and Civilian Pain: The Humanitarian Impacts of Economic Sanctions* (Rowman & Littlefield 1997).

Wintour P, 'UN May Remove Syrian Rebel Group HTS from Terror List if Conditions are Met', *The Guardian* (10 December 2024).

Documents

Case T-315/01 Yassin Abdullah Kadi v Council of the European Union [2005] ECLI:EU:T:2005:332 ECR II-3649.

Joined Cases C-402/05 P and C-415/05 P Kadi and Al Barakaat International Foundation v Council and Commission [2008] ECLI:EU:C:2008:461 ECR I-6351.

UNGA, '2005 World Summit Outcome' Res 60/1 (24 October 2005) UN Doc. A/RES/60/1.

UNSC Sanctions Committee, 'Ombudsperson to the ISIL (Da'esh) and Al-Qaida Sanctions Committee' (main.un.org) Status of Cases <https://main.un.org/securitycouncil/en/sc/ombudsperson/status-of-cases>.

UNSC Sanctions Committee, 'Ombudsperson to the ISIL (Da'esh) and Al-Qaida Sanctions Committee' (main.un.org) Approach and Standard <https://main.un.org/securitycouncil/en/ombudsperson/approach-and-standard>.

UNSC, 'Verbatim Record of the 5599th Meeting' (22 January 2007) UN Doc. S/PV.5599.

UNSC, 'Letter Dated 14 April 2011 from the Permanent Representative of Lebanon to the United Nations Addressed to the Secretary-General' (18 April 2011) UN Doc. S/2011/245.

UNSC, Res 1730 (19 December 2006) S/RES/1730.

UNSC, Res 1904 (17 December 2009) S/RES/1904.

UNSC, Res 1989 (17 June 2011) S/RES/1989.

UNSC, Res 2744 (19 July 2024) S/RES/2744.

72. United Nations expert panels

Caty Clément

I Introduction

Expert panels serve as the 'eyes and ears' of the United Nations Security Council (UNSC) on the sanctioned country, institution or issue. These panels are typically tasked with investigating issues such as the trade in natural resources fuelling the arms trade, assessing compliance with sanctions, evaluating the potential impact of sanctions, identifying sources of financing for targeted armed groups, recommending actions to prevent sanction violations, naming individuals or entities violating sanctions, and monitoring the activities of individuals and entities already listed.

Expert panels and monitoring bodies have served since the late 1990s as indispensable sanctions enforcement tools, which explain why they supported nearly all sanctions committees. Until a few years ago, they had become such a standard component of sanctions that their absence was perceived as a lack of commitment by the UNSC (see chapter). Expert panels proliferated after it was perceived that contentious issues were better raised by independent experts rather than states' representatives. Expert groups are not bound by the United Nations (UN) diplomatic protocols and political consensus, allowing them to provide potentially controversial information that UNSC members may choose to distance themselves from (Carisch et al. [2017]). Despite their success, they have over the years faced due process and political challenges.

II History of expert panels

Contrary to many regional or unilateral sanctions often used as low-key warfare strategies, UN sanctions aim to pursue world peace and improve human welfare. The first expert group was a case in point: it focused on human rights and democratisation with the 'voluntary' sanctions regime against apartheid South Africa in December 1963.

The panels emerged as in the absence of an independent monitoring mechanism, sanctions regimes were often ineffective. For example, the arms embargo in Rwanda was largely ineffective until the establishment of an International Commission of Inquiry in 1995, which engaged in more robust and independent monitoring.

The development of expert groups has been a gradual and iterative process. The evolution had three phases: first, the recognition that sanctions without monitoring were ineffective; second, the understanding that panels needed genuine investigative powers; and third, the importance of professional standards, which were notably promoted by the Group of Friends. First, private companies and UN staff were tested. The UN contracted private companies to recruit its experts: for instance, the Iraq Group of Experts, established in June 1998 under the Oil-for-Food Programme (OFFP), was staffed by Saybolt Nederland BV to provide independent oil inspection agents. Similarly, Kroll Associates were used in Angola (see chapter) in 2001 to second a weakened monitoring group. Second, expert panels also existed independently of sanctions regimes, such as the panel on the illegal exploitation of natural resources in Congo in the early 2000s, which investigated the role of natural resource trade in fuelling conflict before a sanctions regime was established. The Kassem reports, as they became known, named and shamed individuals, companies, and countries, but no sanctions could be implemented in the absence of an active regime. Similarly, the Council also decided to retain the experts in Liberia and Côte d'Ivoire to monitor natural resources after the embargoes had been lifted. In 2024, the expert panel on the Central African Republic too was retained while the sanctions regime was lifted. Third, the contrary occurred after the expert panel of the non-proliferation regime on the Democratic People's Republic of Korea (DPRK) (see chapter) was terminated in early 2024, while the sanctions regime still exists.

Challenges arose, especially after the post 9/11 al-Qaida regime named several hundred individuals, entities, or states. Some of the accused engaged in litigations, which ultimately lead to the establishment of clear evidentiary standards.

III Institutional setup

1 Nomination

The expert panels are part of a broader ecosystem established to support UN sanctions regimes. Panels are subsidiary organs of the UNSC, which determines the substance of the mandate, the number of experts, and the duration of the expert group's activities. The day-to-day oversight of expert bodies is managed by the relevant sanctions committee and the UN Secretariat (UN DPPA [2023]).

The UNSC Subsidiary Organs Branch (SCSOB), which is part of the UNSC Affairs Division (SCAD) within the Department of Political and Peacebuilding Affairs (DPPA), is responsible for recruiting, managing, and supporting the expert groups as well as the sanctions committees. It maintains a roster of experts with the required profiles and, while external candidates are considered, the same experts are often reappointed due to the difficulty of finding qualified individuals. Experts must possess technical expertise, autonomous investigative skills, diplomacy, the ability to educate states and peacekeeping missions on complex sanctions regimes, handle vulnerable sources, and uphold professional standards, including in their own personal behaviour.

SCAD's recruitment process considers the specific expertise required by each mandate. The Secretariat conducts interviews and proposes a list of its preferred candidates to the appropriate sanctions committee. Historically, the Secretariat's expert groups were predominantly composed of Western males, but efforts have been made to increase gender and geographical diversity. Experts are submitted to a 48-hour no-objection procedure, whereby a single committee member can object to a proposed candidate. Over the past decade, objections against specific nominees have been more frequent, reflecting geopolitical power struggles. After 48 hours, the Secretariat's proposal is considered approved. All experts have equal status, although one may be nominated as chair to handle political coordination, which includes asking states to report on actions taken to prevent sanction violations. For a while, when the need arose and when the budget was less tight, the Secretariat hired specific technical consultants for the group.

The experts' independence is crucial; however, it faces important caveats. First, because SCAD nominates experts, handles the expert group's budget, organises their travel, access to the archives, and handles formal communications, SCAD de facto yields considerable leverage over the experts far beyond what one might consider mere administrative support. Second, states can influence the appointment process either by lobbying for their nationals or by vetoing proposed experts who make unpopular proposals to the sanctions committee. A notable example of this occurred in 2007 when the Democratic Republic of the Congo (DRC) expert body proposed that a certification of the origin of precious minerals should be used to separate legitimate from illegitimate mining companies. The proposal faced significant resistance from certain member states and experts were let go, but the idea was eventually enlarged to serve as a corporate due diligence framework and enshrined in international conflict mineral laws. Third, knowing the risks, experts may self-censor and refrain from airing potentially unpopular proposals. Fourth, states have been interventionist in the nomination process of the former non-proliferation (Iran and DPRK) and anti-global terrorist (Al-Qaida and ISIL) panels, whose experts presented themselves by nationality rather than expertise (Vines [2003] 260; Farrall [2009]).

To preserve their independence, experts are hired as external consultants rather than staff, which has implications for their safety. Unlike UN staff members, experts do not receive a UN passport but are issued a travel certificate, which provides less protection than the laissez-passer granted to UN staff. Despite having to take significant risks, especially when working in conflict zones, experts thus face reduced support in the event of harm. Since two experts were killed while investigating the DRC in 2017, the experts' ability to operate independently has been constrained. The loose status also creates challenges with other UN bodies: they may at times be reluctant to share information with expert panels or grant the experts a low travel priority level while they depend on the in-country UN mission to move in conflict-affected areas.

The most effective sanction regimes are those where there is a strong engagement by both the experts and the sanctions committee. Strong engagement by the committee chair, including in the form of visiting missions, may help to offset many political difficulties. The level of engagement between the expert body and the relevant committee varies considerably, ranging from very close to occasional. There was, for instance, a strong collaboration during the late 1990s in the Angola sanctions regime under the Canadian sanctions committee chair, Ambassador Fowler. However, in many cases, contacts may be more occasional at the beginning of its mandate and towards reporting times, depending on the committee's capacity and willingness to engage.

2 *Reporting and oversight*

Each expert body is required to report to the UNSC at the end of its mandate, with interim reports submitted for longer mandates and monthly progress reports. The final report is submitted for public release, while most interim and monthly reports remain confidential. Additionally, confidential annexes listing recommendations of individuals and entities proposed for designations that include sensitive personal details must remain secret to preserve the effectiveness of the asset freeze. The report-writing process is often contentious, as each expert has to sign off on the full content of the report and therefore yields a de facto power over the final report. Disagreements may arise over evidentiary standards, the interpretation of facts, or the timing to publish ongoing investigations. In cases where experts are not independent but represent their country's interests, the process becomes even more politicised, which may lead to the reports being leaked before they are officially released. Once all the experts have signed off on the report, it moves to the secretary of the sanctions committee for submission to the chair of the sanctions committee and political vetting.

All expert groups used to report to their sanction committee whose chair refers the report to the Council. Over the past ten years, this practice has changed and most panels now report directly to the UNSC. There is a key difference between the two despite the fact that the same countries are members of both the Council and the sanction committee. Contrary to the Council, the committees operate by consensus and there is no record of their decision-making processes. Occasionally, committee members have used this opacity to block the release of a report or coerce a panel to modify specific statements. The intention, however, is for the sanctions committees to review the report, debate its findings, and draw from the experts' recommendations before taking the committees' decisions to the UNSC, where sometimes the panel's findings can lead to a revised sanctions regime. However, when no political consensus can be found, sanctions resolutions are often reduced to a 'technical renewal' extending the mandate of the experts with no substantive changes.

Once the expert body's report is approved by the sanctions committee, the chair forwards it to the UNSC for consideration. At this point, the report becomes a public document, typically coinciding with the Council's periodic review of the sanctions regime. However, the Council often refrains from acting on recommendations made by expert groups, and many recommendations go unimplemented. While in some regimes, the panel's recommendations have decisively changed the course of UNSC action (e.g. the DRC regime), in particularly contentious sanctions regimes (e.g. Sudan), these recommendations are often ignored. UNSC member states may decide to act on information from other sources within the UN (special envoys/rapporteurs, peacekeeping, or political missions) or outside. The Council will also decide whether to extend the mandate of the expert body and, if so, whether changes to its terms of reference are necessary.

IV Success and challenges

The effectiveness of expert panels is crucial to the success of sanctions regimes. They have generally investigated everything that allows a state or an illegal armed group to acquire weapons, including in-kind and financial support. As such, they have contributed to highlighting how natural resources have fuelled conflict. The sanctions regimes in Angola, followed by Sierra Leone, Liberia, and Côte d'Ivoire, stressed how diamonds fuelled the conflict and would serve as a blueprint for the Kimberley certification process. Against strong opposition, the panels working on the DRC similarly, after identifying the role played by natural resources (tin, tantalum, tungsten, and gold, in particular) in sustaining or amplifying the conflict, developed concrete due diligence steps multinational companies could adopt to ensure they were not supplied by conflict minerals. These due diligence steps were taken up by the Organisation for Economic Cooperation and Development (OECD) and were included in the US 2010 Dodd–Frank Act, as well as in the 2017 EU regulations.

What makes expert panels effective? Successful monitoring depends on several factors: the capacity to coordinate, the political dynamics within the sanctions committee and the UNSC, and the quality of the investigative process.

1 Coordination

The degree of coordination depends on the mandate, the leadership of the expert panel and the chair of the sanctions committee, personal contacts, and the willingness of states to cooperate. Coordination occurs at various levels:

(1) between the UN sanctions' ecosystem (sanctions committees, Secretariat, within and between expert panels);
(2) with other UN bodies (peacekeeping, political missions, special envoys);
(3) with external actors involved in conflict resolution (e.g. negotiations, peace processes); and crucially
(4) member states, whose cooperation is required under Article 25 of the UN Charter.

While most of the focus to comply rests on the sanctioned country, the full cooperation of member states is critical to the regime's success. Unfortunately, such cooperation is often lacking, even among P5 members. Few respond to requests to submit reports, and those that do often provide single-paragraph letters stating that steps have been taken towards implementation. Some of the world's more robust countries have been particularly reluctant to hold themselves and their economic operators accountable.

2 Political consensus

In many regimes, the three Western P5 (the United States, the United Kingdom, and France) were the sanctions resolutions penholders, which partly explains why China and Russia hold the most reservations on sanctions and expert panels. A few years ago, several panels were paralysed after P5 members threatened to block their renewal. The current erosion of global consensus has had a considerable impact on sanctions regimes: potential sanctions regimes (against Syria or Israel, for example) did not manage to gather P5 support, other panels had to reduce their activities, while the traditionally well-endowed group of experts on non-proliferation has disappeared. Non-proliferation regimes have either been terminated (Iran) or no longer have an expert group (DPRK), signalling a lack of global consensus. This is particularly symptomatic as, until recently, panels addressing counter-terrorism (Al-Qaida) and non-proliferation (DPRK and Iran) were always far better endowed. Their financial support was more than double that of all the other regimes combined. In terms of staff, the panels were not only larger in terms of the number of experts, but they also benefited from the support of several staffers. Their political clout was such that they were able to have more persons or entities listed than all the other regimes combined. Recent budget cuts in the UN have led to late payments and a substantial reduction in travel (Boucher and Clement [2016]).

3 Professional standards

The current fragmentation of the global world order further makes the need for the establishment of robust technical standards for sanctions implementation particularly urgent. The disparity in levels of supporting evidence required between the different panels, the need to protect vulnerable interviewees, and an explosion of listed individuals and entities in the Al-Qaida/ISIL panel spurred efforts to develop professional standards for expert panels (Vines [2003]). The UNSC's Informal Working Group on General Issues of Sanctions ('Sanctions Working Group') has attempted to implement best practices and due process throughout the sanctions cycle, notably through a best practice guide (Carisch and Rickard-Martin [2020]).

Bibliography

Literature

Boucher A and Clement C, 'Coordination of United Nations Sanctions with Other Actors and Instruments' in Biersteker TJ, Eckert SE and Tourinho M (eds), *Targeted Sanctions: The Impacts and Effectiveness of United Nations Action* (Cambridge University Press 2016) 119.

Carisch E and Rickard-Martin L, *Best Practices Guide for Chairs and Members of United Nations Sanctions Committees* (Compliance and Capacity Skills International, New York, 2020).

Carisch E, Rickard-Martin L and Meister SR, 'From Comprehensive to Smart and Fairer Sanctions' in *The Evolution of UN*

Sanctions: From a Tool of Warfare to a Tool of Peace, Security and Human Rights (Springer International Publications 2017) 51.

Farrall J, 'Should the United Nations Security Council Leave it to the Experts? The Governance and Accountability of UN Sanctions Monitoring' in Farrall J and Rubenstein K (eds), *Sanctions, Accountability and Governance in a Globalised World* (Cambridge University Press 2009) 191.

Vines A, 'Monitoring UN Sanctions in Africa: The Role of Panels of Experts' in Findlay T (ed.), *Vertic Yearbook 2003* (Vertic 2003) 247.

Document

UN DPPA, 'Subsidiary Organs of the United Nations Security Council', Factsheet (2023).

CATY CLÉMENT

PART V

OBJECTIVES

73. Sanctions against autocratic regimes

Clara Portela

I Introduction

Scholars generally posit that sanctions are more likely to be successful when imposed against targets featuring a democratic political system rather than an autocratic system (Bergeijk [1997]). This question is of central importance to the study of sanctions effectiveness given that most target countries of sanctions are non-democratic. Only recently, however, have insights from the study of autocracies been transferred to sanctions scholarship, opening up a promising avenue of research. This question became increasingly relevant as African organisations (see chapter on African Union and ECOWAS) established themselves as sanctions senders in the early twenty-first century (Corda [2024]).

II Democracy versus autocracy

The authors of the seminal study *Economic Sanctions Reconsidered* (Hufbauer et al. [2007]) evaluate the target's regime type on a three-point scale running from autocracy to democracy, relying on data from Polity IIId ([2007] 67), confirming that democracies 'are more open to voices advocating a policy shift than autocratic countries. If important internal groups see merit in a policy change, that view is more likely to find advocates within the top circles of a democratic government'. Since democracies have larger selectorates (defined as the set of individuals endowed with political rights within a state), sanctions pose a larger threat to democratic leaders. Democratic rulers have to satisfy majorities of their citizens in order to survive, whereas autocratic governments depend on a small selectorate while constraining the political freedom of the majority. In addition, autocrats have direct control over state resources and are able to protect their supporters from the economic burden of sanctions (Escribà-Folch [2011]). Indeed, the influence over the distribution of scarce goods strengthens the regime's bargaining power domestically, making the continuation of sanctions acceptable if not advantageous (Allen [2005]).

Building on its focus on regime survival, research on dictatorships explored whether sanctions against autocracies can promote democratisation. Marinov found that governments that come under economic sanctions are more likely to lose office because lower economic growth hurts the political survival of leaders. Still, democratic leaders are more likely to be replaced than autocrats: sanctions pressure causes more government instability in democratic than in autocratic regimes (Marinov [2005] 573), with sanctions increasing the probability of leadership destabilisation only by a small margin (Jones [2015]). However, the imposition of economic sanctions can display a negative effect on prospects for a transition to democracy by weakening the opposition and consolidating authoritarian rule because the targeted leadership instrumentalises the economic hardship to restrict political liberties and increase repression (Drury and Peksen [2010]), as illustrated in the case of Iraq (see chapter). Other analyses discriminate between comprehensive and targeted sanctions, positing that sanctions interact with regime type in different ways: targeted sanctions are more likely to succeed when employed against autocracies but will only achieve moderate success against democracies. By contrast, comprehensive sanctions are likely to be more effective against democracies but counterproductive against dictatorships (Brooks [2002]). Sadly, these claims lack conclusive empirical confirmation.

III Autocratic types

Recent advances focus on different autocratic types, highlighting that different kinds of authoritarianism differ from each other as much as they differ from democracy. Barbara Geddes subdivides autocratic regimes into three broad categories to account for their resilience. In military regimes, a group of officers decides who will rule and exercises some influence on policy. By contrast, in single-party regimes, access to political office and control over policy are dominated by one party. Personalist regimes differ from both other types in that access to office depends on the discretion of an individual leader (Geddes [1999] 121). Her study finds that military regimes are generally more vulnerable to pressure than personalist regimes, and that these are, in turn, less resilient than single-party regimes. Because the military elite is more susceptible to splits and displays more readiness to relinquish power in order to preserve internal cohesion, military regimes are more fragile. Personalist regimes are less prone to internal splits, but in turn are very vulnerable to violent overthrow or the death of the leader. Single-party regimes are the most resilient because an organisation exercises some power over the leader, and controls the career path of officials and the distribution of benefits to supporters. Through their control over the allocation of educational and career opportunities, single parties can co-opt the brightest individuals in society and are more likely to broaden their clientele beyond a particular group (Geddes [1999] 124). Their institutional structures enable them to allow greater popular participation without giving up their dominant role in the political system. While more institutionalised regimes tend to rely more on the co-optation of elites and broader segments of society, less institutionalised regimes rely more on narrow support groups and repression to maintain power (Davenport [2007]).

Because autocratic types are connected to specific mechanisms of regime survival, they generate plausible expectations of their vulnerability or resilience to sanctions pressure. The application of Geddesian types to sanctions research suggests that personalist regimes (and monarchies) are more likely to be destabilised by sanctions because they are more sensitive to the loss of external sources of revenue to fund patronage. Single-party and military regimes are, by contrast, more resilient to sanctions pressure because they can increase their tax revenues and reallocate expenditure to increase their levels of co-optation and repression (Escribà-Folch and Wright [2010]; Peksen [2017]). Similarly, the economic costs of sanctions are most likely to entail political costs in personalist dictatorships, with the caveat that the availability of oil revenue renders dictatorships resilient to sanctions pressure, irrespective of their type. These findings can be extended to studies of development aid suspensions as foreign policy tools (Portela and Mora-Sanguinetti [2023, 2025]).

IV Conclusion

While research on autocratic survival established that democracies are generally more vulnerable to sanctions than autocracies (Marinov [2005]; Allen [2005]), early analyses did not contemplate a subdivision of autocracies into regime types. Recent research using Geddes's categorisation of autocratic regimes found that personalist regimes are more vulnerable to sanctions than single-party or military regimes because they are poorly equipped to deal with pressure.

Bibliography

Literature

Allen SH, 'The Determinants of Economic Sanctions Success and Failure' (2005) 31(2) *International Interactions* 117.

Bergeijk P van, 'Economic Sanctions: Why Do They Succeed; Why Do They Fail?' in van Genugten WJM and de Groot GA (eds), *United Nations Sanctions* (Intersentia 1999) 97.

Brooks R, 'Sanctions and Regime Type: What Works, and When' (2002) 11(4) *Security Studies* 1.

Corda T, 'Democratic Sanctions in Africa' in Bultrini A, Giumelli F, Portela C and Sossai M (eds), *International Sanctions in Practice: An Interdisciplinary Perspective* (Routledge 2024) 161.

Davenport C, 'State Repression and Political Order' (2007) 10(1) *Annual Review of Political Science* 1.

Escribà-Folch A, 'Authoritarian Responses to Foreign Pressure: Spending, Repression and Sanctions' (2011) 20(10) *Comparative Political Studies* 1.

Escribà-Folch A and Wright J, 'Dealing with Tyranny. International Sanctions and the Survival of Authoritarian Rulers' (2010) 54(2) *International Studies Quarterly* 33.

Geddes B, 'What Do We Know about Democratisation after Twenty Years?' (1999) 2(1) *Annual Review of Political Science* 115.

Hufbauer GC et al., *Economic Sanctions Reconsidered: History and Current Policy* (Peterson Institute for International Economics 2007).

Jones L, *Societies under Siege* (Oxford University Press 2015).

Marinov N, 'Do Economic Sanctions Destabilise Country Leaders?' (2005) 49(3) *American Journal of Political Science* 564.

Peksen D, 'Autocracies and Economic Sanctions: The Divergent Impact of Authoritarian Regime Type on Sanctions Success' (2017) 30(3) *Defence and Peace Economics* 253.

Portela C and Mora-Sanguinetti JS, 'Sanctions Effectiveness, Development and

Regime Type. Are Aid Suspensions and Economic Sanctions Alike?' (2023) 172 *World Development* 106370.

Portela C and Mora-Sanguinetti JS, 'Aid Sanctions and Hybrid Regimes' (2025) 61(10) *Journal of Development Studies* 1555.

Clara Portela

74. Sanctions against organised crime

Charmaine N. Willis

I Introduction: the emergence of anti-narcotics sanctions

Senders of economic sanctions typically have specific goals in mind when they impose sanctions on their targets (ranging from states to non-state actors). While sanctions have been used consistently for some goals over time (such as defending human rights), other goals have emerged due to changes in the international system and states' domestic politics. For example, in the Global Sanctions Database, sanctions with "other objectives" have increased significantly since the 1990s (Syropoulos et al. [2024] 18). Among sanctions used for "other objectives" are those aimed at countering organised crime, such as drug trafficking. While the United States has been the primary sender of anti-narcotics sanctions since the 1990s, other senders are levying sanctions to address other forms of organised crime. A most notable example is the United Nations Security Council (UNSC) sanctions to counter gang violence in Haiti starting in 2022.

II Anti-narcotics regulations in the United States

Since the beginning of the post–World War II era, the United States has been the most prolific state sender of economic sanctions (Syropoulos et al. [2024] 20). While the US "War on Drugs" began in the 1970s under President Nixon (Guáqueta [2005] 28), sanctions were imposed to restrict the flow of narcotics coming into the country in the mid-1990s. The initial target of the US anti-narcotics sanctions was Colombia, a country whose relationship with the United States largely focused on combatting the production and distribution of narcotics (Guáqueta [2005]). At the time, the Clinton administration was under bipartisan pressure to target countries from where drugs were produced or transported to the United States, and transnational drug trafficking was viewed as threatening US security (Guáqueta [2005] 42). For its part, the Colombian government began emphasising the linkages between armed insurgent groups such as the Fuerzas Armadas Revolucionarias de Colombia (FARC) and transnational drug trafficking, which was the primary source of income for many armed groups in the country (Guáqueta [2005] 45–6). The linkage between armed non-state actors and drug trafficking is also an important aspect of the international community's use of sanctions in the case of Haiti since 2022 (see below).

The legal foundation for the US anti-narcotics sanctions emerged in this context. Three major sets of instruments are used to levy anti-narcotics sanctions in the United States (Rosen [2024] 1). The first is Executive Order (EO) 12978, issued by President Clinton in 1995, which was incorporated into the Office of Foreign Assets Control Narcotics Trafficking Sanctions Regulations in 1997. President Clinton issued EO 12978 using the International Emergency Economic Powers Act, citing the threats to US security posed by transnational drug trafficking, specifically from Colombia (Office of Foreign Assets Control [2014] 3). The Narcotics Trafficking Sanctions Regulations define a person or entity involved in drug trafficking as playing "a significant role in international narcotics trafficking centered in Colombia, supporting specially designated narcotics traffickers (including material, financial, or technological support), owned or controlled by a specially designated narcotics trafficker, or acting for or on behalf of a specially designated narcotics trafficker" (Office of Foreign Assets Control [2014] 3). Individuals determined to be narcotics traffickers may also be denied entry to the United States or denied US visas (Rosen [2024] 1).

The second set includes the Foreign Narcotics Kingpin Designation Act, also known as the Kingpin Act, which President Clinton signed into law in 1999. The Office of Foreign Assets Control (OFAC) created the Foreign Narcotics Kingpin Sanctions Regulations in 2000, which executed the Kingpin Act (Office of Foreign Assets Control [2014] 3). The Kingpin Act's stipulations regarding who may be deemed a specially designated narcotics trafficker and the nature of the sanctions (asset freezes) are similar to those of EO 12978, except that the Act broadens the scope of the sanctions beyond drug traffickers in Colombia to traffickers worldwide (Office of Foreign Assets Control [2014] 3). Beyond individuals and groups in Colombia, the Kingpin Act has also been invoked to sanction entities in Brazil, Mexico,

Myanmar, Nigeria, St Kitts, Thailand, and the United Kingdom, among others (Office of Foreign Assets Control [2000], [2003]).

The last set of anti-narcotics sanctions instruments began with EO 14059, issued by President Biden in 2021. The accompanying OFAC Illicit Drug Trade Sanctions Regulations were issued in 2022 (Illicit Drug Trade Sanctions Regulations [2022]). President Biden issued EO 14059 in the context of the opioid crisis in the United States, intending to stop the flow of fentanyl and other opioids coming into the United States. EO 14059 further expands on the Kingpin Act regarding who may be sanctioned and also includes individuals and entities "who knowingly receive property or an interest in property derived from illicit drug proceeds or used to facilitate illicit drug trade" (Rosen [2024] 1). In addition to the asset freezes and possible barriers to entering the United States prescribed by the previous regulations, EO 14059 authorises the use of financial sanctions on individuals or entities determined to be linked to drug trafficking. EO 14059 also allows the president to deny entry and/or a US visa to any individual "a corporate officer or principal of, or shareholder with a controlling interest in, a sanctioned entity" (Rosen [2024] 2).

To combat transnational organised crime, such as the groups primarily responsible for the current violence in Haiti, the United States also has sanctions instruments specific to combatting organised crime that it at times uses in concert with the above anti-narcotic instruments. For example, President Obama, citing threats to US national security, issued Executive Order 13581 in 2011 to target transnational organised crime (Executive Order 13581 – Blocking Property of Transnational Criminal Organisations [2011]). EO 13581 has targeted groups such as the Zhao Wei Transnational Criminal Organisation, a Laos-based group located within the Golden Triangle Special Economic Zone that has also been involved with drug trafficking (Office of Foreign Assets Control [2018]).

III UN sanctions against Haiti

One of the most recent applications of US anti-narcotics sanctions began in 2022, targeting individuals in Haiti linked to gang activity. While gangs have long existed in Haiti, they have traditionally been linked to political and business elites, but they are now "decoupling from their traditional patrons" and competing for power and resources in Haiti's political power vacuum. The gangs have been associated with violence as well as hindering civilians' access to humanitarian aid and supplies like fuel, food, and medicine. Much like the linkage between armed insurgents and drug trafficking in Colombia described previously, many Haitian gangs are profiting from participating in drug trafficking (Muggah [2023]).

The United States began sanctioning individuals in Haiti in 2020 for human rights abuses and corruption, including gang leader Jimmy Chérizier and the leaders of four of the largest gangs in 2023. Under Executive Order 13818 (focused on human rights), the sanctions imposed an asset freeze on these individuals as well as a ban on entry into the United States (Rios and Seelke [2024] 16). Following EO 14059 about drug trafficking, several former and current Haitian politicians have been the targets of US sanctions since 2022, also resulting in asset freezes and visa bans (Rios and Seelke [2024] 17).

What is notable about the sanctions episode against Haiti beginning in 2022 is that several other entities are imposing sanctions as well. The UNSC issued Resolution 2653 (2022) to impose sanctions against gang leaders in Haiti and individuals and entities who support them, which may include those involved in drug trafficking. The UNSC has called on United Nations members to sanction four gang leaders on its sanctions list, including Chérizier (Rios and Seelke [2024] at 9–10). Additionally, UNSC Resolution 2653 established a panel of experts to assess sanctions compliance as well as to determine which individuals should be added to the sanctions list (Rios and Seelke [2024] 17). Several other members of the international community have imposed sanctions on gang-related Haitian individuals before and above the sanctions imposed by the UNSC, including Canada, the United Kingdom, and the European Union (EU) (Muggah [2023]; Rios and Seelke [2024] 17).

IV Conclusion

Sanctions senders have used a variety of instruments with various goals to combat transnational organised crime, as exemplified by the international community's reaction to the gang-related violence in Haiti. The United

States has attempted to combat transnational organised crime in a variety of ways, including instruments focusing on drug trafficking, transnational criminal organisations specifically, and human rights. US anti-narcotics sanctions appear to be focusing increasingly on combatting the spread of synthetic opioids into the United States, as reflected in Executive Order 14059 (Rosen [2024] 2). Currently, US legislators are focused on China's role in fentanyl-related transnational trafficking, especially involving Mexican cartels (Rosen [2024] 2). Thus, we may see more US regulations regarding drug trafficking soon.

Other sanctions senders have traditionally framed their sanctions to combat transnational organised crime in the context of human rights and democracy, as well as to target gang-related violence specifically. In the case of Haiti, for instance, Canada has sanctioned gang leaders, citing their participation in "activities that have undermined the peace, security and stability of Haiti and that have contributed to acts of gross and systematic human rights violations in Haiti" (Canada Imposes Sanctions against Haitian Gang Leaders [2024]). The EU has similarly cited human rights abuses and concerns for stability in Haiti in its sanctions against the criminal organisations in the country (Council of the EU [2024]). These sanctions measures against Haitian gangs and gang leaders do not place the same emphasis on drug trafficking as the US sanctions. However, given the connections between armed groups and drug trafficking as a source of funding in many parts of the world, it would be unsurprising to see countries and intergovernmental organisations turn to sanctioning individuals prominent in transnational drug trafficking networks to address a variety of international issues, including organised crime.

Bibliography

Literature

Guáqueta A, 'Change and Continuity in US-Colombian Relations and the War against Drugs' (2005) 35(1) *Journal of Drug Issues* 27.

Muggah R, 'Haiti Is on the Brink of State Failure' (Foreign Policy, 17 February 2023) <https://foreignpolicy.com/2023/02/17/haiti-crisis-corruption-criminal-gangs-violence-humanitarian-assistance-state-failure-sanctions/> accessed 30 December 2024.

Rios KI and Seelke CR, 'Haiti: Recent Developments and US Policy' (*Congressional Research Service*, 2024).

Rosen LW, 'US Sanctions: Targeting International Illicit Drug Production and Trafficking' (*Congressional Research Service*, 2024).

Syropoulos C, Felbermayr G, Kirilakha A, Yalcin E and Yotov YV, 'The Global Sanctions Data Base–Release 3: COVID-19, Russia, and Multilateral Sanctions' (2024) 32(1) *Review of International Economics* 12.

Documents

'Canada Imposes Sanctions against Haitian Gang Leaders' (*Canada.ca*, 2024) <https://www.canada.ca/en/global-affairs/news/2024/06/canada-imposes-sanctions-against-haitian-gang-leaders.html> accessed 15 January 2025.

Executive Order 13581, 'Blocking Property of Transnational Criminal Organizations' 76 Fed Reg 44757 (2011) <https://obamawhitehouse.archives.gov/the-press-office/2011/07/25/executive-order-13581-blocking-property-transnational-criminal-organizat> accessed 15 January 2025.

Council of the EU, 'Haiti: EU Sanctions Three Individuals in Relation to the Escalating Gang Violence in the Country' (Press Release, 2024) <https://www.consilium.europa.eu/en/press/press-releases/2024/12/16/haiti-eu-sanctions-three-individuals-in-relation-to-the-escalating-gang-violence-in-the-country/> accessed 15 January 2025.

Illicit Drug Trade Sanctions Regulations, 31 CFR Part 599 (2022).

Office of Foreign Assets Control, 'Blocked Persons, Specially Designated Nationals, Specially Designated Terrorists, Foreign Terrorist Organizations, and Specially Designated Narcotics Traffickers: Additional Designations and Removals and Supplementary Information on Specially Designated Narcotics Traffickers, Foreign Terrorist Organizations' (2000), <https://www.federalregister.gov/documents/2000/12/04/00-30693/blocked-persons-specially-designated-nationals-specially-designated-terrorists-foreign-terrorist> accessed 15 January 2025.

CHARMAINE N. WILLIS

Office of Foreign Assets Control, 'Kingpin Act Designations' (2003) <https://ofac.treasury.gov/recent-actions/20030602> accessed 15 January 2025.

Office of Foreign Assets Control, 'Treasury Sanctions the Zhao Wei Transnational Criminal Organization' (2018) <https://home.treasury.gov/news/press-releases/sm0272> accessed 15 January 2025.

Office of Foreign Assets Control, *Narcotics Sanctions Program* (Department of the Treasury 2014).

UNSC Res 2653 (21 October 2022) S/RES/2653.

CHARMAINE N. WILLIS

75. Sanctions for conflict resolution

John Agbonifo

I Introduction: sanctions and international peace

The United Nations, member states, and regional organisations, such as the Economic Community of West African States (ECOWAS) and the European Union (EU), increasingly rely on targeted sanctions as a non-violent tool for addressing global security issues, particularly conflict resolution (Agbonifo [2021]). Sanctions senders deploy sanctions to achieve one or more of a number of objectives, including conflict resolution, democracy and human rights promotion, nuclear non-proliferation, countering international terrorism, and containing territorial aggression (Dreyer and Luengo-Cabrera [2015]). ECOWAS uses sanctions against unconstitutional changes of government and for conflict prevention and resolution, while the United Nations (UN), the United States, and the EU levy sanctions against human rights abuses, violation of territorial integrity, anti-democratic practices, among others.

Sanctions represent any attempt by one or more parties to change another party's objectionable behaviour through economic and diplomatic means aimed at disrupting or interrupting the target's normal relations (Agbonifo [2017]). Sanctions may put an end to diplomatic relations, cut off trade and investment relations between countries, prohibit the export or import of particular items like arms or natural resources, cut off air travel, block the movement of persons, or freeze assets or bank deposits. The aim is to put maximum pressure on those directly involved in the behaviour that elicited sanctions, as well as those who benefit from it, to change their condemned behaviour (Brooks [2002]). Like a double-edged sword, sanctions can contribute to conflict resolution or conflict protraction. To explore the conflict resolution potential of sanctions, there is a need to focus on the context of sanctions, who uses sanctions and how sanctions are used, and their legitimacy.

II Sanctions effectiveness and conflict resolution

A major study on the effectiveness of sanctions emphasises that UN sanctions aimed at coercing, constraining, and signalling targets are effective about 22 per cent of the time (Biersteker et al. [2013]). Sanctions succeed in coercing targets 10 per cent of the time. However, they do work in constraining behaviour 27 per cent of the time and in signalling 27 per cent of the time. Generally, sanctions are better at constraining the actions of their targets and sending out signals based on norms, but they are not effective at forcing a change in behaviour. Sanctions tend to be effective when three or more sanctions measures are combined (Biersteker and van Bergeijk [2015]). This includes actions like stopping the trade of weapons, banning travel, freezing assets, and restricting certain goods.

Perhaps, a major blind side of the theoretical engagement with sanctions effectiveness was the failure to see how sanctions could be used or are used to resolve conflicts through negotiations (Hudáková et al. [2021]). The focus, instead, was on ratcheting sanctions to deal with the failure to abide by agreements. Thus, the literature ignored the conflict resolution potential of sanctions relaxation. Hudáková et al. [2021] argue that sanctions relief can be used to resolve conflicts, and the authors identify 11 instances of sanctions relaxation by the UN and the EU, articulated in four categories:

(1) making sanctions easier to follow and granting exemptions;
(2) removing certain individuals and entities from the sanctions list;
(3) temporarily halting sanctions; and
(4) partially lifting sanctions measures.

They argue that individual sanctions removals have been used to encourage behavioural changes, promote agreement compliance, shame military leaders, stop troublemakers from disrupting a new government, create divisions between groups, or show that a sanctions programme is coming to an end.

III When do sanctions help resolve conflicts?

The context of sanctions can significantly shape the extent to which sanctions can serve as a conflict resolution tool. In conflicts involving non-state armed actors, achieving conflict resolution through sanctions appears very challenging. Sanctions have increasingly been applied to non-state armed actors given their significant role in international politics (Agbonifo [2021]). Non-state armed actors are unlike state actors and are more difficult to coerce (Biersteker and van Bergeijk [2015]). Sanctions rest on assumptions that do not reflect the nature of non-state armed actors. The factors that make sanctions most successful against states do not translate well to the context of non-state armed actors (Agbonifo [2021]). Thus, failed attempts to coerce targets are associated more with rebel groups than with the state (Biersteker et al. [2013]). Measures like asset freezes and travel bans have limited effect on those who do not have money in foreign bank accounts, do not travel, but have access to the black market for arms (Agbonifo [2021]). Therefore, achieving conflict resolution in this context is quite difficult.

Leadership style is critical to whether sanctions are effective as conflict resolution measures (Agbonifo [2021]). Drawing on Hermann et al. ([2001]), leadership styles are based on how leaders deal with their political environment, whether they listen to new information or are bent on achieving goals. Understanding how leaders respond to limitations, absorb information, and stay motivated to navigate their political surroundings is crucial for identifying their leadership approach. Leaders of non-state armed groups, including Foday Sankoh of the Revolutionary United Front (RUF), Jonas Savimbi of the National Union for the Total Independence of Angola (UNITA), and Joseph Kony of the Lord's Resistance Army (LRA), displayed leadership styles that challenged constraints imposed by sanctions and reneged on negotiated settlements and peace offers. The wars in Sierra Leone and Angola ended only with the deaths of Sankoh and Savimbi. Kony and the LRA have yet to yield to sanctions.

In the context of non-international armed conflicts, the potential of sanctions to achieve conflict resolution is shaped by the leadership of non-state armed groups (Agbonifo [2021]). Ignoring the role of leaders in influencing conflicts would be mistaken, because leaders often determine conflict trajectories. Civil war leaders are aware of the consequences they may face for their actions during war (Prorok [2016]). Such leaders tend to think about the punishment that awaits them when they make decisions. Their decisions are often driven by the desire to avoid punishments like losing power, being exiled, going to jail, or even dying. Leaders who are in charge of wars are expected to face more punishment if the outcome of the war is unfavourable. This makes them less likely to compromise or accept losing terms. These leaders feel pressured to keep fighting even if they are losing, hoping to change the situation and avoid punishment.

IV Limitations of sanctions as a conflict resolution tool

Beyond external limitations to the promise of sanctions as a conflict resolution measure, sanctions themselves sometimes hinder conflict resolution efforts, exacerbating conflicts. Sanctions can inhibit peace processes and post-conflict recovery, constrain peace organisations, undercut negotiations, and entrench divisions between conflict parties. Sanctions are often vigorously deployed with the aim of demonising and isolating targets, promoting entrenched distrust, and becoming 'a factor in locking in the perception among US policymakers and the public that peaceful relations with the target are impossible' (International Crisis Group [2023] 24). Actors can manipulate or leverage sanctions for political capital in the context of destabilising rivalries and political instability. Western sanctions on Zimbabwe aimed at removing Mugabe and the ruling party from power. Former British Prime Minister Tony Blair claimed 'there is no salvation for the people of Zimbabwe until that regime is changed' (Blair [2004]). Sanctions, particularly unilateral sanctions, for regime change deepen domestic instability, and undermine regional peace initiatives and the peaceful resolution of conflict.

Biersteker et al. [2019] emphasise the complementarity of mediation and sanctions as policy instruments for conflict prevention and conflict resolution. The authors argue that the threat or enhanced enforcement of sanctions can provide incentives for warring parties to come to the table and encourage actors to sign a peace agreement. At the same time, however, sanctions can undermine mediation efforts. They point out that the decision to sanction one party and not another could affect the perception of the UN's impartiality, and jeopardise the continued acceptance of

John Agbonifo

mediation. Similarly, the stigmatising effect of sanctions can result in the exclusion of a target from a peace process.

The failure to achieve global consensus in the wake of Russia's invasion of Ukraine demonstrates the key weaknesses of sanctions as a conflict resolution tool. Sanctions are increasingly subject to contestation. Orchard and Wiener ([2024]) elaborate three distinct types of contestation: reactive contestation, or a process wherein certain actors object to or violate norms; proactive contestation, which occurs when actors engage with norms in order to improve them; and interpretive contestation, where actors push for different understandings of global norms. Participation is a condition for achieving recognition and legitimacy for norms, but when some actors are excluded from participation in decision-making, there is an increased likelihood that the excluded will challenge the sanctions interpretively or question the norms that informed them.

Whether sanctions are contested or not is a function of their perceived legitimacy (Palestini, forthcoming). Three legitimacy problems attach to sanctions, including the legitimacy of norms, the legitimacy of the enforcer, and the legitimacy of the measures. The imposition of sanctions is a claim that an actor has violated an international norm, demanding a reaction. The validity of the claim can be disputed, but where the claim is proven, the claimant has the additional burden of showing that the violation legitimises a right to react. Here, the consideration is the status of the norm violated vis-à-vis the status of other norms such as non-intervention and territorial integrity. Similarly, the claimant can be an object of delegitimisation on the basis of the question of who has the right to enforce a sanction. The measures imposed in reaction to norms violations are subject to delegitimisation as well. Are the measures proportional to the violation that they claim to address? Sanctions, even targeted sanctions, often do have unintended consequences on innocent citizens, opening a ground for contestation.

V Conclusion

The importance of sanctions as a tool for conflict resolution has increased over time. Sanctions work through coercion, constraining, and signalling as well as through the relaxation of sanctions. However, sanctions may not be effective in some situations. Sanctions targeting non-state armed groups are particularly challenging. Sanctions in themselves may hinder conflict resolution efforts when used for regime change, or to demonise and isolate targets, promoting distrust. Similarly, the tool is subject to contestation, which weakens its effectiveness.

Bibliography

Literature

Agbonifo J, 'Nonstate Armed Groups, Leadership, and Sanctions Effectiveness' (2021) 14(1) *African Security* 27.

Agbonifo J, 'Sanctions, Conflict Prevention and Peacebuilding: Coercing Non-State Armed Actors in Africa' (2017) 12(1) *Journal of Peacebuilding and Development* 65.

Biersteker T and van Bergeijk PAG, 'How and When Do Sanctions Work? The Evidence' in Dreyer L and Luengo-Cabrera J (eds), *On Target? EU Sanctions as Security Policy Tools* (Report No. 25 EU Institute for Security Studies 2015) 17.

Biersteker T, Brubaker R and Lanz D, UN Sanctions and Mediation: Establishing Evidence to Inform Practice (United Nations University Centre for Policy Research, 18 February 2019).

Biersteker T, Eckert S, Tourino M and Hudakova Z, 'The Effectiveness of United Nations Targeted Sanctions: Findings from the Targeted Sanctions Consortium (TSC)' (The Graduate Institute Geneva and Watson Institute, Brown University 2013).

Brooks R, 'Sanctions and Regime Type: What Works and When?' (2002) 11(4) *Security Studies* 1.

Dreyer L and Luengo-Cabrera J, 'Introduction' in Dreyer L and Luengo-Cabrera J (eds), *On Target? EU Sanctions as Security Policy Tools* (Report No. 25 EU Institute for Security Studies 2015) 15.

Hermann MG, Preston T, Korany B and Shaw TM, 'Who Leads Matters: The Effects of Powerful Individuals' (2001) 3(2) *International Studies Review* 83.

Hudáková Z, Biersteker T and Moret E, 'Sanctions Relaxation and Conflict Resolution: Lessons from Past Sanctions Regimes' (The Carter Center, October 2021) <https://www.cartercenter.org/resources/pdfs/peace/conflict_resolution/sanctions-relaxation-10-2021.pdf>.

International Crisis Group, 'Sanctions, Peacemaking and Reform: Recommendations for U.S. Policymakers' (Report No. 8, 28 August 2023).
Orchard A and Wiener A (eds), *Contesting the World: Norm Research in Theory and Practice* (Cambridge University Press 2024).
Palestini S, 'The Elephant in the Room: Legitimacy and (De)Legitimation of International Sanctions' in Bultrini A, Giumelli F, Portela C and Sossai M (eds), *International Sanctions in Practice: An Interdisciplinary Perspective* (Routledge 2025) 45.
Prorok AK, 'Leader Incentives and Civil War Outcomes' (2016) 60(1) *American Journal of Political Science* 70.

JOHN AGBONIFO

76. Sanctions for human rights and democracy

Stefano Silingardi

I Introduction

The concept of "sanctions for human rights and democracy" encapsulates a diverse and multifaceted practice of measures, including economic restrictions, unified by the possibility of justifying such measures on human rights grounds. These sanctions may serve a variety of purposes, the most common being to promote human rights abroad or to punish a foreign state responsible for grave human rights violations. However, they can also be employed for other reasons related to an unsatisfactory human rights situation in other countries, such as to express the sending state's outrage at human rights atrocities, to prevent a state's own markets from contributing to rights violations, to distance itself from human rights abusers, and to generate pressure for the adoption of multilateral action (Cleveland [2002]). Further, these measures are frequently conflated with sanctions aimed at goals such as the restoration of democracy, good governance, and the rule of law.

The employment of economic sanctions as a means to encourage adherence to human rights norms and democracy represents a relatively modern phenomenon, with individual states occasionally adopting such measures since the 1960s. Examples include the 1960 African States' trade embargo against South Africa (see chapter) in response to its illegal policy of apartheid; the US and European sanctions against Uganda in the 1970s to put an end to the appalling human rights situation in the country; the US and European measures adopted in the 1980s to restrict trade relations with Poland for the arrests and detention of political opponents; and the US and European arms embargo against China following the 1989 Tiananmen Square bloodshed (Dawidowicz [2017]; Bogdanova [2022]). Since the 1990s, this practice has become more prevalent, with the United Nations Security Council (UNSC) regularly resorting to economic sanctions. This often involves determining whether grave human rights violations can be considered a threat to international peace and security, thereby allowing the adoption of such measures under Chapter VII of the United Nations (UN) Charter. At the same time, individual states continue to impose unilateral economic sanctions in response to instances of flagrant human rights violations and breaches of fundamental democratic principles, largely due to the veto power of some UNSC permanent members.

The legality of economic sanctions imposed to address human rights violations and promote democratic governance is subject to nuanced assessment, contingent upon whether such measures have been adopted by the UNSC or unilaterally by individual states. While UNSC sanctions are primarily regulated by the UN Charter, unilateral sanctions are mainly governed by general international law and the law on state responsibility.

II Sanctions adopted by the UN Security Council

It is only from the 1990s that the UNSC developed a consistent practice of imposing economic sanctions to address serious human rights violations. The UNSC can adopt such measures under three situations covered by Article 39 of the UN Charter: a threat to or a violation of international peace and security, and an act of aggression. An analysis of the UNSC's actions reveals that the category of "threat to peace" is commonly invoked to justify the use of such measures. However, it remains controversial whether violations of human rights alone can serve as an independent basis for imposing economic sanctions, or if such violations must be combined with other factors, such as the occurrence or risk of armed conflict. Scholarly opinions on this issue vary, as the UNSC's decision-making is perceived to reflect its inherently political nature (Siatitsa [2022]). The prevailing practice suggests a preference for combining human rights concerns with other goals.

Once the UNSC determines the existence of a threat to peace, it enjoys great discretion in the measures it can take. When serious rights violations are cited to justify a threat, the ensuing sanctions must aim to halt those violations. Yet, the notion of a threat to peace often involves complex, multifaceted situations, with human rights breaches and the promotion of democracy being just two of the key contributing factors. The UNSC has employed targeted sectoral sanctions, such as arms embargoes (see chapter), commodity sanctions (see chapter), and financial restrictions, to address such threats (UNSC

Res 2571 [2021]; Res 2577 [2021]; Res 2588 [2021]; Res 2752 [2024]). Similarly, the imposition of individual asset freezes and travel bans has been frequently employed to mitigate the risk of ongoing and future human rights abuses (UNSC Res 1970 [2011]; Res 2262 [2016]; Res 2428 [2018]).

III Unilateral sanctions adopted by states

As an eminent scholar aptly observed, the risk with centralized UNSC sanctions on human rights abuses is that such measures may be blocked not solely by permanent members' vetoes, but also by the inexistence of a "caring majority" (Pellet [2015]). In recent years, some permanent members (particularly China and the Russian Federation) have often refrained from supporting UN sanctions on human rights grounds. Consequently, individual states have frequently resorted to unilateral measures, including economic restrictions, to address human rights violations and breaches of democratic rule in the absence of UN action.

These unilateral steps can be categorized into two groups: country-based sanctions regimes, which target specific countries and rights violations therein; and thematic (or horizontal) sanctions regimes, which focus on particular themes rather than countries, allowing for the listing of individuals and entities responsible for activities like human rights abuses, regardless of their location or national affiliation.

1 Country-based sanctions

Country-based sanctions represent the traditional approach to sanctioning perpetrators of human rights violations and are employed by many states. The European Union (EU) currently maintains almost a dozen sanctions regimes targeting human rights abuses and the erosion of democracy and the rule of law in specific countries, such as Zimbabwe (Council Decision 2011/101); Iran (see chapter) (Council Decision 2011/235); Belarus (see chapter) (Council Decision 2012/642); Syria (see chapter) (Council Decision 2013/25); Myanmar (see chapter) (Council Decision 2013/184); Venezuela (see chapter) (Council Decision 2017/2074); Nicaragua (Council Decision 2019/1720); Lebanon (Council Decision 2021/1277); Burundi (Council Decision 2015/1763); and Guatemala (Council Decision 2024/254). In May 2024, the EU enacted a new sanctions framework against Russia (see chapter), establishing restrictive measures against those responsible for serious human rights violations, the repression of civil society and the democratic opposition, as well as the undermining of democracy and the rule of law in that country (Council Decision 2024/1484). Alongside individual asset freezes (see chapter on Financial sanctions) and travel bans, this new framework introduces trade restrictions on the export of equipment that could be used for internal repression, as well as on technology and software intended primarily for information security and telecommunication monitoring or interception.

Alongside the EU, other states, including the United States (see chapter), Canada (see chapter), and Australia , have also been active proponents of unilateral sanctions in response to grave human rights violations localized in specific countries. While the targeted countries often overlap, the United States has implemented unique sanctions regimes addressing human rights abuses in Hong Kong (Executive Order 13936 [2020]), Ethiopia (Executive Order 14046 [2021]), and the West Bank (Executive Order 14115 [2024]). In addition, African regional organizations (see chapter on African Union and ECOWAS) typically impose sanctions aimed at promoting good governance and democracy, primarily in response to unconstitutional changes of government, often resulting in membership suspension (see chapter on Membership sanctions; Charron and Portela [2015]).

2 Horizontal (or "Magnitsky-style") sanctions

The recent origins of global horizontal sanctions regimes aimed at addressing the most serious human rights violations can be traced back to the US Sergei Magnitsky Rule of Law Accountability Act of 2012 (Public Law 112-208 [2012]). This Act empowered the imposition of travel bans and asset freezes on individuals believed to be involved in Sergei Magnitsky's death or the corruption he had exposed. The scope of this legislation was significantly expanded in 2016 with the introduction of a separate "Global Magnitsky Act" (Public Law 114-328 [2016]), which granted the US government the authority to impose such measures on any foreign person involved in gross violations of internationally recognized human rights or acts of significant corruption (see chapter on Sanctions to combat corruption).

This US initiative inspired the adoption of similar human rights horizontal sanctions regimes in other countries, including Canada, the United Kingdom (see chapter), Australia, and the EU. The EU introduced the EU Global Human Rights Sanctions Regime (EUGHRSR) in December 2020. This new legal framework enables the imposition of travel bans, asset freezes, and a prohibition on making funds or economic resources available to perpetrators of the most serious human rights abuses worldwide (Council Decision (CFSP) 2020/1999 and Council Regulation (EU) 2020/1998). The regime's scope extends to address a wide range of violations. Alongside the gravest human rights abuses, such as genocide and crimes against humanity, the EUGHRSR also foresees the imposition of targeted sanctions for a circumscribed set of "serious human rights violations", including not only torture but also arbitrary detention. Furthermore, the regime's scope extends to address other human rights violations, including trafficking in persons, sexual and gender-based violence, and violations of fundamental freedoms. However, for these latter categories of rights violations to trigger sanctions, they must be deemed widespread, systematic, or otherwise of serious concern in light of the objectives of the EU's Common Foreign and Security Policy, as stipulated in Article 21 of the Treaty on European Union. Nine other European countries, both candidate countries and non-members, decided to align themselves with the EUGHRSR. Additionally, some other countries, including New Zealand and Japan (see chapter), are preparing or contemplating the introduction of similar targeted human rights sanctions regimes within their own jurisdictions.

Under these emerging horizontal sanctions frameworks, designations have been made against hundreds of individuals and entities across the globe, covering a wide spectrum of human rights violations, some of which are concurrently addressed by multiple jurisdictions — such as the mistreatment of the Uyghur ethnic minority in China's Xinjiang Province.

IV Significance, effectiveness, and criticism

The recent emergence of "horizontal" sanctions regimes, which target human rights violations irrespective of location, represents a significant development in the sanctions toolkit. These align with a shift away from large-scale trade restrictions and other sectoral sanctions — which may inadvertently harm civilian populations — towards more targeted "smart" sanctions (see chapter on Targeted sanctions and sanctions reform process). Horizontal sanctions make it harder for blacklisted leaders to claim that sanctions harm civilians, offer greater flexibility to respond rapidly to human rights violations, and avoid the political costs of country-specific regimes (Portela [2021]). Viewed in this way, horizontal sanctions regimes have been considered an example of the "transnationalization of the law" (Eckes [2022]).

Yet, these sanctions have drawn criticism. Ensuring coherence between horizontal and country-based sanctions can be complex. Sanctions under one of the human rights and democracy sub-regimes within country-based regimes could, indeed, be imposed in addition to sanctions under human rights horizontal regimes, and many of the consequences (such as travel bans and asset freezes) would be the same. At the same time, if an individual is delisted or succeeds in having their listing annulled under one of these regimes, particularly if this is due to lack of evidence, this would necessitate a reconsideration of how the evidentiary standard is met under the other regime. There are also concerns that Western states use human rights selectively as a geopolitical tool, leading to accusations of double standards as certain human rights perpetrators from some countries are listed while other obvious candidates are not. This may partly explain the low adoption rate of this type of legislation among Southern Hemisphere states, many of whom are wary of alienating powerful countries like Russia or China.

The specific criteria and conditions for lifting human rights sanctions also remain unclear, raising questions about whether they primarily have a signalling and deterring objective, or are also punitive in nature (Ruys [2021]). The matter is particularly evident in the case of horizontal sanctions. While country-specific sanctions often share the incentive structure of international sanctions, wherein targets' behavioural change leads to the lifting of measures, the same promise is less clear for horizontal human rights sanctions. For instance, the EUGHRSR does not explicitly specify the expected conduct from those targeted by its restrictive measures.

All of this explains why, even as some states have enacted unilateral human rights sanctions, others view these measures as violations of international law. China, the Russian Federation, and the majority of African states have condemned the use of these sanctions, arguing that developed countries employ human rights as a pretext for economic coercion (Bogdanova [2022]). This debate reflects the contentious and evolving nature of sanctions targeting human rights abuses.

V International legality

When determining the international legality (see also chapter on Legality and legitimacy) of imposing sanctions for the sake of human rights and democracy, a crucial distinction must be made between sanctions imposed by the UNSC and those imposed unilaterally by individual states.

Sanctions enacted by the UNSC are regulated by the UN Charter. As UNSC decisions are legally binding on member states, the international legality of such sanctions should be assessed solely based on whether the conditions laid down in the Charter have been fulfilled. However, the UNSC enjoys wide discretion in choosing the situations in which it will intervene and the measures it can take, owing to its composition and the willingness of its members, particularly the permanent members with veto power. This discretionary power is often caught in the middle of political manipulations and is subject to abuse by interested states, rather than a careful consideration of facts (Siatitsa [2022]).

Nonetheless, this observation does not undermine the international legality of sanctions imposed under Chapter VII of the UN Charter. In this regard, the only significant legal requirement that has emerged in the UN sanctions practice is that the Council can only impose sanctions under Chapter VII for *serious* violations of human rights. This means that not every human rights violation or breach of democratic rule automatically triggers the "threat to the peace" threshold that opens the door to the UN collective security system.

The international legality of human rights sanctions imposed by states, both country-based and horizontal sanctions, is a much more complex issue related to the broader question of the international legality of unilateral sanctions. As there is no dedicated international legal instrument explicitly authorizing or regulating unilateral sanctions, including those for human rights and democracy, assessing their international legality requires engaging with substantive aspects. This includes the nature of the violations they address and their compatibility with other principles of international law, such as the principle of non-intervention, rules on the responsibility of states for international wrongful acts, established principles of jurisdiction as defined by international law, and treaty obligations. The heterogeneous nature of unilateral sanctions imposed for the sake of human rights and democracy further complicates the analysis, as their international legal implications vary depending on their content, the situations they address, and the positions of involved parties. Evaluating the international legality of these sanctions therefore requires a challenging and complex case-by-case analysis to ascertain their compliance with the sanctioning state's international obligations.

The first point to assess is the legal nature of these sanctions according to international law. They could be categorized as either retorsions or countermeasures (see chapter) (Ruys [2017]). Retorsions, being acts of "discourtesy or unfriendliness" not constituting a breach of any state obligation, would be lawful (Articles on Responsibility of States for Internationally Wrongful Acts (ARSIWA) [2001]). However, as human rights sanctions are aimed at remedying human rights violations abroad, they are more likely to fall under the category of countermeasures, which are unlawful reactions to another state's allegedly internationally wrongful act. In this case, they must adhere in principle to the procedural and substantive requirements laid down in Articles 49–53 ARSIWA.

However, the legality of human rights sanctions as traditional bilateral countermeasures is debatable, as it is unclear whether a state can be considered directly affected or injured by human rights violations occurring abroad and against foreign nationals.

As a result, these measures may fall under the category of collective (or third-party) countermeasures (ARSIWA [2001] Art. 54). Additionally, only serious human rights violations can be regarded as breaches of *erga omnes* obligations (or even *jus cogens* norms, such as torture and genocide), while violations of democracy and the rule of law may not meet this threshold, as many legal scholars even dispute the customary nature of these principles.

Secondly, human rights sanctions regimes often set aside the limits imposed by the rules of jurisdiction as defined by international law (Ryngaert [2015]). By targeting situations that present neither a personal nor a territorial connection with the sanctioning states, these regimes allow these states to extend their normative reach to situations that fall outside their jurisdiction or even their sovereignty (see also chapter on Secondary Sanctions and the Extraterritorial Effects of Sanctions) (Beaucillon [2023]).

Furthermore, recent unilateral human rights sanctions have frequently targeted heads of state and other high-ranking officials for abuses relating to their tenure, such as those imposed by the EU and the United States against many Venezuelan, Russian, and Iranian senior governmental officials, or those enacted by the United States against Zimbabwe's President Emmerson Mnangagwa. This raises the question of whether these measures impede the immunities accorded under international law on the personal or functional level, i.e. whether acts were performed in a private or official capacity. At a general level, a distinction must be made according to the type of restrictive measures adopted. Unilateral human rights sanctions that entail travel restrictions on an acting head of state or high-ranking governmental officials whose functions are not of an essentially internal nature present a significant risk of infringing on immunities. However, the compatibility of economic restrictions, such as the freezing of personal assets, with immunities rules remains disputed (Bogdanova [2022]).

VI Conclusion

The use of sanctions to promote human rights and democracy has become increasingly prevalent in contemporary international relations. Such sanctions are frequently adopted by the UNSC, which can characterize human rights violations as threats to international peace and security under Chapter VII of the UN Charter. When the UNSC is unable or unwilling to act, individual states may resort to autonomous sanctions. However, the legality of unilateral sanctions remains widely debated. While UNSC sanctions are primarily governed by the UN Charter and can be deemed legal if they fulfil the Charter's conditions, unilateral sanctions operate in a more contentious legal realm. This is because there is currently no explicit international legal instrument that authorizes or regulates these measures. Assessing the legality of country-based or global "Magnitsky-style" sanctions therefore requires a complex, case-by-case analysis to ensure compliance with the sanctioning state's international obligations.

Some contend that states imposing sanctions for human rights and democracy should adhere to an even higher standard, since restricting rights ostensibly to protect rights can lead to accusations of hypocrisy. The legal status of unilateral sanctions related to human rights and democracy is likely to remain contentious, as long as they are perceived as a challenge to the sovereign prerogatives of states and the decentralized nature of the international legal order. Nonetheless, such sanctions also represent a step forward in global efforts to safeguard fundamental rights, moving beyond traditional constraints on serious violations.

Bibliography

Literature

Beaucillon C, 'Long-Arm Collective Sovereignty Through the EU: The EU Global Human Rights Sanctions Regime Transcending the Limits of the Fight Against Impunity' (2023) 8 *European Papers* 1679.

Bogdanova I, *Unilateral Sanctions in International Law and the Enforcement of Human Rights* (Brill Nijhoff 2022).

Charron A and Portela C, 'The UN, Regional Sanctions and Africa' (2015) 91 *International Affairs* 1369.

Cleveland SH, 'Human Rights Sanctions and International Trade: A Theory of Compatibility' (2002) 5 *Journal of International Economic Law* 133.

Dawidowicz M, *Third-Parties Countermeasures in International Law* (Oxford University Press 2017).
Eckes C, 'EU Global Human Rights Sanctions Regime: Is the Genie Out of the Bottle?' (2022) 30 *Journal of Contemporary European Studies* 255.
Pellet A, 'Unilateral Sanctions and International Law. A Proposal for a New Commission on Unilateral Sanctions and International Law' (2015) 76 *Yearbook of Institute of International Law* 730.
Portela C, 'Horizontal Sanctions Regimes: Targeted Sanctions Reconfigured?' in Beaucillon C (ed.), *Research Handbook on Unilateral and Extraterritorial Sanctions* (Edward Elgar 2021) 441.
Ruys T, 'Introductory Note to the European Union Global Human Rights Sanctions Regime (EUGHRSR)' (2021) 60 *International Legal Materials* 298.
Ruys T, 'Sanctions, Retorsions and Countermeasures: Concepts and International Legal Framework' in van den Herik L (ed.), *Research Handbook of UN Sanctions and International Law* (Edward Elgar 2017) 19.
Ryngaert C, *Jurisdiction in International Law* (Oxford University Press 2015).
Siatitsa I, *Serious Violations of Human Rights: On the Emergence of a New Special Regime* (Oxford University Press 2022).

Documents

Council Decision (CFSP) 2015/1763 of 1 October 2015 concerning restrictive measures in view of the situation in Burundi [2015] OJ L 257/37.
Council Decision (CFSP) 2017/2074 of 13 November 2017 concerning restrictive measures in view of the situation in Venezuela [2013] OJ L295/60.
Council Decision (CFSP) 2019/1720 of 14 October 2019 concerning restrictive measures in view of the situation in Nicaragua [2019] OJ L262/58.
Council Decision (CFSP) 2020/1999 of 7 December 2020 concerning restrictive measures against serious human rights violations and abuses [2020] OJ L410I/13.
Council Decision (CFSP) 2021/1277 of 30 July 2021 concerning restrictive measures in view of the situation in Lebanon [2021] OJ L277I/16.
Council Decision (CFSP) 2024/1484 of 27 May 2024 concerning restrictive measures in view of the situation in Russia [2024] OJ L2024/1484.
Council Decision (CFSP) 2024/254 of 12 January 2024 concerning restrictive measures in view of the situation in Guatemala [2024] OJ L2024/254.
Council Decision 2011/101/CFSP of 15 February 2011 concerning restrictive measures against Zimbabwe [2011] OJ L42/6.
Council Decision 2011/235/CFSP of 12 April 2011 concerning restrictive measures directed against certain persons and entities in view of the situation in Iran [2011] OJ L100/51.
Council Decision 2012/642/CFSP of 15 October 2012 concerning restrictive measures against Belarus [2012] OJ L285/1.
Council Decision 2013/184/CFSP of 22 April 2013 concerning restrictive measures against Myanmar/Burma [2013] OJ L111/84.
Council Decision 2013/255/CFSP of 31 May 2013 concerning restrictive measures against Syria OJ L147/14.
Council Regulation (EU) 2020/1998 of 7 December 2020, concerning restrictive measures against serious human rights violations and abuses [2020] OJ L410I/1.
Executive Order 13936 of July 14, 2020.
Executive Order 14046 of September 17, 2021.
Executive Order 14115 of February 1, 2024.
UNGA Res 56/83, 'Articles on Responsibility of a State for Internationally Wrongful Acts' (12 December 2001) UN Doc. A/RES/56/83.
Sergei Magnitsky Rule of Law Accountability Act of 2012, Public Law 112-208, 126 Stat. 1502 (2012).
The Global Magnitsky Human Rights Accountability Act, Public Law 114-328, Title XII, Subtitle F (2016).
UNSC Res 1970 (26 February 2011) UN Doc. S/RES/1970.
UNSC Res 2262 (27 January 2016) UN Doc. S/RES/2262.
UNSC Res 2428 (13 July 2018) UN Doc. S/RES/2428.
UNSC Res 2571 (16 April 2021) UN Doc. S/RES/2571.
UNSC Res 2577 (28 May 2021) UN Doc. S/RES/2577.

STEFANO SILINGARDI

UNSC Res 2588 (29 July 2021) UN Doc. S/RES/2588.
UNSC Res 2752 (18 October 2024) UN Doc. S/RES/2752.

77. Sanctions for nuclear non-proliferation

ARMEND BEKAJ

I Introduction

The Russian invasion and the war in Ukraine, coupled with subsequent tensions between the North Atlantic Treaty Organization (NATO) and Russia, have brought to the forefront the dangers emanating from a possible nuclear conflict. The latest reports stress that countries such as the United States, Russia and China are undertaking extensive programmes to "replace and modernize their nuclear warheads, their missile, aircraft and submarine delivery systems, and their nuclear weapon production facilities" (SIPRI [2024] 271). Further, India and Pakistan seem to be increasing their nuclear inventories, thus enacting a dangerous regional mimicry of the Cold War arms race. After the US withdrawal in 2018 from the Joint Comprehensive Plan of Action (JCPOA), Iran has been increasing its enrichment capacities, which in the context of the current conflict in the Middle East serves to amplify the dangers of a direct confrontation with Israel (The Jerusalem Post [2024]). Lastly, for North Korea, its military nuclear programme remains central to its national security strategy (SIPRI [2024] 271).

A heightenedproliferation points to the world entering a new nuclear arms race. Worryingly, the normative obligations deriving from the Treaty on the Non-Proliferation of Nuclear Weapons (NPT) have rarely seemed so frail and non-binding. Since March 2023, the direct links between the Nuclear Risk Reduction Centres of the United States and Russia, including on-site inspections, have been suspended. The New Strategic Arms Reduction Treaty (START) expires in February 2026, with no real prospects for a possible extension (The Economist [2023]).

To date, the most common and intuitive response to nuclear armament and proliferation has been the application of sanctions. In recent years, a range of sanctions has been imposed on countries such as Iran, North Korea, India and Pakistan (Parsi [2017]; Esteban and Portela [2022]; Shaikh [2002]). Notwithstanding the "deterrent effect" on starting nuclear weapons programmes (Miller [2014]), or the effect of pushing for nuclear de-proliferation such as in apartheid South Africa (van Wyk [2024]), coercive measures alone often fail to curb nuclear activity. The cases of Pakistan, North Korea, or even Iran currently show that coercive measures may inadvertently precipitate clandestine nuclear activity. Further, governments have been employing novel ways to circumvent sanctions in pursuit of nuclear capacity. Circumvention speaks directly to the (lack of) efficacy of sanctions. Given the changing geopolitical challenges exerted on the international order today, how much room is there to renegotiate a more responsive and efficient use of sanctions?

II From comprehensive towards targeted sanctions

By "sanctions" we commonly understand coercive measures (political, economic, military, technological, financial, or a mix of these) undertaken to punish a state (the sanction target) for wrongful behaviour (Galtung [1967]; Wallensteen [1968]; Miller [2014]). Sanctions as coercive measures are activated when states engage in nuclear proliferation, thereby threatening the nuclear non-proliferation regime (Solingen [2012]; Kaplow [2023]), or when they plan to develop a nuclear programme (Biersteker et al. [2018]; Nephew [2018]).

Until the early 1990s, sanctions were usually comprehensive in scope (Wallensteen and Staibano [2005]). Although such sanctions may have reached their desired objectives (e.g. Iraq in the early 1990s; Lopez and Cortright [2004]), the grave humanitarian consequences for the wider population made them highly unpopular. Instead, we saw a gradual shift away from comprehensive towards targeted or smart sanctions, in order to signify "the use of targeted or selected sanctions, as opposed to comprehensive or general trade sanctions" (Cortright and Lopez [2002] 1).

Sanctions are often employed autonomously (or unilaterally) by individual states against other states as a form of penalisation against the latter's nuclear activities. The former sanctions of the United States against Pakistan and India are a case in point (Bekaj and Chauhan [2024]). However, apart from standing on dubious legal international grounds, unilateral sanctions are often inefficient and ineffective – due to the lack of international consensus, there will be other countries and agencies eager to help nuclear proliferation. By contrast, sanctions are internationally and legally binding when imposed by the United Nations Security Council under Chapter VII of the United Nations (UN) Charter (Charron and Portela [2022] 15–24).

III The interplay between coercive measures and inducements

Comprehensive or targeted sanctions have one common denominator – they are coercive measures against a target state aiming to curb its nuclear activity. Sanctions are instruments of threat, force or coercion through which a target country is pushed or intimidated to change its behaviour. Moreover, with coercive measures, governments are seen to be hawkish and uncompromising with rogue states. Indeed, sanctions are a form of violence (Nephew [2018]).

However, being hawkish doesn't necessarily pay dividends. Empirical evidence shows that, in fact, coercive measures often push target states towards clandestine activities and precipitate their nuclear activity (Dorussen [2001]; Müller and Schmidt [2010]). This has been the case with Pakistan and North Korea, and currently risks repeating with Iran.

To increase the efficiency of results, states may employ inducements (in the form of economic benefits, diplomatic rapprochement or sanction relief) as a means to bring the target state back to the negotiating table or to convince it to abandon its nuclear build-up or proliferation plans (Bekaj and Wallensteen [2024]). These measures are otherwise referred to as "positive sanctions" (Baldwin [1971]; Wallensteen and Staibano [2005]), defined as inducements offered to the target state that aim to establish or deepen engagement. They aim, in other words, to engage, not enrage, and subsequently to involve, not alienate, the target state. It should be underlined, however, that an inducements policy does not always manage to engage with an adversarial side: early attempts by the United States and the European Union (EU) to offer inducements to North Korea and Iran, respectively, did not yield the desired results.

IV Sanctions efficiency in a new world

A greater interplay between coercive measures and inducements (Nincic [2011]) may therefore be warranted, particularly if the international non-proliferation order is to deal more effectively with current challenges.

Firstly, recent UN reports have raised concerns over North Korea's use of cryptocurrency and blockchain channels to siphon off more than $3 billion for their nuclear programme (The Guardian [2024]). Such innovative methods of circumventing the sanctions regime, coupled with the fact that countries such as Russia, North Korea, Iran and China are flouting sanctions imposed by the West (as they see it), may only exacerbate nuclear proliferation.

Secondly, in times of heightened nuclear tensions, consideration should be given to the degree to which sanctions are discouraging regimes from going rogue. Are they perhaps having an inadvertent effect of pushing certain regimes into a corner where they see no alternative but barricade themselves with nuclear proliferation?

V Conclusion

To what degree can a policy of inducements contribute to nuclear non-proliferation? This is a legitimate question to consider, particularly in light of a re-emerging nuclear arms race. A policy of inducements may lead to greater engagement, which provides a potential platform for building trust, reducing tensions and subsequently addressing issues of nuclear disarmament and non-proliferation. Such a policy is not meant to replace coercive measures, but rather to complement them. The objective is to address failures of coercive measures and contribute to greater engagement and security.

Bibliography

Literature

Baldwin DA, 'The Power of Positive Sanctions' (1971) 24(1) *World Politics* 19.

Bekaj A and Wallensteen P (eds), *Sanctions for Nuclear Disarmament and Non-Proliferation: Moving Forward* (Routledge 2024).

Bekaj A and Chauhan R, 'Between a Rock and a Hard Place: Pakistan's Nuclear Weapons and Sanctions' in Bekaj A and Wallensteen P (eds), *Sanctions for Nuclear Disarmament and Non-Proliferation: Moving Forward* (Routledge 2024) 113.

Biersteker T, Eckert SE, Tourinho M and Hudáková Z, 'UN Targeted Sanctions Datasets (1991–2013)' (2018) 55(3) *Journal of Peace Research* 404.

Charron A and Portela C (eds), *Multilateral Sanctions Revisited: Lessons Learned from Margaret Doxey* (McGill-Queen's University Press 2022).

Cortright D and Lopez GA (eds), *Smart Sanctions: Targeting Economic Statecraft* (Rowman & Littlefield Publishers, Inc. 2002).

Dorussen H, 'Mixing Carrots with Sticks: Evaluating the Effectiveness of Positive Sanctions' (2001) 38(2) *Journal of Peace Research* 251.

Esteban M and Portela C, 'EU Sanctions against North Korea: Making a Stringent UN Sanctions Regime Even Tougher' in Casarini N, Fiori A, Kim N, Lee J and Pardo RP (eds), *Routledge Handbook of EU–Korea Relations* (Routledge 2022).

Galtung J, 'On the Effects of International Economic Sanctions: With Examples From the Case of Rhodesia' (1967) 19(3) *World Politics* 378.

Galula N, 'Experts Debate the Urgency of Striking Iran: Is Time Running Out for Israel?' (*The Jerusalem Post*, 21 September 2024) <https://www.jpost.com/middle-east/iran-news/article-820938> accessed 26 September 2024.

Kaplow JM, *Signing Away the Bomb: The Surprising Success of the Non-Proliferation Regime* (Cambridge University Press 2023).

Lopez GA and Cortright D, 'Containing Iraq: Sanctions Worked' (2004) 83(4) *Foreign Affairs* 90.

Miller NL, 'The Secret Success of Non-Proliferation Sanctions' (2014) 68(4) *International Organization* 913.

Müller H and Schmidt A, 'The Little Known Story of De-Proliferation: Why States Give Up Nuclear Weapons Activities' in Potter W and Mukhatzhanova G (eds), *Forecasting Nuclear Proliferation in the 21st Century. The Role of Theory* (Vol. 1, Stanford University Press 2010).

Nephew R, *The Art of Sanctions: A View From the Field* (Columbia University Press 2018).

Nincic M, *The Logic of Positive Engagement* (Cornell University Press 2011).

Parsi T, *Losing an Enemy – Obama, Iran and the Triumph of Diplomacy* (Yale University Press 2017).

Shaikh F, 'Pakistan Nuclear Bomb: Beyond the Non-Proliferation Regime' (2002) 78(1) *International Affairs* 29.

Solingen E (ed.), *Sanctions, Statecraft, and Nuclear Proliferation* (Cambridge University Press 2012).

Stockholm International Peace Research Institute (SIPRI), *SIPRI Yearbook: Armaments, Disarmament and International Security* (Oxford University Press 2024) <https://www.sipri.org/yearbook/2024> accessed 1 July 2024.

The Economist, 'How to Stop a Three-Way Nuclear Arms-Race' (*The Economist*, 31 August 2023) <https://www.economist.com/leaders/2023/08/31/how-to-stop-a-three-way-nuclear-arms-race> accessed 1 July 2024.

The Guardian, 'Cyber-Attacks by North Korea Raked in $3bn to Build Nuclear Weapons, UN Monitors Suspect' (*The Guardian*, 8 February 2024) <https://www.theguardian.com/world/2024/feb/08/cyber-attacks-by-north-korea-raked-in-3bn-to-build-nuclear-weapons-un-monitors-suspect> accessed 1 July 2024.

van Wyk JA, 'Liberation Movements, Sanctions, and Nuclear Disarmament: The African National Congress and Apartheid South Africa' in Bekaj A and Wallensteen P (eds), *Sanctions for Nuclear Disarmament and Non-Proliferation: Moving Forward* (Routledge 2024).

Wallensteen P, 'Characteristics of Economic Sanctions' (1968) 5(3) *Journal of Peace Research* 247.

Wallensteen P and Staibano C (eds), *International Sanctions: Between Words and Wars in the Global System* (Frank Cass 2005).

Armend Bekaj

78. Sanctions in the fight against terrorism

Maruša T. Veber

I Introduction

At the United Nations (UN) level, international terrorism was recognized as a threat to international peace and security by the United Nations Security Council (UNSC) in the 1990s (e.g. UNSC Res 731 [1992] preamble para. 2; UNSC Res 1368 [2001] preamble para. 2). Subsequently, three different types of counterterrorism sanctions were devised by the UNSC: (1) counterterrorism sanctions regimes concerning particular states and incidents; (2) the 1267 sanctions regime whereby member states are required *inter alia* to freeze the assets and prevent the entry into or transit through their territories by UNSC-designated individuals and entities associated with the Taliban, Osama bin Laden or members of Al-Qaida (UNSC Res 1267 [1999] para. 4); and (3) the decentralized sanctions regime 1373 whereby member states themselves identify and enlist individuals and entities associated with terrorism (UNSC Res 1373 [2001] para. 1(c)).

The underlying principle that underpinned the adoption of international sanctions against terrorism is the duty of states 'to refrain from organizing, instigating, assisting or participating in terrorist acts in another state or acquiescing in organized activities within its territory directed towards the commission of such acts', as deriving from the UN General Assembly Resolution 2625 (UNGA Res 2625 [1970] Annex Principle I; UNSC Res 1189 [1998] preamble para. 5; UNSC Res 1373 [2001] preamble para. 9; International Convention for the Suppression of the Financing of Terrorism [1999]). However, due to the lack of consensus, there exists no commonly accepted definition of terrorism under international law (for different definitions see UNSC Res 1566 [2004] para. 3; International Convention for the Suppression of the Financing of Terrorism [1999] Art. 2; European Convention on the Suppression of Terrorism [1977] Art. 1; Directive 2017/541 Art. 3).

Sanctions against terrorism that commonly reflect the two UN sanctions regimes are also regularly adopted by other international organizations and states. The United States has a well-developed counterterrorism sanctions regime, which even preceded and, in some respects, served as a model for the UN sanctions regimes (see also Executive Order [1995]; Moiseienko [2021] 411–15). Similarly, in the United Kingdom (see chapter), two anti-terrorism sanctions mechanisms are in place (see also Anti-Money Laundering Act [2018]; The ISIL (Da'esh) and Al-Qaida (United Nations Sanctions) (EU Exit) Regulations [2019]). The European Union (EU) (see chapter) likewise adopts autonomous counterterrorism sanctions as well as sanctions on the basis of the UN 1267 sanctions regime (see also Veber [2020]; Council Common Position 2001/931/CFSP; Council Regulation (EC) 2580/2001; Council Decision (CFSP) 2016/1693; Council Regulation (EU) 2016/1686).

II UN counterterrorism sanctions regimes concerning specific states and terrorist incidents

The first type of UN counterterrorism sanctions regimes reflects the 'traditional' sanctions mechanisms and has been developed in relation to specific states and incidents. In 1992, the UNSC adopted counterterrorism sanctions against Libya (see chapter) in response to the bombing of two international flights, Pan American flight 103 in 1988 and French Union de transports aériens or UTA flight 772 in 1989 (UNSC Report [1999] paras 15–16; UNSC Res 731 [1992] preamble para. 2). Following the investigation, the main suspects identified for the attacks were Libyan nationals. After the failure of Libya to respond to a request by France, the United Kingdom and the United States in connection with the legal procedure related to the terrorist attacks, as well as its failure to renounce terrorism, the UNSC adopted sanctions against Libya in the form of an aviation ban, arms import embargo, travel ban, asset freeze (UNSC Res 748 [1992] paras 4–5), as well as financial sanctions and targeted economic sanctions (UNSC Res 883 [1993] paras 3–4; Veber [2022] 250).

In 1996, the UNSC adopted sanctions against Sudan in the form of travel restrictions (UNSC Res 1054 [1996] para. 3(a–b)) and threatened the adoption of aviation sanctions (UNSC Res 1070 [1996] para. 3) because Sudan was harbouring terrorists allegedly involved in the attempted assassination of Egyptian President Hosni Mubarak (Charron [2011] 160). The UNSC also responded to other instances of terrorist activities, such as the 2005 bomb explosion in Beirut that killed the Lebanese Prime Minister Rafiq Hariri and 22 other individuals. The UNSC adopted sanctions against those individuals designated as suspects in the planning, sponsoring, organizing or perpetrating of this terrorist act (UNSC Res 1636 [2005] para. 3(b)) and adopted an arms embargo (UNSC Res 1701 [2006] para. 15).

III The United Nations 1267 sanctions regime

Arguably, the most widespread sanctions against terrorism were adopted by the UNSC in response to the activities of Al-Qaeda. In the aftermath of the attacks on US embassies in Nairobi and Dar es Salaam in 1998 by Al-Qaeda, the UNSC adopted a series of resolutions (UNSC Res 1189 [1998]; UNSC Res 1193 [1998]; UNSC Res 1214 [1998]) requesting the Taliban regime in Afghanistan to extradite Osama bin Laden, close all terrorist training camps and cease providing sanctuary for terrorists on its territory (Eckes [2009] 25; Charron [2011] 163). Later, with UNSC Resolution 1267 (1999) at para. 4, it adopted a comprehensive UN counterterrorism sanctions regime in the form of an air embargo and an embargo on funds and financial assets against Afghanistan and the Taliban. Subsequently, UNSC Resolution 1333 (2000), at para. 8(c), expanded this regime to include the freezing of funds of Osama bin Laden and individuals and entities associated with him. Moreover, UNSC Resolution 1390 (2002), adopted in the aftermath of the 11 September attacks, enlarged the reach of these sanctions to any person associated with the Taliban, Osama bin Laden or members of Al-Qaeda (see also UNSC Res 1989 [2011]) and Resolution 2253 (2015) included a focus on ISIL/Da'esh. Thus, the scope of this counterterrorism regime has been extended to cover global terrorist organizations. While these sanctions were designed as measures against the state of Afghanistan, they were transformed into a broader counterterrorism sanctions framework, called the 1267 regime (Keller and Fischer [2009] 257). This sanctions mechanism has a global reach, which means that individuals of any nationality residing anywhere in the world can be listed. A consolidated list, the so-called 1267/1989/2253 sanctions list, was established, whereby member states are required inter alia to freeze the assets (see also chapter on Financial sanctions) and prevent the entry into or transit through their territories by designated individuals (travel ban) and entities associated with the Taliban, Osama bin Laden or members of Al-Qaeda. However, in practice, other terrorist organizations, such as Boko Haram (UNSC SC/11410 [2014]), have also been included on this list. This sanctions regime includes a review mechanism but applies for an unlimited period of time, which means that it is permanent (UNSC Res 1390 [2002] para. 3). Against this background, the 1267 sanctions regime has become the UN's largest sanctions list, constantly reviewed and expanded.

A specific 1267 Al-Qaida and Taliban Sanctions Committee – now the 1267/1989/2253 Islamic State in Iraq and the Levant (ISIL/Da'esh) and Al-Qaida Sanctions Committee – was established pursuant to para. 6 of UNSC Resolution 1267 (1999). This committee has the mandate to maintain the list of individuals and entities as well as to monitor the implementation of sanctions, to make periodic reports to the UNSC and to facilitate cooperation with other UN sanctions committees, and especially Committee 1373 (UNSC Res 1390 [2002] para. 5). The Sanctions Committee considers proposals for listing submitted by member states; such requests must contain a detailed statement of the reasons for the proposed listing and the specific criteria under which the names of individuals, groups, undertakings and/or entities are being proposed for designation (UNSC Res 1617 [2005] para. 4; UNSC Res 2610 [2021] paras 2–10). This sanctions regime includes the possibility to request individual exemptions from travel bans and the freezing of assets, for example, for basic expenses to satisfy essential human needs. Moreover, the UNSC decided to maintain the exemption of humanitarian aid providers from asset freeze measures imposed against Da'esh and Al-Qaida, in accordance with Resolution 2664 (2022) (see also chapter on Humanitarian carveouts).

Maruša T. Veber

IV United Nations 1373 sanctions regime

Another UN sanctions regime was established in the aftermath of the 11 September attacks. Resolution 1373 (2001) required all states to implement different measures to enhance their legal and institutional ability to counter terrorism (Charron [2011] 154), including freezing any funds related to persons involved in acts of terrorism (para. 1(c)). The UNSC at that time recognized the 'need for States to complement international cooperation by taking additional measures to prevent and suppress, in their territories through all lawful means, the financing and preparation of any acts of terrorism' (UNSC Res 1373 [2001] preamble para. 8). With this, it created a general and decentralized 1373 sanctions regime obliging member states to identify and list individuals and entities and freeze their financial resources as well as adopt relevant national legislative measures in the fight against terrorism. This sanctions regime is therefore not limited in terms of its geographical scope and time. Unlike the 1267 sanctions regime, under this regime, there is no consolidated list administered by the UNSC. Rather, listing is decentralized, with autonomous sanctions lists being established by states and international organizations such as the EU. In this respect, it leaves broad discretion to states to develop their own standards concerning the adoption of sanctions (Ginsborg [2017] 88).

The 1373 sanctions regime is part of a broader UN counterterrorism framework established by this UNSC resolution, which requires states to adopt various legislative and other measures at the national level to enhance their legal and institutional ability to counter terrorist activities nationally and internationally (see also UNSC Res 1624 [2005]; UNSC Res 2178 [2014]; UNSC Res 2396 [2017]; UNSC Res 2462 [2019]; UNSC Res 2482 [2019]). The majority of obligations contained in the operative part of the 1373 resolution mirrored the International Convention for the Suppression of the Financing of Terrorism (1999). Against this background, it became known as the first 'legislative' resolution, outlining numerous obligations of states, without, however, defining the notion of terrorism (Ginsborg [2017] 86).

Under the 1373 sanctions regime, a counterterrorism committee was established that is assisted by an Executive Directorate (CTED) (UNSC Res 1535 [2004] para. 2) that carries out its policy decisions and conducts expert assessments of UN member states. Due to the specific nature of this sanctions regime, the mandate of the Counterterrorism Committee does not include listing and delisting procedures as these are handled by states, but includes a wide range of other activities such as the facilitation of cooperation in matters relating to counterterrorism among states, country visits to assess member states' counterterrorism efforts and the implementation of UNSC resolutions, and the facilitation of technical assistance to member states.

V Human rights issues

UN sanctions against terrorism marked an important change in sanctions practices, whereby a transition from state-centric sectoral sanctions to so-called 'targeted' or 'smart' sanctions was made (see Biersteker et al. [2016]). However, such individualization of sanctions has been criticized due to the lack of sufficient mechanisms and legal safeguards to protect the rights of targeted individuals and entities (Cameron [2006]; Keller and Fischer [2009]; Van den Herik [2007]). In particular, their lack of transparent listing and delisting procedures threatened the due process rights of designated entities and individuals under the 1267 and 1373 sanctions regimes (UNGA World Summit Outcome [2005] para. 109). The 1267 regime did not include any specific procedural standards in terms of the notification of listed individuals, listing criteria or delisting processes. These human rights issues were scrutinized by various international courts and bodies.

A landmark ruling concerning the 1267 anti-terrorism sanctioning mechanism was the Court of Justice of the European Union (CJEU) *Kadi* cases, whereby the Court held that UNSC terrorism-related sanctions were not in line with certain fundamental rights under EU law, namely the right to be heard, the right to an effective legal remedy and the right to property (see also chapter on Judicial review (European Union); *Yassin Abdullah Kadi and Al Barakaat International Foundation v Council of the European Union and the Commission of the European Communities* [2008]; *European Commission and Others v Yassin Abdullah Kadi* [2013]). In relation to Resolution 1373, the CJEU decided in the *People's Mojahedin Organization of Iran* case, that there were not sufficient reasons provided by the Council for the listing of persons, groups and entities and that the listing procedure did not respect the right to a fair hearing (*People's Mojahedin Organization of Iran v Council of the European Union* [2008] 130 ff; *Jose Maria Sison v Council of the European Union* [2007] para. 154).

In *Sayadi and Vinck v Belgium* (2008), the UN Human Rights Committee scrutinized the 1267 sanctions mechanism from the point of view of obligations of states in terms of delisting procedures. It concluded that Belgium violated the right to freedom of movement and the right of everyone to protection against arbitrary or unlawful interference with his privacy, family, home or correspondence, and against unlawful attacks on his honour and reputation under Articles 12 and 17 of the International Covenant on Civil and Political Rights, due to its failure to take appropriate steps to remove individuals included in the 1267 sanctions list. Similarly, the European Court of Human Rights concluded in *Nada v Switzerland* (2012) that Switzerland (see chapter) was responsible for a violation of the right to respect private life and the right to an effective remedy under Articles 8 and 13 of the ECHR, as it failed to take appropriate steps in terms of the delisting of designated individuals in the 1267 sanctions regime.

VI Listing and delisting procedures

Criticism and judicial reviews have led to important institutional and procedural changes in the UN counterterrorism sanctions regimes. Several safeguards were adopted in relation to the 1267 sanctions regime, including more specific listing criteria, whereby nominating states are required to provide a 'statement of case' when proposing a listing of a certain individual or entity (UNSC Res 1526 [2004] para. 17; UNSC Res 1617 [2005] para. 4; UNSC Res 1735 [2006] para. 5) with the evidentiary standard being 'reasonable grounds' or 'reasonable basis' (UNSC Res 2253 [2015] para. 16). In addition, an obligation to notify the persons and entities concerned of their inclusion on the list was added (UNSC Res 1526 [2004] para. 18; UNSC Resolution 1735 [2006] para. 6) and a review procedure was introduced by Res 1822 (2008) (paras. 25–26), whereby the Sanctions Committee reviews all names on the sanctions list on an annual basis.

A specific process based on diplomatic protection was introduced for delisting in 2002 (UNSC Guidelines of the Committee for the Conduct of its Work [2002]), whereby a state of nationality of a concerned individual or entity was entitled to request delisting on their behalf. However, later, a specific procedure allowing listed individuals and entities to submit a request for delisting was developed. In 2006, a Focal Point for Delisting (UNSC Res 1730 [2006] para. 1; see also chapter on UN Focal Point and UN Office of the Ombudsperson) was established as a mechanism within the UN Secretariat to receive delisting requests from designated individuals and to facilitate consultations on such requests between the UNSC and relevant member states (UNSC Guidelines of the Committee for the Conduct of its Work [2002] 7–11). Moreover, the UN Office of the Ombudsperson was established in 2009 (UNSC Res 1904 [2009] paras 20–21) with a mandate to receive and recommend action on requests for delisting from the 1267 regime and make recommendations to the Sanctions Committee. Since 2011, the Ombudsperson has been able to recommend to the Committee that an individual or entity be removed from the sanctions list. While a consensus decision of the Committee was previously necessary to remove someone from the sanctions list, since 2011, the removal of an individual or entity as recommended by the Ombudsperson automatically enters into effect unless the Sanctions Committee decides otherwise by consensus (UNSC Res 1989 [2011] paras 21–35; UNSC Res 2610 [2021] para. 62). Committee members can only overturn the Ombudsperson's recommendation by consensus, which has not happened to date. Despite these developments, the delisting system still falls short of guaranteeing relevant minimum procedural guarantees under international human rights law, for example, the right to an effective legal remedy (Ginsborg [2017] 79–80).

VII Conclusion

Sanctions in the fight against terrorism constitute an important part of global sanctions practices. The two most prominent counterterrorism sanctions regimes are the UN 1267 and 1373 regimes, which were developed in parallel in the aftermath of the 11 September

Maruša T. Veber

attacks and continue to coexist. Importantly, these two sanctions regimes have transformed conventional sanctions practices, whereby a transition from state-centric sectoral sanctions to so-called 'targeted' or 'smart' sanctions was made. With this came the increased institutionalization of these regimes in terms of listing and delisting processes; however, both regimes continue to suffer from a lack of due process guarantees (Ginsborg [2017] 86). At the same time, the degree of implementation and the effectiveness of these sanctions continue to be debated (see also chapter on Measuring sanctions effectiveness) (Ginsborg [2017] 96–103). Based on the UN counterterrorism sanctions regimes, other international organizations, such as the EU and states (e.g. the United States and the United Kingdom), regularly adopt counterterrorism sanctions either in the implementation of UNSC sanctions list of designated persons or by creating their own autonomous counterterrorism sanctions lists.

Bibliography

Literature

Biersteker T, Eckert JS and Tourinho M (eds), *Targeted Sanctions* (Cambridge University Press 2016).

Cameron I, 'The European Convention on Human Rights, Due Process and United Nations Security Council Counter-terrorism Sanctions' (Council of Europe 2006) <https://www.statewatch.org/media/documents/terrorlists/docs/Cameron-06.pdf>.

Charron A, *UN Sanctions and Conflict, Responding to Peace and Security Threats* (Routledge 2011).

Eckes C, *EU Counter-Terrorist Policies and Fundamental Rights, The Case of Individual Sanctions* (Oxford University Press 2009).

Ginsborg L, 'UN Sanctions and Counter-Terrorism Strategies: Moving Towards Thematic Sanctions against Individuals?' in van den Herik L (ed.), *Research Handbook on UN Sanctions and International Law* (Edward Elgar 2017) 73.

Keller H and Fischer A, 'The UN Anti-Terror Sanctions Regime under Pressure' (2009) 9(2) *Human Rights Law Review* 257.

Moiseienko A, 'Due Process and Unilateral Targeted Sanctions' in Beaucillon C (ed.), *Research Handbook on Unilateral and Extraterritorial Sanctions* (Edward Elgar 2021) 405.

Van den Herik L, 'The Security Council's Targeted Sanctions Regimes: In Need of Better Protection of the Individual' (2007) 20(4) *Leiden Journal of International Law* 797.

Veber MT, 'Safeguarding Fundamental Values of the EU through the Adoption of Sanctions' (2020) 4 *University of Vienna Law Review* 37.

Veber MT, *Sanctions Adopted by International Organizations in the Defence of the General Interest* (PhD thesis, University of Ljubljana 2022).

Documents

C-402/05 and C-415/05 P Yassin Abdullah Kadi and Al Barakaat International Foundation v Council of the European Union and the Commission of the European Communities [2008] ECLI:EU:C:2008:461.

C-584/10 P, C-593/10 P and C-595/10 P European Commission and Others v Yassin Abdullah Kadi [2013] ECLI:EU:C:2013:518.

Case T-256/07 People's Mojahedin Organization of Iran v Council of the European Union [2008] ECLI:EU:T:2008:461.

Case T-47/03 Jose Maria Sison v Council of the European Union [2007] ECLI:EU:T:2007:207.

Council Common Position (2001/931/CFSP) of 27 December 2001 on the application of specific measures to combat terrorism [2001] OJ L344/93.

Council Decision (CFSP) 2016/1693 of 20 September 2016 concerning restrictive measures against ISIL (Da'esh) and Al-Qaeda and persons, groups, undertakings and entities associated with them and repealing Common Position 2002/402/CFSP [2016] OJ L255/25.

Council Regulation (EC) No. 2580/2001 of 27 December 2001 on specific restrictive measures directed against certain persons and entities with a view to combating terrorism [2001] OJ L344/70.

Council Regulation (EU) 2016/1686 of 20 September 2016 imposing additional restrictive measures directed against ISIL (Da'esh) and Al-Qaeda and natural and legal persons, entities or bodies associated with them [2016] OJ L255/1.

Directive (EU) 2017/541 of the European Parliament and of the Council of 15 March 2017 on combating terrorism and replacing Council Framework Decision 2002/475/JHA and amending Council Decision 2005/671/JHA [2017] OJ L88/6.

Nada v Switzerland (2012) ECtHR 10593/08.

European Convention on the Suppression of Terrorism (27 January 1977) ETS No. 90.

Executive Order No 12,947,60 Fed Reg 5079 (23 January 1995).

International Convention for the Suppression of the Financing of Terrorism (9 December 1999) 2178 UNTS 197.

Sanctions and Anti-Money Laundering Act (23 May 2018).

Sayadi and Vinck v Belgium, Views of the Human Rights Committee of 22 October 2008, concerning Communication No. 1472/2006 UN Doc. CCPR/C/94/D/1472/2006.

UNSC, 'Security Council Al-Qaida Sanctions Committee Adds Boko Haram to Its Sanctions List' (Press Release 22 May 2014) SC/11410.

The ISIL (Da'esh) and Al-Qaida (United Nations Sanctions) (EU Exit) Regulations 2019 SI 466/2019.

UNGA, Resolution 2625(XXV) (24 October 1970) UN Doc. A/RES/2625.

UNGA, 'World Summit Outcome' (24 October 2005) UN Doc. A/60/1.

UNSC, 'Guidelines of the Committee for the Conduct of its Work' (adopted on 7 November 2002, last updated 6 August 2024) <https://main.un.org/securitycouncil/sites/default/files/2024/1267%20Guidelines%20-%20tech%20updates%206%20August%202024%20E.pdf>.

UNSC Resolution 1054 (26 April 1996) UN Doc. S/RES/1054.

UNSC Resolution 1070 (16 August 1996) UN Doc. S/RES/1070.

UNSC Resolution 1189 (13 August 1998) UN Doc. S/RES/1189.

UNSC Resolution 1193 (28 August 1998) UN Doc. S/RES/1193.

UNSC Resolution 1214 (8 December 1998) UN Doc. S/RES/1214.

UNSC Resolution 1267 (15 October 1999) UN Doc. S/RES/1267.

UNSC Resolution 1333 (19 December 2000) UN Doc. S/RES/1333.

UNSC Resolution 1368 (12 September 2001) UN Doc. S/RES/1368.

UNSC Resolution 1373 (28 September 2001) UN Doc. S/RES/1373;

UNSC Resolution 1390 (28 January 2002) UN Doc. S/RES/1390.

UNSC Resolution 1452 (20 December 2002) UN Doc. S/RES/1452.

UNSC Resolution 1526 (30 January 2004) UN Doc. S/RES/1526.

UNSC Resolution 1535 (26 March 2004) UN Doc. S/RES/1535.

UNSC Resolution 1566 (8 October 2004) UN Doc. S/RES/1566.

UNSC Resolution 1624 (14 September 2005) UN Doc. S/RES/1624.

UNSC Resolution 1636 (31 October 2005) UN Doc. S/RES/1636.

UNSC Resolution 1701 (11 August 2006) UN Doc. S/RES/1701.

UNSC Resolution 1730 (19 December 2006) UN Doc. S/RES/1730.

UNSC Resolution 1735 (22 December 2006) UN Doc. S/RES/1735.

UNSC Resolution 1822 (30 June 2008) UN Doc. S/RES/1822.

UNSC Resolution 1904 (17 December 2009) UN Doc. S/RES/1904.

UNSC Resolution 1989 (17 June 2011) UN Doc. S/RES/1989.

UNSC Resolution 2178 (24 September 2014) UN Doc. S/RES/2178.

UNSC Resolution 2253 (17 December 2015 UN Doc. S/RES/2253.

UNSC Resolution 2396 (21 December 2017) UN Doc. S/RES/2396.

UNSC Resolution 2462 (28 Marc 2019) UN Doc. S/RES/2462.

UNSC Resolution 2482 (19 July 2019) UN Doc. S/RES/2482.

UNSC Resolution 2610 (17 December 2021) UN Doc. S/RES/2610.

UNSC Resolution 731 (21 January 1992) UN Doc. S/RES/731.

UNSC Resolution 748 (31 March 1992) UN Doc. S/RES/748.

UNSC Resolution 883 (11 November 1993) UN Doc. S/RES/883.

UNSC Resolutions 1617 (29 July 2005) UN Doc. S/RES/1617.

MARUŠA T. VEBER

79. Sanctions to combat corruption

OLIVER WINDRIDGE

I Introduction

Sanctions can form an important part of the battle against corruption. They allow sanctioning authorities to freeze assets and ban the travel of those involved in serious corruption via emerging thematic and established geographic sanctions regimes. This entry examines the development of these thematic regimes, as well as how geographic regimes can be utilised to address broader issues of illicit finance linked to corruption. It argues for a multilateral approach to sanctions as part of a global anti-corruption toolkit.

II The approach of the thematic regimes against corruption

In a world where domestic accountability for corruption is remote, or nigh on impossible given that it is often those in power engaged in corruption, the use of targeted sanctions as a tool to combat corruption can be an attractive prospect for both governments and civil society groups.

The international sanctions landscape allows for the designation for corrupt acts by individuals and entities through both thematic and geographic sanctions regimes. On the thematic side, these include the US Global Magnitsky Act, the UK Global Anti-Corruption Sanctions regime, Canada's Justice for Victims of Corrupt Foreign Officials Act, and Australia's Serious Corruption Sanctions regime. Of note, at the time of writing, despite mention by European Union (EU) officials, reports by the EU parliament and the efforts of civil society, the EU does not have a similar anti-corruption sanctions regime.

All these thematic regimes operate with broadly the same approach; allowing the sanctioning authority to designate individuals and entities involved in corrupt activities, leading to asset freezes and travel bans within the jurisdiction of the sanctioning authority. The advantage of these thematic regimes is that they allow these sanctioning authorities to designate individuals and entities involved in corruption anywhere in the world without the need for a specific country sanctions regime. The biggest difference between these thematic regimes is perhaps the definition of corruption that allows for designation. For example, the US Global Magnitsky regime takes a non-exhaustive approach by describing corruption as "including the misappropriation of state assets, the expropriation of private assets for personal gain, corruption related to government contracts or the extraction of natural resources, or bribery" (Global Magnitsky Human Rights Accountability Act [2016] title XII, subtitle F). This wide definition leaves significant room for the US sanctions authorities to address various forms of corruption. In contrast, the UK Global Anti-Corruption regime restricts corrupt acts to bribery or the misappropriation of property, thereby creating significant restrictions on the ability of the United Kingdom to address corruption via sanctions (United Kingdom, Global Anti-Corruption Sanctions Regulations [2021]). These differences can lead to obvious discrepancies, where the United States is able to sanction corrupt activities that the United Kingdom cannot because of its narrow scope, thereby creating a patchwork of globalised sanctions. Nevertheless, the emergence of thematic anti-corruption sanctions regimes creates, at least on paper, the potential for a broad sanctions response to corruption.

III The geographic regimes as anti-corruption tools

As mentioned above, running in parallel with these thematic corruption regimes are geographic regimes that are focused on specific states. State-specific regimes have a much wider focus than simply corruption, but they should not be discounted as they can serve as a powerful anti-corruption tool, albeit couched in less direct terms. For example, all the states mentioned above (United States (see chapter), United Kingdom (see chapter), Canada (see chapter), and Australia, as well as the EU) operate a state-specific Myanmar (see chapter) sanctions regime. Under these sanctions regimes, designations can occur for corruption. For example, the UK Myanmar sanctions regime allows for designation for, among other conduct, "undermining democracy, the rule of law or good governance in Myanmar" and "any other action, policy or activity which threatens the peace, stability or security of Myanmar" (The Myanmar (Sanctions) Regulations [2021], regulation 6(2)(a)(i) and (vi), respectively). These regulations do not mention corruption per se, but it is arguable that most, if not all corrupt conduct can be covered within these descriptions.

Similar language is found in most geographic sanctions regimes. The EU provides an interesting example of a blended style of geographic sanctions regime, when it sought to target grand corruption through specific geographic sanctions regimes focused on misappropriation in Egypt, Tunisia, and Ukraine (Portela [2019]). This hybridised approach has ultimately been met with mixed results but demonstrates the ability of geographic sanctions regimes to focus on narrower issues. Nevertheless, the advantage of most geographic sanctions regimes remains the existence of wide language that allows for a broader set of anti-corruption-related designations without the limiting effect of the thematic anti-corruption sanctions regime's definitions. For example, since the UK Global Anti-Corruption regime only covers conduct amounting to bribery or misappropriation of property, this would severely restrict the ability of the United Kingdom to combat wider corruption issues in a situation such as Myanmar. The disadvantages include, as discussed above, that these regimes are state-specific. In the event that the corruption occurs in a state that does not have a geographic sanctions regime, it automatically falls outside of scope.

Underpinning both geographic and thematic sanctions to combat corruption is the underlying reality that both (as with all sanctions) remain, at heart, foreign policy tools. Sanctions to combat corruption will therefore always be weighed on the diplomatic scales of foreign policy, alongside other potential anti-corruption tools including enhanced or improved anti-money laundering action, increased criminal law enforcement investigation and prosecution, and in-country attempts to address corruption at source. Where most effective, sanctions should therefore form part of the anti-corruption toolkit, sitting alongside, not instead of, other actions. This is a toolkit that is even more effective when multilateralised. Taking a global approach to anti-corruption is not just aspirational but essential given the cross-border nature of most serious corruption. Sanctions are a clear and obvious area where this global approach is available; coordinating sanctions across anti-corruption sanctions regimes creates the kind of net that even the most advanced corrupt actor will struggle to escape. This action can best be done by sanctions authorities engaging not only with their own embassies and internal foreign office expertise but also with civil society, who often have troves of information that can be shared and used to underpin designations.

IV Conclusion

Whichever route is relied upon, sanctions provide a form of accountability for corruption that is regularly otherwise lacking. For many, the ideal form of accountability for corruption and associated conduct remains criminal prosecution and ultimately conviction, since it not only allows for criminal responsibility to be established but also raises the potential for the seizure and potential repatriation of ill-gotten gains back to the people from whom they were stolen. But the journey to criminal procedural success is often long and complex. The complicated nature of such cases, combined with the high criminal standard and limited law enforcement and prosecutorial capacity, means that cases languish or conclude before any form of accountability is achieved. It is within this context that sanctions form an important tool that can be immediately deployed with instant effect in the ongoing battle against corruption around the world.

Bibliography

Literature

'Anti-Corruption Sanctions in Numbers: Looking Back at 2024' (CiFAR, 31 January 2025) <https://cifar.eu/anti-corruption-sanctions-in-numbers-looking-back-at-2024/>.

Human Rights First et al., 'Multilateral Magnitsky Sanctions at Five Years' (November 2022) <https://redress.org/wp-content/uploads/2022/11/Multilateral-Magnitsky-Sanctions-at-Five-Years_November-2022.pdf>.

Moiseienko A, Musni M and Van Der Merwe E, 'A Journey of 20: An Empirical Study of the Impact of Magnitsky Sanctions' (International Lawyers Project 2023) <https://www.internationallawyersproject.org/post/a-journey-of-20-an-empirical-study-of-the-impact-of-magnitisky-corruption-sanctions>.

Oliver Windridge

Portela C, *Sanctioning Kleptocrats: An Assessment of EU Misappropriation Sanctions* (CiFAR 2019).
Taylor H, 'All Bark, No Bite? Taking Stock of the UK's Enforcement of Sanctions' (Spotlight on Corruption 2024) <https://www.spotlightcorruption.org/wp-content/uploads/2024/07/Sanctions-enforcement-report-v2.pdf>.

Documents

Australia, Autonomous Sanctions Act (2011).
Australia, Autonomous Sanctions (Designated Persons and Entities and Declared Persons – Thematic Sanctions) Instrument (2022).
Canada, Justice for Victims of Corrupt Foreign Officials Act (2017).
United Kingdom, Global Anti-Corruption Sanctions Regulations (2021).
United Kingdom, The Myanmar (Sanctions) Regulations (2021).
United States, Global Magnitsky Human Rights Accountability Act (2016).